Esin Akalın

Staging the Ottoman Turk

British Drama, 1656–1792

Esin Akalın

STAGING THE OTTOMAN TURK

British Drama, 1656–1792

ibidem-Verlag
Stuttgart

Bibliographic information published by the Deutsche Nationalbibliothek
Die Deutsche Nationalbibliothek lists this publication in the Deutsche Nationalbibliografie; detailed bibliographic data are available in the Internet at http://dnb.d-nb.de.

Bibliografische Information der Deutschen Nationalbibliothek
Die Deutsche Nationalbibliothek verzeichnet diese Publikation in der Deutschen Nationalbibliografie; detaillierte bibliografische Daten sind im Internet über http://dnb.d-nb.de abrufbar.

Cover picture: Painting: Mehmed II, Entering to Constantinople by Fausto Zonaro (1854–1929). Public domain. Source: Wikimedia Commons.

ISBN-13: 978-3-8382-0949-4

Printed in the United States of America

TABLE OF CONTENTS

ACKNOWLEDGEMENTS

There are a number of people in my life to whom I owe gratitude for the support they gave while I was engaged in this study, which was originally a Ph.D. dissertation. I would like to begin by expressing my heartfelt thanks for the invaluable support, assistance, guidance and encouragement I received from Brian Corman, Domenico Pietropaolo and Roseann Runte. Words are not sufficient to express my thanks and appreciation to each one of them, who gave unselfishly of their time and energy.

To Brian Corman, always a source of advice and wisdom, I must extend my special thanks for his guidance. He has been most perceptive, challenging and a thorough reader. With the greatest warmth and regard, I thank Roseann Runte, who, with such generosity of spirit, provided me excellent feedback and most insightful comments during the entire process of writing this book. I am most grateful to Prof. Pietropaolo, whose positive attitude, thought-provoking questions and insightful comments were invaluable for my research.

I acknowledge with special gratitude and appreciation, the financial support provided to me by the Open Fellowships of University of Toronto, and a Travel Grant, which allowed me to do research at the British Library in London.

The most profound acknowledgement goes to my family. My greatest debt, an incalculable one which I cannot begin to repay, is to my husband Oguz, my daughter Derya and my son Kaan. I dedicate this book to them.

Last but not least: thank you Mom and Dad (Guzin and Fethi Kismet) for sending me to the English High School for Girls in Istanbul.

PEACE!

INTRODUCTION

To the eye of the initiated this curtain produces only images
But to him/her who knows the signs, symbols of truth.
Sheik Kusteri[1] *has founded his curtain*
Making it a likeness of the world;
To watch it amuses those who are looking for entertainment,
But those who behold the truth learn a lesson from it.

(An "Ode of the Screen" to a Turkish Shadow Play)

Although the Ottoman[2] culture, before the mid-nineteenth century, engendered neither formal tragedy nor comedy (Halman 17), *Karagoz* (Turkish Shadow theatre), one of the three principal norms of popular performance tradition in the Ottoman Empire, evolved as a comic genre[3]. The world of *Karagoz,* the illusionistic art of the shadow play, reflected the multi-faceted feature of the Ottoman culture and incorporated a total of three hundred and fifty characters, both Muslim and non-Muslim, and non-Turkish but Muslim minorities as subjects. This was an assemblage from various provinces of the Empire such as the "Rumelili" or "Ar-

1 According to an oral tradition, the invention of the shadow theatre is attributed to Sheik Kusteri, a craftsman, who, during the reign of Sultan Orhan I (1336-1359), created the antics of Karagoz and Hacivat in puppet form.

2 The name Ottoman is derived from the Turkish "Osmanli" meaning followers of Osman (Othman), the eponym of the dynasty who were seen as the direct successors of the great Islamic Empires of the past. At the time of its foundation in 1299, the Ottoman State was an insignificant principality occupying a tiny frontier settlement between the worlds of Islam and Byzantium. In a few generations the Ottomans, under the House of Osman, excelled in statecraft and administration, financial policies, land system and military organization and developed into “a centralized and self-consciously imperial state” (Kafadar xi). By the sixteenth century, besides all of Asia Minor, the Ottoman territory comprised the Arab peninsula, Egypt, North Africa, the Caucasus, Crimea, Transylvania, Rumania, Hungary, Serbia, Bulgaria, Macedonia, Albania, Greece, Cyprus, the Agean islands and so on.

3 Some scholars argue that shadow theatre originated in China and was carried West by the Mongols, who transmitted their knowledge to the Turkic peoples of Central Asia. Others raise questions about the Chinese origin of the shadow play tradition. Dutch scholarship maintains that this tradition originated in India or Java. According to Metin And, while the puppet tradition came from Central Asia, shadow theatre did not (And *Culture,* 115).

navut" (Albanian) from the Balkans, "Laz" from the Black Sea Shore, "Kastamonulu" from Central Anatolia, "Kurd" from South East Region, and so on. All of these figures made up a delightful assortment of characters wearing their local costumes and speaking their local dialects. The non-Turkish minorities of the empire such as the Arab, Armenian (*Ermeni*), Greek (*Rum*), Jew (*Yahudi*), French (*Frenk),* Levantine and Persian (*Acem*) each speaking with their own accent as residents of the *mahalle* (quarter) or merely as passers-by, reflected the Ottoman's diverse world onto the *Karagoz* screen. The tradition in the House of Osman was not a national, but a dynastic and multiracial empire in which the Turkish language played a significant role in creating unity. Its varied populations whether Turkish, Muslim, Christian or Jewish were above all else Ottomans, members of a single body politic. Although Islam was a powerful element in the collective consciousness of the empire, the Ottoman system transcended "above all else conceptions of nationhood, religion and race. Alone in its time, it thus gave recognition to all three monotheistic faiths" (Kinross 614). In essence, the world of the Turkish shadow theatre with its individual puppets, each representing the typical characteristics of various groups, was a microcosm of the cosmopolitan city of Istanbul.[4] In its early period of existence, Islam, aspiring to fight idolatry, forbade the representation of living things, especially human faces. Because its worship centred exclusively on the act of silent prayer, drama and music had no place in its liturgy. Representation and animation of human figures were considered an intrusion upon the creativity of God; and imitation of His creatures was the equivalent to sin. Despite the austerity and rigidity of the Orthodox Islamic views of plastic arts and drama, through the ingenuity of the human mind, Shadow Theatre flourished during the Ottoman Empire. As Nicholas Martinovitch points out, "the creative genius of the human spirit" in

---

[4] The flow of action in a typical shadow play was good-natured and based on a broad farce in which humour became a regulative medium of both judgement and compassion.

an effort to overcome religious constraints produced figures which were distortions and parodies of human figures. Moreover, by perforating the puppets, the creators found a way of eliminating their "animate" nature, which would otherwise advocate idolatry (Martinovitch 35).

During his campaign to Egypt, Sultan Selim is said to have asked a puppeteer of a *hayal-i-zil*[5] performance to go with him to Istanbul, so that his son Suleyman I could see the shadow play. During the reign of Suleyman the Magnificent, *Karagoz*, reflecting the cultural vitality of the empire, constituted not only a prominent part of the imperial life, but in displaying a broad spectrum of socio-political, psychological and moral issues, it also fascinated the Ottoman populace. As the neighbourhood (*mahalle)* displayed on the *Karagoz* screen reflected the social pattern of a traditional quarter in the city, the audiences witnessed a parade of images of all typical Ottoman inhabitants, who were noticeable through their ethnic and regional attributes. This was significant because the residents of the *mahalle* were all subject to the decrees issued by the sultan. Their representation on the screen conveyed the reality that there was no distinct separation between the Turkish and non-Turkish/non Muslim populations, who freely mingled with each other. As Evliya Chelebi, the foremost Ottoman travel writer and cultural commentator reported, by the seventeenth century, although Hasanzade, a prominent master of the Turkish Shadow Theatre, incorporated three hundred skits in his repertoire, he had no authority to represent the Ottoman sovereign. The characters were all drawn from common people:

5 While its play technique was imported from the Mamlukes, ultimately, the synthesis of European, Islamic and Turkish traditions gave birth to an indigenous artistic expression in the Ottoman Empire.

> No player would have dared to present to the spectators the silhouettes of the Sultan, of the viziers or of any dignitaries of the Empire. All civil, military or religious authorities were banned from the Shadow Theatre screen either through fear or reverence. This of course did not prevent their being replaced by symbols, which were in harmony with the atmosphere of the 'mahalle' and which veiled their secret identity as well (Siyavusgil 25).

In an empire ruled by an absolute monarchy and a totalitarian regime, while the prohibition to portray the sultan or his *vezir*, did not prevent their representation by symbols, each *Karagoz* show, however, was "a *risque-revue*, as fearless as a militant newspaper" (And, *Karagoz* 67). By a curious irony, though, as Western weekly papers recorded events from the Ottoman court, sultans, *vezirs, agas* and *muftis*, all in their opulent costumes playing out all signifiers of Otherness, populated European stages. Thus, in addition to topical news and political history, a long dramatic tradition kept the Ottoman sultans and their affairs in the forefront of Western minds. Along with Renaissance travelers such as Sanderson, Sandys, Lithgow and so on, London dramatists like Peele, Marlowe, Shakespeare, Heywood and others produced the canonical version of Renaissance thought about Islam and/or the Ottoman Turk. Just like the travelogues, which were not simply a portrait of cities and landscapes in the Orient, but written with a conscious rhetorical effect, Renaissance drama presented a similar ideology displaying standard, received ideas about the Ottoman Empire. As the travelers drew their descriptions of the Ottomans (particularly the sultans and other dignitaries) from a distant and unreliable view of sights that were "forbidden" to the outsiders in the Ottoman Empire, the dramatists based their depictions on this collective store of "knowledge" about the Turks. The moral of Richard Knolles' massive edition of the *General History of the Turkes* (1603), for example, attested to the fact that an "armchair" historian without leaving England could give an account of the historical events of Ottoman/Islamic culture though a collection of erroneous interpretations, representations, attitudes, interests and stereotypes.

Representation of the Ottomans on the English stage can be traced back to the tradition of the English folk plays and the Mummers' Plays with the part of the Turkish knight opposing St. George, performed by an actor in "Herod's vein" and in all likelihood, with a blackened face (Tiddy 14). Despite references to Turkish knights in romances or folk plays prior to the sixteenth century, for the Englishman the Ottoman, as Wood notes, " if he existed at all, was but a shadowy figure inheriting the opprobrium formerly heaped upon the Saracens by generations of crusaders"[6] (Wood 1). The figure of the Turk[7] as a fixed type, loosely representing the "pagan" as such, or the idea of anti-Christian forces, was not simply restricted to allegorical treatments as in a Mummers' Play. Since the terms "Mohammedan", "Moslem", "Arab", "Turk" and "Saracen" were used almost interchangeably as mere theological abstractions within the universe of Western discourse, the distinction between Ottoman and Turk was also neutralized in eighteenth-century dramatic representations. Originally, the term Turk applied only to one of the nomadic peoples in Central Asia. As the *millet* (literally "nation") system of the multi-religious, multinational Ottoman Empire aimed to create one civilization, the Turk was regarded as only one of the representatives of the cultural mosaic of the diverse peoples of the Ottoman society. In the West, while the Turk was synonymous with Muslim, Islam was defined as Mohammedanism. Considering that even in the Age of Enlightenment the *Dictionnaire universel* and the *Dictionnaire de l'académie française* described the word "impostor" as synonymous with Mohammed, the discursive confinement of the Islamic prophet as a "type" led to the polemic use of the term Mohammedanism, as "an insulting European designation" (Said 66).

6 In the 10th and 11th centuries, Crusaders fought the Turks through Anatolia (Asia Minor) to Jerusalem. By the 14th century, as the Holy Land was beyond Christian reach, Turks/Ottomans became the targets of the Crusades. Therefore, the Turk was taken synonymous with Muslim.

7 In the Ottoman Empire, the Turk was “only one, and not necessarily a favoured one of the ‘ethnicities’ ruled” (Kafadar 8) by the dynastic state. An Ottoman gentleman or gentlewoman would always describe himself/herself as "Osmanli", a term used in a dynastic rather than a national sense.

Despite its pejorative connotation, the incorrect definition of Islam was based on the assumption that "Mohammed was to Islam as Christ was to Christianity" (Said 60). Referring to the stereotypical notions generated about the complex society of the Ottomans, who "established one of the longest-lived (ca. 1300-1922), yet least studied or understood, dynastic states in world history" (Kafadar, xi) Naff writes:

> While the Islamic image has always been distorted[8] or misrepresented in the West, the Islamic world of the eighteenth century—particularly the Middle Eastern heartland of the Ottoman Empire, its Arab and North African provinces ... has been a prime victim (Naff 3).

In the course of the analysis of varies dramatic texts, this study aims to shed light on the politics of representation by contextualizing and analyzing the practices of representation of the Muslim/Ottoman Turk on the English stage. The opening chapter analyzes the problems of historiography of the Ottoman Empire in order to reach a historicized understanding of the complexity of Western values and attitudes towards the Muslim/Ottoman Turk. It sets out the foundations of the ideological positions articulated by cultural, religious and historiographical strands in the plays. The following chapters will explore how the Ottoman milieu as a dramatic setting provided for the European audience s a common experience of fascination and fear of Other. With an awareness of how the dramatists operated within the discursive limits of the seventeenth and eighteenth centuries, each chapter offers a detailed consideration of the vital role that European drama played in the formation of Western assumptions and conclusions about the meaning of East/Ottoman/Muslim.

The first chapter, which offers a theoretical, discursive and historical basis for the analysis of specific representations of the Ottoman Turks, lays the foundations of successive chapters, categorized according to the reigns of the sultans depicted in the

8 On the distorted image of Islam in the West, Norman Daniel's *Islam and the West: The Making of an Image*, S. C. Chew's *The Crescent and the Rose*, R. W. Southern's *Western Views of Islam in the Middle Ages* are useful sources.

plays. Essentially, the relevance of the texts in the sphere of the ideological, forms an historical and analytical basis for the representations of Ottomans which have evolved across a range of generic forms.

The most important contextualizing factors which need to be acknowledged in addressing the politics of representation are (a) the relationship between dramatic representations of the Turks and their material world (b) discursive practices that produced knowledge about the Ottomans and their power (c) a cluster of issues revolving around matters of identity and difference. In this context, it must be emphasized that the endlessly repetitive, highly intertextual denial of Ottoman realities in these plays determines in advance the dramatization of the characters. In other words, it is the whole repertoire of imagery and visual effects that organizes the representation of the Ottoman Turks by channeling difference into dichotomies such as Self and Other, West and East, Christian and Muslim. Ultimately, in arguing not only how dialectics shape the representation of the Ottomans and constitute a force in the plots and the stagecraft, but also how they establish the "truth of the matter" (Hall 46), this study draws upon different methodologies by offering a selective overview of a range of theories and arguing for the importance of gleaning certain features from each.

In the representation of Ottoman Turks in English drama (1656-1792), the "Orient" is crucial in the ideological construction of the West. Yet, ironically, the decline of the Ottoman Empire from the eighteenth century onwards also seems to serve the ideological construction of a somewhat abstract, ageographical and ahistorical "Orient" by scholars of the twentieth century who have vigorously allied themselves with studies that explore the relationships among knowledge, power and politics. To offer a specific example, Edward Said's renowned book, to which this thesis owes a great deal, has its own cultural distortion and bias as it refers to the Ottomans only in passing. Said's amply documented scholarship which not only discusses the unified character of the

Western discourse about the "Orient" from antiquity to the present, but which specifically deals with Islamic Orientalism, tells us nothing about the Ottoman Empire (1299-1922). Since there are already difficulties in overcoming the pervasive negative assumptions about the Ottomans embedded in Western understanding, the overgeneralization of the historical interactions of systems and cultures and an unwillingness to confront concrete realities of the past, make the Ottoman case particularly complex. Consequently, in analyzing the representation of Turks in English drama, the aim of this study is not only to seek a solution to the failings of a Eurocentric orientalist history, but also to overcome the historigraphical and methodological problems arising from the current counter-hegemonic "regime(s) of truth" (Foucault 1980, 131) which claim to give voice to the unvoiced. Orientalism as Said asserts, is a "corporate institution for dealing with the Orient—dealing with it by making statements about it, authorizing views of it, describing it". And, this study interrogates the relations of knowledge and power, culture and politics by anchoring its arguments in the empirical depths of the seven hundred years of the imperial experience of the Ottoman Empire, historiographically documented as "the Orient".

Chapter 1: Historical/Theoretical Perspectives

1.1. The Historical Background

> *In the sixteenth and seventeenth centuries the Ottoman state was a world empire which influenced directly or indirectly the lives of millions in the Mediterranean, in East Central Europe and the Middle East. Its geopolitical position, vast territory, ample human and economic resources, its magnificently efficient administration and its army, one of the best organized military machines of the early modern period, gave the Ottoman Empire the status of a world power*
>
> (Agoston 126).

Since its publication in 1978, Edward Said's account, in *Orientalism*, of the Western approach to the Orient has been both pivotal and a major incentive for the growth of work on colonial discourse. In seeking to trace the interrelations of culture, history and textuality, Said, in his widely read and greatly influential book, ultimately leaves the reader with the observation that: "Europe is powerful and articulate; Asia is defeated and distant" (Said 57). Said separates East and West from a wide range of perspectives—political, religious, economic, historical, cultural, etc.—which go back as far as Aeschylus' *The Persians* and conclude with Kissenger, and claims that Orientalism is a "broadly imperialist view of the world" (Said 15). In discussing the East/West relationship from a "general and hegemonic context" (Said 9) Said draws attention to a "geopolitical awareness into aesthetic, scholarly, historical and philosophical texts" (Said 120). He claims that Western political and intellectual domination over the East has defined the nature of the Orient as weak and that of the Occident as strong. Said's model of "'fixity' in the ideological construction of otherness" (Bhabha 8) is for Bhabha[9] a "historical

9 As Homi Bhabha writes in *The Location of Culture*, "[a]n important part of the colonial discourse depends on the concept of 'fixity' in the ideological construction of Otherness. 'Fixity' as a sign of cultural/historical/racial difference in the course of colonialism is a paradoxical mode of representation"

and theoretical simplification" (Bhabha 25). This applies to the Ottoman case from the point of view that Said's ahistorical and ageographical approach to the Orient does not do justice to the historical realities of the Ottoman Empire as a world power in the sixteenth and seventeenth centuries.

What is essentially problematic in *Orientalism* is that it tells the reader nothing about centuries-old Ottoman imperial order. In exploring the relations of knowledge and power, and of culture and politics as the determining elements in defining the worlds of Islam and Christianity, Said refers to the Ottomans only in passing. In his introduction to *Orientalism*, which has widely informed studies of Western encounters with Islam from the time of the Crusades to the present, Said defines his premise with precision and clarity by stating that he will deal with the Near East with occasional reference to Persia and India. He indicates that in his work "a large part of the Orient seem[s] to have been eliminated" such as "Japan, China and other sections in the Far East—not because these regions were not important (they obviously have been)" (Said 17). In his amply documented book, Said begins by confronting the domination of Britain and France of "the Eastern Mediterranean from about the seventeenth century on" (Said 17). He is almost apologetic about the fact his discussion will "not do justice to the important contributions to Orientalism of Germany, Italy, Russia and Portugal" (ibid). Ironically, in his apparent chronological account of Orientalist/imperialist[10] exploration and expansion, Said, as he focuses on the British and French experience of the East, makes a conscious choice not to talk about the Ottoman Empire, historiographically documented as "the Orient". The problem here is that the semantic domain of the concept of power includes the concepts of appropriation and domination, which turn up frequently in Said's characterizations of the will to

---

(66). It does not only connote "rigidity" but also "repetition". Meanwhile, "the stereotype, which is its "discursive strategy ... vacillates between what is already known, and something that must anxiously repeated" (66).

10 The term "imperialism", connoting a universal evil, is one of "Western coinage" (Lewis *Eurocentricism*, 51).

power. Paradoxically, however, based on Said's own appropriation of the domain of the Orient, the six hundred years of the imperial experience of the Ottoman Empire is discarded outright or "when mentioned, is rendered unrecognizable or irrelevant" (Zilfi 4). However, the Ottomans who had excelled in statecraft and administration, financial policies, land and military organization, were a "centralized and self consciously imperial state" (Kafadar xi). As Francis Robinson writes in *The Illustrated History: Islamic World*:

> After taking Constantinople in 1453 the Ottoman Emperors Mehmet the Conqueror (r.1444-46/1451-81), Bayazid II (r.1481-1521), Selim (r.1512-20), and Sulayman the Magnificent (r.1520-66) conquered the fertile crescent, Egypt, and the Hijaz, thus gaining control of Mecca and Medina, Yemen, and North Africa up to Morocco (Robinson 65).

In 1453, the capture of Constantinople, renamed Istanbul, was seen as the realisation of the "apocalyptic prophecies circulating" (Robinson 58) about the new capital of the Ottoman Empire. Istanbul, the location (previously besieged by the Arabs in 668) between Europe and Asia, symbolized the beginnings of the Ottoman Sultan's religious and political power in both the West and the East. In 1500s the Ottoman armies not only began to penetrate Eastern Europe, but with the conquest of Egypt in 1517, the office of the caliphate—reaching back to the Islamic Prophet—which was previously claimed by Mamluk Sultans, officially passed to the Ottoman Sultan.[11] This meant that from the sixteenth to the twentieth century, that is, until the 1922 abolition of the caliphate by Mustafa Kemal Ataturk, founder of the secular Turkish Republic, it was the Ottoman Sultans who, as the heads of Islam, were the sovereigns of the Muslim world. As Lord Kinross writes:

---

11 Before he was given the title "Padisah-il Islam", meaning, The Emperor of Islam, the Ottoman sovereign was referred to as the "Sultan of the Arabs and Persians and the Rum". As for the new title, which is commonly used by historians and others to describe the Ottoman sovereign, the claim for the territorial sovereignty shifts to describe the Sultan as the heir to the great universal Empires of Medieval Islam.

> Of more tangible significance was the transfer to Istanbul of the standard and cloak of the Prophet, relics whose possession symbolized the status of sultans as protectors of the holy places of Mecca, Medina and the pilgrim routes of the Hejaz, hence Islam in general (Kinross 170).

In this context, it is crucial to emphasize that it was only from the nineteenth century onwards that the Ottoman Islamic world system was overwhelmed by forces from the West, driven by capitalism and empowered by the Enlightenment and the industrial revolution. As for 1798, it was a symbolic moment when not only did the leader's standards pass to Europe, but when Western standards, Western armies and Western capital overran the Ottomans with Napoleon's invasion of Egypt, which had been an Ottoman province since 1517.

The Ottoman success in withstanding the Western challenge had continued until the end of the seventeenth century. Yet, the Ottoman defeat at the second siege of Vienna (1683) against a combined Habsburg-Polish army and the subsequent treaty of Karlowitz (1699) marked the beginnings of the long and slow retreat of the Ottoman Sultanate from their European conquests. By the close of the eighteenth century, Western Europe, with its gun-power revolution and superior naval technology was invulnerable to the Ottoman power. Ultimately, as the Ottomans became politically and economically dependent on Europe, they began to adapt themselves to the challenge of Western superiority (Inalcik 1994, 3).

Although Said's main focus is on the post-Napoleonic period in which the European powers have begun the process of imperialism and colonization of the East, his work has been applied to the studies of Western encounters with Islam of different periods. In this respect, his overgeneralization of the Orient is problematic and his general claims, made through a rough historical overview, are misleading. Said's binary opposition of the East and West through configurations such as weak and strong, inferior and superior, etc. should be more "complex and multifaceted" as Vaughan has shown in her historicist analysis of *Othello*, which exemplifies the English concern about the power of Ottoman Islamic imperialism (Vaughan 27). Renaissance curiosity and anxiety about the Ottomans produced an outpouring of texts in the form of travel narratives, historical and political studies, polemical and religious tracts, ballads, poetry, fiction and drama, perhaps the best way of conveying ideas and knowledge about the Turks, who inspired fear and fascination in Europe.

Throughout the sixteenth and seventeenth centuries, while the Christian West was conquering indigenous populations in the New World, the Ottoman power had already pushed beyond the Mediterranean, as far as the walls of Vienna and had even crossed the English Channel. After Columbus' conquest of America, while the Europeans ventured across the Atlantic and Pacific Oceans and "took possession" (Greenblatt 9) of the peoples they encountered, the Ottomans with their formidable army held power over Europe, conquering, capturing and converting Christians to Islam in large numbers. If Christian Europeans, as Greenblatt asserts, "felt powerfully superior to virtually all the peoples they encountered" because of their conviction that they had the "absolute and exclusive religious truth" (Greenblatt 9), there were similar attestations to the Muslim sense of certitude and superiority over the Western world. By a curious irony, Said's radical theory and views about the Orient are clearly evident in the following statement, which represents a construct, not a reality, and his own stereotypical and mythic East of the past:

> The other feature of the Orient was that Europe was always in a position of strength, not to say domination. There is no way of putting this euphemistically...the essential relationship, on political, cultural and even religious grounds, was seen—in the West, which is what concerns us here—to be one between a strong and weak partner (Said 40).

Considering the political significance of the Ottoman-European trade relations and "the fierce competition among" (Naff 100) European countries to appear in treaties as the Ottomans' "most favoured nation", the essential relationship between the East and the West was one in which the Ottomans were "in a position of strength". Ultimately, in Eastern and Western commercial relationships, it was the Ottoman sultan who was the "strong partner" as he ruled the Ottoman lands that extended from Istanbul to Aleppo, a crucial link in the silk route that led to China. Among these lands were Cairo, a trade centre; Jerusalem, the Holy Land; Algiers, "the whip of the Christian World, the wall of the Barbarian, terror of Europe" (Purchas 278) to name just a few. As the Englishman, Thomas Fuller wrote in awe:

> [I]t is the greatest and best-compacted (not excepting the Romane it self in the height thereof) [Empire] that the sunne ever saw. Take sea and land together (as bones and flesh make up one bodie) and from Buda in the West to Taris in the East, it stretches about three thousand miles: little lesse in the extent thereof North and South. It lieth in the heart of the world, like a bold champion bidding defiance to all his borders, commanding the most fruitfull countreys of Europe, Asia and Africa: Onely America (not more happy in her rich mines then in her remoteness) lieth free from reach thereof.[12]

1.1.1. Ottoman-Venetian Relations

> *The Ottoman Empire had inherited the power of the Romans; Neither the Church nor a Christian prince had been able to resume the Roman conquest and unify the entire world. What was at stake in Venetian minds was to anticipate who would establish a universal monarchy. A vision of world history inspired by the prophecy of Daniel was then still popular in Europe. The four pagan monarchies—Babylonian, Persian, Greek and Roman—were to be followed by the establishment of the fifth empire*
>
> (Valensi 1990,180).

In assessing Ottoman-Venetian relations, it is imperative to expand the boundaries of Western historiography by incorporating the Ottoman Empire into the constructions of sixteenth-century world order as a major protagonist, and then to contextualize its role in a commercial zone that stretched from the Mediterranean to the Indian Ocean. As Palmira J. Brummett observes:

12 This quotation from Thomas Fuller, *The Historie of the Holy Warre*, (1639), is quoted in *Islam in Britain* (Matar 14).

> The success of the Ottomans in overcoming the military challenges of European states, in uniting the Holy Land to the rich agricultural heart-lands of Eastern Roman Empire, and in gaining effective control over the outlets to the eastern trade, focused the attention of Europe in a dramatic fashion just when its internal social unity was being fragmented by Reformation. At the same time, the Ottomans developed a navy which threatened European control of the western Mediterranean. These accomplishments reinforced notions of the Ottoman state as a military juggernaut before all else—notions which were articulated in the European diplomatic correspondence and chroniclers for rhetorical political purposes (Brummett 180).

As a commercial empire, since the regime of the Venetian Empire rested upon capital investment in long-distance trade, Venice had entered diplomatic relations with the Ottoman Empire in the second half of the fifteenth century. In fact, among the earliest cultural links between the Ottoman Empire and Europe were evidently those that were provided by Venetian traders and artists. Like the Genoese, Venetians first secured trading privileges in the Ottoman Empire and Ottoman merchants were also a common sight in the Piazza San Marco, as, for instance, they are depicted in Bellini's *Procession Before San Marco.* When Mehmet II, a man of culture, had invited Bellini to paint a portrait of him as well as the frescoes of the Topkapi Palace, the Ottomans with their ceremonial and elaborate costumes were a potent source of fascination and inspiration for the Venetian artist. By the fifteenth century, in the art of Italy, and of Venice in particular, Ottomans would most often be depicted through distinctive modes of dress, which included the turban and other headgear.

What Venice knew about the Ottoman Empire, "she owed to the quality of the dispatches and letters her ambassadors sent during their long sojourns in Istanbul" (Valensi 1990, 177). In Venice, for every patrician that embarked upon a career in politics, the position of "bailo"[13] in Istanbul was the "most prestigious and most important" appointment for which he could hope (Valensi 1990, 177). Venetian ambassadors, bearing the title of

---

13 For an entire series of Venetian "bailo" reports in the sixteenth century, see Eugenio Alberi's *Relazioni degli ambasciatori veneziani al Senato durante il secolo decimosesto.*

"bailo" were the sons of all the most highly educated elite and thus belonged to Venice's erudite circles. As they "stood at an intersection of three spaces, those of empirical observation, political action and humanism" (Valensi 9) they were in a favourable position to appreciate Ottoman culture. Their residency in Istanbul allowed them to make sufficient contacts in the city and "personally collect the most accurate data on the most powerful empire of the times" (Valensi 1990, 176). As every Venetian ambassador was obliged to present a report before a public session of the Senate and in the presence of the doge, Contarini upon his return from Istanbul stated that the Republic has "before its eyes, as in a theatre, a representation of the world, nature, and the laws and styles of various peoples" (Valensi 41). Venetian fascination with the Ottomans resulted in the first instance from the extraordinary power of the Grand Signor and the vastness of his empire. As Valensi concludes, the collection of Venetian accounts covering the Ottomans:

> insisted on the comprehensiveness of every single part of the whole: the empire included 'all of Greece', 'all of Asia Minor', 'all the coasts of Africa and the Mediterranean', 'all the borders of Venetian dominions' and so forth (Valensi 1990, 179).

As Paolo Contarini wrote in 1538: "a large part of Africa, the major part of Europe and a very large part of Asia find themselves today under the obedience of this Empire" (Valensi 180). For Barbarigo three elements made the Grand Signor invincible: "so many territories, so much money, and so much an abundance of obedient men" (Valensi 181). Apart from its opulence and exotic ambiance, the Ottoman Empire, a military giant, was, by the sixteenth century, a source of great anxiety for the Venetian Republic. Particularly in the years following Mehmet II's death in 1481, as the Ottoman fleet began to challenge Venice in the open seas, the Venetians had to demonstrate their effectiveness in meeting the crises of enormous Ottoman danger which had begun to play an increasingly important role in European politics. The Turks are the greatest fighters in the world" wrote Cavalli in 1560; "one should not fight them but fear them" (Valensi 181).

In the second half of the fifteenth century, as the Ottomans set out to make the Mediterranean a Turkish lake, Venice, was the only important Christian power in the region. In that respect no other Christian power had "spent so heavily on defense and war against" (Hale 26) the Ottomans as Venice whose fundamental basis of fortune and power was the Mediterranean Sea.

The Ottoman Empire, which had occupied the heel of Italy in the late fifteenth century and used the French port of Toulon as a naval base in the sixteenth, was in essence a military adversary to the Venetian Republic. In 1453, following Mehmet II's conquest of Constantinople, although the Ottomans' trading, cultural and ambassadorial contacts with Venice had increased, the Venetians were evidently alarmed by the military strength of the Ottoman Empire, which aspired to bring the whole Mediterranean basin under one power.

In the sixteenth century the Ottoman Empire not only posed a serious threat to European sovereignty but also played a great role in rivalries for commercial hegemony in the economic space stretching from Venice to the Indian Ocean. The objectives of Ottoman expansion in its claims for universal sovereignty, Levantine power politics, and the struggle for control of oriental trade, however, were not different than those of "European voyages of discovery: wealth, power, glory, religious legitimation" (Brummett 2).

The Ottoman State's energies for territorial expansion were geared towards acquisition of fertile lands to broaden the tax-base that was used to support the ruling elite. Yet, the Ottoman State was not merely a land-based military state. It was a sea-based power, whose motivation for expansion was directed towards dominating and controlling the trade centres and networks in various commercial zones. And these commercial zones were pivotal for the Venetians' own indigenous merchant networks in long distance trade. In this sense, as "a merchant state endowed with economic intentionality" (Brummett 3), the development of Ottoman sea power was crucial in the reconfiguration of the early sixteenth-century balance of power, which culminated in the subordination of the Venetian Republic.

In 1571, however, a Christian fleet led by the papacy, Venice and Habsburg forces sailing under the flag of the Holy Roman Empire virtually destroyed the ships of the Ottomans in Lepanto. This marked a crucial moment in the history of Venetian Republic. For the Venetian merchants and Genoese captains who competed with the Ottoman traders and ships for silk, spice and other goods in Aleppo and Damascus and Alexandria (all Ottoman provinces by then) the triumph in Lepanto, however, was only symbolical. Like the Venetians, the Ottomans were also a commercial power, whose military ruling class (members including the sultan, his sons and high-ranking dignitaries such as pashas, etc) accumulated wealth that could be and was invested in commercial enterprises. In other words, despite the tendency of European historians to dismiss Ottoman mercantilism in the international scene during the sixteenth century and its commercial hegemony from Genoa and Venice to the Indian Ocean, the Ottoman Empire with its ruling elite military class was a significant merchant state. As Brummett points out, the Ottoman State invested part of its accumulated wealth in trading ventures for profit. Furthermore, the State competed with other states for the control of commercial revenues and designed its foreign policy with a clear purpose of gaining control of sources for commercial revenue rather than simply acquiring land with the intention of colonization and agricultural exploitation (Brummett 5).

Following the Western victory over the Ottomans in Lepanto, although major hostilities were suspended in the Mediterranean Europe and the Ottoman Empire, another danger, piracy the "second form of war" (Braudel 865), persisted. In the first half of the fifteenth century Ottoman sailors were no match for the fleets of the Italian mercantile cities Genoa and Venice, whose state-owned galleys provided unrivalled transport for freight traveling to Alexandria, Syria and Istanbul. In the sixteenth century, however, with the decrease of the Venetian prominence among European countries and the Ottomans' quick revival of sea-power, the "Barbary states were in the same league as naval powers as England and France" (Earle 46). As for Venice, not only had her immensely expensive war of 1570-73 with the Ottomans consumed her wealth, but the Ottoman Empire had now begun to engage in commerce in "Venice's traditional sphere of action" (Hale 38). Following their conquest of Syria, Palestine and Egypt, the Ottomans made an alliance with the Barbary pirates, who placed much of the naval resources of North Africa at their command. As doge Nicola Dona wrote:

> In the days before the war with the Turks, all was grandeur, utility, emolument, commodity, honour ... everyone was interested in sea voyages, in business, in everything appertaining to the existence and good of the fatherland (Chambers 194).

Ultimately, the Ottoman-Venetian wars, had not only increased the interest of the merchants of Marseilles, Ragusa and other places in the Levantine trade, but also had encouraged England to enter directly into trade with the Ottomans. As Nicolo Molin, the Venetian Ambassador to England, wrote to the Venetian Senate in late 1605 about his concerns about the piracies committed with "mixed crews of Englishmen and Turks" in the Mediterranean: "...everything [was] weighed in the scales of Material interest."[14] This correspondence was essentially the embodiment, though simplified, of what was deemed to be the nature of England's 'friendship' with the Ottoman Empire, which was one coveted by all the trading nations.

1.1.2. Anglo-Ottoman Relations

Knowledge of the Turks was "almost nil in medieval England" (Beck, 29) to the extent that even the fall of Constantinople in 1453 had "passed without notice in contemporary English chron-

---

[14] Calendar of State Papers, Venetian, 1603-07—hereafter referred to as C.S.P.—(C.S.P. 140).

iclers" (Wood 1). This was not surprising considering that the efforts of the last Byzantine Emperor Manuel Palaeologus to seek help from the English against the Ottoman Empire were "fruitless" mainly because England had no direct commercial nor diplomatic relations with the Byzantines (Wood 1). Yet the establishment of the Ottoman/Islamic power over what had been the Byzantine/Christian Empire was deeply seated in ideology. Soon, the danger which the Turk represented was revealed to the consciousness of the English, particularly when the Ottomans invaded Europe. Geographically, however, the English were outside the periphery of the Ottoman peril. Furthermore, despite the appeal of the East, with its silks, spices, oils, carpets and mohair, which led to a growing interest in the commercial links with the Levant, England was reluctant to have diplomatic ties with the Ottomans, a nation that was notorious among the Christians as "heathen". As Chew writes in *The Crescent and the Rose*:

> The fact remains impressive that the English government did not enter into diplomatic relations with the Porte till a hundred and thirty years after the fall of Constantinople; and at a much later date James I was reluctant to receive an emissary from the Sultan on the ground that to welcome an infidel would be 'unbecoming to a Christian Prince' (Chew 152).

England's first tentative approach to the Ottoman Empire had occurred in 1553 when Anthony Jenkinson had obtained from Suleyman the liberty to trade through the Ottoman dominions (Hakluyt 62-63). As Chew asserts:

> Anthony Jenkinson's journey ... was probably undertaken with a view of obtaining information regarding the possibility of initiating local trade in Turkey and practicability of tapping some of the trade which came from the further East by way of Mesopotamia or the Red Sea (Chew 151).

The nascent trade that had begun between the Porte and England, however, would cease for the next thirty years for variety of reasons. First, the discovery and the development of the route to the east round of Cape of Hope by the Portuguese had facilitated the delivery of Oriental goods to Europe. Second—as discussed in the previous section on Venetian Ottoman relations—the peril of the Ottoman sea power had reached its zenith following the two wars with the Venetian Republic, which led to the Ottomans' loss of territory in the Aegean and the Mediterranean, such as Cyprus (1570). However, a more constant threat to the English was posed by the fleets of Barbary corsairs who had begun to disrupt trade initiatives by swamping the Mediterranean trade routes leading to the imperial capital Istanbul, Izmir (Smyrna) and Ottoman provinces such as Aleppo and Alexandria. During the suspension of trade with the Ottomans, although the English celebrated the Ottomans' defeat in Lepanto with bonfires and "a banqueting and great rejoycing" as the victory of the Venetians and the Spanish was of "so great importance to the whole state of the Christian commonwealth" (Lipson 335), England's interest in the Turk gradually continued to develop. Unlike France—and other states like Ragusa, Venice and Genoa—which had begun to establish themselves firmly at the Ottoman Porte through the Capitulations[15] (1536), which provided them numerous legal and economic privileges, Anglo/Ottoman relations were delayed to the closing decades of the sixteenth century. It was only in1580 that the English began to push their ventures into the realms of distant power like the Ottoman Empire.

As Sir Thomas Shirley writes in the *Discours of the Turkes (1606-07)*, (Shirley 9-12) it was in the later half of the Elizabethan era that the relations between Protestant England and the Ottoman Empire had expanded. In Minchinton's view, the Mediterranean grain crisis of the 1560s had provided England with her entry into trade relations with powers in that region. Thus, the supply of grain for the Italians and the Ottomans had further fuelled

---

15 Capitulations refer to the legal and commercial privileges granted by the Sultan to the European states allowing the latter's subjects to reside and trade in the Empire exempt from taxes. The capitulations that the Venetians and the Genoese had received from the Byzantine Empire since the eleventh century were renewed by the Ottoman Sultans after the taking of Constantinople in 1453. As for the French, they obtained similar legal rights and trade privileges from Sultan Suleyman I in 1536. For a discussion of England's economic ventures in the Ottoman Empire, see *The Journal of European Economic History* (Eysturlid 614).

the English commercial and economic interest in the Ottoman Empire (Minchinton 7). Once the formal entry of Anglo-Ottoman economic and diplomatic relationship occurred following William Harborne's visit to Istanbul in June 1580, enabling the English to have official access to the Eastern Mediterranean, Elizabethans looked to draw the Ottomans into their export market.

Essentially, the English interest in the "Great Turke" which grew slowly, only began to assume true significance in the final decades of the sixteenth century when the Ottoman Empire entered into a stable economic and political relationship with England following William Harborne's mission to the Sublime Porte (Burian 209). Although William Harborne was successful in receiving a favourable grant from the Sultan, a grant defining the "English liberties on the subject" at the Sublime Porte[16], it was the Venetian and the French ambassadors who would use their leverage against the English. The best means for England to counter the hostility of the Venetians and the French, who jealously guarded their economic rights in Istanbul, was to create a merchant monopoly, the Levant Company, which was initially called the Turkey Company. During the reign of James I, despite the anti-Ottoman sentiments and rhetoric against the Infidel from his Majesty who considered himself one of the defenders of Christian Europe, the survival of the Levant Company founded in Elizabeth's reign became crucial to the development of English exports and power. The economic incentive to fuel commercial relations with the Ottomans was overwhelming for the English considering that a single voyage to their ports (such as Istanbul, Alexandria, Tunis, Algiers and so on) "held the prospect of a profit of up to 300%" (Eysturlid 617).

Despite such outstanding returns arising from the lucrative nature of maritime commerce in the Mediterranean, which attracted wealthy investors in England, the risk involved in these

---

16 The term Porte usually referred as the Sublime Porte is the English rendering of "Bab-i-Ali" (High Porte), which connotes the Ottoman Grand Vezirate and its extension, the Government, in general.

voyages was too high. James I sought to end the English investments in pirate ventures, since they led England to have the reputation of a "nation of pirates" (Eysturlid 618). As for the Ottomans, their ships ranged from North Africa to Arabia and from the English Channel to the Spanish and Moroccan coasts; furthermore, their pirates captured single men and whole families, travelers and soldiers, traders and clergymen (Matar 1998, 5).

Since the first recorded visit of the Englishman, Anthony Jenkinson, to Istanbul in 1533 several merchants and seamen from England had been captured and converted to Islam. The extant records, biographies and autobiographies of England's early modern history repeatedly refer to such British captivities and conversions in the sixteenth century; the Levant Company representatives in Istanbul urged Queen Elizabeth to protect her subjects from any future enslavement in the Ottoman Sultan's dominions. As Epstein quotes in *The Early History of the Levant Company,* ransoming of the British captives had cost England:

> four thousand pounds, and yet divers to this day remain there unrescated of which some (the more to be pitied) have turned Turks (Epstein 242).

"Turning Turk" was not only a puzzling issue but a distressing one for Renaissance England considering the frequency of Christians renouncing their faith for Islam (Matar 1994, 33). One of the topics that Sir Thomas Shirley, an English traveler who had visited the Orient in the late sixteenth century, touched on in the *Discours of the Turkes* (1606-07) was the issue that dominated the English Renaissance concerns of conversion. Although Shirley had no adequate reply, he analyzed the reasons for Christian conversions to Islam. From the beginnings of the Christian-Muslim encounter and the subsequent spread of the Ottoman danger, Islam was seen in the medieval way, as a movement of violence in the service of Anti-Christ. Since there were numerous incidents of English ships being captured by the Barbary corsairs, arrangements were made to redeem the Englishmen who were enslaved in Algiers "lest they follow the example of others and turn Turk" (Harrison 132).

In the *Calendar of State Papers Domestic*, James I, 1619-1629, it was cited that "the pirates of Algiers and Tunis had grown so strong that in a few years they have taken 300 ships, and imprisoned many hundred persons."[17] The *Calendar of State Papers Domestic*, Charles I, 1625-1626, stated: "The Turks are upon our coasts. They take ships only to take the men to make slaves of them."[18] Between1609-1616, it was reported that almost 500 British ships were pursued, captured and their crews enslaved by "Turkish pirates."[19] During the Jacobean period, the Englishmen themselves were also accused of committing piracies in the Mediterranean because of the "lucrative return it provided both business and government" (Eysturlid, 613). Yet, despite the epidemics of piracy in the open seas compounded by the problem of English conversions to Islam, the economic significance of British interaction with the Ottomans in the Mediterranean outweighed its risks. Despite the stream of anti-Turkish rhetoric directed against the "enemy of all Christendom" (Eysturlid 625) and the English fleet's inability to suppress the menace of piracy, enslavement and/or conversion of captives to Islam, the visible result was the growth of Anglo-Ottoman trade; and this meant increased economic power for England.

1.1.3. Franco-Ottoman Relations

The Ottomans were first brought to the attention of France through the crusading expedition of a large body of French knights to aid the King of Hungary against Sultan Bajazed I in 1396 and through the chronicling of the subsequent events. As Froissart wrote in *Les chroniques*, the battle in the Nicopolis Crusade was a complete victory for the Ottomans over the Western knights who had attacked with a rekindled crusading spirit (Kinross 69). This marked the ending of the last of the crusades with a catastrophic defeat by the Muslims in the heart of Christian

---

17 See *Calendar of State Papers Domestic*, James I, 1619-1623, vol 10:12 (hereafter C.S.P. Domestic).

18 C.S.P. Domestic, Charles I, 1625-1626, vol. 1: 11.

Europe. As the biographer of Boucicault, Marshall of France, who was saved at the last moment, put it: "ces chiens de Sarracins, laids et horribles, qui les tenoient durement devant ce tyran ennemy de la foy, qui la seoit" (Rouillard 17).

According to Froissart's records in the chronicles, however, the Duke of Nevers, known as Jean sans Peur, and other prisoners kept by the Ottoman Sultan, were "treated with chivalry worthy of the most civilized prince". Although the French nobles had suffered certain difficulties from "lack of wine and from spicy food 'hors de la nature de la France" they marveled at the size of the Sultan's army, the magnificence of his table" and his concern for justice. Through direct contact with the Grand Turk, the French nobles had realized that "this was not the barbarian enemy of popular imagination" (Rouillard 18). Later in 1453 when Mehmet II began his siege of Constantinople by controlling the Bosphorous and the Dardanelles, Charles VII who was retaking Bordeaux and Rouen from the English had "no desire to waste his strength on another Nicopolis" (Rouillard 22).

Up until the eighteenth century, the Ottomans had no permanent representation in Europe, unlike the Europeans with their permanent representatives in the Ottoman Empire. By the sixteenth century, all the leading states of Christian Europe had been forced to take into account the Ottomans, from a military if not a diplomatic and commercial points of view. Francis I had done so voluntarily as he had sought help from Suleyman I after his capture at Pavia in 1525. As Fatma Gocek writes:

> The contact between the Ottoman Empire and Europe was established in the one direction, from Europe to the Ottoman Empire. As long as the Ottomans maintained their military superiority over Europe, this directionality did not create any problems in the Ottoman Empire (Gocek 3).

By the sixteenth century, the King of France soon established a permanent embassy in Istanbul with the first French ambassador, Jean de La Forest arriving in the capital city in 1536. In 1535 France had formed an alliance with Suleiman through the

---

19 C.S.P. Domestic, James I, 1611-1618, vol. 9: 514.

initiatives of his Grand Vizier Ibrahim—"good friend" (Kinross 204) to the King of France—following the Ottoman conquests of Belgrade and Rhodes. The 1535 treaty, which permitted the French to carry on trade throughout the Ottoman Empire, marked the beginning of a system of privileges to foreign powers known as Capitulations and enabled France to be the predominant and unrivalled foreign influence at the Sublime Porte. In 1579, during the reign of Murad II, King Henri II of France sent Ambassador Baron de Germigny to Istanbul to secure the renewal of Turco-French alliance, confirming the precedence of the French above other ambassadors in the Imperial Capital. The visit also confirmed the privileges of the French protectorate over all the Catholics in the Levant and the holy places of Jerusalem and Sinai under the Ottoman rule. Ultimately, France through her mediation had risen above the rest of Europe to an unchangeable position of influence and prestige at the Sublime Porte in Istanbul.

With no European power did the Ottomans have closer relations than with France as they shared a common bond of hostility to the House of Austria. At the height of Franco-Austrian hostility, the French ambassador had arranged for French ships to re-equip in the port of Istanbul, with the Ottoman fleet wintering in Toulon in 1543-44. As Philip Mansel writes:

> The 'union of the lily and the crescent', as one French noble called it, became one of the fixed points in European politics—although the king of France, conscious of his titles of 'Most Christian King' and 'eldest son of the church', fearful of the criticism of Catholic Europe, evaded the written alliance repeatedly requested by the Sublime Porte [Ottoman government] (Mansel 1996, 44).

Thus, the traditional policy of France was to encourage the Ottoman Empire to become engaged against the adversaries of France and to cooperate with the Ottomans when French interests required it, but never enter into a formal alliance with them. For their part, the French ministers' and diplomats' main reason to befriend the Ottoman Empire was "the desire to protect and propagate Catholicism within its frontiers" (Mansel 1996, 45).

Although the Levant trade was a second cause, the principal motive for d'Andrezel was to ensure that "the power of the Turks remain[ed] an object of fear for the House of Austria" (Mansel 45). Despite their different customs, languages and religion both the Grand viziers and the Imperial ambassadors in their spectacular and highly ceremonial meetings at the Sublime Porte spoke the same language of "power, profit and monarchy" (Mansel 45). As a cycle of 'embassy pictures' revealed the imperial city's political hierarchy and ceremonies, Western artists were commissioned to inform Europe of the "superiority of the ceremonial, customs and etiquette of the Ottoman court" (Mansel 49). In fact, in 1526, when Francis I sought the support of the Ottomans by asking the Sultan to attack the King of Hungary while he fought Charles V, Suleyman I's response to the King of France, revealed an Ottoman sense of superiority:

> I who am the Sultan of Sultans, Soverign of Sovereigns, Distributor of Crowns to Monarchs over the whole Surface of the Globe, God's Shadow on Earth, Sultan and Padishah of the White Sea and the Black Sea, of Rumelia and Anatolia, of Karaman and the countries of Rum, Zulcadir, Diyarbekir, Kurdistan, Azerbaijan, Persia, Damascus, Aleppo, Cairo, Mecca and Medina, Jerusalem and all Arabia, Yemen and so many other lands ... [and] You, Francis, King of the Land of France, who have sent a letter to my Porte (Quoted from Clot, 131).

Suleyman, whose dynamic reign of forty-six years was the zenith of Ottoman political and economic expansion, was:

> at least the equal of his Western contemporaries, Charles V, Francis I and Henry VIII. To the Western world, ignorant of the Ottoman laws and arts, but increasingly familiar with lavish descriptions of the Grand Turk at the head of his conquering armies ... he came to be known as Soliman the Magnificent, and nowhere his reputation was greater than France (Rouillard 67).

In the sixteenth and seventeenth centuries, although the Ottomans had no permanent representation in Europe, Suleyman sent the first representatives to the King of France. The status of Ottoman diplomatic representatives sent to France was restricted to dispatches or rather envoys recruited from heralds, chamberlains and so forth. These envoys, trained in the Palace held symbolic functions such as delivering or receiving letters, acknowledging treaties or attending the coronation ceremonies of European monarchs. The diplomatic contact which had begun with Suleyman's dispatch to Francis I in 1533 was followed by Selim II to Charles IX in 1571, Murad III to Henri III in 1581, Mehmet III to Henri IV in 1601 and to Louis XIII in 1607 and finally Mehmet IV to Louis XIV in 1669. Of these, the last Ottoman representative Suleyman Aga not only aroused great curiosity in France but also invoked a new vogue 'à la turque' at the court of Louis XIV. In 1669 (just before Louis XIV had ordered Molière to write *Le bourgeois gentilhomme*) when the Ottoman Ambassador Suleyman Aga visited the French court, the Sun King went out of his way to impress the representative of the Grand Turk. In a fascinating welcoming ceremony, apart from a lavish feast prepared for the guest of honour, members of the court dressed themselves in fantastically elaborate costumes. As the Minister of Foreign Affairs, Hugues de Lionne wore a long garment "embroidered with a silver Saint-Esprit Cross" (Behdad 37) the King dressed himself in all of his diamonds and wore an "exotic" crown decorated with feathers. Sitting on a silver throne, Louis XIV:

> Paraissait dans toute sa majesté, revetu d'un brocart d'or, Mais tellement couvert de diamants, qu'il semblait qu'il fut environné de lumière, en ayant aussi un chapeau tout brillant, avec un bouquet de plumes des plus magnifiques (Œuvres 10).

By the sixteenth century, general interest in the Ottoman Empire was so great in France that the translations of the treatises written by the historian Paolo Giovio were published in France in 1538 and 1544 (Rouillard 17). Besides this principal source of historical knowledge of the Turks in mid-sixteenth century, a number of internal events of Suleyman's reign were also familiar to French readers through chroniclers or dramatists. The wide popularity of plays written about the Ottomans reflected the history of political, military, economic and cultural relations between the Ottoman Empire and Europe.

In French drama the image of the Grand Signor conveyed through a cycle of plays about Suleyman the Magnificent, beginning with Bounin's *La soltane* (1561), was in a constant state of flux between a powerful and rightful ruler and that of an unnatural despotic Eastern monarch. As Alain Grosrichard wrote in *The Sultan's Court: European Fantasies of the East:* "From the end of the seventeenth century and throughout the eighteenth, a spectre haunted Europe: the spectre of despotism" (Grosrichard 3). In analyzing Montesquieu's conception of the constituents and mechanisms of "oriental despotism", Grosrichard has explored the documentary strata of travel accounts and descriptions of the Ottoman Empire in the seventeenth century. In spite of the fact that the concept of despotism had been around since Aristotle and was used through the Medieval and Renaissance periods with changing connotations, in the eighteenth century "oriental despotism" was particularly fashionable in France. For Grosrichard while Montesquieu had made the concept of despotism a permanent fixture in European political thought, "oriental despotism" was ultimately the concept of fantasy, the fantasy of pure power, through which Napoléon had pursued a mirage of Oriental glory by invading Egypt. Napoléon's Egyptian campaign, characterized by extremes of violence, bloodshed and brutal methods of warfare was conceived in a spirit of rivalry to British imperialism in India. It also extended French military ambitions beyond the limits of Europe to Africa. At last, the fully modernized forces of Napoléon clashing with the Ottoman troops, now lacking military discipline and strength, had marked the triumph of the French against the Ottomans and asserted the hegemony of a "superior" West over an "inferior" East. With the success of Napoléon's army, as a new French ambassador began to seal his country's influence at the Porte, the Ottoman Sultan was anxious to appoint a permanent Ottoman ambassador to Paris, as he could not disguise his fascination with all things French.

1.1.4. Decline of the Ottoman Empire

The eighteenth century marked the culmination of a great transformation in Europe, a revolution in scientific ideas, in philosophical and social thought, brought on by relativism born of geographic discovery and a shift in the perception of the universe due to the progression from Copernicus to Newton. Furthermore, the West had also witnessed the Ottoman failure in two wars against the Russian and Austrian Empires, which were concluded with the treaties of Karlowitz (1699) and Pasarowitz (1718). Since these two wars had led to a shift in the balance of power between the Ottoman Empire and Europe, the Ottomans, in order to maintain their territorial boundaries in the West, had begun to inquire into European military technology. Furthermore, in order to participate in Western diplomacy, they began to dispatch embassies to Europe. As Ambassador Yirmi Sekiz Celebi Mehmet Efendi was sent to France (1721) to inform the French that the "Ottoman State had authorized them to repair the Church of the Holy Sepulcher in Jerusalem" (Gocek 4), this was the "first window opening to the West" (Gocek 5) through France, the cultural centre of Europe and a potential ally to the Ottomans.

In this respect, Ottoman relations with Europe are characterized by two events, each representing a historical turning point for the Empire: the Treaty of Carlowitz (1699), establishing Europe's military superiority over the Turks and Sultan Selim III's Tri-Partite Defensive Alliance (1799) with Britain and Russia confirming the Ottoman defensive posture towards the West. The progression of events between 1699 and 1799 reveals that changes were made within the Ottoman Empire with respect to relations with Europe and the pattern of affairs in their diplomacy. Given Europe's military ascendancy which was confirmed by the Austrians at Passarowitz (1718), the Russians at Küçük Kaynarca (1744) and in Crimea (1783), and by the French in Egypt (1789), the Ottoman Empire ultimately became dependent on the European balance of power. According to Naff:

> in the eighteenth century these determinants were located increasingly beyond the confines of Europe, in the Western hemisphere and Indian subcontinent where the rivalry between England and France unleashed external political and economic forces well beyond the ken or control of the Sublime Porte (Naff 90).

In the eighteenth century, what drastically tipped this balance of power was the difference in the international systems of the state-centred European countries and the Ottoman Empire. In the preceding two centuries, with the rise of strong centralized monarchies in Europe, several Western nations had achieved overseas exploration, colonization and commercial expansion. Furthermore, through the Reformation, by developing a secular, rational outlook, which promoted scientific discoveries, Europe underwent some major technological and industrial revolutions, which led to a more flexible economic system. As for the Ottoman system, it was imperial and Islamic, and foreign relations were inspired by religious precepts and often shaped and influenced by religious authorities. Although these differences complicated and limited the Sublime Porte's participation in and acceptance of alliances with Christian powers, certain trends gradually became apparent in the evolution of the Ottomans' changing relations with the West. In other words, in adopting European rules and concepts, the economic and diplomatic relations between the Empire and Europe underwent a profound change in the eighteenth century. The alignment of Ottoman policies and diplomatic practices with Europe's order of foreign relations led not only to the growth of Ottoman diplomatic missions to European capitals but to an increase in the number of European consular representatives and travelers in the Ottoman domains. Furthermore, as the Empire's economic relations with Europe underwent a profound change in the eighteenth century, capitulations were "no longer an indulgence granted by a seemingly invincible sultan as an expression of his will" (Naff 91). Instead, the terms of the treaties of capitulation were demanded and dictated by European powers, which "often outrageously abused the concessions" (Naff 91). In essence, by the eighteenth century not only its own military, bureaucratic and economic establishments were instrumental in underpinning the power of the Ottoman Empire, but the ascending strength of Europe had begun the further control of Ottoman expansion and drastically tipped the balance. Furthermore, there was a significant loosening of traditional patterns in outlook policy, and the conduct of diplomacy. As Naff observes, although the sultanate's statesmen still harboured feelings of:

> superiority towards Europeans, they were, nevertheless compelled by circumstances to steer a course towards integration with the workings of Europe's state system and foreign relations One of the ways by which the Porte showed its abandonment of the old idea of the inferiority of Europe was its deliberately seeking out and adoption of diplomatic mediation (Naff 93 and 97).

In the eighteenth century, the capitulations were significant not only in the Ottoman Empire's relations with the West, but also in creating a new era of Ottoman diplomacy. The imposition of European diplomatic thought and style ultimately moved the Sublime Porte indispensably away from "traditional Islamic unilateralism" (Naff 103) toward a European-style reciprocity in foreign relations that culminated in the Tri-Partite Defensive Alliance of 1799. From the failure of the second siege of Vienna (1683) on, when the Ottoman Empire was in retreat and needed the diplomatic support of European powers, new capitulary privileges were given mainly for the purpose of gaining political assistance in reciprocation. These capitulations were indicators of the political and economic standing of a particular state at the Empire's capital. As Naff notes:

> The fierce competition among the European powers for the Levant trade in the seventeenth and eighteenth centuries not only led to a significant increase in the number of capitulatory states—at least six in the eighteenth century alone—but as well to the appearance of the "most favoured nation" clause in all the treaties (Naff 100).

Meanwhile since the French (the Ottomans' oldest European friend since the days of Suleyman the Magnificent and Francis I) were highly successful in mediating the 1739 Treaty of Belgrade, they were able to enjoy an unchallenged state of primacy in the Levant. This allowed France to advance her interests against those of Russia, at the expense of the Ottoman Empire, as is attested by the disastrous outcome of the Ottoman-Russian war of 1768-74. England, also considered a friendly nation, regarded the events in the Ottoman Empire of lesser importance until Bonaparte's invasion of Egypt in 1798. Considering the British rivalry with France, England by increasing her diplomatic leverage, charted the way to a Tri-Partite Alliance with the Sublime Porte and Russia irrespective of the centuries of a mutual, deep-seated hostility between the Russians and the Ottoman Empire. Ultimately, by the end of the eighteenth century, the Ottomans' military and economic subjugation to Europe was almost complete.

1.2. Theoretical Approach

> *The success of the Ottomans in overcoming the military challenges of European states, in uniting the Holy Land to the rich agricultural heart-lands of the Eastern Roman Empire, and in gaining effective control over the outlets to the eastern trade focused the attention of Europe in a dramatic fashion just when its internal social unity was being fragmented by Reformation. At the same time, the Ottomans developed a navy, which threatened European control of the western Mediterranean. These accomplishments reinforced notions of the Ottoman state as a military juggernaut before all else—notions which were articulated in the European diplomatic correspondence and chroniclers for rhetorical political purposes*
>
> (Brummett 180).

In his examination of the history of domination and power, Said's focus is on the image of the Arabs in European thought in the post-Napoleonic period when the European powers had begun the process of colonizing the East. Since his definition of "Orientalism" is rooted in nineteenth-century British and French imperial history, Said concentrates on how European and Western writers have developed methods of scholarship by which they "constructed" and "defined" the Other in order to justify the process of continental and British colonization. Modern literary critics who adopt Said's templates of power and domination in interpreting Western literary discourse about the East disregard his historical parameters, which cover only the period from the second half of eighteenth century to twentieth century. Thus, they adopt and focus the post-colonialist discourse from the perspective of power and domination and focusing on the "constructed" image of the East "without its own self-presentation" (Matar 1996,187), and they apply it to the canonical texts of the Renaissance period. The desire to apply Said's theory backwards is not only anachronistic but also misleading considering that the Ottoman Empire and Islam up until the eighteenth century was "beyond colonization and domination" (Matar 1998, 12). As Matar puts it:

> [T]wentieth-century historians and literary analysts of the English attitude towards Islam have ignored this element of power which Renaissance Britons associated with Muslims and through which they defined their relations with them ... [T]hey did not take into account the fact that it was not England but the Ottoman Empire of the sixteenth and seventeenth centuries that was pushing into Europe, conquering Rhodes and Crete, attacking the Spanish, French, Dutch, English and Scottish trading fleets, landing "upon our coasts" impoverishing "that part of kingdom" near the Channel, and enslaving thousands of men and women, many of whom were converted to Islam. Muslims did not see themselves in a subservient position to Christendom, let alone to England (Matar 1998,12).

Matar affirms Bernard Lewis' ideas that the emergence of modern Europe in a "sense defined and delimited by the frontiers of Muslim power in the east, southeast and the south" (Lewis, *Cultures* 13). Furthermore, Matar adds that before the beginning of English colonialism in the eighteenth century, Islam "defined" and "delimited" England (Matar 1998, 14). In the sixteenth and seventeenth centuries Christianity had lost ground in Eastern and Central Europe not only because of the demographic and geographic expansion of the Ottomans,[20] but because the Ottoman Empire presented "a higher civilization than Christendom" (Matar 1998, 15). Since the Ottoman Empire was in a position to offer numerous opportunities to its Christian subjects, those who

20 In the English Myrror (1586), "[t]he puissant kingdom of the Turkes" wrote George Whetstone is "as a scourge sent and suffered by God, for the sins and iniquities of the Christians". For Thomas Fuller, "the cause of causes" for the "infidels" to have advanced so far, was "the justice of God" which had permitted them "to grow into the terrour of the world for the punishment of Christians" (Stradling 34).

sought employment and advancement adopted Islam voluntarily, as it provided them with a sense of imperial power and prospects of success. In Clark's view, while a Christian who joined the Ottoman dominions was "a man run wild", thousands of Europeans converted to Islam either because they "sought to identify with a powerful empire" (Clark 5) or because they were "adventurers" (Lewis, *Europe and Islam* 14) or "opportunists" (Schowoebel 212).

European historiography on the sixteenth century has been structured in terms of the Age of Discovery and the increasing power of Western power that it announced. In that sense:

> Ottoman hegemony in the Levant remains firmly under the shadow of what the empire would become, the late century "Sick Man of Europe" a colonized and imperialized dependence of latter day European dominance (Brummett 2).

It is only in one of the very rare moments of his *Orientalism* that Said refers to the subject of the "Ottoman peril" that "lurked alongside Europe" up until the seventeenth century. He writes that "[f]or Europe Islam was a lasting trauma" (Said 59). In his approach to the Orient, Said chooses to homogenize the East and fails to recognize—let alone particularize—the element of power associated with the Ottoman Empire. Thanks to the work of scholars such as Bernard Lewis, Justin McCarthy, D. M. Vaughan, Paul Coles and recently Nabil Matar, the Ottoman era has begun to receive the attention merited by its significant role in Europe.[21] By focusing on the significance of Ottoman-European relations in the sixteenth and seventeenth centuries, the works of these scholars have revealed a glaring disparity in the relative basis of power, which has been the determining element in the political, religious and cultural struggles between the worlds of Islam and Christianity. Furthermore, in exploring the social, cultural and economic role of the Ottoman Empire, they have shed some light on the scope of the Ottoman impact on Europe and the European fear and fascination of and with the exceptional racial and religious toleration in their administration.

---

21 Considering the scope and wealth of Ottoman archival records, thousands of texts still await interpretation.

1.2.1. Knowledge and Power

> *Herein lies the importance of the Renaissance perspective on Islam in Britain: from the King at Whitehall to a slave in an "Algerine" bagnio, from the university theologian to the cabin boy, Britons recognized that they could not take "possession" of the "Turks". Mediterranean Islam was self-sustained and self-representing because it was militarily formidable and did not consist of lands and peoples—as in the Americas- that could be possesse*
>
> (Matar 1998,13).

Tzvetan Todorov, like Said, also addresses issues that have to do with text and history, knowledge and power, Other and Self but which are less specific to the Orient. In fact, his main subject in *The Conquest of America* is: the question of the Other. For Todorov, we discover the Other in the Self because we are not a homogeneous substance, radically alien to (whatever) we perceive is not us. It is by referring to Rimbaud's "Je est un autre"—on the cultural, moral and historical plane—that Todorov unfolds the "I" and the Other" dynamic. Todorov points to the curious historical coincidence that Columbus's voyage took place in the same year that Muslims as well as Jews were expelled from Spain. In 1492 as Spain had repudiated "its interior Other by triumphing over the Moors and by forcing the Jews to leave its territory ... it discover[ed] the exterior Other, that whole America which will become Latin."[22] That year Sultan Bayezid II proclaimed the Ottoman Empire as a safe haven for Jews[23]. While the discovery of America coincided with the discovery of the Other or the world of Otherness, Spain's overt expansion into the New World "concealed and sheltered an enigma: the enigma of ethical relations

---

22 In *The Conquest of America: the Question of the Other*, Todorov writes about the Spanish conquest as being bent on transgressing existing cultures and civilizations. In *The Morality of Conquest*, he draws attention to the fact that "[w]e simply call barbarous what is not like us" and indicates how Sepulveda was a "defender of the intrinsic superiority of Christian Europe and advocate of the conquest in the name of European civilization" (89-102). Ironically, as the Western world condemned Eastern despotism defined by absence of laws, rules and legality, Columbus' idea of assimilation based on the principle of equality also incorporated the ideology of slavery.

23 See Naim Guleryuz, *The History of the Turkish Jews;* and H. Inalcik, *Turkish-Jewish Relations in the Ottoman Empire.*

between self and other and between disparate cultures" (Dallmayr 33). In fact, throughout history, episodes of cultural encounter between the East and the West have led to attempts to struggle with the issue of relations between Self and Other. As is the case with the discovery of America, the dramatic and devastating form of cultural contact between "two radically opposed paradigms of cultures" has "subscribed to a discursive ethic of cultivation" (Dallmayr 33).

During the Renaissance, paralleling the canonical texts of London playwrights who appealed to sensationalism through drama and imaginary wanderers such as Mandeville, there were other materials, which were informed by the actual British encounter with the Ottoman and Islam. These were descriptions of and many references to the "renegade" who had risen to positions, which he might not have attained in Christendom. Although English diplomats and traders, who interacted with their converted compatriots, did not rebuke them for their apostasy, it was left to the poets and dramatists to challenge the "renegado" through fiction. The dramatists not only "ridiculed and misrepresented their conditions" but depicted the renegades as "a type of generic evil" (Matar 1998, 51) as revealed through Basilisco in Kyd's *The Tragedy of Solyman and Perseda* (1588), the first dramatic presentation of the Christian convert to Islam. While the confrontation of the London audience with Islam took place at a level of fiction and fabrication, the renegade (who met divine retribution on stage) was in fact the most tangible proof of Ottoman's military strength. By the 1600's as Christianity was losing ground in eastern and central Europe and gaining converts in the Americas, the renegade, although vehemently denounced by Western writers was evidence of Ottoman cultural and religious hegemony over Europe. As Daniel J. Vitkus indicates:

> Many Christian sailors and ship-captains had "taken the turban", formally converting to Islam in order to enjoy the freedom and protection of the Barbary ports in North Africa ... In many cases it was the temptation of lucrative employment that motivated Christian sailors and soldiers to turn Turk and become renegade pirates or join the Ottoman army (Vitkus 165).

Within the cultural hegemony of the Ottoman Empire in Europe, what emerged was the frightful paradox for the Westerners of Janissaries (Ottoman army) consisting of men who had originally been Christians. And once "Mahumetised" lamented Nicholas Nicolay, these men became more ruthless against the Christians than were the "natural Turkes" (Nicolay 86). In Marlowe's 1590 play when Tamburlaine at one point converted to Islam he had aspirations to "dominate" the seas and keep in awe "Bay of Portingale/All the ocean by the British shore" (3.3.258-59). At that time, it is highly debatable that Renaissance England would think of "dominating" and "imperializing" the Ottoman Empire. In the sixteenth and seventeenth centuries "imperialist ideologies and prospects were already in the air" writes Bartels, who adds that "they were enmeshed in a cloud of unknowing; their means and ends and their eventual predominance were anything but clear" (Bartels 1997, 48).

As Matar elaborates on the captivity literature produced by Britons who had actually experienced the domain of the Muslims as they had been enslaved yet rejected the appeal of wealth, security and power that the Ottoman government system offered to them:

> These are the texts of men, who like Greenblatt's Columbus, encountered the Other face to face, but unlike Columbus with the Indians, did not take "possession" of the Muslims. Thirteen captivity accounts, from 1573 to 1704, survive which challenge the ideological platform on which contemporary scholarly premises about the English Renaissance encounter with Islam have been raised. In these texts, whose number, incidentally, is higher than the British travelers' accounts of the Muslims, the Briton was not in power, nor was he superior to the Muslim (Matar 1996, 188-89).

Before the beginning of European colonialism in the eighteenth century, Elizabethan England fostered "prospects and projects of English domination" (Bartels 59) to reverse the premises of power. From medieval times up until the eighteenth century, Britain—unlike Spain and Portugal—had not made a single colonial venture in the domain of Islam. During that period, since Britain's imperial drive was directed in the New World, as far as the Orient was concerned, it was limited to a desire to carry out an auspicious trade with the Ottoman Empire. For the English, such economic ventures with the Levant and North Africa, ruled by the Ottoman Empire, were geared towards wealth not to the possession or domination of the Ottoman Turks. Yet, since knowledge about the Ottoman Empire was inextricably enmeshed with relations of power, the Ottomans were subverted discursively and/or dramatically. They could not meaningfully exist outside specific discourses such as historical narratives, travelogues, polemical and religious tracts, news accounts, ballads and drama.

In *The Humanist As Traveler*, Haynes reflects on the Renaissance mode of thinking about history and culture based on George Sandys' account of his travels around Eastern Mediterranean in which the origins of western civilization (Judeo-Christian and Greco-Roman) have flourished. This is also the scene of the confrontation with Islam or what Urs Bitterli refers as the locus of "direct encounter" (Bitterli 29-40) with cultural Otherness bearing in the European mind a far more powerful military and religious threat than the newly discovered cultures of the New World. The engraving on the title page from the first edition of Sandys's book (1615), expresses the allegorical imagination behind it: the Ottoman Sultan in the symbolic plan, is identified by a sign on the pillar as "Achmet, sive tyrannus". Holding the orb of the world and trampling on books and a scale, Sultan Achmet's presence poses a danger to other allegorical figures representing significant powers in the history of the West i.e. "figures of human values and divine promise" (Haynes 16). What is characteristic of Sandys's book as a whole is that, as revealed in its dedication to Prince Charles, Ottoman/Islamic culture is "systematically condemned on theological grounds" (Haynes, 18). Sultan Ahmet represents the scourge of Western civilization, just like the Islamic prophet Muhammed, who in Renaissance humanism, is analogous to a spiritual tyrant.

To a Renaissance thinker, as Islam was considered to be a Christian heresy, the difference between Muslim and Christian was measured not as an historical evolution but as a falling away from the divine truth. Therefore, religious elements, which played such a variety of roles in Western writers' thinking, were an overwhelming force in their consideration of the Ottoman Empire. Christianity was not just the nearest available model of religious behavior, it was an absolute standard of judgement, and judgement quickly took on the meanings of salvation and damnation. The authority of Christianity as a model was so great, and its opposition to Islam so militant and absolute that Islam was understood simply as its negative. As the traveler Sandys's themes and purposes in his dedication revealed, the history of ideas in the Renaissance, including those fostered by humanism, was deeply rooted in specific historical situations such as Sandys's through which he traveled and wrote. Haynes, in locating Sandys's book in the historical context of the travel genre, concludes that:

> Book 1 of the *Relation*, which deals with Islam in general as well as with Turkey and the Turks, is thoroughly shaped by the Christian polemic against Islam...In Turkey he is the exponent of a unified and militant Christendom...Islam is the objectified contrary arrangement in the sharpest and starkest sense, the interpretative principle being one of absolute difference (Haynes 21-22).

Before Sandys developed his "fairly elaborate theory of Turkish culture" (Haynes 21) in the *Relation* in its historical context of the travel genre, Richard Hakluyt, in his *Principal Navigations* (1589), created a new readership interested in the wars with the Turk. His work exemplified previous pilgrimage narratives, broadsides and ballads displaying a Renaissance sense of form with a conscious rhetorical effect with descriptions drawn from a collective store of "knowledge" about the Ottomans. Michel Foucault elaborates on this characteristic of seventeenth-century epistemology when he speaks of "a non-distinction between what is seen and what is read, between observation and relation, which results in the constitution of a single, unbroken surface in which observation and language intersect to infinity" (Foucault, *The Order of Things*, 39-40). The implications of Foucault's assertion are important particularly for the formation and dissemination of ideas about the Ottoman Sultan and his entourage as it was impossible for travelers to approach the object of their study. Since they were always bound by the stereotypes they brought with them, at most their contribution was to bring personal immediacy to the repetition of commonplaces and the collection of knowledge about the Turks. Ultimately, as the English traveler's function was one of verification of what was already known about the Turks, as Haynes puts it "it would have been possible to draw the moral (though less interestingly) without leaving England" (Haynes 65).

One of Said's complex arguments is that not only has the creation of Orient been the outgrowth of the will to power, but that Orientalism is a "style of thought". Fundamental to this argument is his portrayal of the distinction between Oriental and European. The "Oriental" is a "political vision of reality" to be examined, understood, exposed and contrasted with the "European". While the European is a known quantity and familiar, the "Oriental" is its reverse. Hence Orientalism "promoted the difference between the familiar (Europe, the West, 'us') and the strange (Orient, the East, 'them'). This vision in a sense created and then served the two worlds thus conceived" (Said 43-44). What accompanied this vision were value judgements; i.e. the "European was rational, virtuous, mature, 'normal'" and the Oriental was "irrational, depraved (fallen) childlike, 'different'" (Said 40); the West is "rational, developed, humane, superior" and the Orient is "aberrant, undeveloped, inferior" (Said 300). The etymology of the term "Orient" came from Latin *oriens* (meaning "'rising', "rising sun" or the East). It meant all that is not Occident or *occidens* (meaning "setting of the sun"). Ultimately the geographic "topos", through a series of "social and historical turns", came to be an "ideological one" (Lowe 32). In most Western writings, the Orient as a space of infidels and pagans conformed to a traditional structure that opposed the tyranny and licentiousness of the East with the rational, civilized Europe.[24] The term "Europe" was formulated in the

---

24 The cradle of Ottoman power, the birthplace of the empire's commonwealth was Sogut, near Bursa, in the western Anatolian region. In 1299, it was from

nineteenth century as the product largely of Greek thought, Roman law and government, and Christianity. In fact, up until the seventeenth century the accepted mode of expression in Western discourse was to refer to Europe and Europeans as Christendom, Christian Princes and Christian nations (Yapp 135-144). Although the idea of Christendom as a single Christian community was as old as Augustine, it was the power of the Ottoman Empire that prolonged the domination of Christendom as a political and cultural concept.

In short, the implication in Said's work is that Orientalism is a Western style of dominating and having authority over the Orient based upon the ontological and epistemological distinction made between the East and the West. Paradoxically, although Said does not indicate it, the "Orient" to the Europeans primarily signified the Ottoman Empire, which included the Levant - the Arabian Peninsula and North Africa. It is impressive that of the forty-seven plays representing different nationalities in the Elizabethan

---

this small hamlet that great Ottoman leaders emerged to rule the empire for seven hundred years. As for central Anatolia, a series of excavations at neolithic sites has brought new aspects to Europe's roots by locating Catal Hoyuk as its "birthplace" and "cradle" (Erich Feigl, *A Myth of Error: Europe, Turkey and Public Opinion* Amalthea, Vienna, 1999 p.6). Elaborating on the Myth of the "Bull" as the carrier of "Europa", Eric Feigl argues that this is not of Greek, Cretan or of Phoenician origin. As the preface to *Turkish Anatolia-Europe's Mother*, written by James Melaart, the British archeologist and one of the twentieth century's greatest scientists of antiquity, who discovered Catal Hoyuk and "the neolithic roots of real Europe and the entire European civilisation", reads: "The concept of EX ORIENTE LUX is not new, and as every schoolboy since Roman times has known Europe benefited from literate Eastern civilisations: Egyptian, Mesopotamian and Greek, of course ... The story of the bull and the princess Europa ... is of Anatolian origin. The people who created them are of unknown descent. Whether we think of "Prototurks" or not is of no importance (Feigl 11). As Feigl indicates, what matters is that the "southern part of Turkey reaches to the very origins of Europe: Mesopotamia, from which the name "Europe" is derived. Most probably it means "sunset" [which] has the same meaning as "occident" or "Abenland", due to its position as a western peninsula of the continent" (Fiegl 9). The point here is that the history of Catal Hoyuk, which has given the world the name Europe, goes back into the depths of time and is part and parcel of the heritage of the Ottomans as well.

drama, "Turks" were in the majority[25] (Wan166). In a body of plays written about the Ottoman Empire, the ontology of Occident and Orient appears in a consistent manner lending an unwavering coherence to its discourse. Said indicates that the "choice of 'Oriental' was canonical":

> it had been employed by Chaucer and Mandeville, by Shakespeare, Dryden, Pope, and Byron. It designated Asia or the East, geographically, morally, culturally. One could speak of an Oriental personality, an Oriental atmosphere, an Oriental tale, Oriental despotism, or an Oriental mode of production, and be understood (Said 31).

In seeking to expose the discursive relationship between Western scholarship about the Orient and imperialism, Said's discussions, however, do not include women and gender. In that sense, it is important to mention Lady Mary Wortley Montagu's letters, written from Istanbul in 1717, which reveal her encounter with the Ottoman culture, and her challenge and criticism of the received representations of the Ottomans in the travel-account writers who have preceded her.[26] In redressing many of the misconceptions and inaccurate representations of the Ottomans propagated by the seventeenth-century travelogues, Lady Mary deconstructs the inherently authoritative position of their writers. Stephen Greenblatt projects an example of this claim by examining the Mandevillian perception of the East in the medieval period. Although the nationality, actual identity and training of the author who wrote *Mandeville's Travels* was still under scholarly scrutiny (Moseley 13) this textual artifact was written by a European who

---

25 As Louis Wann points out in *The Oriental in Elizabethan Drama*, of the 47 plays about the "Orient", 13 are non-extant.

26 Dr. Johnson's views about travel writers are insightful. He indicates that: "[a]s the Spanish proverb says: 'He who would bring home the wealth of Indies, must carry the wealth of the Indies with him'. So it is in travelling: a man must carry knowledge with him, if he would bring home knowledge". (Quoted from Bernard Lewis, *Some English Travellers in the East*. To cite a few examples of travel writing in the sixteenth and seventeenth centuries: Nicholas de Nicolay, *The Navigations, Peregrinations and Voyages* (1585); Henry Blount, *A Voyage Into the Levant* (1636); Robert Withers, *A Description of the Grand Signor's Seraglio or Turkish Emperors's Court* (1650); John

had never set his foot in Islamic lands. For Greenblatt, the failure to discover the originator of the figure of Sir John Mandeville and to appreciate him as a fictive persona created by a literary artist even "has had its advantages" (Greenblatt 35). Moseley supports this view: "The more one questions Mandeville's truthfulness, the higher one has to rate his literary ability" (Moseley 13). With its fantastic projections of the imagination, its fascination with otherness, this six-hundred-years-old complex cultural work supports Greenblatt's theory that " the author being a European Christian still has the power to represent" (Matar 1996, 187) the Muslim Other. *Mandeville's Travels,* writes Greenblatt, with "its invocations of illusory authorities, its false claims to eyewitness authenticity, and above all its errancy, is an allegory of the text of history" (Greenblatt, *Marvellous Possessions* 49).

Indeed, myths and misconceptions have dominated most Western writings about Islam, the prophet Muhammad and the Qur'anic text. As Knolles wrote in the "Introduction to the Christian Reader", the religion of "the false Prophet Mahomet, borne in an unhappy houre, to the great destruction of mankind" had not only "desolat[ed]" the Christian Church, but had caused the damnation of Muslims as those "millions of soules cast headlong into eternal destruction" (Knolles, A4r-A6d). The pervasive misinterpretation of Islam, even at its most scholarly phase, had its source not only in power relations, but also in history. As early as the 11th century, Erchembert, a cleric of Monte Casino, had described the Muslim armies as "a swarm of bees, but with a heavy hand ... they devastate everything" (Said, 59). Such ideas of terror and devastation soon became inextricably associated with Muslims. For Said what was said about Islam came "not so much for the sake of Islam in itself as to represent it for the Medieval Christian" (Ibid. 60). As misconceptions about Muhammad as an Anti-Christ impostor and Muslims as pagans had flourished during the Middle Ages, these misconceptions were institutionalized

---

Covel, *Early Voyages and Travels in the Levant* (1670); Jean Dumont, *A New Voyage to the Levant* (1696), etc.

in the West in later periods. Hence, Western misrepresentations of Muslims, which were rooted in the Crusades, dominated the European consciousness long after the Middle Ages. In other words, with Muslims as "archenemies" and Muhammed the "archdeceiver", the Christian "holy wars" remained a deeply formative experience in the European relation to Islam. For Christians, however, the primary characteristics of the Islamic prophet Mohammed were not only violence, but also sexual promiscuity (Norman, 274). As Daniel Norman asserts, linking Mohammed with promiscuity was not only an ignorant and/or malicious idea derived from the Muslim conception of Paradise, but it has led to the perception of licentiousness and cruelty being the main characteristics of Muslims. As Edward Aston, in *The Manners, lawes and customes of all Nations* asserted in 1611, "the incredible allurement" of Islam was the prophet's "giving to his people free liberty to pursue their lustes and all other plesures, for by these means, this pestilent religion hath crept into innumerable Nations" (Aston 137). Mandeville, whose accounts in his *Travels* were received as factual in England, condemned the description of Paradise in the Qu'ran as one of the most absurd error of the "Saracens". Given the conventional association made by European Christians between Islam and promiscuity, it is not surprising that the Turk in both the popular and learned texts was not only associated with violence, but also "frequently figured as a sexual/sensual temptation of virtue" (Vitkus 145). In the 1660s when the Qur'an was available in Latin, an imperfect French translation that had appeared in 1649 was "newly Englished, for the satisfaction of all that desire to look into the Turkish vanities" (Moran 1952, 382). Ben Jonson, however, not so much moved by "merely religious prejudice, exhibit[ed] by implication in his poem on the burning of his library, his contempt for the book" (Moran 382). As for Sir Thomas Browne, his opinion was that: "The Alcoran of the Turks (I speak without prejudice) is an ill composed piece, containing in it vain and ridiculous Errours in Philosophy, impossibilities, fictions and vanities beyond laughter" (Moran

382). In 1656 although Isaac Barrow, the teacher of Newton, in his *Epitome fidei et religiounis turcicae*, described Islam in a "fair-minded" manner, he added some "elements of caricature" to his work (Beck 70). Even after the advent of the Age of Enlightenment in Europe, there was not much change in the Christian attitude towards Islam. Now and then, however, attempts, such as those of Boulainvilliers and Goethe, to understand Muhammad helped convey a more sympathetic picture of Islam. New translations of the Qur'an in European languages started appearing, notably with George Sale's (1734) in English and Savary's in French. In Chew's view:

> French is reasonably faithful to the literal sense of the original. But though there is no ground for suspecting any deliberate intentional falsification, there is an all-pervading vulgarizing of the spirit and style of the book. This is due in part to a literary tact and skill and in part to congenital racial and religious antipathy (Chew 451).

Among the writers of the French Enlightenment Voltaire probably had the keenest interest and longest association with Islam. It is probable that Voltaire had gained access to the Qur'anic text through his intellectual encounter with George Sale[27] (Gunny 134). When he wrote *Mahomet ou le Fanatisme*[28](1742), Voltaire's aim was to use Muhammad as a foil to show up the credulity and superstition lying at the root of every religion. In order to do that, he created a character for his tragedy to match the non-Muslims' preconceived ideas of the prophet. Voltaire's focus was to reveal the danger of fanaticism in all religions and all ideologies. He had already used the stage to disseminate ideas that were easily rec-

---

27 According to Chew, Sale's version of the Qur'an with explanatory notes "fixed in the English mind the notion that the Koran is a stupid, verbose and extravagant book" (Chew 481).

28 Voltaire drew certain aspects of Mahomet's character from two historical sources, namely, Henri de Boulanville's *Vie de Mahomet* (1730) and Jean Gagnier's *Vie de Mahomet* (1732). Considering the conclusion of a renewed trade relations between the Ottoman Empire and France, Voltaire encountered opposition from the authorities for the unflattering portrayal of Mahomet on the French stage. He was willing to postpone the performance of the play in Paris in January 1742 because of the Ottoman Ambassador's presence there.

ognizable as subversive. However, even in the Age of Enlightenment, Voltaire could not reveal Islam's emphasis on the value of difference and the integration of the Other. Initially, for Voltaire *Mahomet ou le fanatisme* was a medium to propagate the unorthodoxy he had already given the public with *Zaire*, a play rich in heterodoxy. Unlike his earlier plays, however, since *Mahomet* was confronted with a "particularly determined resistance" (Hanley 95) from different forces, Voltaire set out to win approval for the play by deliberately distorting his representation of Muhammad. As far as its ideological aspect was concerned, Voltaire's tragedy was an overt attack against religious zealots, and a condemnation of religious intolerance.[29] Yet, undoubtedly to the audiences who watched the performance of *Mahomet* in Lille and Paris, and to those who read the play, Muhammad was perceived as a lecherous villain. This symptom of the paradoxical mentality of the Age of Enlightenment was even revealed in the French dictionaries which defined the word "impostor" as "trompeur, affronteur, calomniateur. Mahomet a été un grand imposteur qui a trompé bien des peuples" (Quoted from Gunny, p.4). In *Le Fanatisme ou Mahomet le prophète*, when Voltaire described Mahomet as "artisan de l'erreur" (I.I.), "vil séditieux" (I.IV.), "ennemi du monde" (II.V.), "tyran farouche" (IV.VI.) and "imposteur exécrable" (V.IV.), he acknowledged that the Muslims had a right to complain, given his inimical depiction of the prophet. As David Sox remarks in *The Gospel of Barnabas*[30], however, "no one" had gone "as far as Mu-

29 Essentially, *Mahomet*, constituted Voltaire's "first overt attack on the forces of religious intolerance to be presented on the stage of the conservative Comédie-Française" (Solbrig, 28). The play, however, sparked a heated controversy between the Jansenists and Voltaire. Soon after its cancellation in Paris, Voltaire won approval for *Mahomet* by ingeniously dedicating it to Pope Benedict XIV (Lanson 55).

30 The polemics surrounding *The Gospel of Barnabas* had challenged the very foundation of the Christian belief in Jesus' death and Resurrection. As a major polemical tool, it violated the authenticity of the Gospel tradition and the foundations of Christian theology. Barnabas was a Jewish Levite of Cyprus and one of the earliest Christian disciples at Jerusalem. Despite attempts to link *The Gospel of Barnabas* with the apostle Barnabas and the disputations of early Jewish Christianity, the extant gospel was basically unknown in the

hammad in meeting the Christians half-way" (Sox 25). Yet, even in the Age of Enlightenment, there was little chance for Islam to be given the right perspective.[31]

1.2.2. History and Representation

> *"[A]ll representations, because they are representations are imbedded firstly in the language and then in the culture, institutions and political ambiance of the representer"*
>
> (Said 272).

During the Renaissance, when history did not yet exist as a distinct and coherent discipline, the *OED* defined it as: "A relation of incidents (in early use), either true or imaginary; later only those professedly true".[32] Given the concern of this thesis with the historical representation of the Turks on stage, the numerous instances where history[33] and drama intersect in these plays, foreground "how we make historical 'facts' out of 'brute' events' of the past" (Hutcheon x). Shakespeare's portrayal of "theatre as a history-producing institution" in *Hamlet* and "fore-fronting the power of drama in shaping that record as it sees fit" (Kamps 11) reveal that in its accounts of historical events and interpretations there is much ambiguity in historiographic writing[34]. This ambiguity with its recurring presence in historiography is also a major force in the dramatic representations of the Ottoman Turks.

Muslim world until 1734 when George Sale translated the Koran into English.

31 As David Sox indicates, for Muslims, "Jesus is *the* Prophet before Muhammad and Messiah. For Christians there is no corresponding acceptance of Muhammad" (Sox 125). Yet, again as Sox remarks: "For orthodox Christians, there can be no new revelation after the Incarnation of God's Son. Jesus is God made man- what point would there be in sending a new prophet after that?" (Sox 126).

32 Quoted *Historiography and Ideology in Stuart Drama* (Kamps 10).

33 My purpose here is basically to deal with selected problems of historiography in order to assess how the tradition of representing the Ottomans on the European stage reflects the relationship between Islamic East and Christian West.

34 Paralleling early modern historiography and discourse of canonical texts, the legacy of the Ottoman era is one of distortion.

To pose a relationship between history and drama implies some kind of narrative and textual politics, which are necessarily part of the myriad ways in which the relations of power can be interpreted. Representation of Turks is a source of a distinctive type of knowledge, which is inextricably linked with relations of power between Europe/Ottoman Empire and Christianity/Islam. By employing a Foucauldian framework to his discussion, Stuart Hall elaborates on the application and effectiveness of power and knowledge through discursive formations. Within this discursive approach to power that sustains a "regime of truth" (Foucault *Power,* 131) Hall describes representation as "an essential part of the process by which meaning is produced and exchanged between members of a culture". Consequently, representation "does involve the use of language, of signs and images which stand for or to represent things" (Hall *Representation*, 23). Seen from the Foucauldian perspective, casting dramatic representations as a discursive formation does not simply reflect "real" distinctions between the two cultures, but creates them. According to Hall, the term "discursive formation" refers to the systematic operation of several discourses or statements constituting a "body of knowledge" which work together to construct a specific object analysis in a particular way and to limit the others in ways in which that object may be constituted. Although the internal cohesion for Foucault does not depend on putative "agreement" between statements, this does not undermine the cohesion or the formation of "a body of knowledge" or a "body of truth" around a particular object in a systematic fashion (Hall *Representation*, 191-291). In the case of drama, such a formation includes aesthetic, historical and ideological discourses. Thus the plays, in order to construct the opposition between the "Orient" and the West, display "a range of discursive reserves which employ a whole range of discursive categories" (Ferguson 170) such as fear/threat to cherished beliefs, otherness, and identity.

Linda Hutcheon writes that postmodernism has taught us that "all cultural practices have an ideological subtext which determines the conditions of the very possibility of their production of meaning" (Hutcheon xii-xiii). This applies to Turks and their Western representations in early modern era. Undoubtedly, the Turks with their banners, crescents, "moony standards" (*The Spanish Curate (I.I)*, turbans and brazen head[35], signifying the supposedly Islamic idol "Mahomet", their scimitars, bows and arrows, have stood for a wealth of emotive and mental associations in the Western consciousness. Ultimately, as an "alien" culture and religion perceived as great adversaries to Christendom, the ubiquitous view of the apparently invincible Ottoman Empire, inspired in the West different emotions that ranged from "fear to hostility and awe to admiration" (Artemel 83). Construction of the great literary edifice on the Ottoman Empire in Elizabethan and Stuart times is an indication that the interest in the doings of the Turks was, naturally, intense. As Suheyla Artemel notes, the "impact of the ideas and knowledge about the Turks in England was perhaps most strongly felt in drama" (Artemel 83). This presupposition of a general knowledge about the Ottomans by the English is revealed in Marlowe's account of the tragic story of Sultan Bajazed I in *Tamburlaine* (1590); Robert Greene's depiction of Selim I in *The First Part of the Tragical Reign of Selimus,_Empereur of the Turkes* (1588); Kyd's presentation of Suleyman and the fall of Rhodes (1522) in *The Tragedy of Soliman and Perseda (1599)*; and Shakespeare's reference to the Ottoman court to bring out the superior worth of the English King in *Henry IV*. Inasmuch as more than thirty extant plays were written about the Turks between 1580 and 1642, it is clear that England, like all the leading states in Europe, took into account the Ottoman Empire from an aesthetic, as well as from a religious, political, diplomatic and economic point of view.

English dramatists, like continental writers, often fantasized "in drama and sermon about Christian victory and Muslim defeat" (Matar 1998, 120). In their response to the Grand Turk,

[35] The 'brazen head' appears in Green's *Alphonsus* and also in his *Friar Bungay* (Ward I: 393).

Western writers manifested cultural obsessions of medievalism and chivalry through character, spectacle, visual and dramatic language. As Islam posed a great danger to the continent, the stage was turned into a locus which provided the conversion of the Turk into Christianity. In Robert Greene's tragedy, for example, Corkut, the brother of Selim converts to Christianity before his death. In Thomas Heywood's *The Fair Maid of the West Part II*, Jaffer converts to Christianity because of its higher moral codes, in *The City-Night-Cap* (1624) Robert Davenport conceives of yet another fictional Muslim conversion on stage. But, as Matar observes, by the end of the seventeenth century, England had lost its "eschatological impetus for evangelization" and "subordinated conversion to commercial and trading advantages" (Matar 152) in the Levant.

Representation of the Ottomans in European drama can be best understood as a clear example of the themes and fantasies of medieval history being played out in the "present". In other words, the plays reflect a crusading zeal that stems from pitting a West against an East, Christian against Muslim, European "civilization" against Ottoman "barbarism" (Marcus 6). As Said writes in *Orientalism*, the relationship between Islam and Christianity or East and West has been essentially political and a hostile one from its beginnings (Said 3). By dissecting a discursive Orient of Eastern archetypes and fabricated constructs created by Western scholarship, Said reinforces Anwar Abdel-Malek's observation that Europe by exercising more and more power over the East has produced the "Orientalized Orient" (Said 96). What is problematic about the vision of Orientalism, for Abdel-Malek (who fifteen years before Said analyzed the structure and content of the Orientalist discourse) is that the Orient and the Orientals are "objects" of study stamped with a "constitutive otherness, of an essential character". This "object" of study is "passive, non-participating, endowed with a 'historical' subjectivity, above all non-active ... [an] alienated being, philosophically, that is other than itself in relationship to itself, posed, understood, defined -

and acted- by others" (Abdel-Malek 107-8). Based on these premises and Foucault's method for studying the text as a series of "archival facts" (Foucault Archeology, 79-131) the "archive" being defined by the silent past, representation of the Ottomans on the European stage raises a series of questions. Some of these questions are analytical, others theoretical, still others ideological.

In *Orientalism*, the sweep of Said's theory, which utilizes the concept of the "Orient" and the Other, establishes his position as clearly influenced by Foucault. Said suggests that writings about the "Orient" create and sustain a range of understandings about Eastern peoples as Other.

> In a sense Orientalism was a library or archive of information commonly and, in some of its aspects, unanimously held. What bound the archive together was a family of ideas and a unifying set of values proven in various ways to be effective. These ideas explained the behaviour of Orientals; they supplied Orientals with a mentality, a genealogy, an atmosphere; most important, they allowed Europeans to deal with and even to see Orientals as a phenomenon possessing regular characteristics (Said 42).

Part of the problem of understanding the Ottoman phenomenon on the basis of Said's scholarship is his failure to cover the historical reality of the "Orient". He fails to recognize fundamental differences between the Ottoman Turks and, say, Palestinian Arabs. Yet, he reveals that "representations have purposes" (Said, 273) and function in a specific context that is historical, ideological and cultural. Thus, a theoretical approach to understand the archival repertoire of the Ottoman Empire on the basis of Said's key text on East-West relations seems too speculative to admit any empirical verification. Essentially, Turks as a distortion of the "true", the normal, the European/Christian must be contextualized within their own complex history. Although up to nineteenth century, despite the historian Joseph von Hammer's work, there was virtually no material on the Ottoman point of view available in western languages, the most enduring monument to Elizabethan interest in the Turks was Richard Knolles's *The General History of the Turkes* (1603). The work of a schoolmaster at a grammar school in England, it shared the common goals of Tudor and

Stuart historiography. Knolles's intent in writing the history of the Ottoman Empire was to teach the English "morals, manners, prudence, patriotism, statecraft, virtue, religion, wisdom and truth" (Fussner 59). In his book Knolles introduced the empire of the "Turkes" to his" Christian Reader', as the "Present Terror of the World". In producing 1200 pages of historical account of the Ottoman Empire, as Knolles attached the blame for terror to Muhammed's "gross and blasphemous Doctrines" (Chew 115) in essence, he elaborated on the principal idea that Ottomans were enemies and should be driven out of Europe and the Holy Land. Although he had "never visited" the Ottoman lands and "had little to say about those who had" (Beck, 40), Knolles had a great impact on seventeenth-century thought and imagination. In essence, he was instrumental in the cultural production of meaning about "the Turks". This, of course, raises the question as to how an arm-chair historian 'knew' about the Ottomans who were the figment of his imagination—socially, culturally, and linguistically—except for the threat they posed to Europe. Yet, historiography, like drama, was a form of exercise of power over the Ottomans, and as a propaganda vehicle it was a symbolic resource for promoting Britain's imperial aspirations. Although it is premature to speak of early seventeenth- century England's imperial status, essentially it was a country driven by the economic imperatives of imperial trade, which, in turn, manifested cultural hegemony over the Other. Ultimately, England's colonizing fantasies over the Ottoman Empire were manifested through the "power of the pen" that exhibited an imperialist behaviour in relation to the "known" and the "knower".

History of the Ottoman Empire was evidently a "safe" subject in the European book-markets. In the majority of cases, history was the source of plays dealing with the Turks, for example Kyd's *The Tragedy of Solyman and Perseda* (1599), Fulke's *The Tragedy of Mustafa* (1609) and Goffe's *The Raging Turke* or *Bajazed the Second*' (1631), *The Courgeous Turke or Amurath the First*_(1632), etc. It was Marlowe's *Tamburlaine* (1590) that had marked the beginning of plays about the Ottoman Sultans. In1590 when Marlowe wrote *Tamburlaine*, one of the greatest plays of the Elizabethan era, Ottoman power and influence rode high. Yet, Marlowe's aim in *Tamburlaine*,_which magnified the defeat of the Ottoman Sultan at the Battle of Angora (Ankara) in 1402, at a time when the empire had already expanded at a remarkable rate following this setback, was, solely, ideological. The historical "facts" or contents of drama were culturally produced prior to their incorporation in the dramatic text.

1.2.3. Perspectives on "Oriental Despotism"

In the sixteenth and seventeenth centuries, although the regime of the Ottoman empire was perceived as a tyranny, during the eighteenth century, its image was largely shaped by the concept of despotism.[36] The early eighteenth-century writings in England were mainly based on the ideas of Paul Rycaut, an English ambassador in Istanbul during the reign of Charles II. When Rycaut, who also served as the secretary of the Levant Company between 1661-1667 both in Istanbul and Izmir (Smyrna), wrote his major work, *The Present State of the Ottoman Empire*, it was soon translated to French, Italian, German, Dutch and Polish. In his historical narrative about the Ottoman Empire, Rycaut elaborated on the "the maxims of the Turkish politie", the "most material points of Mahometan religion" and "the Turks' military discipline". Although Rycaut emphasized Ottoman "Tyranny, Oppression, and Cruelty", he concluded that it was because of the existence of tyranny that the Ottoman State had been able to preserve the unity of the Empire against factions and rebellions. Thus, tyranny was not necessarily a bad government regime for Rycaut who identified the greatness of the Ottoman Empire with its tyrannical nature. Rycaut made his case for tyranny with reference to the arbi-

---

36 For discussions of despotism as a persistently dominant concept in Western representations of the 'Orient' see Louis Althusser, *Politics and History: Montesquieu, Rousseau, Hegel and Marx,* also see, Nicolas Antoine Boulanger's *The Origin and Progress of Despotism in Oriental and Other Empires of Africa, Europe and America,* translated by John Wilkes, Amsterdam, London, 1764.

trary management of private property in the Ottoman lands, absoluteness of the emperor and the blind obedience of the subjects of the sultan within his formidable empire.

What puzzled the sixteenth and seventeenth-century observers most was the official and social structure of the Ottoman State, based on the sultan-slave precept, which ordained that absolute authority was derived from the Sultan. From the middle of the seventeenth century, that authority began to be dispensed by the Grand Vizier, who was responsible for administering the affairs of the state, domestic and foreign, including the conduct of diplomacy. Yet, it was the servile disposition of the Ottomans in the Sultan's "Slave Household"—of which the Seraglio provided the prototype—that was the most distinguishing and peculiar characteristic of the Ottoman public and civic life. The sultan's court, which consisted of some three hundred and fifty persons was composed completely of former Christians holding positions from the Grand Vizier to his fellow viziers down to provincial governors, fief holders, tax-collectors and various other executives of different grades. Although some observers focused on the meritocratic principles of the Ottoman State, others condemned the tyrannical nature of the Ottoman government system with its formidable army composed of Christians that had "turned Turk".

As Lord Kinross observes, the strength and importance of the Ottoman governing system which was mainly composed of men of Christian origin:

> lay mainly in the fact that it was non-hereditary, precluding the further rise of a native-born aristocracy and nobility ... and thus safeguarding from political rivalry the absolute power of the sultanate" (Kinross 147).

The Christian-born ruling elite were educated in a highly organized and imaginatively created Palace School, which was essentially secular, yet allowed instruction of the Qur'an and the principles of Islamic theology. While the emphasis in the Palace School was on the statecraft and military science, much attention was paid to the individual merits of the pupils in terms of their ability, initiative and capacity of leadership. Based on the Ottomans' *devshirme* (child-levy) system, they were ultimately rewarded with the highest position of the Grand Vizier or Aga, Chief Janissary- the head of the Ottoman military system. Although the *devshirme* who were at once warriors, statesmen and loyal Muslims would "very voluntarily" as Rawlins wrote "renounce their faith" (Matar 1999, 22), such conversions raised profoundly disturbing questions in the minds of the Westerners who noted that as "Christian-turned-Janissaries" they "became more ruthless against Christians than were the "naturall Turkes" (Matar 1998, 24). Particularly, the militaristic fate of the Janissaries was not only ironic but also a great dilemma for the Christian world, which joined forces against the Ottomans through wars as through discourse. In Lessing's *Minna von Barnhelm (The Fortunate Soldier)* (1765), for example, as Werner, a soldier, put it:

> Our ancestors diligently went after the Turks, and we should do the same, if we are decent fellows and good Christians. Sure, I know that a campaign against the Turks isn't half as much fun as one against the French, but it makes up for it by being that much more meritorious in this life and the next (I.xii).[37]

Lessing's comedy revealed an overt Crusade mentality as depicted in old epics with a Muslim woman being rescued from her own father by a Christian Knight who had been captured and with whom the daughter had fallen in love. This mirrored the essential moral of the Crusades, which partly aimed at liberating Christians and holy places from Muslim power. As Nabil Matar points out in *Islam in Britain*, the intellectual and religious impact of Europe's encounter with the Ottomans was:

> instrumental in defining early modern European culture: from Pope Pius II to Martin Luther and John Locke, from John Calvin to Christopher Marlowe, from John Foxe to George Fox, from Cervantes to Shakespeare, Massinger and Dryden—all reflected, to varying degrees in their writings, on the interaction between Christendom and Islam. Furthermore, all recognized that Christians were converting to Islam more often than Muslims were to Christianity and that the "infidels" challenged Europe not only by their sword but by their religious allure (Matar, 19).

37 Quoted from "Turks on the Eighteenth-Century Operatic Stage and European Political, Military and Cultural History" (Wilson 81).

In analyzing how both historiography and drama tried to undermine the attraction of the Ottoman Empire and shape the image of the Ottomans (in the production, reception, social, political, discursive and aesthetic contexts) two major facts must be taken into consideration: "the higher number of Christian converts and the allure of Islam" (Matar 9). The frequency of Christians deserting their faith and "turning Turke" was a perplexing issue, which Europe had to address. Yet in the Ottoman Empire there were whole populations of renegades, who came from all walks of life. (Matar 1994, 33). These were "men and women, rich and poor, soldiers and priests, friars, bishops, archbishops, and even a Patriarch" (Matar 1994,33). Sir Anthony Shirley, who had traveled through Antioch on his way to Jerusalem, reflected on the English Renaissance concerns with the renegades as he himself was puzzled by the question why these Christians had turned "Turke". As Daborn wrote in his play *A Christian turn'd Turk*, it was "not Diuinity but nature" that caused these converts "which doth in beasts force them to keep their kind" (ll. 1013-1014). Similarly, several writers, whether they traveled or merely imagined the realm of the Ottomans, vilified, ridiculed and denounced the renegades. As Matar notes, for Sir Thomas Shirley, those Christians who called "the Greate Turke Imperator Regni Musselmanni" were blasphemous, since "Musselman" meant believer (Matar, 1994, 36). Thus any Christian who acknowledged "a Mahometan to bee a faythefull belieuer doeth confess himself to be an infidell" (Sherley 5).

Along with theological polemic and evangelism, drama played a crucial role in conveying to audiences the notion of the divine retribution, which awaited the renegade to Islam. While the resonance of crusading ideals grew faint and writers did not even want to reflect on the phenomenon of renegades, they later addressed the issue of apostasy cautiously (Matar 22). As Matar suggests English drama was an anti-propaganda vehicle shedding some light on the relationship of the East/West which is riddled with stereotypes and fabricated constructs:

> The way that English dramatists, preachers, theologians and others confronted Islam and Muslims was by fabricating images about them-by arranging protagonists and geography in a manner that was disembodied from history and cultural surroundings. In the imaginatively controlled environments of the theatre and the pulpit, Britons converted the unbelievers, punished the renegades, and condemned the Saracens. As long as the sphere of the action was fabrication, the victory was won by the Christians. Outside that sphere, Englishmen and Britons treated Islam as a powerful civilization which they could neither possess nor ignore (Matar 20).

In Venice as elsewhere, there existed, however, an entire literature prophesizing "the divine punishment to be visited on the states of the Grand Signor" and announcing "his imminent conversion to Christian truth" (Valensi 15). The ambassadors' reports, however, which were more realistic and immediate, were written with rationalist rigour. They knew the fault-lines where the Ottoman system might weaken of its own account. Thus they assured Europe that in spite of the apparent power of the Ottoman state, the possibility of revolution was inherent in a system "largely dependent on the fanatical devotion of converted Christian slaves" (Hale 438). Venice was an active participant in the international affairs of the West with its *bailos* in Istanbul sending reports to Europe condemning the arbitrary power of the Grand Turk. The Empire was presented as an example of the dangers in the absolute rule of one man.

Ultimately, the Ottomans evolved their unique system of civil service by drawing on the services of their conquered Christian population, such as the Greeks, Armenians, Serbians, Albanians, etc. They created this system by reflecting on the principles of slavery to which the Turks in their earlier history and in other lands had submitted and "under which they had thrived" (Kinross 614). "Unnatural as such enslavement might appear in the eyes of the West" writes Lord Kinross, "it proved in its own context to be an enlightened and practical formula" (Kinross 614). The strength of the Ottoman government system lay mainly in the fact that it was non-hereditary, which in turn, hindered the further rise of a native-born aristocracy and nobility. This system put into practice mainly safeguarding the absolute power of the sultanate from political rivalry. As Lord Kinross elaborates on the Sultan's Slave Household system, it involved, using to the full the qualities and skills of the Sultan's Christian subjects, to the benefit of the Empire and indeed the slaves themselves. For soon they came not to resent but to value their enforced status, for the privileges which brought to them and which were denied to the Moslem-born. Deprived of their own families to become part of the Sultan's 'family', they developed into a nonhereditary ruling class, reared on the principles of meritocracy alone. Here was an elite which, through the first centuries of the Empire helped to secure the power and to ensure the stability of the Ottoman dynasty, relieving the state from the disruptive rivalries and nepotist forces of any hereditary aristocracy, Moslem-born. Moreover, the Sultans themselves ceased as a rule to contract legal and dynastic marriages, breeding their progeny instead through women of the Slave Household, reared in the Harem, and those for better or worse, introducing mixed blood into the veins of the Ottoman dynasty (Kinross, 615).

Particularly, the enslavement of women, which functioned as a symbol of the "uncivilized" practices of the Orient, was a sign of "barbarism" or rather "Oriental despotism" for the Western world. As Valensi notes while the words "despote", "despotique" and "despotisme" appeared in the French Dictionary for the first time in 1720 (Valensi 2), it was Montesquieu's *Lettres persanes* (1721) and *L'esprit des lois* (1748) that had made the idea of despotism a permanent feature in European political thought. In fact, the idea of despotism, which had been formulated in Aristotle's time, had passed through the Medieval and Renaissance periods with Montesquieu making it fashionable again in Europe. Bodin in his *Six Books of Commonwealth* (1576) had described despotism as a form of monarchy in which the Prince was the master of lives and properties of his subjects by war and conquest in a just war. Later Hobbes in his *Leviathan* (1651) had written that if a dominion was acquired by conquest, it was "despoticall" as the dominion of the master (conqueror) over his servant (subjugated) which had come into being through a "covenant of obedience" (Hobbes 140-42). As the definitions of despotism implied the arbitrarines of the government system, the entire population of the Ottoman Empire was perceived as the "captives" or rather slaves of the Sultan. Since notions about the harem, polygamy and the presumed oppression of women were linked to despotism, representations of women in the sultan's *seraglio* were overdetermined both by sexual connotations of their writers and by ideological assumptions for the need of the Western hero to come and rescue them from the sultan.

In the eighteenth century, however, Lady Mary, through a high degree of assimilation in the Ottoman culture, praised the civility and refinement of the Ottoman women and idealized their liberty. What was particularly significant about representations of the Ottoman sultans, however, was that they were primarily based on *The General Historie of the Turkes* (1603). Thus, the dramatic texts, in one way or another, represented history and as such they were examples of historiography. In other words, they were as much about writing a history of issues about the Ottoman Empire, its culture and its society, as they were about representing it. In essence, the ideological impact of the narrative and discursive structure of historical re-presentations was particularly revealed through ideas and fictions revolving around concepts of "tyranny" and "Oriental despotism".

In response to historical forces, however, some changes occurred in representations of Ottomans in eighteenth-century English drama. Indispensably, the progression of events between 1683 and 1798 revealed that the military, economic and political power of the Ottomans was shifting to a European system of alliances. In that sense, the eighteenth century was a time of change in establishing new patterns and trends for the Ottomans in their relations with the West. Following the Treaty of Karlowitz, the Ottoman ruling circle's immediate focus on its domestic affairs and its laying down of a strict policy of peace in foreign affairs was not only a sign of its waning power, but also its economic and diplomatic relations with Europe. Thus, with the diminution of the Ottoman military prowess followed by long periods of relative peace (from 1718 to 1798), the Ottoman-European relations underwent a profound change. What this meant for the Western world was that the sultan was no more an invincible ruler who could act out of his will. Thus, the historical role of the feared villainous sultan on stage was relegated to an underling in order to champion the noble and generous pasha with moral virtues. This was not the portrayal of the conquerors who had once threatened the survival of the West. As the ascending strength of a web of European alliances began to check further the Ottoman expansion and the balance in political, military and economic power, what then began to dazzle the aesthetic imagination of the eighteenth-century Europe was the sultan's *seraglio*, waiting to be called upon the stage.

While most of the Western sources treated the "exotic" East as a vast cabinet of curiosities, in the eighteenth-century plays, it was the seraglio (which featured as an obligatory "topos" in travel literature and paintings of the century) that attracted the curiosity of Europe. In fact, most of the seventeenth- century accounts of the Topkapi Palace were written for Louis XIV, who was fascinated with Oriental despotism. The Topkapi Palace referred to as the *seraglio* in the West, as a microcosm of the despotic Ottoman Empire with its enslaved pages, secluded and cruel eunuchs, was made to contrast with the benign ideals of the absolute monarchies in Europe. The accounts of the *seraglio*, however, as revealed in the dramatic texts, were exceedingly fantastic since the narratives about the inaccessible royal residence of the Ottoman sultans were solely based on the fantasy and gossip of Western travelers. Consequently, at the root of some serious historical errors that had been transmitted by the West throughout the centuries, lay an intense fascination with a variety of cultural practices, ideologies and socially constructed codes of the harem. During the Enlightenment, such constructions of the fantastical Other perceived through lenses of violence, cruelty and excessive sensuality were necessary to counter the project of a rationally based Western society. As the progression of events between 1699 and 1799 revealed, in the Ottoman Empire's destabilization period, heroic themes displaying the strength and the military powers of the Ottomans were now overshadowed by plots revolving around fratricide, regicide or romances in the *seraglio*. In the eighteenth century, while the *seraglio* themes became more suitable for musical plays than for tragedies, the Ottomans still continued to fascinate audiences not only through their harem stories, but by the extravagant costumes and the magnificent staging of these plays.

Ottoman costumes, which featured as exotic elements of drama, particularly appealed to the European curiosity about the Orient. While the standard visual image of the Ottomans was essentially formed through the illustrations of the travelers' accounts, one of the first books about the Ottoman costumes, *Costumi e Modi Particolari de la Vita de Turchi* (1545) was written by an Italian named Bassano da Zari. Although the illustrations of da Zari's book are missing, as Ribeiro points out, for the Europeans the descriptions of the Ottoman women's dress seemed to have proved "a potent source of fascination" (Riberio 20) since it was their "forbidden" aspect that appealed to the West. Since the most sacred and exalted place in an Ottoman household was the harem it was "hidden from a man's eyes so was as talk within it was beyond the reach of his ears" (Peirce 113).

In the years between 1450 and 1550 the first written sources about the harem were based on the reports of the *bailos* following the establishment of the Venetian Embassy in Istanbul. As Necipoglu observes, in the second half of the sixteenth century, the Venetian reports about the *seraglio* were complemented by the Habsburg, French and English ambassadorial accounts and the observations of Christian Westerners affiliated to the Ottoman court as merchants, slave pages and dignitaries. The first manuscript dedicated solely to the Topkapi Palace was written by Ottovio Bon, the Venetian *bailo* living in Istanbul as the representative both of the Senate and of Venetian subjects resident in the city. As Goodwin points out: "Of all the accounts by Western diplomats and travelers between 1453 (when Constantinople fell to Mehmet II) and the end of the seventeenth century, Bon's is the most reliable in every aspect" (Bon 13). Bon's *Decrizione del Serraglio del Gransignore* (1608) written under the spell of the of the palace's architecture and institutional system was the fullest and most accurate account as affirmed by Turkish scholars (Ulucay xvii). Therefore, it was much appreciated by its plagiarizers as well. Robert Withers (1625) passed off an English translation of Bon's work as his own; and John Greaves (1653) included the "Withers" text in his own book. As Goodwin puts it, considering that Bon felt no need for sensationalism, as his book revealed none, it was the "integrity" of the Venetian bailo that had enhanced the "authority" of the book (Goodwin 14). Like Thomas Dallam of the sixteenth century who had the privilege of entering the Pearl Kiosk to install an organ, a gift from Queen Elizabeth I to Murat III, Bon, who came from a distinguished family in Padua, had left invaluable information about the Sultan's court. In the sixteenth century Bon was the only foreigner (other than Dallam) who had actually the visited private residences of the Sultan's palace, where only the highest-ranking officer at the sultan's court could enter. Yet, it was still impossible for him to visit the women's quarters as no male could ever set foot in the harem other than the eunuchs.[38] Although it is possible that the plays written about the *seraglio* were based on these narratives, even a source such as Bon's could not reveal any information about the harem.

1.3. Conclusion to Chapter One

The complexity of writing one culture by another, based on an inevitable indeterminacy of knowledge, is the main argument of

---

38 Evidently, in 1910 Abdurrahman Seref Bey was the first male ever to penetrate the walls of the harem which was officially dispersed in 1909. Following the disbanding of the harem in the Topkapi Palace, polygamy was officially abolished in 1929.

this chapter, which posits that the resulting process of representation is inevitably ideological and furthermore epistemologically a delicate matter. My concern in this chapter is not as much the historical reality of events and state of affairs of the Ottoman Empire as the reality of the mental structure of the writers manifested through historiography, representation and discursive formations.[39] Since the Crusades, the historical circumstances surrounding the rhetoric and logic behind the European approach to the Turk seem to have sprung from the Western perceptions of Islam. Inscribed in a "play of power", discursive practices about the Ottoman Muslims, in the periods examined, are "linked to certain strategies of relations of forces supporting and supported by types of knowledge" (Foucault 1980, 194 and 196). Based on Foucault's[40] premise, "large groups of statements" which have given a certain kind of knowledge about the Ottomans and Muslims, are governed by a set of assumptions, conventions and systems that share common political drifts and patterns in the Christian West. That is to say, in struggling with the military, territorial and religious ascendancy of the Ottomans in the sixteenth and seventeenth centuries, Western representation and knowledge are put to work through discursive formations to regulate the power of the Ottoman Empire. In the case of drama, such a formation includes aesthetic, historical and ideological discourses. The plays, in order to construct the oppositions between the "Orient" and the West, display "a range of discursive reserves which employ a whole range of discursive categories" (Ferguson

---

39 Foucault says that "[w]henever one can describe between a number of statements, such a system of dispersion, whenever, between objects, types of statements, concepts or thematic choices, one can define regularity (and order, correlations, positions and functionings, transformations) we will say, for the sake of convenience, that we are dealing with a discursive formation (Foucault *Archaeology,* 38).

40 Foucault has been highly influential across a number of disciplines as far as the term discourse is concerned. He "uses the term discursive formation in away that seems roughly interchangeable with *discourse*" (Hawthorne 49). Although the term 'discourse' is normally used as a linguistic concept, for Foucault who has given it a different meaning, "discourses are large groups of statements" defined by "strategic possibilities" (Foucault *Archaeology,* 37).

170) such as fear and threat to cherished beliefs, Otherness, and identity. Caught up in the interplay of knowledge and power against the Ottoman Islamic threat, the Christian West through discursive practices has sustained a "regime of truth" in producing certain conceptions about the Ottomans whose system of government is essentially defined as tyrannical and despotic.

My purpose in this chapter is not merely to introduce the theoretical approach of this thesis and to give an overall view about textual representations of Ottoman Turks and Islam through European versions of history, politics and discourse. By introducing the representation of the Ottoman Empire through Western Christian ideology it is my intention to explore the foundations of the negative images of the Ottomans and perceptions which have led to discursive contradictions and tensions within both its historical and the dramatic contexts. I believe that the problem of textual representations of the Ottomans arises from multiple causes, such as the limitations of the Orientalist approach to history, the nature of colonial discourse that embraces both history and drama and the structures of textual domination to reverse the Ottoman power. At best, the analysis of texts not only reveals a curiosity about the habits and customs of the Ottomans, but it also indicates an effort to discover what was at the root of their power. At worst (although aesthetically and politically ingenious) they are ideological constructs, which reinforce cultural, religious and sociopolitical differences on stage in order to overcome, emulate and ultimately surpass the Ottomans. Yet, contrary to Edward Said's assertion, representations of the Orient cannot be generalized and taken as serious descriptions of the Ottomans as "weak", "defeated" and "inferior". In postulating important theories about the East and West relations and speaking for the Orient itself, Said has his own specific, political concerns. As he seems to reintroduce the East through his own identity and the discourse of his own culture, he reveals a power relation correlated to his field of knowledge. For Foucault, whose discourse analysis has provided the basis for Said's theories of Orientalism, "[w]hat makes power hold good, what makes it accepted, is simply the fact that it traverses and produces things, it ... forms knowledge, produces discourses" (Foucault 1980, 119). Todorov, in addressing the problematics of alterity at the epistemic level stresses the importance of a dialogue between cultures in which neither voice is reduced to the simple status of object. While Todorov's theory of alterity through discovery and subjectivity is useful, the theoretical orientation of this thesis will be primarily based on Said's *Orientalism*. What constitutes a great challenge to adapting Said's theories to the arguments is that when Said examines the identity and difference structures of the East and West by addressing historical, material and ideological issues, he treats the Ottomans as if they existed outside of history. The paradox here is that the Ottoman Empire carries within itself the burden of an imperial past, which includes its centuries' rule of Eastern lands such as Egypt, Palestine, Jerusalem, etc. Therefore, the Ottoman identity, which cannot be equated with a single race, culture or religion, is a puzzle that perhaps he cannot solve. Considering the pluralistic and open-ended nature of the Ottoman past, Said's generalization of Orientalism as a constant and monolithic discourse poses a further challenge to his thesis and becomes problematic as noted by critics such as James Clifford, Lisa Lowe, John Mackenzie and several others.

According to Foucault, for whom representation, knowledge, "truth" and discourse are "radically historicized" (Hall 46), things have meaning and are "true" only within a specific historical context. Foucault believes that discourse produces forms and practices of knowledge, which differ radically from period to period with no necessary continuity between them. In the sixteenth and seventeenth centuries ideological formations exercise significant historical influence in depicting the Ottoman Islamic culture, identity, beliefs, values which are constructed within the Eurocentric representational paradigm. In the eighteenth century, although the ideological frameworks of Western thought which are used to define a discursive meaning with perspectives on the Ottoman Muslim persist, due to historical forces, the Ottomans ultimately, undergo a process of "colonization". Once defeated, once the threat they posed is safely in the past, the sultans become models of Enlightened virtue against which European despots are measured. However, just as the "Turkish" garb donned by Louis XIV is false and fanciful, so are other interpretations, often superficial and erroneous.

Chapter 2:
Rise to Power: The Great Conquerors

2.1. Sultan Bayezid (1389-1402)

Faithless, and furious Bajazet's Armes now fly,
As swift as Thunderbolts dart through the sky;
In Adrianople plants his haughty Throne,
To make all European Crownes his Owne.
Constantinople twice with sieges tires
And twice he takes it only in desires
Till Tamerlane for all his bloody paines,
Rewards the Monster with a Cage, and Chaines.

(Knolles 124)

As "[M]odern history" writes Lord Acton, "begins under the stress of the Ottoman conquest" (Paul Cole, preface), up until the end of the sixteenth century, the Ottoman threat to the Christian world was at its gravest and most intense. In the mid-fourteenth century, when the Ottoman Empire invaded Europe, the threat and danger, which they represented to the Christian West was soon revealed to the European consciousness. In their conquests outside the European Continent, Westerners did not encounter any major opposition, with the exception of the Ottoman Empire, which by the sixteenth century had emerged as a decisive military power both on sea and land. Yet, since religious diversity within their empire made the Ottomans among one of the great imperial powers in history, as a "new-life force" in the Orient, their contribution to history was twofold:

> First, through their early successor-sultanates they revived and reunited Islam in its Asiatic lands; then through the imperial Ottoman dynasty they regenerated the European lands of Eastern Christendom. As agents of continuity, uniting East with West, they filled a void by the disintegration of the Arab Empire in Asia and of the Byzantine Empire in Europe, to evolve within it a new and creative Ottoman civilization (Lord Kinross 613).

2.1.1. *His haughty Throne*

In 1389 when Murad I (1359-1389) won the Battle of Kossovo at the cost of his life, his elder son Bayezid I was proclaimed on the battlefield the fourth sultan of the Ottoman Empire. Milosh Obrovitch (the son-in-law of Prince Lazar) who had plunged a dagger into Murad's breast, in a pretense of submission to the sultan, was avenged by the Ottoman soldiery. As for Bayezid I, he was quick in coming to terms with Prince Lazar's son Stephen Bulcowitz, who gave his sister Despina in marriage to Bayezid. During Bayezid's reign, since the Ottomans did not have any conflict with the Serbians, Bulcowitz undertook to command a contingent in the Ottoman army and to furnish the Serbian troops whenever and wherever Beyazid required them. While the Ottoman victory in Kossovo had established Ottoman rule in the Balkans, as faithful allies, the Serbians fought with the Ottomans in Nicopolis against the Crusaders and in Angora against Timur.[41] The reign of Sultan Bayezid (1389-1402), nicknamed Lightning or Thunderbolt for his swiftness in transporting his troops across Europe and Asia, corresponded to the rise of the Ottoman's autocratic centralized state, which supplemented its territorial expansion. In this "well-defined and distinct period" (1300-1600) of centralization and expansionism, referred to as "the classical period" (Inalcik 1), the Ottomans' social and cultural structure was conceived as,

> a true 'Frontier Empire', a cosmopolitan state, treating all creeds and races as one, which was to unite the Orthodox Christian Balkans and Muslim Anatolia in a single state ... The Ottoman conquest in the Balkans ... coincided with a time of political fragmentation, when many independent kings, despots and lords of small Balkan principalities did not hesitate to seek outside help in the settlement of their own local disputes. In the midst of the anarchy prevailing in the Balkans only the Ottomans pursued a consistent policy, and only they possessed the military strength and centralized authority necessary for its execution (Inalcik 7).

---

41 Serbia was not incorporated in the Ottoman Empire by Beyazid, but remained an automous vassal state until its annexation to the Ottomans in 1457 by Mehmet II.

According to Herbert Adams Gibbons, who elaborates on the rise of the Ottoman state, "the growing Ottoman power might have been easily crushed by a resolute body of crusaders with a single aim" if it were not for the "ingrained animosity of the East and West, of the Greek and Catholic Churches"(Gibbons 128). After the failure of the union of the Greek Orthodox Church with Rome, not only did each Balkan prince accept one by one Ottoman sovereignty, but also the Byzantine Emperor Emanuel Palaeologus became a virtual Ottoman vassal seeking the sultan's support to hold the Byzantine throne. Initially, none of the Christian states opposed the Ottoman expansion in the Balkans or in Asia Minor. Venice and Genoa signing treaties with the Byzantine Emperor to defend him against all enemies, excluded "the magnificent and powerful lord of lords" Sultan Murat" and his Turks" (Kinross 55). This, however, was later replaced by an alliance, "against that Turk, son of unrighteousness and evil, and enemy of the Holy Cross, Morat Bey and his sect, who are attempting too grievously to attack the Christian race" (Kinross 55).

During his thirty-year reign, however, Murad I had handled the Christians of his empire "with a tolerance striking in its contrast with the attitude of their own fellow Christians" (Kinross 59) and through a process of assimilation. As Lord Kinross writes, Murad:

> [C]ountenanced no persecution of Christians, and apart from the Janissaries, enforced no conversions to Islam. The Orthodox Patriarch himself testified in a letter to the Pope in 1385 that the Sultan left to his Church complete liberty of Action ... Murad I sowed the seeds of a multiracial, multireligious, multilingual society which was to function effectively under the rule of his successors to come (Kinross 59).

Gibbons indicates that the Ottoman conquests were not "raids" but rather "part of a plan of settlement" and that the Ottomans "were not raiders. They were empire-builders" (Gibbons 149). He also adds that in the fourteenth century since the people in the Balkans would rather accept "the rule of the Osmanlis to that of their neighbours [as] ... "Ottoman domination was preferable" (Gibbons 135) to that of the other states. Moreover, what had strengthened the position of Murad in Europe was the internal struggle amongst the Palaeologus family in the Byzantine Empire and the Venetian war with Genoa and Hungary (Gibbons 155).

Following the prestige and power that he gained in Europe, Murad I turned his attention to the expansion of authority in Anatolia (Asia Minor). In 1362, he captured Angora and the Galatian village from the frontier principality of the Germiyan, a Muslim dynasty. The western and northern territories of the House of Germiyan became Ottoman following the marriage of the emir's daughter to Murad I's son. Soon, as the independent Muslim rulers in Anatolia each recognized the Ottoman Sultan as their suzerain, Murad crossed over to Europe and made Adrionople (Edirne) in Thrace the first "real" capital of the Ottoman Empire.

As Gibbons indicates, Murad, in spite of the crusades projected against him, had been careful not to draw upon himself the attention, much less the ill-will, of the western Christian princes (Gibbons 182). As for his son Bayezid, not only did he fight the Christian knights, but he also set upon the first Ottoman subjugation of the Byzantine Empire. Meanwhile, as he placed great importance upon the idea of extending the Ottoman sovereignty in Anatolia, he faced a great challenge from Timur, the new ruler of a powerful empire in central Asia and Iran. Six years before his notorious defeat to Timur, Bayezid had won a complete victory over the Christian forces, which had camped together in a new Crusade against the 'Turks' in Nicopolis. As Froissart records in *Les chroniques*, this battle at Nicopolis in 1396 marked the end of the last crusade with the catastrophic defeat of the Christian Knights at the heart of Europe (Kinross 69). Following his capture of important strongholds in the Byzantine Empire, Bayezid intensified the blockade of Constantinople by building and strongly fortifying a castle on the Asian side of the Bosphorous. While his attempt to capture the city was deterred by the lack of Ottoman naval power at this time, Boniface IX's appeals for a crusade to defend the capital of the Byzantine Empire "fell on deaf ears":

> Richard of England was fighting for his throne, Florence was in a struggle with the Visconti, the Duke of Burgundy and the Duke of Orleans were disputing the regency of France. Only Venice and Genoa were vitally interested in the fate of Constantinople (Gibbons 236).

Later, with the arrival of French Marshal Boucicault and the two naval Republics of Venice and Genoa, although Bayezid's fleet was defeated, the inhabitants of the city afflicted by six years of Ottoman siege and near starvation were ready to surrender themselves to the sultan. While John Palaeologos was willing to make a treaty to give up the city to Bayezid, the Tartar army of Central Asia led by Timur came to his rescue. During the time that Murad and Bayezid were winning an empire in the Balkans, Timur, a new and world-shaking conqueror—a descendant of Genghiz Han—had begun to rule the greater part of the Muslim world including Persia. Furthermore,

> [T]he upper valleys of Tigris and Euphrates, the steppes between the Caspian and Black Seas, Russia from the Volga to the Don and Dnieper, Mesopotamia, the coasts of the Indian Ocean and the Persian Gulf, and the western and northern India were his path of conquest (Gibbons 244).

As Timur and Bayezid confronted each other near Galatia, the Battle of Ankara marked a change in the course of history in terms of being the only crushing defeat experienced during the first three centuries of Ottoman history and as "the only instance where a sovereign of the house of Osman ha[d] been captured" (Gibbons 254). Following the victory at Ankara, while Timur and his hordes swept across Anatolia, the Princes in Europe insistently began to seek the favour of the leader of the Tartar army. As Gibbons writes:

> Henry IV of England wrote to him most cordially, and expressed the hope that he would be converted and become the champion of Christianity (Gibbons 259).

As for Manuel Palaelogos, once he found out the news of Bayezid's defeat, he rushed home from Europe to expel the Ottoman colonists from Constantinople and to close their tribunal. Meanwhile, he sent an ambassador to Timur offering to acknowledge his sovereignty, and volunteering to pay him the tribute that had been given to Bayezid (Gibbon 259). Since Timur had no plans to organize his conquests into a world-empire, following the death Bayezid in 1403, he returned to Samarkand with a plan to conquer China.

The topic in this section is not about Timur the Lame, who defeated Sultan Bayezid in one of the epic battles of history, on a plateau north of Ankara, the present-day capital of the Republic of Turkey. The concern of this section is with the European approach to the representation of an Ottoman sultan on stage. Yet, without a historical perspective on Timur, not only does the meaning of texts written about Bayezid remain obscure, but their contemporary allusions would also be lost. According to Gibbons:

> Like the earlier conquerors of his race, Timur was a raider. Satiety came with destruction and victory, that is satiety for the particular conquest in which he was engaged. So he turned his back on Constantinople and the glittering possibilities of a European invasion (Gibbons 260).

The portrait of Tamerlane that Sir William Temple drew in his essay, entitled *Of Heroick Virtue* was, however, full of praises for "the greatest Conquerer that was ever in the World". As he wrote about "the great Hero of the Eastern Scythians or Tartars",

> He was, without Question, a great and Heroick Genius, of great Justice, exact Discipline, generous Bounty, and much Piety, adoring one God, tho' he was neither Christian, Jew, nor Mohametan, and deserves a nobler Character than could be allowed by Modern Writers to any Person of a Nation so unlike themselves (Hill 2:66-67).

In Marlowe's first Tamburlaine play both Bajazeth and Zabina cursed "Mahomet, that mak'st [them] thus/The slaves to Scythians rude and barbarous" (III.III 270-271) and abandoned their religion. Timur, however, like Bayezid, was a Sunni (or orthodox) Muslim. Yet, unlike the Ottoman Sultan, Timur had never been a menace to Europe. Rather, for Western contemporaries, his abrupt eclipsing of the Ottoman power "meant that Christianity was avenged" (Rouillard 19). Had it not been for Timur, Constantinople would have fallen into the hands of Bayezid who had defeated the Christian Knights at Nicopolis. As Knolles put it, Tamerlane had ultimately been able to coop up the Turk in a "little Iron Cage, like some perilious Wild Beast". This was "Rare example of the uncertainty of worthy honour, that he unto whole ambitious mind, Asia and Europe, two great parts of the World were too little" (Knolles, Vol I, 152-153).

2.1.2. European Crowns

In 1594 when "Tamberlane" in "breeches of crymson vellvett (Greg *Henslowe's Diary*) took centre stage in the Admiral's Company production of *Tamburlaine The Great* to utter the lines:"the ripest fruit of all, / That perfect bliss and sole felicity, / The sweet fruition of an earthly crown" (II.VII. 20-29), Queen Elizabeth I had sent to the Ottoman Sultana Safiye, (Murad III's *haseki* and mother of the heir-apparent Mehmet III) a jewel in her own likeness (Peirce 219). This was a decade after the establishment of Anglo-Ottoman diplomatic relations in 1583 with the arrival of William Harborne in Istanbul as the English ambassador. As was normal at the installation of every ambassador, in 1583 Harborne carried with him gifts and letters from the Queen to be presented to Murad III (1574-95). Later in 1593, however, during Edward Barton's ambassadorial term, when the Queen sent a second set of letters and gift to the Sultan, the royal package was accompanied by a special letter and royal gifts for Safiye Sultan, usually referred to as Sultana in the contemporary European reports.

Richard Wrag, a member of the English delegation to Istanbul listed the inventory of gifts from the Queen of England to Safiye Sultan. Apart from "a jewel of her majesties picture, set with some rubies and diamants", the gift package included "3 pieces of gilt plate, 10 garments of clothe of gold, a very fine case of glass bottles, silver & gilt, with 2 pieces of fine Holland".[42] While Marlowe's *Tamburlaine* demonstrated on stage the symbolic violation

42 From Wrag, *A Description of a Voiage to Constantinople and Syria* quoted by

and shame of Sultan Bayezid's Serbian wife (Maria Olivera Despina), this was a friendly moment in the politics of diplomacy between the English Queen and Safiye Sultan.[43]

In the sixteenth century, although diplomatic relations with the Ottoman Empire were kept alive through the establishment of regular European embassies in Istanbul, royal women created their own diplomatic channels across the Empire through the exchange of letters and gifts. Throughout the reign of her son Mehmet III (1595-1603), Safiye enjoyed the all-powerful position of *valide* sultan or "sultana mother" as she openly took part in the government of the country. Meanwhile, she carried her diplomatic relations with England through correspondence and the exchange of gifts with Elizabeth I who, in 1593, was delighted to receive a "princely attire" in Turkish fashion made of "cloth of gold very rich" (Skilliter 146). The gift also included "two ritch wraught handkerchers" (151), "an under gowne of cloth of silver, and a girdle of Turkie worke, rich and faire" (146). Since the "attyre for the head with the earrings" (Skilliter 154) were lost during the delivery of Safiye's gift to the Queen, in 1599, Safiye made up for the missing item by sending Elizabeth I another robe accompanied by two sets of magnificent headdresses adorned with rubies, pearls and diamonds. As for the Queen's royal present to Safiye, it was a beautiful coach sent by a ship named *Hector* which also carried Elizabeth's famous accession gift to Sultan Mehmet III—an organ accompanied by the famous organ-maker Thomas Dallam of Lancashire (Skilliter 149).

Rosedale, *Queen Elizabeth and the Levant Company*, 16—quoted from "Three Letters from the Ottoman 'Sultana' Safiye to Queen Elizabeth I" by S.A. Skilliter.

43 Participation in diplomatic affairs was a common activity for royal women in the states of Turkish origin. In fact, it was a tradition for Turkish rulers to send female elders of the dynastic family, especially their mothers, as emissaries and intercessors to negotiate with other rulers such matters as the empire's eastward expansion or the division of states (Peirce 219). While women were employed as intercessors and succeeded in reaching effective and peaceful settlements, up until the sixteenth century, the increasing seclusion of the royal family in the Ottoman's Imperial Harem had caused the end of their function as ambassadors.

On stage if Tamburlaine wooed Zenocrate with offers to mount her "on steeds swifter than Pegasus", the mythical winged horse of antiquity, "ivory sled[s]" drawn by milk-white harts and garments "made of Median silk" adorned "with precious jewels" (I.II.94-98), the England of Elizabeth I was an ardent suitor of the Ottoman Empire. A letter written by the agent of the English monarch revealed that the Queen was anxious to incite Sultan Murat III "to make common cause with her" against the Spanish Habsburgs:

> The King of Spain [who] relying on the help of the Pope and the idolatrous princes, design[ed] to crush the Queen of England and then to turn his whole power to the destruction of the Sultan, and make himself a universal monarch (Creasy 49).

Although impressed with the Queen's "wisdom to govern", the sultan, would not take up her proposition to act in alliance with England against Spain. Shortly after, with the defeat of the Spanish Armada, not only would England be victorious, but Elizabeth I would undoubtedly feel relieved that Murad had not collaborated with the Queen of England in fighting her fellow Christians.

2.1.3 Monster with a Cage

> *And to manifest that he knew how to punish*
> *the haughty, made him to be shackled in Fetters*
> *and Chains of Gold, and to be Shut up in an Iron*
> *Cage made like a Gate, in such sort that he might on*
> *every side be seen*
>
> (Knolles, Vol. I, 152)

In the late sixteenth-century when theatre-going Londoners were watching Tamburlaine tormenting the caged, defeated and humiliated Bajazed with more than ordinary zeal, the Ottoman populace in Istanbul, in a magnificent ceremony was celebrating the power and splendour of their twelfth sultan, Murad III. In varying degrees, both of those spectacular moments share striking similarities with the politics of today's superpower rivalry and demand for sensationalism. Each moment captures the *OED* definition of 'spectacle', "a person or thing exhibited to or set before the public gaze as an object either (a) of curiosity or contempt (b) of marvel and admiration" (*OED*).[44] To the English eye, if the spectacle of a caged Ottoman Sultan on stage provoked curiosity and contempt at the very least, victorious Tamburlaine as a kind of substitute for Prester John, inspired admiration. Since the time of the Crusades, the Christian West, prompted by large-scale wishful thinking had created the legend of Prester John, a Christian monarch who had lived in the Orient and who might one day defeat the Muslims. In the European imagination, Timur (although neither a Christian nor in any way an ally of the Europeans) stood for Prester John, as the admired saviour who had succeeded in defeating Bajazed near Angora at the beginning of the fifteenth century.

Towards the end of the sixteenth century when Christopher Marlowe, to the delight and wonder of the audience, created a "spectacular" entrance of the Ottoman sultan with "two Moors drawing Bajazet in his cage" (4.2.1sd),[45] Richard Knolles' *The History of the Turkes* was not yet printed. Yet, Elizabethan England even prior to Richard Hakluyt's *Principall Navigations, Voyages and Discoveries of the English Nation* (1589), which appeared just before *Tamburlaine* (1590), had already fashioned in the public minds the contrast between the "English civility and the 'barbarism' of the exotic Other" (Vaughan 39) prevalent in earlier travel narratives.

As for the Ottomans, judging from the magnificently-staged fêtes, pageantry and spectacles, which involved the physical manifestation of the Sultan's person to his subjects, they knew how to evoke the power of their monarchs by celebrating and recording their triumphs in war and conquest. Just like Queen Elizabeth who said: "We princes are set on stages in the sight and view of

---

44 Quoted from "Before *Othello*: Elizabethan Representations of Sub-Saharan Africans" (Vaughan 27).

45 The first production of *Tamburlaine* is unknown. According to Henslowe's *Diary*, the Admiral's Company produced several performances of *Tamburlaine* in 1594, 1595 and 1598. The 'j cage' is listed in the group of properties.

all the world" (Greenblatt 57), the sultans of the sixteenth-century created spectacular Ottoman Festivals, which lasted more than forty days to impress the world by displaying their might and glory. Yet, if the Queen financed revel costumes of Turks for entertaining masques, particularly after the Ottoman setback at Lepanto these representations "tended to exoticize their subjects" (Bartels 1993, 55) through a fascination that oscillated between fear and emulation. In essence, Elizabethan England exhibited "a polarity" that could only be understood and "brought under control and into meaning by prospects and projects of English domination" (Bartels 1993, 59). Marlowe not only subverted these "prospects" dramatically by portraying the magnified humiliation of an Ottoman sovereign on stage, but he also pioneered the staging of the great divide between West and East, self and other through constructed images of difference. Marlowe's visual image of the Turk was likely formed through illustrations of travelers' accounts in which the significant signs and symbols in European iconography were the turban (*sarik*), the crescent moon (*hilal*) and the curved sword (*kilic*), referred to in the West as the scimitar. The image of the 'Turk' based on distinctive codes of dress was derived from Italian sources such as the anonymous engraving entitled *Omnium Turcarum Imperatorum Effigies* (Denny 8), which depicted the first thirteen Ottoman sultans, including Bayezid I.

The varied populations of the Ottoman Empire, whether Turkish, Muslim, Christian or Jewish, were called Ottomans after the dynasty. Although, Europeans erroneously referred to the Ottoman Empire as "Turkey", as if it were a national state, the multinational subjects were members of a single body politic. In fact, while "Turk" was a pejorative term applied to Anatolian peasants, the realm as a great body was composed of diverse peoples (Turks, Greeks, Serbs, Franks, Levantines, Kurds, Armenians, Arabs, etc.) with the sultan as head. In that regard, the Ottoman celebrations for centuries—to quote the prominent Turkish scholar Metin And—brought together the ruler and the Ottoman subject "in a mystic communion, and served a most political purpose by the physical manifestation of the Sultan's person to his subjects" (And 133). Like the English Queen, the Ottoman Sultan was a performer of a larger dramatic event in which the populace was the audience. This analogy between the two sovereigns brings to mind the myth of the "king's two bodies" which, according to Ernst Kantorowitcz, implied that monarchs like Queen Elizabeth were corporeal both in their own mortal flesh and legally as the head of the state. Based on this theory, which gained particular prominence in the Elizabethan era, while the king had two bodies, "a body natural" which died, "a body politic or corporate" (Rolls 2) which lived on. This mythic dimension of English sovereignty reflected to some extent the Ottoman sultan's imperial ideology that authorized and exalted him through descriptive terms such as the "shadow of God" or "king of kings" (*shahinshah*). While the elaboration of the Ottoman ruler as *padishah* (great king) meant subordination of the sultans' Turkic' image and identity as *khan* to a broader Islamic political legitimacy, public ceremonials were legitimizing devices to celebrate the empire's conquests. Although following Suleyman II's reign there was a lapse in the military activities of the sultans, the image of the sovereign skilled in the arts of war "informed sultanic ceremonial in most sedentary sort" (Peirce 172). Thomas Dallam, the English organ-builder who installed Elizabeth I's gift to Sultan Mehmet III, described the Ottoman sovereign's retinue as including two hundred pages, one hundred mutes and one hundred dwarfs each holding a scimitar. While a bow and a quiver of arrows lay beside the sultan's throne, he,

> satt in greate state, yeat the sighte of him was nothinge in Comparison of the traine that stood behinde him, the sighte whearof did make me almoste to thinke that I was in another worlde (Dallam 69).

The elaborate Ottoman spectacles sought to incorporate realistic portrayals of battles with engines shooting missiles and armed men attacking their opponents. The ultimate defeat of these opponents bore witness to Ottoman superiority in arms, a superiority well known in Elizabethan England. When Marlowe, magnified on stage the defeat of Bayezid in Ankara, Ottoman power and influence was riding high. This was a time when the empire had already expanded at a remarkable rate following its setback in Lepanto (1571). In fact, it was against the backdrop of the Ottoman might, that Marlowe portrayed a military adversary:

> So from the East unto the furthest West
> Shall Tamburlaine extend his puissant arm.
> The galleys and those pilling brigandines
> That yearly sail to the Venetian gulf,
> ...
> Keeping in awe the Bay of Portingale,
> And all the ocean by the British shore;
> And by this means I'll win the world at last. (III.III.246-9 &258-9)

Marlowe's repeated allusions to topical events and perils in the Mediterranean revealed that his ideas were fixed upon the conditions of his own day, rather than that of Tamburlaine. Very few pageants in sixteenth-century Europe could possibly have exceeded in splendour, duration and extravagance Murat III's 1582 feast. There are at least four German descriptions of this particular festival as a total performance and at least three independent accounts in French of which one was translated into English. Today, one of the manuscripts containing only the prose text[46] composed for the delectation of the Ottoman Sultan is kept in Vienna, a city twice besieged by the Ottomans. In this context, it is surprising that in the seventeenth century when an Austrian gentleman commissioned an artist to complete a cycle of paintings about the Turks on the ceilings of a residence near Graz, his subject was not the glorification of Sultan Murat III (Denny 6). Instead, it was the story of Bayezid held by Timur and paraded in an iron cage.

In European performances, Tamerlane (known to history as Timur the Lame as he walked with a limp, whether due to an inborn paralysis or to a wound in a battle) fed Bayezid with crumbs

---

46 The original copy with 427 full-page miniatures is kept at the Topkapi Palace.

from his table and used him as a block to mount his horse or as a footstool to his throne. He also kept the Ottoman sultan in a cage until he was driven to such despair that he dashed out his brains against the bars. There is no historical foundation for the legend that Bayezid and his wife Despina had committed suicide in such indignity. Considering that Bayezid's suffering in captivity had broken his spirit and his mind, Lord Kinross writes the Sultan was "dead from an apoplectic seizure" (Kinross 76). Other sources point to poison hidden in his ring. Yet since the cage episode was more dramatic and more sensational, as Giovanni Botero wrote in 1630: "how [Bayezid] died, our stages have instructed Mechanical men" (Botero 508).

The fabrication of the iron cage legend, according to the nineteenth-century historian Joseph von Hammer, owed its origin to a misunderstanding of the Turkish word 'Kafes' recorded by the chroniclers. Voltaire, in his *Essai sur les moeurs* also treated the idea of the iron cage as a fable (Voltaire *Oeuvres,* 12:90-91). Von Hammer confirmed that the story of the iron cage came from a misunderstanding of the word "kafes" which meant "litière grillée"(Von Hammer 2:96) The word "kafes", apart from its literal meaning "cage", also referred to the covered and curtained litter carried between two horses. The primitive origin of the whole fable—evidently due to a wrongly translated passage from Turkish to Latin- thus made its way into history books.

As Samuel Chew writes in *The Crescent and The Rose,* the "[s]ubsequent legend" of Bayezid's death in captivity was "elaborated by Byzantine and Latin historians [who] magnified his humiliation" (Chew 469). U.M. Ellis-Fermor indicates that each writer added "something to the saga" of Bayezid "unknown to the Oriental authorities" (Ellis-Fermor 28). The story of Bayezid's exhibit in an iron cage was first elaborated in Pope Pius II's *Asiae Europaque Elegantissima descriptio* written in 1534 (Chew 469). According to Ellis-Fermor whether the cage story was drawn from Pius II's "own imagination" or not "it was instantly adopted by other historians"(Ellis-Fermor 29). The story of Tamburlaine's feeding of Bajazet under his table originated in Andrea Cambinus' *Libro dell'origine de'Turchi* (1529) (Chew 469). Scholars point to the German Phillipus Lonicerus' *Chronicum Turcicorum* (1556) as the source for Marlowe's play[47] in which (to the delight of his spectators) he outlined events without testing "by comparison with the authentic oriental traditions" (Ellis-Fermor 35).

In the case of Knolles, who addressed the Ottoman sultan with the resounding words "Behold, Bajazet, the terror of the World" (Knolles 152), the English historian "did not hesitate to transfer semi-legendary matter from the pages of the novelists to his *History*" (Chew 114). Marlowe established the nature of the Sultan's death on the English stage, which was later repeated in Knolles' *General History of the Turkes* (1603), exemplifying the tendency for legend to be treated as historical fact. The fable of Bayezid was popular long into the eighteenth century. Before Nicholas Rowe wrote his *Tamerlane*, based on the work of Knolles (Clark 3), John Dryden alluded to the legend in *The_Conquest of Granada* (1670): "I'll cage thee, thou shalt be my Bayezid/On no pavement but thee will tread/And when I mount, my foot shall know thy head". Dryden in *An Evening's Love* also compared a lover's heart to a bird in a cage: "'Tis a meer Bajazet; and if it be not let out ... will beat out the brains agains the Gates".

As Louis Wann asserts, "this indispensable part of the legend was an indication of how historians could raise a mountain out of a molehill"(Wann 436). Dramatic texts revolving around the Timur and Bayezid story are fictional. Artistic ideals allow or even encourage deviations from reality for the sake of literary and ideological considerations. Yet, each fictitious episode is subjected not only to a process of repetition as but also to a process of transformation whether it be linguistic as the translation of the story or generic as in Handel's *Tamerlano*. Although the fictional quality of the plays is taken for granted, both the process of repetition

---

47 See *The Oriental in Elizabethan Drama* (Wann 177) and *Tamburlaine the Great* (Marlowe 33).

and the process of transformation that are found in the Timur and Bayezid story are ideological and arise from historical forces.

The story of Bayezid's humiliation lived on in Handel's and Nicola Haym's *Tamerlano*. Vivaldi and Scarlatti also wrote on the subject. Handel's opera version incorporated a multiple intertextuality, both material (with its linguistic, musical, scenic and costumic signs) and structural (that is generic). Although there were other versions of the story such as the seventeenth-century French play *Tamerlane ou la mort de Bajazet* by Jacques Pardon, the basis for Nicola Hayms's libretto was Augustino Piovane's text on Bayezid and Timur. What was significant about Nicola Haym's libretto was its presentation of a noble and human Ottoman sultan, echoing Froissart's account of Bayezid in *Les chroniques* written after the Nicopolis Crusade in 1396 and anticipating Mozart's passionate yet wise and compassionate, Selim Pasha. According to Froissart, not only were "the prisoners kept by Bayezid ... treated with chivalry worthy of the most civilized prince" but also the French nobles through direct contact with the sultan had marveled at his generosity, hospitality and concern for justice. As Clarence Dana Rouillard puts it "this was not the barbarian enemy of popular imagination" (Rouillard 18).

2.1.4. Tamerlane (1702)

Nicholas Rowe's popular play *Tamerlane*, which was performed 196 times between 1714-1747 and 88 times between 1747-1776[48] enjoyed a huge success in London. While it made its debut at the Lincoln's Inn Fields Theatre in 1702 with Betterton in the title role, later, as a "stock play" (Johnson *Lives* 77), it was performed annually at various London playhouses on William III's birthday (4th November) and on the anniversary of his landing in England (5th November 1688). At the Queen's Theatre in Dublin (Boas 12) *Tamerlane* was revived in London "as late as 1815" (Johnson 77) with Edward Kean playing Bajazet. According to the *Drury Lane Calendar (1747-1776)* in which the chronological lists

48 See *British Drama-1660-1779: A Critical History* (Kavenik 120 and 164).

are arranged according to theatre seasons rather than calendar years, David Garrick, one of the managers of Theatre Royal during that period had inherited from his predecessors a repertory with which he and his audiences were familiar, and in which each actor felt home in his own niche.[49]

While Garrick was often criticized for reviving old plays rather than producing new ones, *Tamerlane* responded well to the popular taste. With Barry usually in the role of Bajazet[50] *Tamerlane*, played annually on November 4th and November 5th, was "as good as the best that the century had to offer" (Calendar xxvii). In fact, *Tamerlane* "was the tragedy which Rowe valued most, and that which, by the help of political auxiliaries, excited most applause" (Johnson 77). Rowe, like his predecessors and his contemporaries, used Ottoman history to explore issues of ideology and government in his own day. One reason playwrights commonly did this might have been to attract audiences, appealing to the contemporary interest in history and controversy. Plays about the Turks satisfied both tastes simultaneously. Another related reason was that sensitive contemporary political issues could be touched on indirectly. Ultimately, historiography and drama served well to undermine the power and prestige of the feared and disdained Other while shaping its image in production, reception, social, political, discursive and aesthetic contexts. Matar suggests that English drama was an anti-propaganda vehicle shedding some light on the relationship of East and West, which was riddled with stereotypes and fabricated constructs:

> The way that English dramatists, preachers, theologians and others confronted Islam and Muslims was by fabricating images about them by arranging protagonists and geography in a manner that was disembodied from history and cultural surroundings ... As long as the sphere of the action was fabrication, the victory was won by the Christians. Outside that sphere, Englishmen and Britons treated Islam as a powerful civilization which they could neither possess nor ignore (Matar 20).

---

49 See *Drury Lane Calendar* (1747-1776), xxvi.

50 The other actors who played Bajazet were Berry, Mossop, Wilkinson, Palmer, Holland, Smith and Reddish (*Drury Lane Calendar* 329-30).

Marlowe had written *Tamburlaine* two decades after the Ottomans' defeat in Lepanto, which Europe had celebrated with bonfires, sermons, and even poetry such as King James I's boyhood verse about the defeat of the Turks as God's triumph over Satan. In staging his play in a London public theatre, which was accessible to a mixed audience of both lettered aristocrats and illiterate citizens, Marlowe for "topical interest" had also invented "a mythical siege of Vienna" (Chew 472) by the Ottomans, anticipating by more than one century its first siege in 1529. A century later when Rowe created his own version of the Bayezid story in his popular play, regularly performed in London (and prior to Handel's *Tamerlano*, he made no reference to the siege. In reality, at the time of Nicholas Rowe's retelling of Bayezid's story, the Ottomans' second attempt at the siege of Vienna in 1683 had ended in a disastrous defeat against a combined Habsburg-Polish army. Yet, as Raymond Williams insists, drama is as constitutive of "reality" as any other form of discourse. To limit its political meaning to a specific topical reference is to fail to analyze the broader ideological implications embedded in the play.

Rowe's *Tamerlane*, however, which was an "allegorical eulogy" of King William III (Canfield 45), the hero of Glorious Revolution, provided an analogy to the diabolic representation of Bayezid and Louis XIV.[51] As Rowe declared in his dedicatory letter to the Duke of Devonshire, Tamerlane, the Tatar Conquerer, "who gave Peace to the World" was the prototype of the ideal sovereign, his Majesty William III, who stood against "tyranny and oppression" (Rowe 17) typified by Louis XIV. Yet as Samuel Johnson pointed out, England's,

> quarrel with Lewis has been long over, and it now gratifies neither zeal nor malice to see him painted with aggravated features like a Saracen upon a sign (Johnson 77).

In his dedication, although Rowe virtually admitted that the characterization of his Tamerlane was an implicit panegyric on

---

51 On the aspects of political allusions in *Tamerlane*, see "A Key to Rowe's Tamerlane" (Thorp 124-127).

William III, the two Eastern rulers, in representing a model king and a cruel tyrant respectively, stood for much more than either historical or contemporary personalities. In Rowe's play, the conflict between Beyazid as a "satanic figure" and Tamerlane depicted "as God's champion" was an emblem of what J. Douglas Canfield refers as the "eternal struggle of good and evil" (Canfield 57). According to Canfield, the prototypes of Messiah and Satan in Rowe's text constituted a dramatization of the struggle between Mercy-Revenge, Tolerance-Prejudice, Compassion-Hatred. Ironically, though, when the English writers manifested an interest in portraying Tamerlane, they reinforced their own prejudices against the Turks "in order to control, manipulate, even to incorporate what is a manifestly different world" (Said 12).

In the "penny plain" engraving[52] taken from the 1815 edition of Rowe's play, published by John Fairburn in London, Edward Kean with his "blackened face" signified both "exoticism ... and barbaric cruelty" (Vaughan 31). The "elaborate curved scimitar, bejeweled turban with its large aigrette ornament and the undercoat" that Kean wore, clearly revealed "the stereotyped nineteenth-century image of an oriental potentate" (Denny 7). The visual image of the Ottoman sultan in the "penny plain" print was significant in terms of recalling Bajazet's suicide with a dagger in Jean *Magnon's Le grand Tamerlan et Bajazet*, published in 1648. In this French tragedy, which was one of the repertory plays of the Hôtel de Bourgogne in 1646-47, Bajazet, although exposed in "une cage de fer" (Rouillard 480) did not end his life by dashing out his brains against the bars. Instead, as soon as his chains were removed, he stabbed himself with the dagger that was handed to him.[53] While the seventeenth-century French version of the Tamerlane-Bayezid story complied "with the popular conception Oriental horror" as Rouillard concludes, the suicide of the Ottoman sultan(which flatly contradicts the facts related by all

52 As Denny indicates there was also a "tuppence coloured" version for those with more ample means (Denny 7).

53 In Handel's opera he dies by taking poison.

Ottoman historians and by von Hammer) at the end revealed "its absurdity" rather than of its horror" (Rouillard 481). Rowe's *Tamerlane* ends with the exit of "Bajazet guarded" (V.I. 359) as Tamerlane sends him to his "Doom":

> Closed in a Cage, like some destructive Beast,
> I'll have thee born about, in publick View,
> A great Example of that Righteous Vengeance
> That waits on Cruelty, and the Pride like thine. (V.I.346-350)

2.1.5. Conclusion

As Samuel Johnson asserts, "virtues of Tamerlane" were "arbitrarily assigned to him by his poet". When Rowe wrote his tragedy, although, the "quarrel with Lewis" was over, the "fashion" still called "to accumulate upon [Bajazet] all that can raise horror and detestation; and whatever good was witheld from him, that it might not be thrown away, was bestowed upon [Tamerlane]" (Johnson 77). For Foucault, while "politics is war pursued by other means" (Sexuality 93), Bayezid's story is a vivid example of how history was transformed in fiction, which in turn became, in the popular imagination, reality and thus played an important role in epistemology by reversing the premises of political power. In fact, "in any given culture and at any given moment", says Foucault "there is always one 'episteme' that defines the conditions of possibility of all knowledge whether expressed in a theory or silently invested in practice" (Foucault *Order*, 168). Based on that assumption, if representing a caged Bayezid on the European stage was "linked to certain strategies of relations of forces supporting and supported by knowledge" (Foucault *Power*, 194-6), then it was the dynamics of intercultural intertexts in their myriad ways that made the Ottoman Sultan especially liable to the kind of Orientalism that Said describes.

The "Orientalist" images of Beyazid in the European, and specifically, in the English imagination, must be contextualized by recognizing their intertextual character. For Kristeva the text is "a permutation of texts, an intertextuality: in the space of a given text, several utterances, taken from other texts, intersect and neutralize one another (Kristeva *Desire*, 36). The texts revolving around the Timur and Bayezid story across different centuries and cultures are fundamentally intertextual. As Said points out:

> In the system of writing about the Orient, the Orient is less a place than a 'topos', a set of references, a congeries of characteristics, that seems to have its origin in a quotation, or a fragment of a text, or a citation from someone else's work on the Orient, or some bits of previous imagining or an amalgam of all these (Said 177).

While Stephen Heath points out that the text is "far from being a unique creation of the author as originating source...every text is always (an)other text that it remakes, comments, displaces, prolongs, reassumes"(Heath 24). What constitutes the intertextuality of the Bajazet episode as a paradigm for other European texts written about the Ottoman Turks is that, in undergoing a process of repetition, it exists as an ongoing interplay between identity and difference. In constructing and defining the Other, it includes discursive practices and codes which lay the foundations of the conditions of later texts. For Barthes any text is an intertext with "a new tissue of past citations, [b]its of code, formulae, rhythmic models, fragments of social language, etc. [that] pass into the text and are redistributed within it (Barthes 1977, 39). The ramifications and ideological implications of representing the defeat and the humiliation of the Grand Turk on the European stage are obvious. Intertexts constructed by imaginings, fabrications, echoes and transformations of different texts revolving around Sultan Bayezid are varied.

2.2. Sultan Mehmet II (1451-1481)

I who to kingdomes, Cities, brought their fate
The terror of the trembling world of late
Yield to the greater Monarch Death, but am
Yet proud to think of my immortal fame
Greater than Alexander, once I
Or him that Camps of Romans did destroy.
I vanquished the victorious Greeks, and I
Destroyed Epyrus, and fierce Tatary.
From mighty me, th'Hungarians had their doom
And the report reached ye proud walls of Rome.

(Knolles I:229)

In Orientalism, which revolves around such ideas as history, culture and the geography of power (colonization), Said's persistent claim of unchallenged Western hegemony emphasizes the dominance of imperialism of a single character. For Said Orientalism is a "political doctrine willed over the Orient because the Orient was weaker than the West, which elided the Orient's difference with its weakness" (Said 204). In deemphasizing what Lisa Lowe calls the "heterogeneity of imperialisms" (Lowe 5) Said's work lacks historical precision and disregards the question of hegemony as a process, which is neither static nor monolithic. As Foucault states, "power does not function in the form of chain". It circulates and is never monopolized by one centre. Power is "deployed and exercized through a net-like organization" (Foucault 1980, 98), which is rooted in particular contexts and histories. Thus, hegemony and domination are not permanent forms of power that radiate from one single direction, one specific source. The geography of power or rather colonization, which derives from the Latin word "colere" meaning to cultivate or put to use, is a "process by which the frontier of a less technologically developed or less organized civilization—and organization is also a technique- yielded before a civilization whose technological equipment was superior" (Verlinden ix-xiv). In that sense, different societies at different historical moments appropriated new territories to build their civilizations:

> [T]he ancient Greeks pushed into the Mediterranean perimeter; Rome reached as far as England; the Germanic tribes penetrated into Gaul; and William the Conqueror invaded England changing its nature forever (Vaughan 13).

Like the Italian City Republics, which had initiated medieval colonizations in the Holy Land, the Aegean, the Ionian and even the Black Sea, the Ottomans had similar ambitions for imperial possessions. As the historical accounts of ancient and medieval politics are abundant with stories of invasion, occupation and subjugation from the sacking of Rome to the Norman Conquest, the Ottomans, building their civilization, soon became participants of the "conquest culture".

2.2.1. Conquest of Istanbul

Following the conquest of Istanbul, on 29 May 1453, by (Fatih) Mehmet, known to history as "the Conqueror", the loss of the city to the Ottoman Empire would reverberate in European literature for centuries to come. While Istanbul was a city of "world's desire" (Mansel 1), as Emanuel Chrysloras described her:

> Constantinople is situated on a commanding point between Europe and Asia ... By her interposition, the two seas and the two continents, are united for the common benefit of nations; and the gates of commerce may be shut or opened at her command ... encompassed on all sides by the sea, and the continent, is the most secure and capacious in the world. The walls of Constantinople may be compared with those of Babylon: the towers many... (Gibbon 182).

When he was enthroned in 1451 as the seventh sovereign of the Ottomans, the Western world had no high opinion of the nineteen-year-old Mehmet II. Yet, his conquest of Istanbul is celebrated as the turning point between the Middle Ages and the Modern Age. First founded in the seventh century B.C., Byzantium was refounded anew in 324 A.D. by Constantine the Great. Until its capture by Mehmet II, Istanbul, the largest city of modern Turkey, had endured several attacks and sieges,

> [B]y Goths (378 and 476), Huns (441), Slavs (540, 559, 581), Avars (617), Persians and Avars (626), Arabs (669-79 and 717-18), Bulgarians (813, 913 and 924), Russians (four times between 860 and 1043) and Pechenegs (1087). It had never recovered from its sack by a Western crusade in 1204, organized by a commercial rival Venice. As the city reverted to the Byzantines in 1261, repeated defeats of the Byzantine Empire by Muslim enemies, and civil wars between rival emperors, had reduced the city's population from a peak of 400,000 inhabitants to about 50,000 Greeks—or 'Romans' as they were still proud to call themselves (Mansel 3).

Today, the Turkish Republic still calls its citizens of Greek origin *Rum* (an Arabic term with an echo of Rome), but there was no Turkey, either as a geographical or as a political entity until the end of the World War I. The name "Turkey" was first used in a Latin Crusading chronicle of 1190 (Lewis 13) to mark the geographic locations of the Turkish speaking populations and polities. "Turkey" first appeared in English in Chaucer in 1369. Thus, it became the common designation in Western (though not Turkish) usage to refer to the lands of the Turkish Muslim Seljuk Sultanate of Anatolia and the Ottoman Empire as Turkey or "Turchia". Despite this Western discursive practice, as fifteenth century Ottoman writings reveal, the common title for "Turkey" was *diyar-i-Rum* or the Land of Rum. In Muslim usage of medieval times, the *Rum* were the Byzantines who ruled over the eastern remnant of the Roman Empire. Yet, following the Seljuk Sultanate's defeat of the Byzantines in Manzikert in 1071, *diyar-i-Rum* referred not only to the conquered and colonized lands of Anatolia, but it also embraced territories in Europe, Asia and Africa. The term *Rumi* distinguished the Turco-Muslim populations of *Rum* from the rest of the Muslim world and from other Turks. As Cemal Kafadar indicates:

> Being a *Rumi* Turk also implied belonging to a newly emerging regional configuration of Islamic civilization that was on the one hand developing its own habitus in a new land and on the other engaged in a competition to establish its hegemony over a rival religio-civilizational orientation (Kafadar 2).

If the formation of extensive Latin dominions in the Eastern Mediterranean after the fourth crusade in 1204 can be regarded as one of the pre-conditions of the Renaissance, the revival of learning in classical culture gained a further impetus after the fall of Constantinople. With the rediscovery of ancient classical knowledge, the Western world, which had defined itself in the successive phases of Hellenic, Roman and Christian, adopted a new way of looking not only at the past, but also at the major events of the time. In the fresh perspective of new learning through the revival of ancient texts (translated by Muslims), the European Hellas, had now been invaded by an Asiatic tyrant—in this case the Ottoman Sultan and his troops. For Bernard Lewis, "this equation, however, inappropriate, continued to affect the European perceptions of events" (Lewis *Eurocentricism*, 48) within the Ottoman Empire for a long time to come.

In Edward Gibbon's opinion "Mahomet the Second must blush to sustain a parallel with Alexander or Timour" (Gibbon 834). Yet, as many writers contend, Mehmet II, had a "reputation as a supranational hero like Alexander the Great, whom different nationalities could invoke as a protector" (Mansel 12). Compared to the conquests led by Timur, who was quick to overrun Anatolia, the Ottoman expansion was slow. Yet, as an empire which embodied in its political and social structure all races and creeds, it was phenomenal that it endured for seven hundred years.

When the "Ottoman Empire emerged from the decaying corpse of the Eastern Roman Empire" (Phillipides 3) the Byzantine Empire was undergoing internal problems. The fall of the city "passed without notice in contemporary English chroniclers" (Wood 1). It was the civil strife with revolts, usurpation, religious crisis, social injustice and crippling taxation that presented an ideal situation for the rising Ottoman Turks. Although the last Byzantine Emperor Manuel Palaelogus had sought help from the English against the Ottoman Empire, his efforts were "fruitless" (Wood 1) because England had no direct and commercial relations with the Byzantines. At the time Mehmet II conquered the Byzantine capital, the English, following the Hundred Years' War, had just begun their so-called War of the Roses, which lasted from 1453 to 1485. As David Hume writes, historians declare that no part of English history since the Norman Conquest is so obscure as that of the War of Roses. According to Hume "[T]he deep cloud that covers that period is a scene of horror and bloodshed, savage manners, arbitrary executions and treacheries, dishonourable conduct of all parties".[54] He claims that Shakespeare in *Henry VI* and *Richard III*, brings before us the brutal aspects of that horrid drama of history, the ghastly realities of the historic theatre itself, and makes their representation tolerable to modern spectators. The War of Roses, which killed off large numbers of turbulent feudal lords and quickened the desire of the middle class for strong, stable government, ended with the union of the two rival branches of the Royal family, the Lancasters and the Yorks. As for the conquest of Istanbul, it led the Ottoman Sultan to unite the two continents, Asia and Europe, and make himself the Sultan of the Arabs, the Persians and the *Rum*. In other words, when Mehmet II passed through the Adrionaple Gate in Istanbul, the English were occupied with a civil war, which ultimately contributed to autocracy in the country and led the Tudor sovereigns to become absolute rulers. As for France,

> Charles VII was retaking Bordeaux and Rouen from the English even as Constantinople was falling, and had no desire to waste his strength on another Nicopolis. Even later, he remained deaf to the more fervent appeals of Pope Calixtus III. But it must not be thought that France was unmoved by this catastrophe (Rouillard 22).

For England, however, the establishment of the Ottoman/Islamic power over what had been the Byzantine/Christian Empire was one of the most ideologically-laden threats to its identity. In *Henry V*, it was Hal, grandfather to the first king of the Tudors who aspired to emulate the Ottoman Empire. As he wooed the French King's daughter, he pled with her to prove "a good soldier breeder":

> Shall not thou and I, between Saint Dennis and Saint George compound a boy, half French, half English that shall go to Constantinople and take the Turk by the beard? (V.II.209).

---

54 Quoted from *The Great Events by Famous Historians* (Rossiter 72).

2.2.2. Memory and Identity

As Edward Said writes in a recent article: "Memory and its representations touch very significantly upon questions of identity, of nationalism, of power and authority". Said says that " Far from being a neutral exercise in facts and basic truths, the study of history, which of course is the underpinning of memory ... is to some considerable extent a nationalist effort premised on the need to construct a desirable loyalty to an insider's understanding of one's country, tradition and faith" (Said *Critical Inquiry,* 176). A powerful link between history and memory and the manipulation of the past in order to mold the present is mostly notable in plays written about the Ottoman Turks who are represented on the European stage as West's Other. It is common knowledge that the manipulation of the past often entails the use of stereotypes and prejudice in constructing alterity. Although the Ottomans, with their turbans, their scimitars, their bows and arrows have stood for an abundance of emotive and mental associations in the Western consciousness, alterity derives its power not from specific images, but from its epistemology.

Despite the attempts of Western historiography or iconography to "barbarize and delegitimize" (Kafadar 38) the "Turks" or "Turkish Empire" (as referred to in Western discourse), the grand plan of Mehmet II was geared towards creating one civilization within the empire. In the Ottoman system, the Turk was regarded only as one of the representatives of the cultural mosaic of diverse peoples, each with their own religious, linguistic or political affiliation. The ruling class was composed of "Muslims (some by conversion) who spoke Turkish (though not necessarily as a native tongue), affiliated (some voluntarily some involuntarily) with the dynastic state" (Kafadar 4). The Turk was "not necessarily a favoured one of the ethnicities" (Kafadar 4) ruled by the House of Osman. Yet, ironically, from the point of view of Western historiography and consciousness and based on the "us/them" configurations, assumptions and presumptions on national or individual levels were based on the idea that it was the barbarous "Turk" who had oppressed the non-Turkish, non-Muslim Other.

The English historical plays about the Ottoman Empire are predominantly based on stories narrated in *The History of the Turkes*. Evidently, the moral of Richard Knolles' monumental work attests to the fact that an "armchair historian" without leaving England has been able to give an account of the historical events in the empire. Besides Knolles' disapproval of the "tyrant Mahomet" and "all his works and ways" (Bronson 100), the English historian in his work gave "life" to collective memories of the Tamburlaine-Bayezid episode, the fall of Constantinople, the legend of Irene, the career of Scandenberg, etc. As Samuel Chew argues, Knolles' "verbose" and "mercilessly long (twelve hundred pages) ... compilation" of *The History* is not devoid of "prejudice" as "his purpose was propagandist" (Chew 114). In Samuel Johnson's opinion no historian could "justly contest the superiority of Knolles."[55] For Henry Hallam, however, it was unfortunate that he had chosen to write of "a remote and barbarous people about whom none desire to be informed" (Quoted from Chew 113).

Whether or not the English historian composed his monumental work as a propaganda vehicle, the truth of the matter was that Mehmet II, who desired to meld occidental influences with the tradition of Islam had a propagandist aim as well. Like his great grandson Suleyman I, Mehmet II's utopian ambition was to revive the Roman Empire by uniting Constantinople with Rome. His "imperial project" (Kafadar 97) to seize the rest of the Italian peninsula following his conquest of Otranto continued until his Mehmet II's death. Ultimately, he saw himself as a universal sovereign personifying Turkish, Islamic and Byzantines traditions. As an important patron of European artists, Mehmet initiated a series of vigorous cross-cultural artistic contacts with Venice. He invited celebrated artists such as Matteo de Pasti, Gentile Bellini and Constanza de Ferra to Istanbul and attempted to attract Leonardo da Vinci and Michelangelo to the services of the Ottoman

55 See *The Rambler* 122 (18 May 1751).

Court (Necipoglu 424]. During the period that Bellini spent in Istanbul as a guest of Sultan Mehmet, he was fascinated not only by what he saw in the capital city but also by the Ottoman art. As Riberio writes of Bellini:

> In his well-known painting of a Turkish artist, now in the Isabella Gardner Museum, Boston, Bellini's attention to his subject's costume of sumptuous brocaded velvet is influenced by the manner of Turkish and Persian miniatures (Riberio 190).

When Mehmet II's image, constructed by Bellini, circulated in European courts, the triple crown on the painting was based on a "ready model, the papal tiara with its three tiers, especially the famous one which Caradossa had made for Pope Julius II" (Kurtz 251). Though crowns were not worn in the Islamic world, where the Caliph or the sultan appeared on all occasions with a turban, in 1480 the Venetian artist had put three crowns on Mehmet II's portrait medal. These multiple crowns were symbolic of the lands ruled by the sultan: Asia, Greece and Trebizond, where a Byzantine dynasty had reigned until 1461.

In essence, the iconography of such headgear or helmet crowns fulfilled certain propagandistic functions such as conveying "Ottoman imperial claims to a European audience through a Western discourse of power" (Necipoglu 402). In the sixteenth century, Agostino Veneziano's published engraving depicted Suleyman the Magnificent in a fantastic headgear in the "shape of a papal tiara" (Kurtz 249). The iconography of the woodcuts and the engraving was aimed at conveying Ottoman claims of sovereignty to a European audience "through an intelligible Western vocabulary" (Necipoglu 425). As Necipoglu writes:

> Three Venetian woodcuts and engravings by Agostino Veneziano depict Sultan Suleyman I with a fantastic headgear that could almost be dismissed as a figment of Orientalist imagination ... However, these prints are truthful graphic records of a spectacular golden helmet produced... by Venetian goldsmiths in 1532 ... this fantastic helmet-crown clearly constitutes the main subject of the series of Venetian prints depicting Suleyman that are thought to be based by Titian (Necipoglu 401).

While the Ottoman court was actively involved in a network of patronage that produced these art pieces in Venice, the reputation of Suleyman's quadruple gold crown served as the basis for an iconography with multiple interpretations: emperor, sultan, pope and caliph. In the sixteenth century "[m]any a European already saw the *Grand Seigneur* as the supreme head of all the believers, Muslims, Jews and Christians alike"(Feigl 42). Later, in mid-seventeenth century, as an anonymous German engraving depicted Mehmet IV (1648-1687) adorned with the same helmet crown, this was a "proof that in Europe the idea of a universal ruler ... 'sultan-emperor-pope-caliph' had at least entered into legend" (Feigl 42). In fact, when Michael Kritoboulos, a Greek historian, gave an account of the conquest of the Byzantine capital and dedicated his book to Mehmet II, he regarded him as a Caesar, and as a legitimate successor to the Byzantine emperors (Phillipides 10). Pope Pius II affirmed that for Mehmet's claim to be legitimate, he would have to be a Christian. He wrote to the sultan "offering him baptism, so that he might become, under papal protection, the greatest of Christian Princes ... Pope Nicholas V is said to have prayed for the conversion of the Sultan, after suitable instruction"(Kinross 115).

Mehmet II's utopia to create a universal *imperium* was later replaced by a "national" one. Istanbul, soon became the capital of an empire, which came to control a great territory, from Belgrade to Yemen and from Crimea to North Africa. Later, when Suleyman the Magnificent ruled between 1520-66, an era generally considered the golden age of the Ottoman power and prestige, he challenged the Hapsburg's claim to the title of Caesar. Suleyman I not only shared Mehmet II's imperial aspirations to create a world empire, but he expanded the latter's enthusiastic patronage initiatives with European artists mainly Venetian.[56] According to the

56 The Ottoman Court's enthusiastic patronage of European artists who offered their services in return for lucrative rewards, stopped, however, in the mid-sixteenth century because of an attitude of "unquestioning confidence in the superiority of Ottoman culture that produced the 'classical' masterpieces of art and architecture" (Necipoglu 424) in Istanbul.

Venetian Ambassadors, wisdom and a sense of justice were qualities repeatedly found in most sultans of this period. This was because these qualities were entrenched in the sultans' education and knowledge of literature (Valensi, 184). In 1518 Mocenigo wrote that: "Sultan Selim I was considered a 'justman' who, nurtured by 'The Life of Alexander', wished to imitate his feats and become the master of Asia, Africa and Europe" (Valensi 184). Suleyman the Magnificent—known as the Lawmaker—was, as Minio spoke of him, a "philosopher" with a "good knowledge of his law" who as a reader of Alexander "devoured glorious examples of the past" (Valensi, 184). In essence, as Bernard Lewis puts it:

> The Turks who entered Constantinople were not simple barbarians as depicted by some Western writers, but the heirs and carriers of an old and high civilization—that of classical Islam, to which they themselves had added a not inconsiderable contribution (Lewis 103).

In 1453, when Mehmet II rode across the marbled court of the much-ruined imperial palace, he indulged in melancholy reflections on the "impermanence and instability of this world, and of its ultimate destruction" (Lewis 6). Tursun Beg, a veteran of the conquest and Secretary to the Sultan's council, was with the Sultan as he wandered through "this mighty structure fallen in ruin" (Lewis, 8). As he wrote in his biography of Mehmet II, there was a great sadness in the Conquerer's voice as he cited a Persian poet: "The spider weaves curtains in the palace of the Caesars/The owl calls the watches in Afrasiab's towers" (Kinross 110).

When Mehmet II aspired to emulate and surpass the achievements of Alexander the Great and Caesar, Rome had already lost its powerful position. While Venice could not foresee the fall of Constantinople to the Ottomans, "[e]veryone knew that the Venetians and the Byzantines had long entertained the heartiest dislike for each other"(Setton 4). Yet,

> the fall of Constantinople struck Western Christendom with a sense of doom. Lamentations arose from all those lands, which had done so little to save it—the more so as an eleventh-hour effort do to so, with a papal armada of Venetian galleys, had failed to penetrate farther than the shores of the Aegean (Kinross 111).

Constantinople, the original "new Rome" had long evoked in the Venetians, a search for "ancient identity and grandeur". As the Venetians saw themselves as the city's "Catholic restorer and the true heir of Constantine" (Chambers 18) for Venice, Constantinople continued to be an inspiration. For example, St. Mark's basilica was modeled upon the church of the Holy Apostles in Constantinople, which still evoked memories of its Byzantine past and splendour. As for Mehmet, "the true image of what was to be the fundamental feature of this state" was under his rule, was "a cosmopolitan empire" (Kinross 112). Although the Christian church was now subordinated to the Islamic State, the empire was at once secular and religious. In fact, Mehmet II's "task was not to destroy the Byzantine Empire, but to bring it to new life on a new Ottoman pattern" (Kinross 112). The system devised by Mehmet was to organize religious minorities into *millets*, or nations, which were self-governing communities that preserved their own laws and practices under a religious leader. Although these *millets* would not have the privilege of the ultimate sanction of political freedom, they would have peace and prosperity under the Ottoman rule. Mehmet also required that,

> [S]ide by side with the ulema, the Islamic authority, there should reside within the walls of Istanbul the Greek Orthodox Patriarch, the Armenian Patriarch, and the Jewish Rabbi (Kinross 113).

While the sultan's main task was the rebirth of a new capital in this strategically important city, multinationalism became the essence of his centralized government. Since there were not enough Turks to populate the city, he transferred people from all parts of Asia and Europe. He personally went to Bursa to select Turkish merchants and artisans and had artists and craftsmen transported from Konya, the Selchuk capital in Anatolia. He also had Armenians, who were prominent in the Eastern Anatolia as jewelers, craftsmen, tradesmen brought to the capital. Some areas of the city never lost their Greek population. Yet, Mehmet, who appreciated Greek culture also "imported Greeks" (Mansel 9) to Istanbul, understanding the prosperity that they would bring to the city. Mehmet also appealed to many "immigrants from Salonika, with its large Jewish community, and Jews from Europe on a substantial scale". Thus, soon "[t]he Jews, with their own *millet*, were to become the third largest element in the capital after the Moslems and the Christians" (Kinross 117). Yet, as much as Mehmet identified himself with Alexander and nurtured diversity within the cosmopolitan *diyar-i-Rum*, in the eyes of the Christian West, the city of Constantine had "turned" Turk.

2.2.3. The Christian Hero (1735)

Iskender, the Pride and boast
Of that mighty Othman host,
With his routed Turks, takes flight.
From the battle fought and lost
On the day of Pentecost,
Leaving behind him dead,
The Army of Amurath

(Longfellow, *Tales of Wayside Inn,* Part III)

As Christopher Tyerman argues *in England and the Crusades (1095-1588)*, England had lost its idea of a Crusade against the Muslims during the reign of Elizabeth I. Yet, "the memory of crusading lingered in academic, literary and antiquarian circles"(Tyerman 369-70). It is in this spirit that George Lillo, in the dramatis personae of his play, *The Christian Hero* (1735) lists the "Turks" (Amurath, Mahomet, Osmyn, Kisler Aga) and the "Christians (Scandenberg, Aranthes, Amasie and Paulinus) separately and ends the play with the victory and glory of the Christian hero over the Ottomans. In 1735 when *The Christian Hero* opened at Drury Lane, featuring William Milward in the title role and James Quin as Amurath, it played with "tolerable success" (Steffenson 215) for three nights and then completely disappeared from the stage. As Aaron Hill wrote in the *Prompter* "the Pulpit seems the properest Theatre for such Representations, and the clergy the properest actors in the religious drama" (Hill 29). In Lillo's dramatization of the opposition of faiths, it is Amurath's daughter Hellena, who becomes enamoured of the Christian hero, in the tradition of the old epic. As she tells her confidante, Cleora:

How long shall Amurath, my awful Father
Tho' press'd and overwhelm'd with Disappointments,
Provoke the Malice of his adverse Stars,
And urge his own Destruction; whilst in vain
With unrelenting Hatred pursues,
Who, Heav'n protects, th'ever victorious Hero of Epirus. (I.I.23-28)

The victorious hero in the play is Scandenberg, to whom Knolles refers as "the most valiant and fortunate King of Epirus" (Knolles 248). Yet, it is not only Amurath (Murat II, father of Mehmet II) who stands between Hellena's hopeless love for him. Scandenberg is already in love with Althea, the Christian heroine who has fallen captive to the Turks. A common denominator in captivity themes revolving around the Ottomans is that the Christian woman is taken captive (usually by Barbary corsairs or during sieges and conquests) and is temporarily separated from her lover who voluntarily follows to rescue her. In spite of numerous variations, the desire for the Christian hero to penetrate the Seraglio in order to rescue his lover is quite popular in eighteenth-century abduction plays. As a general rule, while the motif of captive lovers draws attention to the oppressive energies of the captor, the ultimate goal is to undermine the power of the sultan through master-slave configurations. The idea of the powerful sultan is a disruption of Christian oneness and unity as well as a threat to Western identity. In that sense, captivity as a dramatic theme reinforces the inescapable otherness of the Ottoman sultan, who is linked with cruelty, oppression, tyranny, lasciviousness, etc.

Unlike Eliza Haywood's *The Fair Captive* in which Alphonso arrives in Istanbul to redeem his captive mistress Isabella, *The Christian Hero* is not set in the capital of the Ottoman Empire. It is set on "*The Plain and Mountains near* Croia, *the Metropolis of* Epirus", or rather Albania, during the reign of Murad II. As Gibbon describes Mehmet II's father: "The justice and moderation of Amurath is attested by his conduct and acknowledged by Christians themselves" (Gibbon 188). As for Mehmet II, within the historical time frame of the play, he has not yet conquered Istanbul. Instead, he has captured Aranthes, a loyal follower of Scandenberg—the Albanian hero—and his daughter Althea, a "second Lucrece" who "In Mahomet shall find another Tarquin/As Cruel and remorseless as the first" (IV.I.6-8). In the play, "Mahomet drest like Scandenberg" will enter Althea's apartment "fast'ning the door on the Inside (IV.I). To Althea's cries: "Father! Arathes!Haste/And like Virgins preserve your Daughter/Come Castriot, come" (IV.I.62-65), those who respond for rescue are ironically Amurath, Visier and Kisler Aga who presume that they have captured Scandenberg. With the turn of events in *The Christian Hero*, however, the audience will be completely relieved as Althea will be freed, reunited with Scandenberg and blessed by Aranthes, "Prince of Durazzo/Who derives his high Descent from Charlemain, that most/Illustrious Frank", (I.I.191-3)

As Lillo writes in the Prologue "there's not a theme so dear/As virtuous freedom to the British ear". Critics acclaim, however, that the subject matter of *The Christian Hero* does not lend itself to the contemporary political situation in Britain, as it raises no issues relevant to the eighteenth- century concerns of the country. Scandenberg's tirades against "arbitrary Tyrants" (II.I.113), the "Number of [Amurath's] Slaves" (148), and "Religion by the Sword" (154) versus his own "Love of Liberty" (173) were, however, familiar to those members of the audience, who had read about the "maxims" of the Ottoman Government, as outlined by Paul Rycaut. Although, by the end of the seventeenth century, the concept of absolutism had lost its credibility in England among intellectuals (such as Locke), nonetheless, as Rycaut had written:

> But not only is Tyranny requisite for this people, and stiff rein to curb them, lest by an unknown liberty they grow mutinous and unruly, but likewise the large territories and remote parts of the Empire require speedy prevention without processes of law, or formal indictment; jealousie and suspicion of misgovernment being license and authority enough for the Emperour to inflict his severest punishments: all of which depends on the absoluteness of the Prince (Rycaut 3).

Lillo ends *The Christian Hero* with the rhetoric of the ideal of political liberty by drawing a contrast between England and the Ottoman Empire:

> And Kings are Gods on Earth but while, like Gods,
> They do no ill, but reign to bless mankind.
> May proud, relentless Amurath's Misfortunes
> Teach future monarchs to avoid his crimes. (V.V.16-20)

Historically, Scandenberg, a renegade of Albanian origin, was raised and educated in Murad's palace. To the surprise and chagrin of the sultan, however, he had "proclaimed himself the avenger of his family and country [while] the names of religion and liberty provoked a general revolt" (Gibbon 203). As Aranthes put it, if other Christian Princes would "unite/Afflicted Europe wou'd no longer groan/Beneath [Amurath's] Yoke and mourn her Freedom lost" (I.I.298-300). Scandenberg (1404-1468), the Albanian hero, was the son of the hereditary prince of a small district in Albania (Epirus). His original name was George Castriota or Katriotes. As the Ottomans called him Iskender (Alexander) Bey, in Western discourse this was corrupted to Scandenberg. When his father, John Castriot, was unable to contend with Murat II's power, he had submitted to the Ottoman conditions of peace and tribute. George was taken to the Ottoman capital as a youth and given the best advantages of training and education at the Palace School. Soon he was showered with favours from Murat II and given an army to command. The reduction of his father's principality in a small province, was compensated by the award of the rank and title of *sanjak beyi* (governor of the chief administrative unit of the empire). During the time that Iskender Bey rose to high military rank and personal favour with Murat, he had "served with honour in the wars of Europe and Asia" (Gibbon 202). Yet, during the confusion of Ottoman defeat in Croia, he escaped the battlefield. Under his command, Scandenberg's standing militia of Albanian chieftains, which included adventurers from France and Germany, successfully resisted the power of the Ottoman conquerors Murat II and his son Mehmet for over two decades. Upon receiving aid from Venice, Naples, Hungary and the Pope, Scandenberg finally asked Pius II for refuge in the ecclesiastical state, dying as a fugitive on the Venetian territory. Lillo captures on stage the biography of the Albanian Prince.

> Have I not been a Father to thy Youth?
> Did I not early form thy Mind to Greatness,
> And teach thy Infant Hands to use Arms?
> Th'o the unerring Maxims of our State,
> (The only Rule of Right and Wrong in Courts)
> Had marked thee for Destruction; still I spar'd thee.
> Trusted, belov'd, advanc'd thou hast betray'd me:
> First seized my Provinces you call'd your own,
> Then join'd my Foes to rob me of my Fame;
> The perjur'd *Uladislaus*, fierce *Hunniades*,
> And the *Venetians*, who have since forsook thee. (II.I. 82-93)

The first notable information about Scandenberg appeared in Peter Ashton's *Shorte treatise upon the Turkes Chronicles* (1546).[57] Gentleman's translation of Jacques de Lavardin, *The Historie of George Castriot, Surnamed Scandenberg, King of Albanie. Containing his famous acts, his noble deeds of Armes, and memorable victories against the Turkes for the faith of Christ* (1596), covered an extensive biography, citing continental sources upon which the story of the Albanian hero was based. In a sonnet titled *Upon the Historie of George Castriot, alisas Scandenberg,* Edmund Spenser declared him "The scourge of Turkes, and plague of infidels/Thy acts, O Scandenberg, this volume tells" (Spenser 603). For Spenser, Scandenberg, who had stood between Mehmet II and his aspirations for conquests in Eastern Europe, merited "a mere triumphant feate" (Spenser 603). Marlowe had used Calvin and Thomas Fortescue's (1571) "scourge of God" concept through the career of the Muslim conqueror Timur, who was the rod for the chastisement of the Ottomans. In that sense, the scourging that Scandenberg had equally administered was a justifiable act. Although it is hard to grasp Marlowe's idea of God in *Tamburlaine* with his confusing allusions to Jove, Jupiter, etc., in England, he

---

57 For contemporary biographies, see Edward Gibbon's *Decline and Fall of the Roman Empire* (Chapter 57, viii, n156).

had turned Timur (a devout Muslim) into a Renaissance subject by depicting him as the saviour of Europe in traditional Christian terms. In his play, as a sacrilegious rebel, while Marlowe could challenge all "gods" with cautious references to Christianity, ultimately he had a freer hand to condemn Islam.[58]

Samuel Chew draws attention to an entry in the *Stationers' Register* for *The true historye of George Scandenberg as yt was lately playd by the right honorable the Earle of Oxenforde his servantes* (Quoted from Chew 477). According to Samuel Chew, there were conjectures based on some weak evidence, that Marlowe might have been the author of this lost play entered in the registry in 1601. In *The General History,* Scandenberg casts a shadow on Mehmet the Conqueror as Knolles devotes almost half of his chapter on "Turkish Emperor" to the Albanian Prince. Therefore, it seems "logical" to assume that Marlowe would have chosen to write on the "successive subjects" of heroes who triumphed over the Ottoman Empire (Chew 478). Yet, whether or not Marlowe left a "Scandenberg behind" (Chew 478), the story of the Albanian hero, to whom the Pope referred as the "champion of Christ" (Kinross 132), would reverberate in Europe in the centuries to come. As Gibbon indicates, Scandenberg "must be justly praised as a firm and able champion of his national independence". As for the rebellion of the Albanian Prince, "[I]n the eyes of the Christian" it was "justified by his father's wrongs" (Gibbon 201-6).

Scandenberg was a figure of greater epic stature than the Ibrahim of Mlle de Scudéry's novel of 1641. The source for Lillo's character was the English translation of *Scanderberg the Great*, a romantic novel by Anne de la Roche-Guilhem written in 1688. Similarly, Thomas Whincop's unperformed tragedy, *Scandenberg: or Love and Liberty,* written before 1730 but not printed until 1747, and William Havard's *Scandenberg* (1733), which was not

---

58 For a discussion of Marlowe's position towards Christianity, see *Christopher Marlowe, Complete Plays*, Edited by Irving Ribner with an introduction and notes.

well received by the audience, were derived from the same source. [59] In the play, although Lillo asserted his values on political liberty, *The Christian Hero* was essentially a religious drama reaffirming the glory and victory of the Albanian Prince who had fearlessly resisted the Ottoman Empire. However, the greatest irony in the Scandenberg story, was that, while the news of victory of George Castriot, who defied the Ottoman Empire and took arms against it, spread throughout Europe, the *grand vezirs* who ruled the Ottomans during the entire seventeenth century (The Koprulu Family] were all Albanian renegades. In sum, since the 1500s twenty-six *grand vezirs* of Albanian origin had taken office in the Ottoman Empire. Yet, a distorted perspective and biased approach towards the Ottomans, who had posed a great threat to Europe since mid-fourteenth century, constituted and ignored vast areas of historical reality.

2.2.4. Irene (1749)

> *Upon the mount where old Musaeus sung,*
> *Sits the gruff turban'd captain, and exacts*
> *Harsh tribute! In the grove where Plato taught*
> *His polish'd strain sublime, a stupid Turk*
> *Is preaching ignorance and Mahomet.*
>
> Sneyd Davies[60] (1744)

In 1675 when Neville Payne wrote in *The Siege of Constantinople* that "The Turk must take this town and the Pope/Will have a rival Bishop in the World" (I, p. 8) the Ottoman Empire, despite its capture of important fortresses in Europe, was no longer deemed a serious threat to the West. Yet, the spectre of papism still hung over England. Rather than dwelling on the anti-Islamic polemic, Payne changed the image of Mehmet the Conqueror from that of

---

59 The earliest books on Scandenberg in French were G. Gaulteron's *Commentaire d'aucunes choses des Turcs et du Seigneur George Scandenberg* (1544), a translation from the Latin of Paolo Giovio; Jacques de Lavardin's *Histoire de Georges Castriot, surnomme, Scandenberg,* chiefly drawn from a Latin biography; and Montaigne also referred to Scandenberg in the *Essais*.

the cruel tyrant into a benevolent and virtuous ruler. Though he was an absolutist ruler, in *The Siege of Constantinople*, Payne described Mehmet as,

> ... a Prince of such a mighty soul:
> Vertues in him contend for Victory
> And each of them in turn do gain a triumph. (V, p. 86)

Payne ended his play with the words that "we must your vertue, and the Sultans praise" (87). As Voltaire indicated, the Ottoman Sultans did not rule arbitrarily. On the contrary, they were sworn to obey Islamic laws that protected individual rights and were guaranteed by the power of the largely autonomous *muftis* (See Kaiser 18). Since religious toleration of other faiths was central to the Ottoman government system, when Johnson wrote his *Irene*, Greeks like other non-Muslims within the Ottoman capital enjoyed wealth and privilege, their religion having been protected since the days of Mehmet II.

In the eighteenth century however, many English writers remembered the plight of Greece—which like Albania, Egypt, etc. was then an Ottoman province—through the panegyric of Ancient times. Eliza Haywood, for example, in *The Fair Captive* (1721, constructed and positioned the "barbarous" Ottoman Empire antithetical to the Western norms of "civilized" Europe.

> Greece, who to all the world around her taught
> Ingenious Arts, Morality and Arts
> Now quite forgets herself, the use of letters.
> And all involved in Clouds of Ignorance
> Still mournful, brooding o'er her learned Ruins
> Her tuneful Streams are lost, her Fountains silent. (I.I)

Haywood built her characters upon the dialectical interplay of identity and difference and constituted the European culture against a defined Other which she referred as "this savage rage" (I.p.3), "cursed infidels" (V. p.44) and so on. In *The Fair Captive* it was the Spaniard Alphonso who echoed Johnson's Aspasia. On

60 For Davies' verse-epistle, see Dodsley's *Collection of Poems*, (the "new edition" of 1782), vol. 6:160.

asking Demetrius "Is Greece delivered? Is the Tyrant fall'n", she lamented "O Greece! Renown'd for Science and for Wealth/Behold thy boasted Honours snatch'd away (V.III.42-3). As he arrived in Istanbul to redeem his captive mistress, for Alphonso the city itself conjured up the image of the "fair captive" in the hands of the rapacious and treacherous Turk:

This Heavenly clime, this Earthly Paradise
This Beauteous Mistress of the Eastern world,
Should drag the Chains of Arbitrary Power.
Spite her Pomp, the drooping still laments
Her ravish'd Freedom and her lost Estate. (I.I)

Heywood's description of the city was not only restricted to images of violation later echoed in Johnson's *Irene*:

From ev'ry Palace burst a mingled Clamour,
The dreadful Dissonance of barb'rous Triumph,
Shrieks of Affright, and Wailings of Distress.
Often when the Cries of Violated Beauty
Arose to Heav'n, and pierc'd my bleeding Breast. (I.I)

In their rhetoric, not only did these playwrights echo one another, but they sounded more like the philhellenic poets of the nineteenth century.[61] In *Irene* it was Demetrius, the Greek hero, who told Leontius that:

... Now ghastly Desolation
In Triumph sits upon our shatter'd Spires
Now superstition, Ignorance and Error
Usurp our Temples and profane our Altars. (I.I.66-9).

As Heywood put it, "this rugged, barbarous Scythian Crew" like "ravenous Beasts of Prey" came rushing down to "Fix the Standard of their strolling Prophet" (I.I. p.2). In that sense, the idea of apostasy which ran through John Milton's Restoration poem *Paradise Lost*, in which Satan is named a "great Sultan", echoed in *Irene*. Milton's work was clearly in Johnson's mind since *Irene* was charged with similar anxieties of temptation leading to the

61 See *Fair Greece Sad Relic: Literary Philhellenism from Shakespeare to Byron* (Spencer 247-67).

Christian captive's "renoun[ing of] her Faith" (I.II) and "Receiving the faith of Mecca" (I.III). For Johnson, if Irene's ambition for worldly glory and temptation for wealth and riches was Satanic, the Sultan himself was doomed to "Idolize th' Apostate" (IV. Vii. 11). In *Irene* Johnson did not merely argue against the Greek captive girl's willingness to become an apostate to the Christian faith. As an ideological construct, the play reinforced on stage the cultural and religious differences of the Ottomans with the Western world.

Johnson's reconstruction of a collective memory of the conquest of Istanbul on stage some three hundred years after the fall of the city and his representation of the Ottomans as an evil empire played a dual role. On the one hand, the play provided a sense of continuity between the past and the present by arousing sympathy felt for a city, which was obviously seen as a captive in the hands of the Ottomans. On the other hand, it allowed Johnson to make arguments against apostasy and for "Grecian liberty against Turkish tyranny" (Spencer 253). Although it was Knolles, who had provided the essential material for his tragedy, the English dramatist, anachronistically, attributed to Greeks of the fifteenth century feelings of devotion to liberty. Furthermore, the dramatic plot of *Irene*, which was conducted on behalf of the liberty of Greece, had an obvious contemporary thrust with respect to British national identity struggling for "...the glorious Cause/The Cause of Liberty, the Cause of Nations" (I.II.8). Johnson's *Irene*, however, attracted little attention from critics and scholars because it was a "dull play" (Moran 1956, 87).

The popular story of Irene, which first appeared in England in Painter's *Palace of Pleasure*, originated in Bandello's *Parte de le Novelle del Bandello* (1554). In 1566 when William Painter wrote an Elizabethan version of the story of Irene derived from the tenth novel of Bandello's collection published in 1544, he referred to Mehmet as "barbarous cruel Prince" (Painter 197) of "terrible nature" (Painter 191). He assured his readers that they would be touched by the story which depicted "the beastly crueltie of an

Infidell louver towards his Ladie" as "Mahomet one of the Turkish Emperours, executeth curssed crueltie/Upon a Greek maiden, whome he tooke prisoner, at the wynning of Constantinople" (Painter 190). In 1594 George Peele first gave the story its dramatic form in *The Turkish Mahomet and Hiren the Fair Greek*. Later on, it took its place in Knolles' *The General Historie of the Turkes* which Johnson greatly admired (*The Rambler* 122). Irene captured the imagination of other playwrights such as Gilbert Swinhoe in *The Tragedy of Unhappy Fair Irene* (1658), Neville Payne in *The Siege of Constantinople* (1675) and Charles Goring in *Irene or the Fair Greek* (1708). Prior to Swinhoe's version of the tragedy and an anonymous play titled *Irena* written in1664, Thomas Goffe in *The Courageous Turke or Amurath the First* (1632) and Lodowick Carlell in *Osmond the Great Turke* (1657) also used the story of Mahomet II taking Constantinople as sketched out by Knolles.

For Nichol Smith none of these plays "owes anything to another, nor did they provide anything to their great successor" (Smith 236-37). Berna Moran, however, draws attention to the similarity of Johnson's *Irene* to the anonymous play *Irena, A Tragedy*. According to Moran since the similarity is not only confined to the outlines of the story but also observed in some of its details, "the claim that he neither knew nor used the anonymous *Irena* cannot be accepted" (88). In fact, prior to Swinhoe's version of the tragedy, both Goffe and Carlell portrayed Mehmet II and dealt with the theme of a captive Greek girl (Despina in Carlell's play) being the victim of the tyrant Sultan enamoured of her beauty and torn between virtue and weakness. In Goffe's play although the characters Mehmet II and Irene have been replaced by Murat I and Eumorphe respectively, in the "Argument" at the beginning of *The Courageous Turke*, the captive girl's name was kept as Irene.

At a time when Johnson was engaged in writing the story of Irene, in which the Christian heroine struggled between the forces of "worldly glory and allegiance to Christianity" (Smith 111), in France, Jean Sauve de la Noue was also working on the same theme. Upon seeing the play, Voltaire made it the subject of a very interesting letter. Voltaire, who at that time was writing about the Ottoman Sultan in his *Essai sur les moeurs* reversed: "[T]he traditional picture of the tyrant and the cruelties of his siege of Constantinople, repudiate[d] the Irene story, present[ed Mehmet II] as a highly educated, enlightened monarch" (Bronson 116). Like Voltaire, Joseph von Hammer and Edward Gibbon, asserted that the fable of Irene (Mehmet's cutting of the Greek maiden's head in front of his troops) had no place in history. Yet, Johnson, like his predecessors, would alter the past to suit contemporary needs.

Ironically, when both *The Fair Captive* (1721) and *Irene* (1749) were performed so England heard the cries of "violated beauty" and "wailings of distress" from a city "clouded in ignorance", this actually was a time when the Ottoman capital regaled with Tulip Festivals held in the sweet waters of Asia. The tulip, the flower of Anatolia, which was introduced to Holland by the Ottomans, was a symbol of a dawning renaissance. Thus, the reigns of Sultan Ahmet III (1703-1730) and Mahmud I (1730-54) were known as the Reign of the Tulip, reflecting an era of enlightenment, liberal reform and rational inquiry. During this period, extravagant tulip and *helva* festivals were held in Istanbul with the whole city, illuminated and festooned with garlands of flowers. As the Ottoman elite with a love of the *beaux arts* feasted in social gatherings with philosophical symposia, poetry recitals, dancing, shadow plays, etc., poets wrote panegyrics to Istanbul, the seventh heaven, a mine of happiness "peerless of cities, thou jewel beyond compare" as the celebrated Nedim would say. As the sultan's doctor Daniel de Fonseca, who lived in Istanbul between 1702 to 1730, put it, everything in the city was full of "politesse et agrément" (Mansel 182). And Lady Mary Wortley Montagu agreed: "I am almost of opinion that they have a right notion of Life; they consume it in Music, Gardens, Wine and delicate eating"(Montagu 142). While peace reigned for many years within the dominions of the empire, the spirit of the age was epitomized in an inscription placed on a kiosk at the Topkapi Palace:

> May Allah bless this kiosk and may there be rejoicing here,
> May this Kiosk of Happiness be replete with happiness! (Quoted from Mansel 180).

Although, in the eighteenth century, the image of the Ottoman Empire had declined from what it was when the thinkers of Renaissance had viewed it with fascination coupled with caution, territorially, the empire's realms were well-nigh intact. In fact, contrary to the Ottoman's military decline and deterioration in the economic, political, scientific and educational fields, culture in the eighteenth century, particularly the architectural and other branches of art, continued to grow and develop by creating new styles, new schools. In the European thought, however, civilization meant the Occident.

2.2.5. Conclusion

Just as Aristotle equated the West with freedom, independence and the rule of law and designated its neighbours as "barbarians" associated with tyranny and slavish submission, Herodotus, described the customs of the Scythians in their "oppositeness" of the Greeks themselves described them as "typically barbaric" (Visser 42). Similar notions of difference inform Sandys's treatment of the European and the Turk, as is evident in his description of the Greeks in his *Relation of a Journey begun A. Dom. 1610*:

> A nation so excellent that their precepts and examples do still remaine as approued Canons to direct the mind that endevoureth vertue. Admirable in arts, and glorious in armes; famous for government, affectors of freedome, euery way noble: and to whom the rest of the world were reputed Barbarians (Sandys 77).

According to the humanist traveler Sandys, although the Greeks had declined from their original greatness, they were "still thoroughly comprehensible and likeable" and still accorded "an honoured place in the European family" (Haynes 76). Since the Turks belonged to a culture that was "radically foreign", they were not described in their own terms. On the contrary, they were "firmly locked into their identity as the antithesis of Europe and the scourge of God, their culture (ultimately springing from the notion of the imposture of Muhammad) is a distortion of the true, the normal, the European/Christian" (Haynes 76). Unlike the Greeks, the Turks had no genetic relation with the Turks and Europe. The European/Ottoman relation was one of stark opposition, not evolution, and Europe was "what the Greeks—and later the Romans and others—called their own homeland" (Eurocentrism, 47). From this perspective, the portrait of the Ottoman civilization as complex, powerful and advanced corresponded to the medieval notion of Muhammad and Islam as the antithesis of Christ and Christianity.

Upon Mehmet II's conquering of Constantinople, however, the Ottoman Empire presented itself as heir to the Eastern Roman Empire and the leader of the Islamic world. As a cosmopolitan empire, the Ottoman system embodied among its population "all races and creeds, living together in order and harmony" (Kinross 112). With fall of the Byzantine emperor in the fifteenth century, although the Christian Church was subjected to payment of tribute, in return, its community was "still to enjoy freedom of worship, and retain its own observances and customs of life" (112). The Ottoman system was devised and established in such a way that it protected the status of religious minorities. Throughout the entire empire each "nation" or *millet* constituted of self-governing communities preserved their own laws and usages under a religious head such as the Greek Orthodox Patriarch, the Armenian Patriarch and the Jewish Chief Rabbi, all of whom resided side by side with the *ulema*, Islamic authority. As Vitkus writes:

> [M]ost English were unaware of the Muslim rulers' policy of toleration, which allowed Jews, Christians and Muslims to live together peacefully within the same community. This policy differed radically from that of England, where the norm was religious persecution and where very few Jews or Muslims were permitted to maintain residence. In Spain, too, persecution and intolerance was the rule (Vitkus 161).

From the standpoint of the Western world, the fall of Constantinople to a Muslim power generated a widespread and an ongoing interest in Ottoman affairs. The abundance of books and other printed material about the Ottomans in the centuries to come demonstrated that Islam occupied the minds and imagination of the Christian West. Furthermore, the presence of the Ottomans in the Mediterranean and the extension of their rule over large parts of South-Eastern Europe and North Africa deeply affected Westerners politically and culturally. Consequently, calls for Christian unity and resistance against the Ottoman Empire became a recurring theme in the West ultimately leading to a political formation of the Holy League in Europe to fight the '"infidel" and "alien" Turk. Perplexity or rather fear of the Ottoman power was intensified by and recorded in an outpouring of texts in Europe. These texts, however, did not exist in isolation from one another or from the culture that produced them. Rather, they were "porous" structures, which communicated with other texts and with what Greenblatt refers to as "the complex network of institutions, practices and beliefs that constitute the culture as a whole" (Greenblatt 1991, 6).

By the time Shakespeare had literary fantasies of "taking the Turk by the beard" (V.V.209) in *Henry V* or displayed a Venice imperiled by a threat from the Ottomites in *Othello*, the Ottoman Empire posed a serious threat to European sovereignty. Moreover, it played a great role in rivalries for commercial hegemony in the economic space that stretched from Venice to the Indian Ocean. By the mid-eighteenth century, however, when English playwrights wrote plays revolving around apostasy and represented the Ottoman Turk as a distortion of the true, the normal, the civilized European/Christian, the Ottoman military and economic power had begun a steady decline. Yet, Western dramatists continued writing about the conquest, captivity and conversion themes, which embodied the worst fears of Europe.

2.3. Sultan Suleyman (1520-1566)

Magnificent Solyman mounts on his father's throne
With Christian Slaughters formidable growne
Rhodes, Naxos, Paros felt his cruelty.
And the Sweet shores of the Tyrrhenian Sea.
The Hungarian Territories did he invade.
And fierce attempts on fair Vienna made.
Till from the Walls of Sigeth meanly come.
Th' Aspiring Tyrant crept to his lonely home.

(Knolles, Volume I. 381)

2.3.1. Magnificent Solyman

Suleyman the Magnificent (also known to history as *Kanuni*, the Lawgiver) was the ruler of the Ottoman Empire at the height of its glory and strength. A conqueror of many lands, his fleets dominated the Mediterranean and his armies laid siege to Vienna. The term "Magnificent" (*Muhtesem* in Turkish), derived from the Venetian reference to the *Gran Signor* as *magnifico* in their chronicles, was not used by the sultan's Chancery. To his Ottoman contemporaries and successors Suleyman was known as the Lawgiver (*Kanuni).* This was because criminal, administrative and constitutional laws (*kanun*) that had been compiled and validated during the reigns of prior sultans were systematically arranged and regulated during Suleyman's era. It was during his reign that that the codification and standardization of the *kanuns* were harmonized with the *Shari'a* by establishing the Chancellor (*Nisanci*), the key figure in central bureaucracy, as the secular counterpart of *Seyhulislam.* As J.M. Rogers asserts:

> Conqueror, administrator, patron, uxorious husband, even tragic hero in the eyes of subjects and adversaries alike, Suleyman's exploits justify his epithet 'the Magnificent' far more than the vain show of Francis I or Henry VIII, the campaigns of Charles V, the petty struggles of the princelings of central and eastern Europe, the desperate excesses of Ivan IV of Muscovy, which more than merited his epithet 'the Terrible', or even the achievements of his contemporaries Babur and Humayun in India (Rogers 24).

In the sixteenth century, the dynastic conflict between the Habsburgs, Germany and Spain and Francis I of France and the religious strife between Lutheranism and the Protestant states had effectively prevented the realization of a Europe united under a single religion and a crusade against the Ottoman Empire. Meanwhile, in European politics, Suleyman II's influence was so profound that he even "played a more decisive part in the struggle between Charles V and Francis I than did Henry VIII of England" (Merriman 2). His dynamic reign of forty-six years, was not only the zenith of the empire's political and economic expansion, but it was also the golden age of Ottoman culture and creativity (Atil 17). As Lord Kinross described Suleyman, who took a personal interest in the educational, artistic and scientific activities of the state and made enormous contributions to administrative, judicial and diplomatic tasks,

> The Grand Turk was a Prince of the Renaissance, outdoing in the magnificence of his court and of his style of living many of those in this Golden Age of Western Christian civilization. He outdid them not only in his personal character, but in his wise judgement of the character of the others (Kinross 257).

Suleyman was the son of Selim I, who had conquered Egypt in 1517 and won the title of the "Protector of the Holy Cities". While some writers maintained that his mother was a Circassian or a Georgian, other sources such as Ogier Ghiselin de Busbecq, Joseph von Hammer and Cagatay Ulucay indicate that she was the daughter of the Khan of the Crimean Tatars. The reports of the Venetian ambassadors shed light on the appearance of Suleyman and "it is significant that Titian should have painted him in his "Ecce Homo" in 1543 and Veronese in his "Marriage at Cana" some fifteen years later (Merriman 32). As Bartolomeo Contarini described him in 1520, he was "a wise Lord, fond of study, and all hope for good from his rule" who had been raised in the "ways and manners of the Turkish *gentilhomme par excellence*" (Merriman 33).

The Ottoman Empire had a complex patron/client relationship and cross-cultural contacts with Venice. This was particularly fruitful in terms of publicizing to Europe Suleyman's bejewelled costumes, accessories and other "props" displayed in ostentatious ceremonies. The image of Suleyman was not only a curious sight to his rival monarchs in the political sphere, but also to the wider public thanks to popular prints, news pamphlets and, ultimately, drama. Although Venetian-made imperial regalia such as crowns, scepters and orbs had been foreign to the Ottoman tradition of sovereignty, in this era, the production of thrones, horse furnishings and other precious items of inestimable value served as the iconography of Suleyman's power (Necipoglu 401). Suleyman's renowned Venetian headgear, the production of which was orchestrated by his Grand Vezir Ibrahim Pasha through his links with the *doge* Andrea Gritti, aimed to display the sultan's magnificence to the world.[62] As the Venetian *bailo* Marcantonio Barbaro wrote of Suleyman's reign: "Since the fall of the Roman Empire, no prince ever brought under its rule as many provinces and kingdoms as the Ottomans did today by the force of their armies" (Quoted from Valensi 180.) Subsequent to the sultans' goal to make the Mediterranean an Ottoman lake, no Christian power in the region had "spent so heavily on defense and war against" (Hale 26) the Ottoman Empire as Venice whose fundamental basis of fortune and power was the sea.

For a long time Suleyman (like his father Selim I and his Grandfather Bayezid II) followed a policy of peace with Venice. Suleyman's Grand Vezir Ibrahim was also a firm supporter of the

62 In the anonymous Venetian woodcut (1532), Suleyman's quadruple gold crown symbolically represented each of the kingdoms over which he ruled. Set with rubies, diamonds, pearls, an oblong emerald, a large turquoise and a plume, the crown was made by a consortium of Venetian goldsmiths. Since the head made in the tradition of Durer portrait was a type, it did not project the appearance of Suleyman himself (Kurtz 257).

sultan's policy of peace with the Venetian Republic. As for Venice, the "ambivalence" of the policies of the Republic towards the Ottoman Empire was "well known" (Valensi 17). This ambivalence had its most interesting representation in *doge* Andrea Gritti, an outstanding figure in Venetian history. Gritti had an illegitimate son (named Alvise) by an Ottoman woman during his diplomatic appointment in Istanbul. Not only was Alvise Gritti the godson (*beyoglu*) of Suleyman the Magnificent, but he also held a position in the palace as the Keeper of the Sultan's Jewels, as he settled in Istanbul like many Europeans who made fortune in the capital city. While Alvise had the best education in Venice available to the sons of the Italians of High Renaissance, he was also entirely at ease with the Ottoman culture and prospered in the wealthy district of Pera, which resembled an Italian city with Catholic churches and its piazzetta, the Galata Tower. Alvise's allegiance to Suleyman was clearly evident as he fought along with the Sultan in the Hungarian campaign in 1528 and the siege of Vienna in 1532. In fact, while Gritti played an important role in Suleyman's anti-Habsburg policy in Hungary and eastern Europe, he was a principal intermediary in the Ottomans' diplomatic relations with the European powers.

2.3.2 Barbaros

The Ottoman state was essentially a land-based military state with its energies for territorial expansion geared towards acquisition of fertile lands to broaden the tax-base that was used to support the ruling elite. During Suleyman's reign, the empire as a sea-based power also gained numerous victories and began to dominate and control the trade centres and networks in various commercial zones. In the sixteenth century the Ottoman Empire initiated naval campaigns against Venice mainly because of the influence that Barbaros Hayreddin Pasha (known as Barbarossa in the West) had on the palace. Unlike Suleyman and his Grand Vezir Ibrahim, Barbaros Hayreddin Pasha, a naval commander of the Ottoman Empire, favoured war against the Ottoman's great maritime rival. Hayreddin was the abler of the two red-bearded Barbaros brothers, both seafarers. Yet it was his brother Oruc Reis (Aruj) that the eighteenth-century English audience knew well through John Brown's popular play *Barbarossa* and Francis Gentleman's *Zaphira* (1754).[63]

The father of the Barbaros brothers was Yakub, a *sipahi*, who after a career in the Ottoman army, had retired in the island of (Lesbos), "a notorious centre of Christian piracy" (Kinross 218) commanding the entrance to the strait of Dardanelles. As corsairs and traders, the Barbaros brothers, born in the island of Midilli (Mytelene), soon became effective leaders of the Moors, who had fled North Africa in 1492. While these Muslims who were expelled from Spain provoked piratical raids against the southern coasts of Spain, Oruc Reis would subdue the local chieftains at the Barbary coast of North Africa and liberate Algiers and other ports from the Spaniards. Brown's *Barbarossa*, which was performed forty-three times between 1754 and 1772[64] and revived at the Drury Lane and the Covent Garden in 1804[65] is set at a Royal Palace in Algiers. The title character is a villainous usurper, a tyrant who is ultimately overthrown by Selim, the Prince of Algiers. In the play Selim disguised as Achmet seeks help "from Ferdinand of Spain, t'invade Algiers ... to conquer and dethrone" (I) Barbarossa. Ultimately as in Voltaire's *Merope* (1743) and Arthur Murphy's *Grecian Daughter* (1772), Selim, the "true" ruler is restored to power through various turns of fortune based on multiple disguises (Kavenik 173).

In Brown's *Barbarossa*, it is the "Gen'rous Selim" who kills the usurper and restores harmony to the kingdom by forgiving the "bloody Tyrant" and announcing that "Algiers is free/And Tyranny no more" (V). Historically, however, Oruc Reis died (in action

63 *Zaphira* revolved on "the same story as Dr. Brown's play of *Barbarossa* (which it preceded in the representation) and was not ill received" (*Biographica Dramatica* 429).

64 See *The London Stage*: *1600-1800 IV*, 1747-1776.

65 Also revived in New York in 1793. See *A History of English Drama* (Nicoll III: 82.

against Spain) in 1518 as the sultan of Algiers, a position which had been granted to him by Suleyman's father, Sultan Selim. Later, his brother Hayreddin recognized the Ottoman sultan as his suzerain. Suleyman, at once detecting a depth of political wisdom and military genius in Hayreddin, gave him the title of Grand Admiral (*Kaptan-i-Derya* meaning Captain of the Oceans) and had an entirely new fleet constructed for him. The English spectators of *Mustapha*, a tragedy acted at the Theatre Royal in Drury Lane, read from the inscription distributed to them at the performance:

> In the Year 1534, Solyman sent Barbaross the Pyrate, then in league with him, to invade Africa, where he did much mischief both in Africa, and the sea-coasts of Italy, and the Islands of the Mediterranean. He after conquered the Kingdom of Tunis; and by his Arts as well as Arms caus'd himself to be proclaim'd King.[66]

Piracy, as Braudel writes was a "second form of war" (Braudel 865) in the Mediterranean. In the first half of the fifteenth century, Ottoman sailors were no match for the fleets of the Italian mercantile cities Genoa and Venice, whose state-owned galleys provided unrivalled transport for freight travelling to Alexandria, Syria, Istanbul and England. During Suleyman's era however, with the quick revival of sea power, the "Barbary states were in the same league as naval powers as England and France" (Earle 46). Following their conquests of Syria, Palestine and Egypt, the Ottomans had made an alliance with the Barbary pirates, who placed much of the naval resources of North Africa at their command. The Ottoman victories in the Mediterranean under the command of Barbaros Hayreddin Pasha not only caused an increased interest of Marseilles, Ragusa and others in the Levantine trade, but it also encouraged England to enter into direct trade with the Ottomans.

While the Ottomans had good trading relations with commercial cities like Florence, Ancona and Ragusa, which had no possessions in the Levant, they ended the Venetian domination in

66 See the inscription for *Mustapha* (*History of the Life and Death of Sultan* 16).

the Aegean Sea through a series of campaigns led by Barbaros. Ultimately, it was Barbaros's victory at Preveza (1538) against a Holy League under the command of Andrea Doria, Charles V's admiral that established Ottoman supremacy in the Mediterranean. As J.M. Rogers indicates, while Andrea Doria was a "*condottiere* by origin", the "navies of Europe had little moral superiority" in terms of employing corsair admirals.

> For much of the sixteenth century there was no clear distinction between piracy and commerce or event between individual clashes at sea and those of a fleet under the orders of a government. Recruitment on both sides was a constant problem and explains, for example, the high proportion of slaves in Barbary galleys, and of criminals in Ottoman, French and Spain fleets (Rogers 13).

The Ottoman naval campaigns were instigated mostly by political motivations in order to secure shipping and to prevent Habsburg territorial expansion. Thus the defeat of the strong allied European amphibious force was followed by annual naval campaigns led by Barbaros, who would dominate the eastern Mediterranean and the coasts of Italy, France and Spain. Essentially, the Ottomans had "no desire to discourage trade and warred with Venice and Genoa arguably only because of their military bases" (Rogers 15). Yet, some thirty years after the Preveza victory and following the Ottoman's capture of Cyprus from Venice, when a European naval coalition under the command of Don John of Austria, won victory over the Ottoman Empire in Lepanto (1571), Venetians would be first to hear of the Ottoman defeat. Even after the Western victory in Lepanto, Venice still had anxieties as to whether the empire could appropriate the whole world and claim itself as a universal monarchy. While Venice ultimately withdrew from the imperial European alliance, Charles V's campaign "to bribe Barbarossa away" (Kinross 227) from Suleyman's service, was without success. Although it was common for *condottieri* "to be ready to be bought" (Rogers 14), Barbaros, known as the "King of the Sea", was described by a Spanish historian as "the creator of the Turkish navy, its admiral and its soul" (Kinross 223). He remained loyal to the Ottomans. Like his brother Oruc Reis, depicted in *Barbarossa*, Barbaros Hayreddin was a "Mighty Warrior" (I) who ruled Algiers following his brother's death. Much admired and feared by his Italian contemporaries, Barbaros' turbanned portrait with a brocade caftan, most likely drawn by Gian Maria di Andrian Gian-Battista (Rogers 52) in 1533, encouraged Agostino Veneziano to issue prints of the Ottoman admiral along with the images of Charles V, Francis I and Suleyman.

2.3.3. Ibrahim

As Barbaros Hayreddin's career in the seas began during the first years of Suleyman's reign, the sultan was busy conquering Rhodes and campaigning against Austria and Hungary. When he was not busy with the business of government, Suleyman pursued his favourite sport, falconry, accompanied by his chief falconer Ibrahim (Greek born) who was exactly the same age as Suleyman. Despite the claims and envy of older *vezirs*, Suleyman raised Ibrahim from the post of chief falconer and *has odabasi* (the Head of the Privy Chamber) to the position of Grand Vezir (1523-1536). To everybody's astonishment the two friends became virtually inseparable. In *The Tragedy of Solyman and Perseda*, Ibrahim as Erastus is referred as Soliman's "other best-loved" (III). In Thomas Kyd's *The Spanish Tragedy*, the story of Erastus and Perseda, which is presented as a play-within-a play in Act IV, carries with it many parallels with and similar phrases from *The Tragedy of Soliman and Perseda*. Despite the controversy that surrounds the authorship and source of *The Tragedy of Soliman and Perseda* (entered in the Stationer's Registry in 1592) most scholars ascribe it to Kyd, whose representation of "Soliman, Emperor of the Turks" fluctuates between that of a magnanimous and rightful ruler and a melodramatic villain. In the early scenes of the play, Suleyman displays those qualities of civility and kindness with which popular reports in the West were inclined to credit him. In the end, Kyd turns him into an oriental despot whose death is caused by the deadly poison on the lips of

Perseda; suffers the postmortem vengeance of the dead heroine. As Chew writes, Suleyman's death,

> at the moment when Rhodes has fallen to him does so great a violence to history that it is difficult to believe that, witnessing it, even an Elizabethan audience, indifferent though it may have been to most such liberties, was undisturbed; for the fact is that forty-four years elapsed between the fall of Rhodes and the death of Solyman [sic] (Chew 497).

What is also significant is that while Suleyman took Rhodes in 1522, his campaign against the Persians was in 1534-6. Yet, Act I.III and Solyman's debate with his counselors in Act I.V. point to his recalling his armies from Persia and Russia to lay siege to Rhodes. In fact, not only is the historical background of the play anachronistic, but in the tragedy which revolves around Ibrahim, referred to as "brave Erastus", Perseda, "his Rhodian dame" (I) is also fictional. The story of Ibrahim was told in a sixteenth-century prose tale in Jacques Yver's *Le printemps d'Yever, contenant cinq histoires discourues par cinq journees, en une noble compagnie, au choteau du printemps* (1572). Kyd's tragedy was based on Henry Wotton's translation of *Le printemps* as *A Courtlie Controversie of Cupid's Tales* (1578), which was a fairly faithful reproduction of Yver's version. In *Soliman and Perseda* Kyd, following the main threads of Wotton's Erastus-Persida-Soliman plot, gave the fictional character Perseda a position of central importance and constructed Erastus on the historical character of Ibrahim.

The English audience was also familiar with Ibrahim's character through Sir William Davenant's *The Siege of Rhodes*, Dryden's *The Conquest of Granada*, based on Mlle de Scudéry's romance *Almahide* and *Ibrahim*, and Elkahan Settle's *Ibrahim The Illustrious Bassa*. In these heroic plays, in which a clearcut conflict of love and honour shapes the action, the dramatists modeled their heroes on Ibrahim, the rival of the sultan preferred by the beautiful Christian heroine. Obviously, the dramatic motive of an Ottoman sultan falling in love with a Christian woman was a common theme in Western drama since it was based on historical fact. As an exceptionally intelligent and capable person and a close companion to Suleyman, not only had Ibrahim been raised to the highest possible post in the palace, but he had also married Suleyman's sister Hatice. As an imperial *damad* (son-in-law), which meant that the sultan could bestow upon him unlimited favours, Ibrahim accumulated a lot of wealth. Mansel draws attention to the sultan's special treatment of Ibrahim:

> [C]ostume was governed by dynastic priorities. Whereas his predecessors had worn camelot or mohair, Suleyman wore cloth of gold. Although in theory it was reserved for the sultan alone, as a special favour he permitted his beloved Grand Vizier, Ibrahim Pasha, to wear 'gold brocade and on campaign a suit of cloth of gold' (Mansel 66).

Ibrahim's splendid palace built from Suleyman's Privy Purse (today restored as the Museum of Turkish and Islamic Art) in the Hippodrome in the present day Sultanahmet region with its renowned Blue Mosque, was similar to that of the sultan. Like the sultan he had unprecedented authority to call up the Divan, act independently and command armies. *The Tragedy of Soliman and Perseda* captures Ibrahim's special position as a Christian slave risen to power through the palace system and his bond with the sultan. As Soliman tells Erastus:

> Thou shalt be captain of our Janissaries
> And in our council shalt thou sit with us
> And be great Soliman's adopted friend
> ...
> For what are friends, but one in mind in two bodies" (II)

For Erastus "Soliman" is kind", but he laments that "God is lost, if faith be overthrown". (II)

> No marvel, then, if I have little mind
> Of rich embroidery or costly ornaments:
> Of honour's titles, or of wealth, or gain:
> Of music, viands, or of dainty dames (III).

When Soliman takes Rhodes he ensures Erastus that "for his sake only" he shall spare the island from "spoil, pillage and oppression/Than Alexander spared warlike Thebes/For Pindarus:or than Augustus/Spared rich Alexandria for Arias' sake" (III).

The first account of the career of the historical figure of Ibrahim was available to Europe in French in Paolo Giovio's *Histoires*, published in Lyon in 1522 and later in Paris in 1570. Giovio narrated the humble origin of "Abrim Bassa" (son of a Greek sailor of Parga), his rise to eminence as the all-powerful *grand vezir* and his fatal end. The cause of Ibrahim's sudden death led to many speculations, one of which pointed to Suleyman's favourite Hurrem (known to the West as Roxelana), who had all-powerful influence over the sultan. As Hurrem detested Ibrahim, it was perhaps no coincidence that the *grand vezir* was strangled once the ambitious and wilful Hurrem moved in. Hurrem was jealous of Ibrahim's intimate friendship with the sultan and his power, which she aspired to exercise herself. Yet, as André Clot points out:

> Harem intrigues and popular rumours on their own, however, would not have been able to win over a man as self-willed as Suleiman. Everything indicates that Ibrahim's own behaviour, particularly some recent errors he had committed, exerted a decisive influence (Clot 96).

It was no secret that following his capture of Tebriz from the Persians, Ibrahim had adopted the title of and asked his commander-in-chief to address him as Sultan Ibrahim. In fact, his incredible arrogance and extravagance was such that the Venetians, taking Ibrahim's boastings of "It is I who govern" at face value dubbed him "Ibrahim the Magnificent". Thus, a day came when Ibrahim, the *grand vezir*'s "existence became unbearable to the *padisash*" (Clot 96), the sultan, known as the "Shadow of God" on earth. While Ibrahim's usurpation of the title of sultan was something that Suleyman "could hardly ignore even though he might disbelieve for a while" (Donaldson 112), the *grand vezir* 's fatal end was linked to his disloyalty to the sultan. While Ibrahim's life was as full of strange events as highly-coloured romance, and almost incomprehensible in its rapid changes, it captured the minds of the Europeans through wild imaginings. Paradoxically, while Ibrahim had played a crucial role in bringing the Ottomans into friendly contact with Europe, his death was "inflated into speculation or ill-informed gossip" through the reports of European diplomats (Rogers 11). Essentially, the brilliant career of Ibrahim, who accumulated enormous wealth through trade monopolies shared by Andrea Gritti of Venice, sheds light on the exercise of different means of political power in an absolute monarchy. As Hester Donaldson Jenkins indicates:

> Ibrahim's importance in [Ottoman] history lies partly in the great diplomatic changes and the conquests which he achieved together with Suleiman, and partly in the fact that he was the first grand vizir taken from the people who exercised much power, and that with him began the rule of vizirs and favorites which became a very important fact in later [Ottoman] history (Jenkins 118).

From the reign of Mehmet II, *vezirs* were drawn with few exceptions from the slave elite and thus in many respects they were the male parallels of the women in the harem. The Venetian Bailo Marcantonio Barbaro wrote about the 'Kapikullari' (Slaves of the Porte), who were men of Christian origin:

> It is a matter of deserving consideration that the wealth, strength and government, in short the entire state of the Ottoman Empire be based on and put into the hands of people all born in Christ's faith, who by different means have been made slaves and transferred to the Mahometan sect. (Valensi 179)

In the Ottoman dynastic state, promotion of the slave elite to the *vezirate* was the zenith of a well-defined career path.[67] It involved inner palace service, which culminated in one of the prestigious offices in the outer palace service. Later, the official received a provincial governorate and hence rose to more prestigious governorates or even to admiralty. He could then go on to hold one or both of the highest ranks below that of the *vezir*, such as the governor-generalships of Rumelia and Anatolia. After reaching the high post of *vezir*, he progressed along the *vezirial* hierarchy and then, upon retirement, dismissal or death of the incumbent, to the grand *vezirate*. While one of the prestigious positions was that

---

67 Among grand vezirs who were not drawn from the slave elite, were Karamani Mehmet (1477-81), Candarli Ibrahim (1488-99) and Piri Mehmet (1517-23). For the military/administrative career paths of the vezirs see Kunt, *The Sultan's Servants: The Transformation of Ottoman Provincial Government, 1550-1650.*

of the Agha of the Janissaries, his military/administrative career was considered "like a craft that had to be learned through observation and experience no matter how bright the individual might be" (Peirce 72).

Another significant aspect of the Ottoman heritage was the sharing of power among family members. The dynasty's unusual survival had much to do with "its careful guard against dissipation of that power" (Peirce 18). Prior to the foundation of the Ottoman Empire, the earlier Muslim states of Turkish-Mongol origin had all fallen prey to fragmentation and disintegration resulting from successive divisions among male dynasts. In order to prevent similar divisions and collapse in the rule of the territories of a vast empire, the Ottomans took drastic measures in the politics of handing down the patrimony from one generation to another. While the main tension revolving around the issue of dynastic inheritance was intergenerational, the process of having a rightful claim to the Ottoman throne involved a number of legitimate and constitutional options, which included the succession of the eldest son or the eldest living male of the dynasty (Peirce 19). Considering the rivalry of the heirs, however, most successions were marked by executions and strife followed by further violence which continued after the sultan's accession to the throne. In order to repress the claims of collateral dynastic lines, by the mid-fifteenth century the practice of fratricide was codified "[f]or the welfare of the state" (Kinross 138). Also legitimized at this time was the shift of authority from the sultan to the grand vizier to preside over the Council of State—referred as the *Divan*. Despite the Grand Vezir's great "grace and honour" (Bon 37) in presiding over the *Divan* and managing state affairs it was the sultan who:

> sometimes cometh privately by an upper way to a certain window, which looketh into the *Divan*, right over the head of the Chief Vizir; and there sitteth (with a lattice before him, that he may not be seen) to hear and see, what is done in the *Divan* (Bon 38).

2.3.4 *Mustapha (1609)*

By assuming an intimate role within the Ottoman dynasty, Grand *Vezir* Ibrahim Pasha's power, which emanated from his status as the highest-ranking member of the slave elite, shared striking similarities with Hurrem (born Alexandra Lisowska). The daughter of an Orthodox priest of Ruthenian/Ukranian origin, it was her playful temperament that had won Hurrem (meaning the joyful one) her Turkish name. Yet it was to Ogier Ghiselin de Busbecq, the ambassador of the Emperor Frederick to the Porte, that Hurrem, by mistake, owed her name Roxelana (meaning Ruthenian maiden).

Up until Suleyman's reign the Ottoman sultans had only married royal Muslim brides or Christian ones such as Orhan wife's Theodora, the daughter of the Byzantine Empire and Beyazid's wife Despina, a Serbian Princess. Hurrem was the first harem woman to be freed and made a legal wife. In *Mustapha*, David Mallet captures this "breach of ancient custom":

> E'er since the time inhuman Tamerlane
> In Bajazet's insulted Queen, dishonour'd
> The majesty of empire, future Sultans
> Have shunn'd the marriage-tie
> ...
> Which made it a state-maxim. (I.I)

Roxelana, however "not being the Sultana Queen, that is wedded to the Sultan, she fear'd the more, that at the Death of Solyman, Mustapha would be Emperor". Thus "[t]he first thing she had to do was to prevail on the emperor to wed her; for being his Queen, would effectually disinherit (as we say) Mustapha" (*The History* 21-22). Like the exuberant festivities of his sons' circumcision ceremonies, the splendid wedding of Suleyman and Roxelana aimed at representing graphically the Ottoman supremacy in the sixteenth century.

The lavish wedding ceremony of Roxelana, a cultural heroine familiar to Europeans through chroniclers and dramatists, was a sign of Suleyman's unfaltering love for a woman to whom he would be exclusively devoted for over a period of forty years. A clerk at the Genoese Bank in Istanbul wrote that his marriage to Hurrem was celebrated with splendid festivities that lasted a week:

> A most extraordinary event took place this week in the town, absolutely unprecedented in the history of sultans. The Great Signor Suleiman has taken for his empress a woman called Roxelana ... amid much rejoicing. The ceremony took place in the Seraglio and the festivities anything we ever witnessed ... There was a public procession ... the principal houses are gaily illuminated ... houses are festooned with garlands ... and everywhere there were swings in which people swing by the hour with great enjoyment ... tumblers, jugglers and a procession of wild beasts and giraffes with necks so high... (Clot 70).

According to what his sources told the Hapsburg ambassador Busbecq, this marriage proved that Hurrem, like Ann Boleyn, had the advantage of controlling the sultan's emotions by "love charms and magic arts" (Busbecq 49). In *Mustapha* Mallet captures Suleyman's infatuation with Hurrem as the sultan "burns for Roxolona's charms!" to the extent that "Not all the fabled power of herbs or spells/Could raise it to more height" (I.I).

As Mansel indicates, "[f]rom behind the harem walls" Roxelana "exercised greater influence then the Queen of England" (Mansel 85). After giving Suleyman three sons (Selim, Bayezid and Cihangir), Hurrem began to scheme ways to get rid of Prince Mustafa, Suleyman's eldest son from a previous favourite. Like Rogers, many critics suggest that "Hurrem's support of her other sons against Mustafa was not unreasonable" (Rogers 20). Suleyman's first-born son was an extremely popular prince and loved by the Janissaries. All those around him were unanimous that Mustafa was the brightest star of the House of Osman. As the Ottoman historian Pecevi wrote: Mustafa was "the envy of all the princes in his gloriousness...nearly all the soldiers were of one heart and mind to love him" (Quoted from Peirce 81). While Busbecq spoke of Mustafa's "remarkable natural gifts", the Western world was aware that Mustafa, as a "marvelously well educated and prudent" prince would make as good and as powerful a sultan as Suleyman (Clot 155). Yet, along with the efforts of Suleyman's *damad* grand vezir Rustem Pasha (married to Suleyman and Hurrem's daughter Mihrimah), Hurrem played an instrumental role in Mustafa's downfall in order to secure the reversion of the throne to her own son. The plot against the innocent prince included the false accusation that he would be reaching an agreement with the Shah of Iran to overthrow Suleyman. As *The History of the Life and Death of Sultan Solyman the Magnificent, Emperor of the Turks, And of his Son Inscrib'd to the Spectators of Mustapha*, acted at the Theatre Royal, in Drury Lane indicated, in order to persuade the sultan of Mustafa's treason, Hurrem had "got counterfeit Letters convey'd to the sultan, that shew'd that innocent Prince in a false and guilty Light (24).

The most circumstantial account of Mustafa's death reached western Europe through one of the famous letters of Busbecq. Although European accounts of Mustafa's death contained "as much unsubstantiated gossip as historical fact" (Rogers 21) the first published narrative of the event was by Nicholas Moffan, a Burgundanian whose *Soltani Solymanni Turcorum Imperatoris horrendum facinus* (1555) was translated in *The Palace of Pleasure*. The tragic tale of this palace intrigue soon became immensely popular in western Europe in portraying Suleyman as an unreasonable tyrant. For example, according to historic records, although Suleyman had no brothers, in *Soliman and Perseda*, his fictional brother Haleb is killed by Amurath who in return is killed by the sultan: "That makes the brother butcher of his brother" (I.I). The fratricidal episode of Soliman-Haleb-Amurath in the play, which echoed Shakespeare's *Henry IV, Part II* was, however, inspired by contemporary history as Kyd wrote *Soliman and Perseda* at a time which corresponded to Murad III's (1574-1595) strangling of his brothers on his accession to the throne.

While the primary sources of knowledge in western Europe of the Mustafa story were Moffan and Busbecq, Hugh Gough's *Ofspring of the house of Ottomanno* was based on Batholemaeus Georgeiewitz's *De Origine Imperii Turcorum* (Moran 22). Following the two translations of the original Latin edition, Gabriel Bounin's

La Soltane (1561), the first French tragedy based on an Ottoman theme and revolved around Mustafa's death. It was written at a time when Suleyman was alive. Another French tragedy, *Solyman II*, dealing with the same topic, was written by George Thilloy (Rouillard 430) in 1608. In England, the first tragedy on Mustafa's death was the anonymous Senecan drama entitled *Solymannidae Tragoedia* (1582) written in Latin (Chew 500). It was followed by Fulke Greville's *The Tragedy of Mustapha* (1609), Roger Boyle's *The Tragedy of Mustapha* (1665) and David Mallet's *Mustapha* (1739).

According to William Smith Clark, the source for Boyle's tragedy is Knolles' *The General History of the Turkes.* As for Mallet's *Mustapha,* while it is based on Knolles's historical account, the dramatist has also made use of Greville and Orrery's works (Starr 285-287). In Mallet's *Mustapha,* set in "the Sultan's Tent, in a large plain near Aleppo, where his army lies encamped", Rustan, the Grand *Vezir* and the Mufti open the play. As the inscription compiled for the spectators of *Mustapha* informed the viewers, the sultan:

> When he was first seated in the Turkish Throne ... for several Years reign'd as a benign Prince. But being corrupted by the artifices of Roxolana, and the impious Designs of Rustan his Grand Vizir, who wedded a Daughter of Roxalana's, began to dip his Hands in Blood (*The History* 4).

As Mufti tells the Grand Vezir, he has traveled to Aleppo (in Egypt added to the Ottoman domains by Suleyman's father) all the way from Istanbul, as "Such prompt dispatch/Great Roxalana's mandate had enjoin'd" (I.I). Rustan acknowledges the unprecedented power of Hurrem: "Indeed you owe/And I no less, all duty to her Highness" (I.I). Although he has considerable authority secured by his marriage to a princess, as he tells the Mufti: "My influence waits on hers. You know she gave/Her daughter to my bed" (I.I). When Rustan informs the Mufti that "She holds Prince Mustapha her deadly foe" (I.I) the doctor of the Muslim Law is in awe:

Mustapha! The favourite
Of our redoubted Lord! His eldest hope!
Sole pledge the fair Circassian left his fondness!
How will she root him from a father's love
Who holds him dear for virtues that renown
And dignify himself? (I.I)

As the audiences of Mallet's *Mustapha* are informed: "Circassia is a Province that extends from the Bosphorus to the Eastern Shore of the Exuine Sea, famous for its beautiful women" (*The History* 15). In Sir William Davenant's *The Siege of Rhodes*, Suleyman refers to Mustapha's mother, whom Hurrem has ably eliminated from the Harem: "Mustapha does shine/Who is the pledge of my Circassian Wife" (2.IV.III. 323-25). Following a long struggle and countless intrigues Hurrem has been able to expel Mustapha's mother Mahridevran from the palace. In the Mallet play as Rustan sums up Roxolana's situation:

If Mustapha succeeds his Royal Sire
She falls forever! Sinks from what she is,
Empress and consort of unbounded sway,
Dower'd and declar'd to so-sinks into a slave! (I.I)

Thus Roxalana "must destroy or perish" (I.I). Despite her own son Zanger (Jihangir)'s pleas to her to save his "lov'd brother from the shameful fate/That hovers over him" (IV.IV) Roxalana proceeds to procure the death of Mustapha. Meanwhile she chastises Zanger for him to come to grips with the reality of the family faction, which is central to the dynastic politics of the absolute monarchy: "Awake, expand thy views/To greatness, and deserve my noble cares". She tells her son:

...I know thy follies.
Deaf to ambition's glorious call and blind
To sovereign power that spreads its dazzling charms,
The ruling sceptre, starry diadem
Before thy fight and now within thy reach (IV.IV).

When Zanger asks his mother what crime Mustapha has committed to deserve his ruin, she is quick to respond that it is "His birth-right" (IV.IV). Roxolana fears Suleyman's first-born, Mustapha, the heir-apparent, who was born: "To reign thy master: he might live to see/A slave in Roxolona" (IV.IV). In the final scene of the tragedy, following the Mutes' sign for Mustapha to retire for his "eternal parting" (V.VI) as they bring his body on stage, Zanger stabs himself: "Alas! My brother -dead! -Look here, just heaven! / I could not save -but I can perish with thee" (V.VII). As "Solyman to the last of his Life regretted the Loss of his Sons Mustapha and Zanger" (*The History* 27) the play ends with the sound of the thunder as Solyman invokes the heavens:

> Justice divine! Discharge it here -on me-
> On her. It cannot err: we are both guilty (V.VII).

Historically, while the army and the clerisy unanimously concluded that Mustafa had been executed by the baseless accusations of Hurrem and her fellow-conspirator Rustem, Mustafa's tragic end was undoubtedly a stain on Suleyman's reputation. Prince Mustafa's death had an enormous effect on the Ottoman troops who revered him. Writers and artists within the empire bewailed his loss. Europe, as Clot asserts, "breathed a sign of relief":

> It was known that the heir to the throne had been intelligent, courageous and ambitious. After Suleiman's conquests, what limits could there be to the expansion of the empire under a sultan with such talents? ... His disappearance did not totally dissipate all the anxieties because next to nothing was known about the other sons of Suleiman. The most dangerous one, however, was no longer among the living (Clot 159).

Although the European historians have agreed on reporting the death of Jihangir as suicide, following the strangling of Mustafa he died of grief. In fact, Busbecq in his letter also attributed the death of Mustafa's step-brother to "shock and terror, rather than suicide" (Rouillard 426). Jihangir's death as a suicide contradicted the facts as related by all Ottoman historians and Joseph von Hammer, the European historian, who could read Ottoman sources. Also, unlike the play, in which Rustan is killed by the soldiers, historically, following Muspafa's death Rustem Pasha was immediately dismissed from the grand *vezirate*. Upon

Hurrem's plea for mercy, however, Rustem resumed his *vezirate* in two years time. In the popular view, Hurrem's role as maternal advocate of her own sons had ensured that Selim succeed Suleyman upon his death in 1566. In Rogers' view "whatever part Hurrem played in the Mustafa affair her behaviour was probably not conspicuously worse than that of her female contemporaries" (Rogers22).

Mallet's *Mustapha* was first performed at Drury Lane on 13 February 1739. This play, which captured the essence of the tragic story of Prince Mustafa, was performed (*Biographica Dramatica* II, 64) fourteen times[68] with Quin playing Solyman, Milward Mustapha and Butler Roxolana. As for the role of Mufti, played by Winston, his words were surely telling:

> Inflam'd with zeal,
> And holy hatred to the foes of heaven,
> Jews and Christians, who pollute our pious land,
> I would have wrought that boy to prompt his father
> In giving the sword those infidels (IV.I).

These words did not subscribe to the reality of the Ottomans who ruled an intensely pluralistic (ethnically and religiously) society and based their policies and actions on the premise of religious tolerance. Although the execution of Mustafa, had given the West ample material to portray Suleyman as villain, it was nevertheless a Renaissance commonplace that the Turk was "Bloody and cruel". As Chew writes:

> Prejudices against the Turks reached climax in the oft-expressed notion that they were incarnate devils or at any rate the chosen followers of Satan, that they all derived from hell or were all going there (Chew 141).

2.3.5 The Siege of Rhodes (1656)

The first publication about the Ottoman Empire in England was a translation of Guillaume Caorsin's *Obsidionis Rhodioe Urbis Descriptio* (1481) which depicted Mehmet II's attempt to conquer

68 See *The London Stage: 1600-1800* II, 760-62.

Rhodes in 1479. In 1482 John Kay's translation of Caoursin was dedicated to "the moste excellente, most redoubted, and most cyrsten kyng: King Edward the fourth"(Moran 1964, 11). While Suleyman II's siege of the island took place during the time of Henry VIII, Sir William Davenant wrote *The Siege of Rhodes* (1656) during the Commonwealth, it was revived at Lincoln's Inn Fields during the time of Charles II.

Alwin Thaler, writing about the historical importance of *The Siege of Rhodes* observed that Knolles' account of the siege was to be generally considered the main source of Davenant's play. In his Preface to *Gondibert*, however, Davenant emphasized the importance for the poet to work with good knowledge of the material he was handling, and he drew upon a variety of other works in writing *The Siege of Rhodes*. He took pains to relate the details of the historical siege from Thomas Artus' *Continuation de l'Histoire des Turcs* (1612). Besides Artus, other possible histories that Davenant might have used as sources for the siege were *Giacomo Bosio's Dell'Istoria della sacra religione et il militi di San Giovanni Gierosolimitano* (1602) translated into French in 1629, and Jean-Jacques Boissard's *Vitae et Icones Sultanorum Turcicorum* (1596). Ann-Mari Hedback draws attention to the fact that the picture of Roxelana in Knolles' book was a reproduction of that in Boissard. Despite this, she rules out Boissard as a possible source for Davenant since the story of the siege in the quarto "occupies only a page and a half" (Hedback 1). According to Hedback while Davenant has followed the outline of the siege sketched by Knolles, he drew Suleyman's character from Artus' account of the sultan. She observes that:

> Davenant's Solyman is a heroic figure, victorious and raised above every one else both in valour and honour. Ianthe speaks well of him and in the end also Alphonse has to admit that Solyman is his superior not only in arms but also in courtesy. This is not the picture of the Turkish Emperor that we find in Knolles: the English historian is mostly concerned with Solyman's violence in conquering one Christian nation after another (Hedback l).

Davenant captures the spirit of the early Crusades as he opens the play with a display of the military insignia of several countries including France, Germany, Spain, Italy and England. The Order of the Knights is placed on one side and the crescent of the Ottomans on an Antique Shield is set on the other. Villerius, a Knight of St. John, who is in command of the forces successfully defends the fort from the Ottoman assault together with Alphonso, who is fighting with the Rhodian Knights. As Ianthe (a fictional character), leaves her home in Sicily to join her husband Alphonso, she is taken prisoner and brought before the sultan. Although Solyman is enamoured of her, he sends her back to her husband. In the play, the Ottomans, because of the bravery of their Sicilian ally, are initially repulsed. As the tide of war finally turns, the Rhodians' only hope becomes Ianthe, who has sold her jewels to buy arms. Suleyman eventually sends Alphonso and Ianthe back to Rhodes, leaving the terms of the island's surrender to the discretion of the virtuous Ianthe. Not only does Ianthe escape the supposed lust of the sultan, but also a general amnesty allows all the Knights of St. John free egress from Rhodes:

> No fames free voice, nor lasting Numbers can
> Disperse, or keep, enough Solyman (II.V.VI.)

Although *The Siege of Rhodes*, a full-fledged heroic play, revolves around Suleyman, the historical prototype of Davenant's heroine Ianthe was Queen Henrietta Maria (Hedback lii-lvii), the leader of French *preciosity* who introduced ideas of love and honour to the English court. In laying the "excellent groundwork" for the love and honour formula in *The Siege of Rhodes*, when Davenant introduces the Fleet of Solyman the Magnificent and his army to represent ideas of greatness and virtue on the Restoration stage, he portrays the loyalty of the Bassas towards their sovereign:

> Majestick Sultan! At you feet we fall:
> Our Duty 'tis and just
> To say, you have encompass'd us with all
> That we can private trust
> Or publique Honours, call. (II.III.i.)

Davenant, like Fulke Greville, the English statesman and poet, who in his *Treatie of Warres* had written about the problem of

Turks being "first in unity" while "Christians divided stood, in schism and sect among themselves", (Chew 100) stresses this point in his preface to the play:

> In this poem I have revived the remembrance of that desolation which permitted by Christians princes, when they favoured the ambition of such as defended the diversity of religions (begot by the factions of learning) in Germany, whilst those who would never admit learning into their empire ... did make Rhodes defenseless (Hedback 6).

In his account of the siege, although Knolles did not relate the despair and spirit of rebellion among the Rhodians, according to Artus, the citizens who had lost faith in the Knight's ability to save the island, had threatened the Grand Master to take the matter in their hands. In historical sequence of events, when Suleyman came to the throne, the island of Rhodes had been in the hands of the Knights of St. George of Jerusalem for over 200 years. The city of Rhodes, with its formidable fortifications, was, in effect, a pirate state governed by a Byzantine governor, who had repudiated his allegiance to the Byzantine government. Following Rhodes' conquest by the Knights Hospitallers of St. John of Jerusalem, who had left the Holy Land after the fall of Acre in 1291, the Order regarded it their sacred duty to continue the onslaughts of the crusaders. The Order of Knights composed of Frenchmen, Germans, Englishmen, Italians, Castilians, Aragonese and the men of Auvergne and Provence was divided according to the language spoken. While they were charged with the duty of defending the walls of the island, the Knights soon learnt to be expert seamen and trained fighters and became "the terror of every Moslem sailor who put to sea in the Eastern Mediterranean" (Bridge 53). They attacked Ottoman merchant ships, confiscated merchandise and tortured the crew (Yucel 25). As Merrimen writes:

> When Moslem prisoners were taken, they were usually butchered. In 1320, we are told that 6250 Turkish captives were slaughtered in cold blood; a fanatical Englishwoman on her way to the Holy Land is said to have killed a thousand of them with her own hand. The story is hard to believe, though it is supported by contemporary evidence. In any case it is indicative of the spirit of the times (Merrimen 60).

In the sixteenth century since Rhodes was the strongest of the fortresses, the Divan was divided on the idea of attacking it. Following Suleyman's correspondence with the Grand Master, Phillip Villiers de l'Isle Adam, the sultan was finally challenged to put Rhodes under siege. Following the siege of the island which lasted one hundred and forty-nine days, Suleyman conquered Rhodes forcing the Knights into a peace treaty after their surrender of the island. Ultimately, Suleyman had achieved what Mehmet II had tried and failed to do in Rhodes. His son Selim II would take Cyprus, which the Venetian Republic had acquired in 1489.

In 1604, when *Othello*'s first recorded performance took place, the Ottoman conquest of Cyprus in 1570 had already provoked retribution by the armada of the Holy League on a large scale leading to a victory at Lepanto. In Shakespeare's tragedy, the Dukes, Senators and Officers of Venice realize:

> Th' importancy of Cyprus to the Turk;
> And let ourselves again but understand,
> That, as it more concerns the Turk than Rhodes. (I.III. 20-22)

In *Othello* when Shakespeare portrays the "Ottomites" as an unrelenting, calculating danger yet an invisible power kept offstage, "The Turkish preparation [is made] for Rhodes" (I.III.14):

> We must not think that the Turk is so unskillful
> To leave that latest which concerns him first,
> Neglecting an attempt of ease and gain
> To wake and wage a danger profitless. (I.III. 27-30)

Othello, like the Ottoman invasion, is a menace to the safety of Venice and dies having "turned Turk". The Moor of Venice stabs himself, ultimately in an attempt to destroy the Other:

> And say besides that in Aleppo once
> Where a malignant and a turbaned Turk
> Beat a Venetian and traduced the state,
> I took by th' throat the circumcised dog[69]
> And smote him thus. (V.II)

As the overwhelmingly negative view of the Ottoman Turk as the Other prevailed in the late Elizabethan era, the opposition between English civility and Oriental barbarism helped define England, which was in search of a common ground in religion and politics. In fact, throughout the period of 1640-1687 "English writers were comparing events in England and the (Ottoman Empire]" (Beck 67) and discovering significant similarities. First of all, both states had experienced dramatic social and economic problems and had undergone major change and upheaval in their systems of government. Second, England had lived through the English Civil War and the beheading of Charles I. In fact, when Paul Rycaut came to Istanbul as the Ambassador's secretary, he wrote that the turbulent times just before his arrival to the Ottoman capital enabled him to "understand how King Charles the Glorious Martyr was put to death"(Rycaut 77).[70]

During the same period while both states were faced with issues such as the succession to the throne, popery and factionalism, writers even criticized the Stuarts and the Catholic monarchs of Europe in a spirit of comparison with the Ottoman Empire. For example, in his *Political Reflections on the Government of the Turks* (1656) Francis Osborne, writing about the Ottoman system, admired:

---

69 As Daniel Vitkus states, Othello's suicide speech echoes the opening lines of James I's poem about Lepanto written in 1585 and published in 1591: "bloodie battle bolde /... Which fought was in Lepanto's gulfe / Betwixt the baptiz'd race, / And circumcised Turband Turkes" (ll.6-11). (Vitkus 149). Same discourse is also present in Aphra Behn's comedy, *The False Count.*

70 Sir Paul Rycaut, *The History of the Turkish Empire From The Year 1629 to the Year 1677. Containing the Reigns of the last Emperours, viz. Sultan Morat or Amurad IV, Sultan Ibrahim and Sultan Mahomet IV* ... This is the continuation, by Rycaut, of Knolles' *General Historie* in the edition of 1687. (*The Turkish History with Sir Paul Rycaut's Continuation.* Sixth Edition).

> [T]he Ottoman practice of subjecting ecclesiastical power to civil power. The Ottoman state was no more brutal and tyrannical than the monarchies of Europe. With the Ottomans power depends upon merit rather than birth; hence the Ottomans are free from corruption and idleness, the ruination of Christianity (Osborne 289-95)

Davenant's play, revolving around a historical siege, aimed at portraying a strongly united Ottoman Empire contrasting to Christendom split into factions. In the play Alphonso, the Christian hero admitted that the "Great Turk" was superior to him not only in arms, but in valour and courtesy. Despite the common charge of cruelty and barbarity leveled at the Ottoman Empire:

> The constant admiration in travel writings, not only of Turkish civil and military discipline but of fine moral qualities, could not fail to lead intelligent readers to some readjustment of values, especially when such admiration frequently evolved into sharp criticism of French or Christian institutions (Rouillard 643).

In writing *The Siege of Rhodes* (1656), one of the most influential and pioneering works of the Restoration drama, Davenant was "quick to perceive the preferences of popular taste and gratify them" (Tupper xi). Thus, he chose for his subject Suleyman the Magnificent whose reputation was nowhere greater than in France. Meanwhile, French influence was dominant in England during the reigns of Charles II (1660-1685) and James II (1685-1688). Particularly when Charles II and his court returned to England many literary men who had followed their patrons into exile in the days of the Commonwealth began to imitate the French writers with whose works they had grown familiar. During their years spent in France many English writers came into direct contact with the French literary world in which many authors had turned to Ottoman history for subjects. Since the most widely known of these works was Mlle. de Scudéry's heroic romance, *Ibrahim, ou 'l'Illustre Bassa* (1641), in writing *The Siege of Rhodes,* Davenant who was acquainted with contemporary French literary fashions early in his career drew from it "his types of character, motives of dramatic action, heroic sentiment and the rest"(Child 166-173).

In his essay of "Heroic Plays", Dryden wrote that Davenant was forced to introduce examples of "moral virtue" in order not to offend the Puritans. This moral virtue was in line with what the French classicists were trying to present in their drama. In his preface to *The Siege of Rhodes*, when Davenant wrote that he tried to "advance his characters of virtue in the shapes of valor and conjugal love", he was in keeping with the ideas of the French classicists. In raising Solyman above others in valour and honour, Davenant had introduced heroic motives on the English stage in which virtue became victorious over passion. From the point of view of the audience, pleasure arose in theatre from admiring the virtue of the hero as he resisted and overcame adversity. As the central issue in the play was the struggle between love and honour, Davenant also revealed this conflict through Roxolana, whom he also rose to a heroic stature:

> To all the world your virtue known
> More than the Triumphs of your Sultans' Throne. (2V.VI. 93-4)

Initially, Roxolona, with the "Turkish embroidered Handkerchief in her left hand, and a naked Ponyard in her right" (2. IV.III) taunted Ianthe, whom Davenant portrayed as a model Christian wife and praises her courage and beauty. Roxolona who was actuated by a jealousy towards "her rival, the Sicilian Flow'r" (2.V.VI.17) wanted revenge and sought it by plotting against Solyman and Ianthe. In the end, however, with her "virtue try'd" on stage, Roxolona's seeming wickedness was transformed to goodness:

> If Roxolona thus revengeless proves
> To him such a beautious Rival loves,
> It does denote she Rivals can endure
> Yet think she is of my heart secure. (2 V.VI.178-80)

After the Restoration, when Samuel Pepys "went to Sir William Davenant's Opera, this being the fourth day that it hath begun and ... today was acted the second part of *The Siege of Rhodes*" he recorded in his diary that Davenant's play was "very fine and magnificent" (Pepys 46). As one of the pioneer works of Restoration drama, and particularly, of heroic drama, *The Siege of Rhodes*, in many ways marked "the beginnings of a new era"(Thaler 624-41). Although Samuel Pepys saw women on the stage for the first time in 1660 at the Theatre Royal (Nicoll 70), the first appearance of an actress on the English stage was Mrs. Coleman in the role of Ianthe in D'Avenant's "opera" of 1656 (Nicoll 70). The fact remains that it was *The Siege of Rhodes*, which had led to the establishment of actresses on stage and had caused the boy-actors to vanish away (Nicoll 71). Despite Davenant's representation of Solyman as a noble and generous Turk, however, the image of the Ottoman sultan as a bloody and tyrannical ruler, would retain their popularity in the Restoration and eighteenth-century plays.

2.3.6. Conclusion

One of the primary aims of this thesis is to unfold the intricate relationship between historiography and historical representations of the Ottoman rulers in the plays. It is self-evident that partiality in historical knowledge and conflicting accounts of historical events and interpretations of their causes and significance at cross-purposes threaten each other's credibility. Yet, as Norman Itzkowitz, summarizes the frame of mind of the West until the Second World War, the prevalent attitude towards the Ottoman history was that knowledge of the Ottoman language was unnecessary since "anything worth knowing could be found in European sources" (Itzkowitz 77). Ottoman Turkish was unnecessary, as anything worth knowing, was to be found in European sources. Evidently, Knolles, whose sources were wholly Western[71] was irritated by the Ottoman sources "from whom the greatest light for the continuation of the Historie was in reason to have been expected, [they] being ... rather short, rude notes ... hard if not impossible to reconcile" (Beck 41). Itzkowitz, the twentieth-

---

71 As Brandon Beck notes Knolles' sources were "Giovio, Latin translations of Ottoman chronicles, so called, by German authors, Minadoi, Lavardin (The

century historian, locates the root of this attitude to Western bias as reflected in Kipling's words: "You'll never plumb the Oriental mind/And even if you do, it won't be worth the toil" (Quoted from Itzkowitz 77). As Itzkowitz maintains:

> It was the rare European who tried to remove the blinkers of prejudice in order to better view the Ottoman world in which he worked, lived and traveled. If, in the 16th century he stood in awe of the might and grandeur of the Ottoman Empire, he did so grudgingly in spite of himself. Whatever, admiration, he may have felt for the military colossus was quickly over-ridden by fear and hatred (Itzkowitz 84).

In *The Siege of Rhodes* Davenant's representation of Suleyman reveals that he has not embraced Knolles' historiography uncritically. Yet, ultimately, his heroic drama revolving around the Ottoman sultan, appropriates not only the substance or content of early seventeenth-century historiography, but also its varied conceptual and methodological schemes. These are based on ideological interpretations of history. In his exploration of the literary and subjective sources of historical interpretation, Hayden White aptly observes that the contents of "verbal fictions", be they literary or historical, "are as much invented as found" (White 82). Evidently, historians' accounts of the past reflect their personal interests and vision of past events. As they can infer particular facts about the past from the evidence available to them, the way they give meaning to those "facts" is a function of their own creative imagination. Thus, these historical "facts" or "contents of verbal fictions", which are not constrained by particular cognitive requirements, are culturally produced prior to their incorporation to the dramatic text. Whether or not the descriptions and interpretations of historical subjects are culturally biased—thus unfair—the historical content of drama is also ultimately an ideological production. From Terry Eagleton's perspective, in ideological representations, "the text reveals in peculiarly intense, compacted and coherent form the categories from which those representations are produced (Eagleton 85).

Historie of George Castriot, London, 1956) and Boissard (Vitae et icones sul-

In *The Siege of Rhodes,* Davenant legitimized and substantiated the power of Suleyman on stage and downplayed his negative qualities as sustained in Knolles' historical narrative. Despite his various innovations for the stage, it was nevertheless impossible for the Restoration dramatist to erase or even minimize simulations of historiographical practices, which were expressions of ideological interpretations of history. Even casting aside epistemological worries and concerns about cultural biases as to how the Ottomans were conceived in the European mind, the fact of the matter was that they constituted, in an almost archetypal sense, "the Muslim Other" for the Christian West:

Chorus: Our Swords against proud Solyman we draw.
His cursed Prophet and his sensual Law. (I.I.85-86).

---

tanorum, Frankfurt, 1596)" (Beck 41).

Chapter 3: Shifts in Power: Period of Destabilization

3.1. Sultan Osman II (1618-1622)

Osman, thy gentle nature far declined
From Turkish tyranny, and pride of mind;
Which made heaven raise, thee and extirpate them
The proud Usurpers of thy Diadem,
O! Would all Princes, when their States are blest
With power, and empire think their interest
In those their blessings, held but by the grace
Of Gratitude and Goodnesse and no place
Is held without them long, they some would trie,
That Truth prevails past their Policie.

(*The Historie,* 1638 edition)

The Ottomans knew under Suleyman I a power, wealth and splendour without equal. During his forty-six years of reign, while the Ottoman sovereign led his army on a dozen campaigns, he also intervened in quite diverse fields of artistic, cultural and educational operations. Under his rule, the number of *madrasahs* (each like a real university) provided the most advanced education of the era, particularly in the field of science (medicine, astronomy, mathematics, chemistry, geography, etc.) producing the greatest masters of sixteenth century. The works created in the field of architecture during his reign even today preserve their characteristics of beauty and live as monuments that have gained the admiration of the world.

In the seventeenth century, however, the House of Osman began to show a significant falling-off in its grandeur. When Osman II (at the age of fourteen) became the sultan in 1618, he displayed a desire to emulate his great ancestor Suleyman, particularly in military glory. Instead, he became extremely unpopular partly as a result of major losses sustained in his brief campaign against Poland in 1621. Particularly because the Janissaries and the

Sipahis were of great menace Osman II, the sultan announced a pilgrimage to Mecca, with a maneuver to raise and train a new army in Syria. However, he was soon deposed and strangled by the Janissaries, who had turned into chief power in the Ottoman Empire.

3.1.1. Tyranny

The above verses citing "Turkish tyranny" and set beneath the engraving of Osman II in Richard Knolles' *The Turkish History: Beginning from Mehmet III and Continued to this Present Year 1687* were composed long after the death of the English historian Knolles in 1610. Knolles' history book (1603) which came at the end of Elizabeth's reign was dedicated to the new king James I who had serious anxieties about the Ottomans' political, religious and military power. Through a narrative of campaigns, wars and conquests integrated into the reigns of the sultans, Knolles described how from the earliest states of the empire, the Ottomans could turn the best of their Christian subjects into powerful slaves, loyal to their sovereign. The best became "Janizaries ... the greatest strength of the Turkish Empire" and thus the basis of tyranny:

> The Grand Seignior's government is so absolute, as they all tearm themselves his slaves, and no man, how great so ever can assure himself of his estate, no not of his life. (*The Historie* 1638 Edition, 1390)

Noting how the Ottomans built their Empire on a system of slavery which sidestepped its "natural subjects" and relied instead on their Christian subjects, Knolles wrote:

> the better part of them whom we call Turks (but are indeed the children of Christians, seduced by their false instructors) ... There is not one natural Turk among all those that bear authoritie...Turks live in Anatolia, all of them either merchants or of base and mechanical trades, or poor laborer with spade and pickax -and such like peoples unfit for the wars (Knolles 349).

In an earlier work entitled the *Rėpublique* (1576) Jean Bodin, focusing on Islam as "an example of civil harmony" (Beck 47), made a more rational analysis of the intellectual and moral capacity of the Ottoman Empire in terms of its combination of slavery and nobility:

> For as concerning the Turks' Praetorian Soldiers, and those youths which are taken from the Christians as tribute ... I never accounted them slaves ... They all alone enjoy the great honours, offices, and priesthoods ... All their posteritie afterwards being accounted base except their vertue and noble acts they maintain the honour of their grandfathers, for the Turks alone of other people measure true nobilitie by vertue, not by descent or the antiquitie of their stocks: so that the farther a man is from vertue, so meuch the farther hee is...from nobility (Bodin, *Six Bookes* I:44).

Before he died at the beginning of the reign of Ahmet I (1603-1617) Knolles translated Bodin's *République* and published it with the English title *The Six Bookes of a Common Weale* (1606). His own book about the long history of war and statecraft in the Ottoman Empire was successful in imprinting the image of "Turkish tyranny". Since Knolles wrote for the advancement of the "Common State of Christendom" (Beck 40) his book remained popular well into the seventeenth century, with numerous new editions. Paul Rycaut, during his tenure as secretary to both the English Ambassador in Istanbul and The Levant Company, bridged the gap between Knolles's continuations in 1623 to 1640 in *The History of the Turkish Empire from the Year 1623 to the Year 1677*. As Rycaut's historical narrative began with the year 1623, it dealt with Ottoman "Tyranny, Oppression and Cruelty". Rycaut's contention was that while tyranny was a bad regime, it had its advantages such as the case with the Ottoman's military system, which had brought greatness to the empire. Ironically, though, Sultan Osman II—victim of first regicide in the Ottoman Empire—had been subject to the tyranny of his military corps, the Janissaries, who virtually dominated the capital and brutally subverted the power of the sultan. For an Ottoman prince to become a legitimate sultan, it was necessary to him to have the support of the Janissaries, who were a fundamental factor in succession. In Osman's case, the Janissaries who upheld a supreme power, deposed and murdered the sultan to bring his uncle Mustafa to the throne.

There were three causes of the regicide of Osman. Failure in his brief campaign against Poland culminating in his poor relationship with much of the military, his advisors' policy of increasing both his and their own power, and his marriage to the daughter of the *Mufti* (Muslim theologian). The Janissaries, the infantry and the *Sipahis*, the household cavalry, were of great menace to the sultan and the imperial treasury. Meanwhile Osman was badly advised by his Grand Vezir Dilaver and his entourage to suppress these military troops through a maneuver, which involved raising and training a new army in Syria. The advice involved Osman's leaving for Mecca with his personal retinue under the pretense of a pilgrimage. Thirdly, by marrying the daughter of the *Mufti* Esad Effendi he transgressed a dynastic tradition in the House of Osman. Ultimately, the twin problems of political factions and the power of the mothers of his rivals to the throne only facilitated Osman's deposition and murder at the age of eighteen.

When Osman's father Ahmet I died in 1617, his brother Mustafa was brought from his long confinement to succeed him. This was a break from the principle of succession of son to father, which had lasted fourteen generations over the previous three centuries. The rationale behind this shift from primogeniture was based on Ahmet's sons being too young to rule the empire. Although Mustafa had reached an age necessary to ascend the imperial throne, he suffered from a mental infirmity, mostly attributable to the long seclusion, which had deprived him from contact with society. Mustafa's enthronement was not merely a breach of the centuries old tradition of succession. His incompetence was so apparent that in three months the teenager Osman, was proclaimed the sultan. A letter written to James I to inform the English King of Osman's enthronement read:

> This paternall Empire and Monarchicall Kingdome hath almost untill this present blessed time beene alwaies hereditarie, from Grandfather to Father, from Father to Sonne, and so cursively in that manner: but having regard unto the age and yeeres of Our Great and Noble Uncle, Sultan Mustafa, hee was preferred and honoured to sit on the Ottoman Throne...[72]

Since Osman had resented the insertion of his uncle into the line of succession, first he dismissed Mustafa's grand *vezir* and limited the precedence of the *mufti*, both of whom were responsible for his uncle's enthronement. There were, however, other challenges to Osman's reign. First of all, the significant amendments made in the pattern of succession to the throne during the reign of Ahmet I owed a great deal to efforts of Kosem Sultan, *haseki* (wife) to Osman's father. In the Ottoman dynastic system, the palace intrigues of the reigning sultan's mother played an important part in the destiny of the sultanate. Although Osman's own mother Mahrifuz Sultan was alive when he was enthroned in 1618, she did not reside in the palace during her son's reign.

> What seems likely is that Mahfiruz fell into disfavour, was banished from the palace at some point before Osman's accession, and never recovered her status as a royal concubine (Peirce 233).

Mahfiruz's banishment thus eliminated a great obstacle to Kosem's own efforts to ensure the enthronement of Mustafa rather than Osman, Ahmet I's first born son, who posed a great threat to Kosem's ambitions for her own sons. Kosem's fear was that should Osman succeed his father and should he produce his own sons, he would likely execute his brothers and her own sons Murad, Kasim and Ibrahim—all brothers to Prince Bajazet portrayed in Racine's renowned tragedy. Ultimately, the motive behind Kosem's lobbying efforts to ensure the accession of Mustafa rather than Osman was to maintain the security of her own sons

---

72 Purchas, Samuel. *Hakluytus Posthumus or Purchas His Pilgrimes*, 9:407-8. The letter is an addendum to Robert Wither's The Grand Signiors Serraglio, which is a translation of Ottaviano Bon, *Decsrizione del Serraglio del Gran Signore.*

who would provide her with a long career as *valide sultan*.[73] Since his childhood, however, Kosem was successful in cultivating a good rapport with Osman. In return, the young sultan enjoyed her friendship and honoured the relationship.

Other than Kosem, who was influential in the domestic politics of the empire, the real threat to Osman's reign was the Janissaries, a body of regular infantry, known as *Yenicheri* in Turkish, meaning "new troops". Referred to as Janissaries in the West, the standing army of the empire constituted a remarkable organization with the military elite manifesting a freedom of spirit and action unmatched by any other organized group. In fact, the Janissaries were the group which came least under the "subordinating influence" (Lyber 92) of the Ottoman system. They were instead instrumental in the political upheavals within the empire:

> In the time of battle, however, they drew an invincible line behind which the person of their sovereign was safe as in an impregnable fortress ... Yet their *esprit de corps*, resting on consciousness of power, made them feared at all times. They took an active part in determining the destinies of the empire in two ways—by limiting conquests, and by influencing the succession to the throne (Lyber 93).

The Janissary corps was repeatedly gratified by the Ottoman court and flattered in imperial proclamations while numerous favours were showered on them for their bravery in battles. While their supreme commander, the Aga of the Janissaries, lived in splendid palaces, the complex of the military barracks extending between the Suleymaniye Mosque and the Golden Horn was one of the power-centres of the city. Since the Ottoman administrative system lacked a parliament and a senate, the Janissaries sometimes acted as their equivalent in terms of expressing the social, economic and political discontents of the populace. Although the *vezirs* and *ulemas* manipulated the Janissaries in order to

---

73 In this major work, as Rycaut had little to say about the harem institution, he completely omitted mention of *valide sultans* who had unprecedented power and means to sustain their sons and their own authority. Although he devoted an entire chapter to Kosem Sultan, he omitted to mention that her central role in the harem stemmed from being the mother of the sultan.

achieve their political ends, they were essentially their own power group representing the patriarchal system of the capital. When they overturned their *pilav* cauldrons, this was a sign of mutiny in the empire. During their uprisings, they would set up their cauldrons on a large open space near their barracks and use them as rallying points to demand for more pay and power—two principal causes for their unrest. Particularly, the Janissaries had a vested interest in changing sultans, whose accessions meant a monetary bonus (donatives) for each member of the corps.

Following the report of the Janissaries' murder of Osman in 1622, the English eyes were fixed on events in Istanbul with news circulating about the first Ottoman regicide through pamphlets such as *The Strangling and Death of the Great Turke ... 1622)*[74]. Ultimately, the strangling of Osman II became the subject of two English tragedies towards the end of the second half of eighteenth century - Cornelius Arnold's *Osman* (1757) and Francis Gentleman's *The Sultan or Love and Fame* (1770). Gentleman's play, which was rich in heroic elements, represented Osman as an ideal character of heroic drama. What was significant to Cornelius Arnold's *Osman* (1757) was his creation of a "Procession from the Marriage" of the sultan and Aphendina, Mufti's daughter.

3.1.2. Osman (1757)

Cornelius Arnold's *Osman* written in 1757 and "founded on a catastrophe which happened at Constantinople in the year 1624" (*Biographica Dramatica* 108) depicts the chain of episodes linked to the murder of the Ottoman sultan. There are, however, chrono-

74 The Strangling and Death of the Great Turke ... A wonderful story, and the like never heard of in moderne times ... and yet all to manifest the Glory and Providence of God, in the preservation of Christendome in these Troublesome Times printed in London on 15 July 1622; A true relation of the murther of Osman the Great Turke, and fiue of his principal Bashawes, and of the election and coronation of Mustapha his uncle in his stead ... (1622); and A True and faithful relation, presented to His Majestie ... of what lately happened in Constantinople, concerning the death of Sultan Osman, and the setting up of Mustafa his uncle (1622).

logical deviations relevant to the question of historicity. First of all, the catastrophe that Arnold refers to in his tragedy took place in 1622 not in 1624. Following Osman's death his uncle Mustafa remained on the throne for fifteen months. The effective instrument of government during this time was the sultan's mother. In Osman, Arnold captured the devastating rivalry and violence in the saray through the character of Kiosem, who collaborated with Osman's rivals in order to put her son Murad on the throne. This was significant given that the women's energies in the harem were solely directed towards producing an heir for the Ottoman dynasty. For women in the harem to acquire the title of regency (*valide sultan*) upon the death or deposition of the sultan was the principal aspect of their life, great tension surrounded the issue of dynastic inheritance. As matriarchal power was at the heart of political life in the seventeenth century, obviously, mothers vigilantly protected their sons. And historically, Kosem Sultan who survived the threats to her life during the second reign of Mustafa (1622-1623) played a fundamental role in the politics of the era—even taking charge of the reign of her seven- year-old grandson Mehmet IV following the death of another son Ibrahim.

Arnold's characterization of Kosem, the most powerful and colourful woman to rule the Ottoman harem, had wider political implications and allusions to her well-known influence in the government affairs during the sultanate of women. Kosem Sultan was ultimately an emblem of the Ottoman dynastic matriarch. She exercised her official power and sustained her career by means of her carefully designed networks within the structure of Ottoman politics and society. Despite Kosem's resumed power, her status, like that of all other women in the Ottoman Empire however, derived entirely from the male on whom she depended or to whom she was related. Kiosem, through her son, shared an inherited nobility. Yet there were limits to her sovereign role. As Pierce indicates:

> Ottomans were ever mindful of the custodial limits of women's power: when a royal woman appeared to act in her own self-interest rather than in the interest of her son or of the dynasty as a whole—when she acted to exploit rather then to preserve sovereign power—the public did not hesitate to decry her activity as illegitimate and corrupt (Peirce 17).

In *Osman* Kiosem plays a great role in terms of informing and providing the reader with the means of imagining the internal functioning of the harem and the palace and of relationships among its residents. Kiosem's soliloquy in her Apartment in the Seraglio in Act II Scene V gives the reader a glimpse of the ulterior goals of the mother of an heir to the throne and reflects her aspirations for power as well as her vigilance in protecting her son:

> To what End serve myself corroding Cares?
> Whilst Osman gains th'Affection of the Court,
> The populace, and ev'ry Order -Amurath,
> My son, neglected, dreams away his Life,
> Or immaturely falls—for fall he must,
> E'er Osman's Head can hold the Crown secure:
> Then what if I by subtle Stratagem
> To save my Amurath, bring Death on Osman;
> The Janizaries, cover'd with Disgrace,
> Resent his Treatment in the Late Campaign-
> I'll fix my spies, observe their ev'ry action,
> Sow discord by Degrees, fill them with Terror,
> And raise 'twixt him and them such Jealousy,
> As from the slightest Rumour may be blown
> (By addding proper Fuel) to Rebellion.
> ...
> If Amurath reigns, the Pow'r is lodg'd with me:
> If Osman - Perish th'abject, dastard Thought!
> Better meet Death, attempting Sov'reignty,
> Than linger Life in absolute Subjection:
> For Life's no Life for me, devoid of Power. (II.V)

In the play, although the main focus is on the tragedy of Osman, its plot hinges on a love triangle, which provides an indirect cause to the tragic end of the sultan. The central theme in the play revolves around the relationship between Osman and Aphendina, Mufti's daughter, which culminates in marriage. The love triangle in the tragedy, however, consists of the love of both Mirza and Aphendina for Osman. The outcome of the action is the suicide of both women following the murder of the sultan. Although *Osman* is set against a background of political intrigue, uncontrolled passions such as love, jealousy and revenge effect the tragedy in which the plot is primarily forged by Kiosem to subvert the power of the sultan.

The play opens at a camp with Osman launching a war against Poland. While Osman is obliged to retire with heavy losses because of a mutinous camp of soldiers who lack courage and discipline, the Lieutenant of the Janissaries describes Osman to the Aga as "matchless youth" who is "great" in Science as in Valour/As many languages did grace his tongue". The Lieutenant and the Aga of the Janissaries are amazed at Osman's "powers" and his "Courtesy" which add "Lustre to his Sword" (I.I). As for Osman, he is in "The Sultan's Pavillion in his Camp" reading a letter from Aphendina, his childhood friend and the daughter of Mufti Ashad (Esad Efendi). Osman tells Ashad that because of "the late Dispatch" sent to him by "faithful Aphendina" he is ready to treat for peace with the Poles: "She loves me, Mufti, sues for my Return/And I'm resolved to honour her Request" (I.II). Osman is ready to transgress the cultural hierarchies in the empire by marrying the Mufti's daughter so that: "all the World may hail the Sultan's Choice" (I.II). When the news that "Mirza no longer/Reign's in her Sov'reign's Heart" (II.I) reaches the sultan's first haseki whom Arnold refers as Sultana Queen this gives Kiosem an opportunity to benefit from Osman's change of heart. She helps Mirza thunder vengeance on Aphendina to fulfill her political aspirations and construct her own social and political order. Meanwhile the revolt of the Janissaries culminates in their overthrow of the Janissary Aga and the Lieutenant for "their Attachment to his Majesty". This ensures the future of Kiosem's political power. Thus she partakes in the operations of the Janissaries who are determined to rise in further rebellions. Kiosem also collaborates with other state dignitaries who are cast aside by the Sultan for new favorites. She tells the Bassa of Bosnia whom Arnold casts as "a Partizan of Kiosem: "Let's lose no Time; Occasion on the Wing/Beckons away, to snatch glorious Prize" (III.II). The prize for Kiosem's toil is "The Royal Diadem on Amurath's Head" (V.III) which is realized following the imprisonment of Osman at "The Seven Towers" (Yedi Kule). Since the enthronement of her son makes Kiosem the valide sultan, she ultimately is at the apex of the power-structure of the palace.

Historically, Kosem Sultan was raised to the apex of the palace structure from her initial position of a Greek-born slave girl. Like Suleyman I's wife Hurrem, she succeeded in subverting the power of the Ottoman sultan, stereotyped in the Western representations as the oppressor/tyrant/owner. As the complexities and controversies of gender/power relations and sexual politics of the Ottoman traditions reveal it, the status of the sultan was, in fact, vulnerable to being the oppressed/victim/object. In the final scenes of *Osman*, Arnold captures this paradox in the Ottoman system through Kiosem's soliloquy at *The Seraglio*:

> That nought transcends the Genius of a Woman:
> E'en Man, who stiles himself Creation's Lord,
> And boasts superior Knowledge and Address,
> Is but a Dupe -'Tis Kiosem governs all-
> My son, my Amurath reign! -But, ha! How reigns... (V.III)

While the sultan's harem was exclusively composed of slave concubines, upon the accession of their sons to the throne the mothers were freed automatically from slavery. Other than the *valide sultans*, the only inhabitants[75] of the *saray*, who were not slaves were the princesses—sisters and daughters of the sultan. Contrary to the *valide sultans'* prominence, universally esteemed positions and legitimate scopes of power, in the hierarchy of the harem, the princesses were insignificant figures. In essence the Ottoman governing system was made up of Turkish, Byzantine, Persian and traditional Islamic components.

---

75 As for Muslim women they were absent within the ranks of the harem. As Pierce indicates: "One of the key features of dynastic politics—reproduction through concubinage rather than legal marriage—suggests that the freeborn Muslim woman was an anachronism in the harem" (Peirce 143).

> The origin of Turkish element is obvious, because it was the basic form of the rule of the nomads who rode into Anatolia and ultimately created the Empire. Perhaps the most important aspect retained from the Turkish system was the idea of merit and ability as the basis of authority (McCarthy 105).

One of the features that marked the domestic politics of Osman II's reign was his radical move to contract marriage with a high-born Muslim woman named Akile, who was the daughter of the mufti, Esad Efendi. The popular discontent about this marriage which took place only a few months before Osman's death in 1622 is well documented in foreign sources.[76] Thus, Arnold's Osman is compatible with verisimilitude in terms of portraying this historically documented marriage in the Ottoman dynasty. For Osman, the Mufti's daughter is "qualified to grace [his] Throne/And nuptial Rites shall constitute her Empress" (II.V). He knows, however, that this marriage will "thwart the Empire's Laws/Which do inhibit Marriage to the Sultan" (II.II). In Act III which takes place in the Council Chamber (Divan) Osman gathers the state dignitaries who include the Vezir, Agha of Janissaries, Kizlar Agha (Chief Eunch), Captains and Bassas to seek their blessings on this marriage. Ultimately Arnold in his Osman—though "not acted" (Biographica Dramatica 108) on the English stage—recreates a procession of marriage to reflect a historical moment:

> This Day be sacred in our Turkish Annals,
> Which makes the peerless Aphendina mine. (IV. I)

Weddings in the Ottoman Empire were ceremonial events in their own right. Particularly the weddings of sultan's daughters were celebrated with great pomp and magnificence. For example, in 1623 when Osman's sister Hanzade Sultan was married to the Aga of the Janisssaries, her elaborate bridal procession was escorted among the cheering crowds in the streets of Istanbul by

---

76 See Deshayes de Courmenin's *Voyage de Levant* (161), Michel Baudier's *Histoire generalle du serail et la cour de grand seigneur, empereur des Turcs* (530), Paul Rycaut's, *The Present State of the Ottoman Empire* (155-56), Francois Petis de la Croix's *Etat general de l'empire otoman,* (105) and in M. d'Hosson's *Tableau général de l'empire ottoman* (7:63).

the vezirs of the sultan. According to privy purse accounts, however, Mufti's daughter Akile, a high-ranking Muslim woman, whom Arnold names Aphendina, never entered the harem of the imperial palace. Peirce elaborates on this point as such:

> Certainly, this freeborn Muslim woman of great status would have been an anomaly in the household composed of slaves, and her presence disruptive of the harem's established hierarchies ... Demonstrated here is the paradox of the royal harem: it gave birth to and nurtured the most powerful and august family of the empire, perhaps even of the entire Islamic world, yet it was beneath the dignity of a freeborn Muslim woman to enter it (Peirce 106-7).

In *Osman*, the Grand Vezir praises the young Osman for his decision to marry Ashad's daughter as he speaks adamantly against the custom that militates against the sultans' marriages to their royal consorts:

> Our former Emp'rors, despotik Ravagers!
> Preying on Beauty with relentless Will,
> Have glory'd in a Latitude of Action;
> While you great Sir! Their Junior far in Years,
> Descending from your Arms one beauteos Bride,
> Relinquishing the Sex for her alone. (IV.I)

Obviously, in the Western thought what tied the notions of the Other together was the idea of the harem as a nexus of sensuality and slavery. As a result, Western perceptions of the harem as an institution in terms of gender, space and politics easily fell sway to value-judgements. Writing about the myths and realities of the sultan's harem, Peirce clarifies that sex, however, was "not a random activity" in the imperial harem:

> Sex for the Ottoman sultan, as for any monarch in a hereditary dynasty could never be purely pleasure, for it had significant political meaning. Its consequences—the production of offspring—affected the succession to the throne, indeed the survival of dynasty ... Sex in the imperial harem was necessarily surrounded with rules, and the structure of the harem was aimed in part at shaping, and thus controlling, the outcome of the sultan's sexual activity (Peirce 3).

In that sense while the Ottomans could not easily abandon their restrictive laws and customs enforced by the Shariah Law, which allowed polygamy, sexual relations between the sultan and his women were "embedded with in a complex politics of dynastic reproduction"(Peirce 3). Ultimately, Arnold in *Osman* was successful in terms of depicting that the political status of women in the empire depended on the matriarchal power of *valide sultans*. Furthermore, through his portrayal of a wedding ceremony, he revealed to the reader a rather unique event—other than that of Suleyman and Hurrem's marriage—that constituted a radical break with most of the Ottoman past.

3.1.3. The Sultan (1770)

> *The Sultan, or Love and Fame, was printed in Jan. 1770; from the advertisement prefixed to it, it appears that it had been acted at this theatre in the preceding April by very bad performers—it was written by Gentleman ... he tells us that his plot is founded on Turkish history, and that it mostly adheres to facts ... this is a dull T.—the language is very unnatural.*
>
> (Genest 5:249).

What seems to be one of the sources to Arnold's play is another tragedy on Osman, *The Sultan, or Love and Fame* written by Francis Gentleman. This assumption is based on the fact that while Gentleman's tragedy was written in 1753 (*Biographica Dramatica* [3:306]) Arnold's *Poems on Several Occasions*, which includes Osman was printed in London only in 1757. Unlike Arnold's *Osman*, however, which was not performed, Gentleman's tragedy was acted at the Theatre Royal in Haymarket in 1769 and "met a very favourable reception by ... numerous and polite Audiences" (Advertisement, *The Sultan*). Although Gentleman's play was printed in 1770, as the dramatist indicates in the introduction of the text, the play was performed in various theatres such as those of York and Scarborough after 1754.

As much as Gentleman claims to adhere to "facts" and bases his plot on "Turkish history", the major fantastical element in the tragedy is Osman's suicide at the end of the play. Although the play deals with the theme of Osman's deposition followed by Mustafa's accession the throne, Arnold's detailed account of the practices and mores of the sultanate surpasses Gentleman in its accuracy particularly in terms of his treatment of the role and power of the *valide* sultan. Arnold's case is indeed surprising considering that mention of *valide sultans* were omitted by a number of influential Western writers such as Ottavio Bon, Michel Baudier and Paul Rycaut in their descriptions of the sultan's palace. In their descriptions of the harem and the Ottoman court, these writers attribute various aspects of the *valide sultan*'s authority to the principal concubine. In Peirce's view, these writers who even had tenures in Istanbul and should have known the difference between *valide sultan* and *haseki* nevertheless blended the two so that "their readers would find it more satisfying to believe that power lay with the sultan's concubine rather than with his mother" (Peirce 117).

As is evident in Gentleman's play in the dramatic representations of the harem, women also compete passionately for power and influence as royal consorts of the present sultan rather than as the mothers of future sultans. Rather than a story of regicide, Gentleman's heroic drama revolves around the jealousies of the saray. His plot is driven by Almira's "peace destroying jealousy" (I.I). Osman's royal concubine who rages at being cast aside by the sultan for a new favourite Aphendina[77]. In her fury though Almira calls Osman "fickle", "false", "faithless", "cruel, "relentless tyrant", she has also "long retained in amorous bonds", "Solan, a leading pillar of the state" (I.I), the Agha of the Sipahis. Women's rivalry for the sultan's love and deadly struggles for power in the palace are all too real. Yet, within the structure and nature of the harem where women are confined and guarded fiercely by the eunuchs the idea of Almira (referred to as Sultana Queen) having a lover merely colours other fictions and fantasies of the harem. Even as the jealousy of Almira for Aphendina drives the action in the first act, Osman's appointment of Omar as the new Grand vizier arouses the fury and jealousy of Orasmin who now consid-

---

77 Another reason why Arnold might have used Gentleman's play as a source is that he also uses the name Aphendina, which in fact is only a derivation of "Efendi" somehow equivalent to "Sir".

ers himself an "outcast slave" (I.II). Thus, he plans vengeance against Osman by joining forces with Almira, for "love forsaken turns bitter rage/No instrument more fit than female hate/To wing destruction with resistless force" (I.II). Mostly, what plays into the hands of Orasmin is the rage of the "collective band" of Janissaries who are "Prepared to spread destruction throu' the land" (II.II) as Effendi informs the sultan.

In the play, rather than the Janissaries, it is Orasmin and his collaborators who plot against Osman in order to bring his uncle Mustafa to the throne. As Solan informs Almira,

> Orasmin, faction's most adventurous son
> Full of that consequence which power bestows
> And holding us but secondary means,
> With bold ingratitude has breathed a vow,
> To settle Mustafa in regal way. (IV.I)

Mustafa, however, is a "known established foe" to Almira who only "deserves [her] hate" (IV.I). Since Orasmin has underestimated the Sultana Queen's power she immediately withdraws her forces from Orasmin who has plans of raising Mustafa to the throne. As she tells Solan:

> Shall proud Orasmin then dispose the crown,
> Nor ask concurrence of Almira's voice?
> Have I employed my friends, and pledged my faith
> To pour treasure forth in golden dreams?
> Cast all my weight into the public scale
> To be so insignificant at last. (IV.I)

In the eyes of Almira, while Orasmin is now an "Audacious traitor" Osman is "No longer victim to [her] jealous heart" (IV.I). Compared to Arnold, Gentleman lacks information about the vital presence and influence of the *valide sultan* over factions in the Ottoman government. Instead, he captures in his work the influence of the royal consort. Moreover, his play dramatizes the power of the Janissaries—one of the most effective armed forces of the times.

Historically, the Janissaries' ominous power in determining the succession to the throne even provided Europe a great service on several of these occasions. For example, in the sixteenth century they had played a great role in the death of Suleiman I's two ablest sons, Mustafa and Bayezid in order to put on throne Selim II, who was drunken and dissolute. It was under Selim's rule that Europe had defeated the Ottomans at Lepanto. Nevertheless, Selim II, whom Robert Greene had depicted in *The First Part of The Tragical Reign of Selimus* (1594) had come to power at the peak of the Ottoman Empire. Prior to Osman's reign, the power of the Janissaries, who represented the specific interests of the empire, was visible in the streets of Istanbul. In 1514, they had obliged Selim I to abandon an attack on Persia by threatening mutiny and even firing on the sultan's tent. Particularly when Selim I tried to strengthen his ties with their Arab subjects—after his conquest of Cairo—the Janissaries forced him to return to Istanbul. In 1529 they had forced Suleyman to raise the siege of Vienna as they wanted to return to Istanbul.

In Osman's case, evidently, he had not been able to respond sufficiently to the avarice of his corps with rewards that would ordinarily be payable upon their victorious return from a battle. Furthermore, there was a chronic depletion of the Imperial Treasury arising from the deposition of Mustafa and with the advent of a new sovereign. In a short time, the Janissaries had benefited from two substantial accession bonuses. Predominantly incited by avarice, they had begun to resent the adolescent sultan, blaming him for failure in the war against Poland. The Janissaries, however, were largely to blame for Osman to treating for peace after heavy losses. *The Sultan* captures these historical realities. When Effendi informs Osman that the Janissaries pose a serious threat to both the sultan himself and the empire at large, Osman replies:

> Is it not plain, but for their coward hearts
> Or what is worse, their factious stubborn minds
> Which stood in opposition to my will
> Ere this I had subdued the Polish king,
> And trod the barbarous Muscovite to earth.
> When passing the confines of the sea
> I might even sent such powerful navies forth

> As would have spread my conquests over the main,
> And made even Britain strike her flag to mine;
> Whilst I at land laurell'd millions led
> To sure subjection of the Christian world.
> But crosses, opposed, by this rebellious crew,
> Perplexed with mutinies and endless jars
> I was obliged ingloriously to stop
> And stain my honour with imperfect peace. (I.II)

At this point it is interesting to note that even at a time when the Ottoman military threat had begun to wane, the perception of the Ottoman power was still alive. When Gentleman wrote *The Sultan* in 1770 the West had witnessed the Ottoman failure of two major wars against the Russian and Austrian Empires which were concluded with the treaties of Karlowitz (1699) and Pasarowitz (1718). Yet, in numerous variations, fear of Ottoman conquest and of conversion to Islam remained pervasive in Europe:

> Our arms have taught the Christians to revere,
> And bow before the sons of holy Mahomet:
> We spoke in thunder and made all obey:
> ....
> If in our proud success, by force of arms,
> The Koran's influence had spread around
> And taught those Christians to obey its laws:
> Our prophet then in Paradise had smiled
> To see a world converted by his sons. (I.II)

As McCarthy indicates, however, religious tolerance was both a practical and a legal necessity " for the Ottomans.

> Islamic law commanded that Christians and Jews (called *dhmmis*, 'people of the Book', those who believed in the Bible) be allowed to practice their religions. The non-Muslims were legally bound to pay a special tax in lieu of military service, but could worship in their churches and keep schools, religious organizations and other elements of their religions. As an Islamic Empire, the Ottoman Empire necessarily conformed to this Islamic law. There was also a practical base for this tolerance. The Ottomans ruled over a vast territory populated by members of different Christian sects. Even if they wanted to force by conversion, it might have proved impossible and certainly would have caused revolt. As long as his subjects accepted his rule, it was in the interests of the sultan to leave them in peace (McCarthy 127).

In essence, while the Ottomans' career of conquest was aided by the social and political conditions of the defending countries, as

Inalcik, mirroring McCarthy's views, asserts: "the empire emerged at the same time, as protector of the Orthodox Church and millions of Orthodox Christians. Islam guaranteed the lives and property of Christians and Jews, on the conditions of obedience and payment of a poll tax. It allowed them free exercise of their own religions and to live according to their own religious laws" (Inalcik 1973, 7). Yet, if the Ottoman system was tolerant, it was also complex. Although the *millet* system which operated with the greatest liberality and tolerance towards each religious group (the Greek Orthodox, the Armenian Gregorians, other Christian sects and the Jews), the Ottomans' *devshirme*-run system presented a different picture. The *devshirme* (Ottoman administrators and military men) system, which was a "model of meritocracy" (McCarthy 126), demanded conversion to Islam. While this practice based on the Islamic Law, was not "a theoretically legal one", nevertheless, it was "a pragmatic system" (McCarthy 99) which allowed sultans to rule efficiently.

In Osman II's case, however, his enemies included many of the most powerful *devshirme* in the Ottomans' administrative and military system. When he was enthroned as a young boy, while Osman cherished dreams of his ancestors' martial glory, he launched a war against the advice of his ministers. When he returned to the capital with heavy losses, nevertheless he claimed victory. In Act I Scene II, Gentleman skillfully depicts Osman's claim to victory on stage: "Enter Osman... in triumph; with a procession of Tartars, Bostangis, Janissaries, Polish hostages, officers of the Seraglio, Dervises, Banner of Mahomet, of war, and of the empire, &c.&c.&c."

> Subjects, the toils of war are now no more;
> All cheering peace again displays her smiles,
> (Like summer-suns succeeding wintry skies,)
> And spreads around a universal joy. (I.II)

The Janissaries, however, highly resented Osman and complained that due to the failure in battle "the reward payable for a head of an enemy severed in battle was no more than a single ducat-and for this a man was expected to risk his own head" (Kinross 292). Osman's advisors convinced him to devise an elaborate scheme to secure his sovereignty. Ultimately, under the cover of an advocacy for reform, Osman agreed to recruit a new troop, "a large Asiatic army to serve the Sultan" (Kinross 293) and to suppress the Janissaries. This grand plan initiated by Osman's tutor Omer Efendi and his Grand Vezir Dilaver Pasa,[78] involved the sultan's meeting with his new corps in Damascus on his way to Mecca to perform pilgrimage. As *The History of the Turkes* maintains:

> Delavir Bassa, a man of great wit and courage, lately called from the Eastern parts, where he had long governed with honour, who came in though late, yet in a very brave and warlike equipage, above all his other captains, was suddenly made great vizier ... If his majesty would pull up his spirits and follow his advice, he would provide him with a new soldiery about Damascus, of the Coords (Kurds), men ever bred in the frontier, with hardness and warre of great courage and experience; and that of them he should erect a new militia... (2: 971).

When the ulterior motives of Osman's holy visit to Mecca by transporting the royal treasures were soon detected, they triggered the sultan's deposition and murder by the Janissaries and the *sipahis*. *Sipahis* (horsemen) of the Porte were another component of the Ottoman military institution.[79] As they massed together at the Hippodrome, the Janissaries and the *sipahis* conducted their sultan, who in fact was the commander-in-chief of the entire army, to the prison of the Seven Towers (Yedikule). As a young and inexperienced sultan who lacked the foresight and

---

78 In *The Sultan* Gentleman names the *vezir* and the *mufti* as Omar and Effendi respectively. As for Arnold, the name of the *Grand Vezir* in his play is Dilaver.

79 *Sipahis* were the permanent cavalry, who were better educated than the Janissaries. While their organization was older than that of the Janissaries, their members did not constitute one single body. Since the *sipahis* had the privilege to acquire wealth and to rise with rapidity, up until the seventeenth century they did not cause much trouble to the sovereign. The *sipahis* of the Porte had their own generals, who supervised the administration of all their affairs.

discretion of such an ambitious venture, Osman made a final plea before his death:

> My aghas of the sipahis, and you the elders of the Janissaries, who are my fathers, with a young man's imprudence I have lent ear to bad advice. Why do you humiliate me in this way? Do you want me no longer? (Kinross 294)

Sir Thomas Roe, Ambassador to the Ottoman Porte between 1621 and 1628 described the death of Osman on May 19, 1622 as the Janisaaries broke into the Saray: "a strong knave stuck him on the head with a battle-axe and the rest leaping upon him, strangled him without much ado" (Roe 45-52). In Gentleman's tragedy, the dramatic sequence of events follows the historical ones to a great extent. As the Janissaries "fill the Hippodrome with dreadful show", Solan and "the Sipahis" (III.I) wait for Osman at the palace gate. Yet Osman escapes death at the hand of the mutes who "seize him to put on the bow-string" (V.I). Seeing this, Aphendina stabs herself. Although the redeemed Solan reaches the prison to save the sultan from Orasmin, Osman too stabs himself with his last words being:

> Oh! Mahomet, stretch forth thy holy hand
> And lead me to thy paradise above. (V.I.)

This is paradoxical considering that—based on Islamic faith—the fate of anyone committing suicide, would be the misery and anguish of hell. Nevertheless, Gentleman who portrayed Osman as the appointed "successor" (IV.II.) of the Prophet, seems to have a broad knowledge of Islam:

> This world affords no punishment for thee;
> But in the next- observe prophetic truth,
> Mark it, and tremble at the awful sound,
> When Israfil shall rouse the awakened dead. (IV.I.)

By the time Gentleman's *The Sultan or Love and Fame* had contributed to the success of the Haymarket Theatre season in 1769 (Genest 250) attempts were made in the Christian West to understand the Islamic faith. In fact, in the eighteenth century, new translations of the Qur'an in European languages had started to appear notably by George Sale in English (1734). Yet, though there was "no ground for suspecting any deliberate intentional falsification" of the Qur'an, there was "an all-pervading vulgarizing of the spirit and style of the book" (Chew 451). The purported "fact" about "Mahometanism" was that women, unlike men had no souls. In 1792, Mary Woollstonecraft, writing about women's subordination in the context of the "Mahometan" institution of the harem had even intensified this spurious "fact" of Muslim theology. Furthermore, even as late as 1877, it was pronounced in the *Englishwoman's Review* that "to him she [was] a mere animal" (42). Yet, the truth of the matter was that, as much as women's sexuality was recognized in Islam, there was a great emphasis placed in the Qur'an on the spiritual equality of both men and women. In that sense, by committing suicide, Aphendina like Osman too had no chance for the "paradise above".

3.1.4. Osman on the French Stage

The turbulent events of 1622 in Istanbul, were turned into French tragedies several decades before their dramatizations in England. When Denis Coppée, a Flemish bourgeois of Huy, published *L'assasinat du sultan Osman* in Liege, he was also honoured as "being the first Belgian to write anything for the theatre to be printed in French" (Rouillard 488). Evidently, the dramatic events during the short reign of Osman II had caused a great stir in the West. As was the case in England, a number of French pamphlets as well as dispatches in *Le mercure* provided readers with news of great interest, excitement and curiosity. Beginning with the death of Ahmet I, through pamphlets such as *Discours véritable de la mort du Grand Turc,* printed in Paris in 1618, France was already informed that, although Osman was favoured by a group of dignitaries, the Janissaries and the Grand Vezir had acclaimed his uncle Mustafa. *Le mercure* had informed its readers about the revolt of the Janissaries and the Sipahis and the subsequent murder of Osman. Following oral reports of the French ambassador M. de Cesy, soon all this information was transferred to the stage through Copée's play. When Denise Coppée wrote a play about the murder of Sultan Osman II, he promised his audience/readers to offer "[t]he double satisfaction of witnessing their fill of horrors and felicitating themselves that they are not Turks or Mahometans" (Rouillard 489). As Rouillard puts it:

> That the play did give satisfaction, at least on the score of thrills provided, is evidenced by a number of admiring sonnets to the author...Hollogne describe[d] the "mille plaisirs" he experienced in reading the play (Rouillard 489).

By dramatizing Osman's tragedy for his audience, Coppée assured them that he would not allow them "to forget to ridicule and condemn as well as shiver and shake" (Rouillard 489). In his prologue to the play, in which he represented the Janissaries as a sinister force, Coppée also told the audience that he trembled at the horrors he contemplated in "ces Turquesques malheurs" and added that:

> In the course of the world from cradle to tomb no more tragic events can be found than will here be seen. The murder of Caesar "n'est rien qu'un baisemain à ceux-ci comparé". (Rouillard, 489).

In the play, which revolved around two sultans, Mustafa and Osman, Coppée—who ironically was killed in 1632 by a "mysterious assassination"—(Rouillard 488) mostly made use of Ottoman history from both *Le mercure françois* and an account from *Lettres du père Pacifique de Provin[s]*, who was an eye-witness to some of the incidents (Rouillard 493). While le père Pacifique's own prayer was that "France may profit by these woes 'de nos voisins' and remain faithful to her Prince" (Rouillard 487) he provided the readers with the exact titles and roles of important civil and military officers in the Ottoman Empire. The local colour that Coppée created on stage through the title roles Selictar (*Silahtar*) Aga, Kissilar (*Kizlar*) Aga, Capi (*Kapi*) Aga, Janissary (*Yenicheri*) Aga, the Boustangis (*Bostancis*) Ussin Bacha (Huseyin Pasha) were also derived from the same source.

In France, another retelling of Osman-Mustafa story in dramatic form took place in 1647 when the tragic event of the Ottoman regicide provided the plot for Tristan l'Hermite's *Osman*. For Rouillard, Tristan's play indicates no borrowings or even knowledge of Coppée's earlier work. In his view *Osman* is "certainly the finest of all the tragedies based on Turkish history that were written before 1660" (Roullaird 496). Based on Rouillard's summary of Tristan's play it seems that the French dramatist made a good use of Ottoman history. The play revealed with great success Osman's bitterness over the ominous power of the Janissaries despite their lack of courage and discipline and their idleness and greed, which culminated in his death. The Janissaries, who played an important role in Tristan's work, were an inauspicious threat to Osman's power. In the first act of the play:

> Déjà le Janissaire ému par la Cite
> Est contre le Serrail à demy revolté.
> Il ne faut qu'un pretexte à ces âmes cruelles,
> Qui brûlent de désir pour les choses nouvelles... (Quoted from Rouillard 501-502)

Tristan who gave a certain amount of authenticity to *Osman*'s historical and geographical references, set his tragedy at a clearly defined place:

> Le Théâtre est la façade du Palais où Sérail, ou il y a une Porte au milieu qui s'ouvre et se ferme, à costé une fénêtre, ou l'on pourra tirer un rideau, lors qu'Osman recoit les plaintes des Janissaries" (Rouillard 32).

He incorporated into his play the role of "La Fille du Mouphti", Mufti's daughter, an authentic Turkish figure who became "Sultane Reyne" by marrying the sultan. He also made allusions to veils worn by Muslim women and used specific terms such as turban, scimitar, mosque, Divan, the Seven Towers and so on. Gentleman also refered to *Bostandjis* (gardeners) who cared for the garden and grounds of the sultan's palace and rowed his boats (*caiques*) when he wished to enjoy the splendid scenery of the Bosphrous and the Sea of Marmara. Ultimately, twenty-five years prior to the staging of Racine's *Bajazet* (1672), Tristan succeeded in creating a much more genuine Ottoman atmosphere on the French stage.

3.1.5. Conclusion

It is a commonplace that in the Western thought slavery is considered as a lack of power and a lack of freedom. Obviously, the terms "slave" and "slavery" sound most unnatural—to say the least—in modern sensibilities. Yet, in the Ottoman slave system, women in the harem and *kapi kullari* (slaves of the gate) gained great power and riches. Although lack of freedom was the defining quality of slavery, a slave could rise to high status, live in a palace and have personal authority over many slaves. As it was the case with Osman, sultans were even killed if they went too far against the *devshirme*. As Justin McCarthy explains: "The word 'slavery' creates images in most minds of African slavery in the New World. Slavery in the Ottoman ruling class was very different, as was slavery in Islam in general. The *devshirme* were slaves who could rise to become leaders of the empire, even to the highest position below the sultan, the Grand Vezir. So with the disadvantages of their slave status came real power, often great wealth, and a comfortable life" (McCarthy 110). Similarly, the Janissaries, which formed the main part of the salaried standing army, were somewhat similar to the feudal levies of Europe. However, though the Sultan called the Janissaries, "my sweet lambs" to their face, he knew that they could turn into "ravenous wolves" (Mansel 24).

By the time Osman II was enthroned in 1618, the unsurpassed Ottoman power and prestige was in jeopardy with the Janissaries being both the cause and symptom of crisis. While the Ottoman Empire survived its internal difficulties including violent factionalism within the ruling class, a break from the Ottoman conquests was quite a relief for the English King who had plainly worried about Osman II's attacks in the Ukraine and in Poland. The reign of James I shared the atmosphere of plot and treachery, which had surrounded the Elizabethan era. Unlike James I, who had survived the "Gunpowder Plot", a scheme to blow up James with all his chief ministers and subjects in the Houses of Parliament, Osman II had fallen victim to the Janissaries. He shared a fate of regicide with Mary, Queen of Scots who, upon the order of Queen Elizabeth, had received the stroke of death from the hand of the headsman. As for Osman, the sixteenth sultan of the Ottomans, "being young and strong he had put up a good fight" (Kinross 294) before the news of his death reached the mother of Mustafa, who was behind this regicide. Ultimately, what she aspired to was to achieve the title of *valide* sultan (Mother Queen), which would give her unprecedented power in the empire.

In the general populace of the Ottoman Empire, the distribution of power in the family was based on a generational divide in which juniors were subordinated both to their male and female elders. Such generational distinction through which matriarchal elders could enjoy the respect of and authority over males, mirrored the dynastic structure of the Ottoman imperial life in which senior women of the dynastic family were known to exercise an extraordinary degree of power and political effectiveness (Peirce vii). As Paolo Contarini, the Venetian ambassador to the Ottoman court during Murat III's reign (1574-1595) indicated, "all good and bad came from the queen mother" (Peirce vii) who had the power to create and manipulate domestic political factions, to negotiate with foreign monarchies and to act as regent for her son.

As the rise to power of the imperial harem revealed the political influence and public prominence of the dynastic women, the "sultanate of women" (*kadinlar saltanati*) began with the reign of Suleyman II (1520-1566) and ended with the death of Sultan Valide Turkhan in 1687, mother of Mehmet IV. While women in the sixteenth and seventeenth centuries played a central role in the "public culture of sovereignty", (Peirce vii) female power was inextricably linked to the changing "configurations of status and authority" (Peirce viii). Although the supreme political authority in the legal and constitutional sense was ultimately patriarchal (power being hereditary through sons only), women played key roles in functions of sovereignty as revealed in the figure of Kosem Sultan. Although Suleyman II's wife Hurrem (Roxelana) was the woman of the Ottoman dynasty best known in Europe, it was Kosem, the wife (*haseki*) of Sultan Ahmet I—Osman II's father—who was remembered as the most powerful woman in Ottoman history. Unlike Hurrem, whose main influence stemmed from being a *haseki* or the mother of sultan's children, Kosem's power emanated from being the mother of the reigning sultan(s), a position that she held for twenty-eight years (1623-1651). This period covered not only the reigns of her sons Murat IV and Ibrahim, but also the early years of her Grandson Mehmet IV (1648-1687).

In sum: Osman, one of the elder brothers of Murad IV, was assassinated mainly for his efforts in the state to put political reforms into effect. If implemented, Osman's reforms would have struck at the heart of the government system that had come to control the Ottoman state since the time of Mehmet II. While his plans for putting "a new Turkish Empire into effect" (McCarthy 176) meant taking a stand against the power of the *devsirme* and women in the harem. However, the radical plans of the Ottoman sultan cost him his life, as effectively captured on the European stage.

3.2. Sultan Murad IV (1623-1640)

> *[A]n occurrence that took place in the seraglio not more than thirty years ago. The Compte de Cezy was then the ambassador at Constantinople. He was apprised of all the details of the death of Bajazet; and there are numerous persons at Court who remember having heard him relate them when he returned to France. The Chevalier Nantouillet is one of this number. And it is to him that I owe this story and the project that I undertook of composing a tragedy out of it.*
>
> (*Complete Plays of Racine, 2* and *3*)

Upon Osman's death in 1622, his uncle, Mustafa, was put on the throne. A year later, when Murad (at the age of twelve), was quietly substituted for Mustafa, he became for some time the mouthpiece of his mother Kosem, who held the real power with energy and ability. Many years were to pass before Murad—one of Osman's younger brothers—was old enough to take the reins of authority and to produce great internal reforms in the empire. Murad, soon, grew to be a vigorous and ruthless ruler ready to combat the violence of his rebelling army and civil confederates. As his contemporary Evliya Chelebi described him: "Never was there a modern prince so athletic, so well-made, so despotic, so much feared by his enemies and so dignified" (Kinross 302). If Louis XIV's motto "L'état, 'c'est moi" was an expression of his own self-willed absolute authority, Murad IV's cruelties and tyrannies to rescue his empire from anarchy and division were legendary within and without the Ottoman state.

In *Bajazet*, Racine puts an imaginary site before his king, distancing it culturally and spatially from the French court. His play carries a set of images not only from Murad IV's court located in the Imperial Capital Istanbul, but his *seraglio*. In the play, Amurath, the absent sultan, who is far from "Byzance" (Istanbul) warring against "Babylonia" (Baghdad), is an off-stage representation of Murad IV. In a corpus of plays written about the Ottomans, dramatists use different techniques for creating/representing the Other. In all of the plays, however, the Ottomans are homogenized into a collective *they*, which, usually is distilled even further to the "iconic *he*"—the Sultan (and in some cases *she*, the Sultana). Anything that the cultural Other does is depicted as "an instance of a pregiven custom or trait" (Brown 662) marked by instances of superiority and inferiority. Thus, in a given natural order of cultural difference, the characteristics of the Ottomans are represented through a system that incorporates discourses of domination. Racine's ultimate concern that governs his dominant discourse in *Bajazet* is not intended to create a process of difference so that he can mark off the Ottoman Turk as different, thereby inferior. Although the subject of Ottoman fratricide that he deals with in the play can readily come to be identified as deviant and cruel, Racine's major concern in *Bajazet* is his claim to power and authority. By focusing on multiple sources of cultural energy such as desire, kinship, authority, as Racine turns the stage into a space of difference, he represents and debates power and resistance in terms of dominance and surveillance in the sultan's palace and his harem.

This fictional spatial world into which Racine allows Acomat, the Grand *Vezir*, free admission while the sultan is away warring, is the world of the Ottoman East projecting fantasies of a dark, threatening Otherness. Ultimately, Racine's references to the Ottoman political and social institutions, which sustain poetic imagery and provide the play's Oriental context, bear witness to the picturesque appropriations of Otherness. The exotic fantasies revealed in the play provide "mise en scène of a cultural appropriation of the spectacular aspects" (Greenberg 75) of Otherness. The exterior extravagance of the bejewelled and enturbaned exotic costumes, onomastics and bits of local colour are all external to the psychology of the characters and the conflicts of the action. Just like Antoine Galland whose *Mille et une nuits* (1707-14) weaves an endless series of tantalizing events, loves, deaths, voyages and magical transformations, Racine as a Western writer is a voyeur from a distance. Ultimately, he aspires to unveil the Ottoman sultan's harem by emphasizing on two excesses (love and power) which lead to death.[80]

On 5th January 1672, following its highly successful first performance at the Hôtel de Bourgogne, Racine's *Bajazet*[81] received "royal approbation from Versaille"[82] (McGowan 11). Performed in "superb Turkish costume" with La Champmeslé playing the part of Atalide, Champmeslé that of Bajazet and Mlle d'Ennebaut as Roxane, the play became so successful that Corneille's supporters had difficulty hiding "their fury at Racine's accomplishment"

---

80 For a discussion of the conjunction of these excesses see Allen Wood, "Murder in the Seraglio: Orientalism in seventeenth century tragedy" in *Papers on French 17th Century Literature,* 1979-80, pp. 91-107.

81 Racine's *Bajazet* was first translated into Turkish by Ahmet Resit Bey in 1934 during the Turkish Enlightenment Period following Ataturk's foundation of the Republic of Turkey. A second translation of the play by Resat Nuri Darago was published in 1946 by the Turkish Ministry of Education.

(McGowan 11). Although Mme de Sévigné, immediately after seeing the play, received it enthusiastically, she later joined the devotees of Corneille in challenging Racine of "fausse turquerie"—that is for not making "Bajazet sufficiently Turkish" (Knight 28). Like Mme de Sévigné, whose opinions of *Bajazet* fluctuated from admiration to harsh criticism of the "frenchified Turks" and the "bloodbath" which ended the play (McGowan 12), other critics set out to disprove Racine's claim to historical truth. Barbier d'Aucour and Donneau de Vise in *Le mercure galant*, a journal set up in 1672, for example, began to transmit to their readers a formidable amount of accumulated evidence to prove Racine's "facts" wrong. In fact, *Bajazet*'s success was mainly due to the topicality of the theme rather than to its novelty. The audiences were familiar with the Ottoman affairs through weekly newspapers like *Le mercure de France* and *Gazette* by Robinet, which attentively recorded events from the Ottoman Court, ranking "second to Versailles as far as public interest in its affairs [was] concerned". (McGowan 19). In addition to topical news and political history, what kept the Ottomans and their affairs in the forefront of French minds, ultimately, was the curiosity of the spectators to see the exotic Other that had established a long tradition of Orientalism on the French stage through works such as Mainfray's *La Rhodeiene* (1621), Mairet's *Le grand et dernier Solyman* (1635), Dalibray's *Le Solyman* (1637), George Scudery's *Ibrahim* (1643), Desmares' *Roxalane* (1643), Le Vayer de Boutigny's *Le grand Selim* (1645), Tristan L'Hermite's *Osman* (1647) and Jacquelin's *Le Soliman* (1653).

3.2.1. Bajazet (1672)

In 1672 when Jean Racine set his gaze towards the *seraglio*, the fictional world that he created on stage was different from the chambers and anterooms characteristic of his plays. Unlike his

---

82 On 22 January 1672 a special performance was given at Versailles as part of the celebrations of the wedding of Monsieur with Elizabeth-Charlotte of the Palatinate.

other tragedies, which were based on earlier historical, biblical or dramatic texts, Racine's plot in *Bajazet*, revolved around a contemporary subject. As Racine claimed, "the subject of this tragedy [was] not yet to be found in any printed history" yet "nonetheless very true". In his first preface to his tragedy, Racine included oral testimonials and affirmations to his story. Thus, apart from M. de la Haye, the current ambassador to the imperial capital, various dignitaries attested to the "truth" of Racine's researched data just like the collection of statements in the *Turkish Secretary (1688)*[83] which included the following: "We have examined the History of Gulbeyaz and her lover... We give it our Approbation" (Quoted from Yeazell 261). As most of these highly regarded disclosures were "charmingly evasive" (Yeazell 261), they served to undermine the historical authority of Racine's dramatic venture.

Yeazell argues in her *Harems of the Mind* that the "greatest fantasists of the harem" draw attention to the "imaginary status of their creations" (Yeazell 8). In *Bajazet*, however, Racine reveals a rather paradoxical position. In writing a tragedy set in the harem and anchored on an eye-witness report, Racine announces that this is "a very true story" from Istanbul. Ironically, though, the basis for the verisimilitude of Racine's *Bajazet*, is ultimately a discursive artifice. In insisting on the authenticity or rather the "truth" of his subject matter, Racine asserts that:

> The main thing that I was concerned with was not to alter anything in the manners and customs of the nation. And I have taken great care to put forward nothing, which does not conform to the history of the Turks and to the new History of the Present State of the Ottoman Empire translated from the English (Solomon 3).

In *Bajazet*, regardless of how the events progress, Acomat, the Grand *Vezir*, plans a terrible surprise for Amurath, as the sultan's brother, "Bajazet/To-day will mount on the throne, with him Roxane" (I.I.94-95). Since Murad IV has a Grand *Vezir* named Ha-

83 *Turkish Secretary*, J.B., Joseph Hindmarsh and Randal Taylor, London, 1688, is a summary of information and fables about the Topkapi Palace with a list of dates and signatures of various people in Istanbul claiming to the "truth" of a set of Testimonials.

fiz Ahmet Pasa it is possible that Racine has named his fictional character Acomat after Ahmet. Yet, unlike Racine's Acomat, who plots against Amurath while the latter is away warring, Hafiz Ahmet Pasa, known to be responsible for administering all affairs of the state—domestic and foreign- including diplomatic affairs, was Murad's brother-in-law, to whom the sultan was especially attached. In fact, in 1632 during a revolt when the Janissaries tore the Grand Vizier Hafiz Ahmet to pieces, Murad was not only moved to tears by his death, but he declared that the mob would suffer a terrible vengeance. From the first moment of his reign Murad faced conflict with the Janissaries who were a serious threat to the Empire. Fearing the fate of his eighteen-year old brother Sultan Osman whom the Janissaries brutally murdered in 1622, Murad's resolution from henceforth was a policy of either "kill or be killed" (Kinross 303).

In *Bajazet*, despite Acomat's plans to kill Amurath, the state of affairs the moment the action ends presents a different scenario. Before Acomat has a chance to flee in the galley, which he has prepared beforehand, Roxane utters her famous line "sortez" to Bajazet and he walks out of the main room to be strangled by the mutes. As for Roxane, she is assassinated by Orcan carrying the orders of Amurath, who like the King of Pontus in *Mithridate* and Thesis in *Phèdre* is an absent ruler and acts like a *deus ex machina*. Like the gods who destroy both the guilty Phaedre and innocent Hippolytus, in *Bajazet*, through cruel fate or rather through fatal order that Amurat's brother and Roxane, a favourite of the sultan, are executed. Ultimately, though, it is Amurath—portrayed simultaneously as absent on the stage yet present in the text—who is effective in the execution of Bajazet and Roxane.

In *Bajazet*, Racine, by focusing on multiple sources of cultural energy such as desire, kinship and the politics of authority, turns the stage into a space of difference to represent and debate power and resistance in terms of dominance and surveillance in Murad IV's palace. In the play, although Murad's brother Bajazet, chooses death rather than the opprobrium of marrying Roxane

(II.III.631-2), nevertheless, with Amurath in power, there is no escape from death for the fraternal heir, who poses a political threat to the sovereign. In the Ottoman dynastic system, collateral lines are eliminated not only to avoid a direct challenge to the authority of the sultan during his lifetime, but also as a means of protecting his children from the sovereign's siblings. Thus, Bajazet is destined to be a victim of fratricide, an act defined by Naima, an Ottoman historian, as of "tyrannical cruelty ... an unjustifiable martyrdom" which showed "no mercy towards the blameless prince" (Naima, 2:187). Although Racine chose to demonstrate on stage the horror of fratricide from a historical perspective, Bayezid had already been killed three years prior to Murad IV's Baghdad campaign. Thus, technically speaking, it is another brother of the Sultan, Prince Kasim, who merits representation in Racine's tragedy.

As the state of affairs at the beginning of the action reveals, Racine in dramatizing "a very true story" from the Ottoman capital, ignores the historical time frame. Instead, the enunciating conditions of the dramatic action are achieved in a mythical time. In reality, by the time Murad made his second Asiatic campaign in 1638 to recover the city of Baghdad, to which Racine refers as Babylonia, Bayezid's news of death had since long drowned amidst the triumphal cheers of the populace celebrating Murad's victory in Revan (Erivan) in 1635. That is to say, three years before Murad IV made his campaign to Baghdad, he had already given his discreet orders to strangle not one but two of his brothers—Bayezid and Suleyman. The timing of his victorious entry to the imperial city was planned in order to divert attention from the execution of these two princes. In 1638 the new celebrations for the reconquest of Baghdad—depicted in the play—were to mask the death of another brother, Prince Kasim. Despite Racine's powerful staging of an historical fratricide in *Bajazet*, "the enunciation conditions" (Pavis 4) of his text are "fictional"—that is to say not only the "space and time of the dramatic discourse are those of a fiction" but also the temporal indicators of dramatic events in the play do not correspond to actual chronicled incidents. Although the entire spatial-temporal construct that functions within a text is the prerogative of its author, it is Racine's own insistence on the verisimilitude and historical precision of *Bajazet* that makes the reader aware of the historical moment.

From the beginning of the action, Amurath is presented as commanding the army in the act of besieging Babylon. Meanwhile he has prevailed over both his principal rivals, Bajazet and Ibrahim, though the latter is not a major threat because of his mental deficiencies. Although one solution to Amurath's predicament is to eliminate Bajazet, a formidable opponent, the assassination has to be delayed until the sultan establishes himself with the army. Because of his own fear of the Janissaries the sultan must secure their allegiance before he attempts to eliminate the fraternal heir (I.69-74). While the diachronic succession of events in the fictional world of the play ultimately lead the audience/reader to a state of affairs in which the sultan is the only surviving power in the palace, in reality this is not the case. What is missing from Racine's historical data is that it is the mother of the reigning sultan, the Greek-born Kosem, who is the most effective instrument of government. As for Roxane (Ruksan), although Racine designates her to a position of supreme political authority, she has no conception of government other than the model that Amurath has impressed upon her. Roxane, as a slave girl is alien to the royal blood and knows that "the custom of the sultans is not my own" (I.III). She is, however, anxious to subvert the sultan's law by breaking her fidelity to him. Swayed by ambition and desire, which allows her to dominate Bajazet's world, she asks the prince: "Do you realize that I hold supreme sway over your life?" (I.II.I). Ultimately, Racine's tragedy is "but that of power and subjection" (Barthes 100). But if strife for power is the strife for difference, spectacle, fiction, play and harem function all in the same way in their epistemological domains with discourse leading to false knowledge. While characters are captives of a physical as well as a linguistic space, spectators/readers too are forced to divide their faculties and move back and forth to follow "an interregnum of ownership" (Hoffman 106) while Racine claims power and authority over the "facts" inscribed in his work. Racine's devotion to verity, as genuine as his revelation of the absence of any published document on his story, indicates a conflict. In other words, despite his efforts to give specific factual and historical details to render his source more authentic, ultimately what is fundamental to his play is that it is constructed on the basis of "Europe's collective imagination of the harem" (Yeazell 10).

In *Bajazet*, both power as representation and representation as power permeate a veiled world with a desire to master an absence in history. A vezir, a royal prince and a concubine all seek to replace the sovereign. If Roxane, is "raised in the Seraglio" and thus knows "its hidden ways" (IV.7), Racine in trying to discover the exercise of power and the cultural dynamics of desire in the harem, is also trapped in the complex labyrinth of an undiscoverable world. Although his knowledge of the *seraglio* is based on images, myths, talk and gossip, his determination to meander through its dark corridors constitute a constant challenge to his discourse of domination. The non-absolute form of power that he takes hold of in the world of the play, the fiction, the harem, notwithstanding prevails. As a consequence, imagination and fantasy triumph once again on stage surviving the author's absolutist claim to truth in representing a cultural and spatial difference—the harem.

The purpose of this section on Jean Racine's *Bajazet* is not merely to analyze the methods of his construction of the play and his fashioning of difference, but more to elaborate on the dramatized events of his tragedy noting particularly contradictions and absences. Essentially, the task of this analysis is to demonstrate the very incompleteness of Racine's historical data and to fill in those unuttered concepts that constitute the very essence of his tragedy, which he claims to be based on "a very true story" from Istanbul.

3.2.2. Seraglio

In the Western discourse *seraglio* is used as a vague term synonymous with the *harem.* While this is a term coined mainly through Western fantasies of women as "literally being locked up in the harem" (Yeazell 2), seraglio is a derivation of the Latin word *serraglio* "a cage for wild animals" (Penzer 15). Extending around an area of 600 000 square meters on the site of an ancient Byzantine acropolis down to the shores of the Golden Horn and the Marmara, the *saray* menagerie indeed housed wild boars, bears, elephants, giraffes, lions, tigers, gazelles, deer etc. In 1530 two Ambassadors from the Holy Roman Emperor Ferdinand I had even reported seeing ten lions and two tigers in the first court "fettered with golden chains and roaring terribly" (Freely 35). Just like the display of elephants and giraffes in the first court during feasts, this is, as an Ottoman chronicler puts it, a "demonstration of magnificence" (Freely 35). According to Yeazell it was due to linguistic perplexity that the Italian words *sera,* "a bar" and *serrare,* "to lock up" were "mistakenly associated with the Turco Persian" (Yeazell 2) words *sara* and *saray* meaning palace. Whether or not, however, it was by an erroneous etymology mainly arising from women's confinement that the English *seraglio* and the French *serai* came to signify both the *saray* and the women's apartments, it was the Ottoman princes who were literally incarcerated in the Cage *(kafes).*

The total confinement of royal princes in the kafes[84] as a way of protecting them from dynastic fratricide, began during the reign of Mehmet III, who was the last sultan to enjoy a public role as a prince. During the next five reigns spanning from 1603 to 1648—those of Ahmet I, Osman II, Mustafa I, Murad IV and Ibrahim—all male members of the dynasty spent their lives within the *kafes* to come forth only if and when they ascended the throne. Since no son of any of these sultans would reach the traditional age to be sent to provincial governorships, stewards were dis-

---

84 For an elaboration on the *Kafes* (Cage) see *The Harem* (197-200).

patched to oversee the affairs of provinces, which the princes were nevertheless assigned to by formality (Peirce 98). In the Ottoman state, the death without male heir of the three sultans who succeeded Ahmet I was one of the reasons for abandonment of the principle of succession of son to father. When Osman was deposed and executed in 1622 he had left no sons (one died in infancy). The only male members of the dynasty were Osman's five minor brothers. The fact that Mustafa was reinstalled despite his proven incompetence suggests that the statesmen of the time considered it necessary to avoid placing a child on the throne if at all possible. Yet, since Murad IV had perforce ascended the throne at the age of twelve, evidently, in the seventeenth century princes did not have an opportunity to grow to adulthood before being tossed onto the throne, nor were they able to produce heirs who might reach adulthood before their own accession. "In this unstable environment, the political involvement of mothers was the glue that held the dynasty together" (Peirce 101). Yet, in European thought, the notion of despotism incarnate in the harem was inextricably tied with women, depriving them of souls and reducing them to weak beings with no ambition and power. Racine, however, kept Bajazet solely under the captivity of Roxane, who had not yet progressed through the hierarchy of the harem system, he was far from providing authenticity.

Based on the accounts of Jean-Claude Flachat, who held "the distinction of being the first foreigner to see" (Penzer 44) the entire *saray*, a "high wall" (Penzer 48) was built all around the *kafes*, which was inhabited by the sultans' sons, who were next in line to the throne. According to Flachat—a manufacturer who settled in Istanbul for fifteen years (1740-55) and accompanied the Compte de Castelle, the French Ambassador at the Porte during the installation of some mirrors sent by Louis XV to Mahmud I (1730-1754)—the suite of the princes was built "like a long citadel" (Penzer 48). There were no windows on the first floor, though those on the second floor overlooked the Sea of Marmara and the Bosphorous, which Racine cited as the "Black Sea Channel".

Carefully guarded by eunuchs both within and without, heirs remained in the *kafes* without ever leaving the building situated in the heart of the harem, almost opposite to the suites of the *valide* sultan. While the *kafes*, "luxuriously built" (Penzer 199) with the most exquisite tiles, had its own beautiful courtyards, baths and gardens that the princes, apart from deaf mutes could enjoy the company of women, the Ottoman heirs to the throne, were treated with utmost severity. Similarly, women, who could accompany these princes in the *kafes*—on condition that they could not bear any children- suffered the fate of the heir—apparents in terms of not having the liberty of ever leaving their confined space.

In Racine's case, what triggered his interest in the harem was Compte de Cezy's eye-witness report on the "seraglio". In both his prefaces, when Racine lavished excessive care to preserve Ottoman habits in an attempt at moral and sociological verisimilitude, elaborating on the sultan's family and including several historical details, he was, however, far from actually deepening the spectator's knowledge of the sultan's palace. Despite his care for precision in portraying an authentic story by not altering "anything in the manners and customs of the nation", he completely omitted the total confinement of the royal princes in the *kafes* even though the Compte de Cezy had informed several people that:

> Several times he even saw Bajazet, who was allowed sometimes to take a walk on the seraglio cape, along the Black Sea Channel. Compte Cezy used to speak of the prince's good looks (Solomon 3).

As impossible as it sounds for an incarcerated prince to take a walk along the Sea of Marmara cleaving its way into the swirling waters of the Bosphorus, Bajazet, as Racine constructed his character, could not be an experienced and dedicated warrior. According to Racine, the prince had gained the admiration of the Janissaries (I.I.117-122) who had already killed Amurath's older brother Osman (II.I.487-92). Since his childhood, Bayezid, however, had been a captive prince in the *kafes* in the inner palace. In other words, when the policy of keeping young princes as a precaution to save their lives from fratricide was established in

1618, Bayezid was only seven years old. As captive princes were totally cut off from outside world, it was not plausible at all for Bayezid to become a soldier let alone have military prowess. Such an assertion infringed upon Racine's claim for verisimilitude.

Despite the fact that the Ottoman sultan's palace[85] was a vast and encompassing site governed by political hierarchies and royal protocol, Racine's intense gaze on the seraglio ruled by the logic of fantasy, pierced through all liminal figures and mediating boundaries, both physical and moral. First of all, the harem, which concealed women from the eyes of the alien men, was a sacred space created for the sultan's presence. When Racine opened his play in "Stamboul" with Amurath away "on Babylon's plains" (I.I.45), Osman and Acomat had already transgressed boundaries and entered "forbidden precincts" (I.I.4). Although the presence of these men in the "seraglio" would be punishable by death, Racine had freely broken "the rigid laws/That guard the harem" (I.I.206-7). Thus Acomat could "have free admittance" (l.203) to an Ottoman sacred precinct and even "look upon Roxane" (l.204), a favourite concubine of the Sultan. Acomat, the Grand Vezir, and his friend Osman, however, had no consanguinity with Roxane and Atalide—the latter a princess of royal blood—who resided in the private quarters of the sultan. Yet, Racine, by creating a fictional world for the stage, guided these men to the

85 Originally, the sultan's palace was referred to as Yeni Saray (New Palace). In 1818 when Mahmut II (1809-39) had a summer place built by the Marmara Sea, the new palace, in its entirety comes to be known as the Topkapi Palace, literally meaning the *Canon Gate.* Topkapi was an old gate that has once stood at the top of Sarayburnu, *the Seraglio Point,* a peninsula that covered the entire royal residence. Surrounded by a high wall called *Sur-i-Sultani* (Imperial Wall) which was fortified with towers, the Topkapi Palace—referred to as the *Saray*—was built in thirteen years (1465-1478). The historical peninsula on which the entire complex was built had seven gates, four of which were on the side facing the Marmara Sea that opens up to the Bosphorous. Since the divisions of all the large buildings were regulated by these gates, the *saray* was also known by the name *Bab-i-Humayun,* the Gate of Majesty or the Sublime Porte, which was the seat of the Ottoman government. The private apartments of the Royal household which incorporated both women and men's residences were beyond the Gate of Felicity called *Bab-i-Saadet.*

"forbidden" women through "a secret passage" (l. 211). Thus, it was Racine's own voyeurism that dispersed the spell and dissipated the mystery of the most private, forbidden quarters of the sultan's palace, which architecturally and politically projected the power of the sovereign.

> With the exception of the sultan, only those who [are] not considered to be fully adult males [are] routinely permitted in the inner worlds of the palace: in the male harem household, boys and young men, eunuchs, dwarves, and mutes; and in the family household, women and children ... he highest officials of the empire—the grand vizier and the leader of the religious hierarchy, the mufti (also known as Sheikh-ul-Islam) might meet personally with the sultan, but only with his permission and in well guarded areas just inside the gate separating the inner third courtyard from the semipublic second courtyard. On the rare occasion when the sultan desire[s] or [is] forced to meet with members of the 'outer' government or ordinary subjects, the audience [is] held outside [the] gate. [Peirce 11]

According to the accounts of a Turkish historian Dursun Beg, the Harem was surrounded by such high walls and was so closely guarded that had the sun not been female—considering that the Persian word for sun (Sems) is female—even she would not be able to enter the Sultan's palace.

> [S]o secret and jealously guarded was the harem and all that happened inside it that nothing of any consequence whatever was definitely known (let alone seen) until after the deposition of Abdulhamid II in 1909. And even since that date, the number of people who have visited any of the closed rooms is mere handful [Penzer 19].

In the inner world of the sultan's palace,[86] which was divided to sections *selamlik*[87] (men's residences) and *haremlik*[88] (women's residences) one's status was marked by the extent to which one

86 There exists a rich corpus of archival documents, both Ottoman and European on the Ottoman sultans' palace. Barnette Miller traces the history of the palace from its foundation to its abandonment as a royal residence. Similarly, reconstructions of the harem by Leslie Peirce and by N.M. Penzer are based on a wide range of primary sources and unpublished archival documents.

87 *Selamlik* signifies the domain of the husband. Since the word selam without the suffix *lik* means 'greeting or 'salutation' this is the one place in the household to receive guests]

88 The suffix *lik* connected to the noun "harem" denotes the portion of any Muslim household allocated to the wife, her children and the servants.

can penetrate the interior of another's household and most of all that of the sultan. The more intimate one's service to the sultan in the inner world, the greater was one's standing in the outer world. In *Bajazet* Racine's desire for proximity to the ultimate source of power coincided not only with the physical absence of the omnipresent sultan, but also without the corps of eunuchs who fiercely guarded the inner palace from the outside world.

> So the fantasy, which appear[s] as the hidden core of ideological reality, itself discloses a paradoxical core: an impossible Real which it reveals and disguises at the same time. At the centre of the fantasy there is a hole: the place of the despot is a vanishing point, evoked and veiled by ... the gaze ... the omnipresent and terrible despotic gaze which nobody can see. (Grosrichard xxi).

What was beyond fantasy was bequeathed with a formidable mysterious power—a power subject to the curiosity of numerous Western authors writing about harem.

3.2.3. Sultana

In the Sultan's palace, which was an authoritative space, a space of power representing a hegemonic imperial ideology, women were excluded from the central ceremonial space designed for the dominant male order. Although the higher the women moved in the ruling hierarchy, the closer they came to the locus of that power and built networks of influence, ultimately they belonged to a private space, the harem, which was a constant "challenge to visual desire" (Yeazell 22). Harem is derived from the Arabic word "haram" meaning that which is unlawful, forbidden. Just like Mecca and Medina, which for centuries had been the forbidden cities that could be entered under the constraints of some prerequisites, the word "harem"[89] in the noun form of "haram" indicated a spatial prohibition. As Peirce puts it:

---

89 Since "harem" is also used in the context of women of a Muslim man, it indicates a sexual prohibition in the sense that these women are forbidden to any men except their husbands. While unmarried women are "free" for their prospective husbands, married women are naturally "haram". Also, just as the women of Muslim men are called "harem", so are the women of the sultans.

> The word *harem* is a term of respect, redolent of religious purity and honor, and evocative of the requisite obeisance. It is gender-specific only in its reference to the women of a family. (Peirce 5)

Despite women's seclusion and protection in a space considered sacred as the word harem also meant "holy", "protected" and finally "sanctuary" (Peirce 5) when it came to distribution of power in the Ottoman dynasty, it did not stem from a simple male/female dichotomy. As Leslie Peirce stresses, gender segregation in the sultan's palace did not prevent "the articulation of hierarchy of status and authority among women, parallel to that which existed among men" (Peirce ix). First of all, the political legitimacy of a women's power was solidified in the usage of the title "sultan" meaning "authority" and "dominion" carried by both males and females of the dynasty. The usage of the ungendered title, which encompassed the entire royal family—male and female—indicated the fact that the Ottoman's notion of sovereign power was "a family prerogative" (Peirce 18). Again, contrary to western discourse, however, in which the Ottoman ruler was always referred to as the "sultan" and his wife as the "sultana"—Westerners' feminized version of the title—in the Ottoman tradition the proper title of the monarch was "padisash" or "hunkar". The Ottoman ruler's formal title consisted of "Sultan" together with "Khan" (i.e. Sultan Murad Khan); such a dual title was an emblem of the Ottomans' dual heritage—Islamic and Central Asian. In formal address, princes and princesses were referred to as "*shehzade* sultan", principal concubines as "*haseki* sultan" and the reigning sultan's mother as "*valide* sultan". While in the male gender the title came before their given name, in the female gender (such as daughters, mothers and concubines) the title followed the given name i.e. Sultan Suleyman versus Hurrem Sultan or Mihrimah Sultan, their daughter. As Peirce notes, the growth and change of the title "sultan" reflected shifts of power among royal women with the erosion of the favourite concubine over the seventeenth century. The title of the "sultan" was replaced by *kadin* or *haseki*, which designated less prominent members of the royal family. Only the mother of the reigning sultan—-though initially a concubine of nonroyal blood—was addressed as *valide* sultan (Mother Queen) as a means of guarding against the dispersion of her matriarchal power within the dynasty. As Peirce points out:

> In the first half of the seventeenth century, when queen mothers frequently acted as regents for their minor or emotionally disturbed sons, virtually the only sultanic prerogative inaccessible to them was personal command of the Ottoman military (Peirce x).

This was the case with Kosem Sultan who as the ultimate power behind Murad IV's throne enjoyed the prestigious and powerful career of the *valide sultan.* Kosem, *haseki* (wife) of Ahmet I, who died at the age of twenty-seven, was brought to public attention when her son Murad IV ascended the throne. In *Bajazet,* Roxane's aspirations for power ultimately mirror the renowned Valide Kosem Sultan. Although the criminal nature of Roxane's passion for Bajazet stems from a desire for supreme authority, critics' views that she has already "inherited the power" of the sultan through the "legitimate and official passing of the scepter " (Romanowski 853) are as preposterous as her own fantasy of marrying Bajazet. In fact, the ultimate threat to Amurath's power came from the fact that despite giving her all that attention, he had not made Roxane any promises of marriage nor was he expected to do so (I.III. 303-4). Although it was the politics of reproduction based on slave concubinage rather than legal marriage that legitimized female power in the palace, the thought of securing that position through the reigning sultan's brother, was a fatal thought, that of a traitress, the consequence of which was death. Furthermore, in the seventeenth century, the principle of succession of son to father had been changed to the automatic succession of the eldest male in the dynasty. Therefore, despite her desperate aspirations, Roxane had no chance of being a Roxelana or a Kosem. Against Ottoman dynastic policies and royal protocol, Racine, however, bestowed upon her the title of sultana, effectively made her participate in the political interregnum and the conspiracy, compete for dominance, plead for bargains to acquire power, practice her authority by sending Bajazet to his death. Ultimately, Roxane was only a foil to the supreme political authority of these historical women, whose superior status as the most important and powerful member of the dynastic family was recorded in history.

In his first preface, Racine was lavish in his particular care and preservation of Ottoman habits and character with a claim to sociological verisimilitude of the harem. In his second preface he expanded on the first by giving a brief history of the sultan's family as well as several historical details. In composing a tragedy about Bajazet based on a story related to him by the Chevalier du Nantouillet, who in turn had heard it from the French Ambassador to the Sublime Porte, Racine emphasized that on his return to France, the Compte de Cezy informed several people of "Bajazet's love and the Sultana's jealousy" (Solomon 3). As Yeazell asserts: "while Racine bases the execution of Bajazet on contemporary reports, the passionate rivalry of his heroines appears to have been his own invention. (Yeazell 173). Indeed, as the psyche of Roxane revealed the status of a typical harem woman, who in her desire for power turned out to be a great schemer selfishly manipulating those around her, she was ultimately a fictional character, not a historical one. As for her rival Atalide (Adalet), sources indicate that in Bajazet's lifetime there was no such historical character of dynastic lineage. (Arikan 8-9). Consequently, Atalide was also a fictional character just like the attendants Fatima (Fatma) and Zara (Zehra) whose names conveyed a rich texture of the "onomastics of Otherness" (Wood 95), central to cultural representations of difference.

Although Racine treated the harem, as "his theatre of jealousy" (Yeazell 172) with the rivalry of Roxane and Atalide driving the action, it was private desire that generated the competition in the play. Meanwhile a historical contextualization of Cezy's reference to the "Sultana's jealousy" clearly pointed to an official position that was jealously guarded by the non-fictional Kosem Sultan. Historically, what contributed to her fame or rather blame was her power to sway the fate of the Ottoman Empire by favouring one son over the other. Furthermore, as a doting mother, she had jealously guarded her sons from the harem favourites mainly to spare herself from the danger of their interference in her effective rule of the empire. Kosem indeed shared with Hurrem her infamous reputation for preserving her own power at the expense of the sultan or the dynasty. As the mother of the sultan, Kosem ruled the empire. In Racine's case, his choice of the name Roxane—a deviation of Roxelana's name—and titles were, of course, manifestations of his authorial power. Apparently during his absence, Amurath had left his favourite concubine in command of the affairs and bestowed upon her the honour of sultana. Such a thought was as fantastical as Acomat's strategy to have Bajazet proclaimed sultan by Roxane:

> ... Whom Amurath chose
> As fairest that array which fill'd
> His court, from Europe and Asia gathered
> In countless numbers, who alone has fixed
> The sultan's heart, they say, whom he has named
> Sultana, though no son she yet has borne him. (I.I.96-101)

What Racine, however, enunciated here was the paradox that after the fifteenth century the mothers of all the Ottoman sultans had been slave concubines rather than Muslim princesses. In other words, Ottoman sultans had neither claim to nor any interest in the purity of a Turkish lineage through marriage with royal women considering that the majority of the Ottoman dynasty, were the offspring of slave women, who constituted the ruling elite. During the foundation of the Ottoman Empire sovereigns married daughters of elite families and noble women of Turkish origins, later on in order to eliminate rivalry with the Turkish tribes, the Ottomans' marriage policies were redesigned and reconstructed.

In the fourteenth and fifteenth centuries, Ottoman rulers and their sons contracted interdynastic marriages with both the Christian powers of Rumelia (Balkan) and Muslim powers of Anatolia (Asia Minor) mainly to maintain the state's military and diplomatic status. In order to strengthen shifting alliances, most marriages were arranged at the conclusion of battles as an emblem of the defeated party's submission and vassal standing. While the royal marriages of the fourteenth century were arranged mainly with Christian women from the Byzantine and Serbian royal houses, in the fifteenth century, marriages were made primarily with Muslim women from principalities in Anatolia, such as Germiyan, Aydin, Saruhan, Jandar, Karaman and Dulkadir. Right before the creation of a centralized empire in 1453, by abolishing all Muslim Anatolian and Christian Rumelian neighbouring dynasties, a final interdynastic marriage was made by Mehmet's father with the daughter of George Brankovitch, King of Serbia. During the late fourteenth and fifteenth centuries, however, with the growth of the Ottoman claim to the status of world-empire, there were no princesses left in the neighbouring countries that could equal the sultan in status. In other words:

> [N]o power was seen as worthy of such an intimate bond with the mighty and august sultanate. It was doubtless this posture of superiority, in conjunction with a growing preference for concubinage that kept Ottomans from contracting marriages with other Muslim dynasties. (Peirce 30).

A widespread belief among European observers (Busbecq 29) attributed the decline or rather the elimination of dynastic marriages to the notion that the Ottoman sultans wished to refrain from repeating the tormenting and degrading experience of Bayezid I and his wife as depicted in Christopher Marlowe's *Tamburlaine.* Yet, the "logic" behind this explanation that "it would have been less an assault on royal dignity for a slave woman than a queen to be mistreated" or rather humiliated is, as Peirce indicates "perhaps more European than Ottoman" (Peirce 38). Another European explanation for the decline of dynastic marriages was based on the Western assumption that it was only in the case of contracting marriages with high-born women that the dowry bestowed by the sultan became the property of the wife. According to Ottavio Bon:

> The reason why the Queens are not now, nor have been of late years, espoused, is, not to dismember the King's patrimony of five hundred thousand chicquins a year. For *Sultan Selim* having allowed so much to the Empress his wife (to the end that she might spend freely and build churches [mosques] and hospitals, so that by all means she might be honoured and esteemed) made a decree that all his successors should do the like, if so they purposed to be married to their Queens. But now the said revenue being otherwise employed, the *Bashaws* do endeavor, as much as in them lies to keep the *Grand Seignor* from marrying ... Howsoever, married or not married, the mother of the heir is by every one called and acknowledged for Queen, and presented with many rich presents from all great personages; and hath continually at her gate, a guard of thirty or forty black eunuchs, together with the *Kizlar Aga* their master, whom she commandeth, and employeth in all her occasions; and so all the other *Sultanas* (Bon 50).

Contrary to the absence of such legal guarantees in Europe as those "afforded by Islamic law to the financial estates of legal wives" (Peirce 38), concubines also had the luxury and the right to accumulate enormous amounts of wealth. In other words, wives who had recognized lineage were feared to have vested interests in their own family affairs that could interfere with their loyalty to the sultan. Thus gradually almost all offspring of the rulers were born of concubines who enjoyed legitimate matriarchal authority—yet solely pertinent to the interest of their son or the broader dynasty and the state as a whole.

Technically speaking, Racine's Roxane, too, was a *potential* mother of a royal offspring who could give her a royal status higher than that of the sultan's own sisters, aunts and other princesses of the dynasty. In fact, the hope of achieving such status was vested in every concubine taken into the harem. This elevated status could provide her with stipends much higher than those who had blood relations to the sultan. In *Bajazet*, Amurath had no fears of Roxane's vested interests in her own family affairs. Roxane might be devoid of lineage but she was not devoid of disloyalty to the sultan, who, in return, had no reason to suspect her betrayal. When her love for Bajazet whom she had never seen, was awakened by Acomat as an alternative that would assure her a privileged place, Roxane was willing to declare him sultan in return for his love (I.II.251, 255-56). Acomat's strategy in suggesting Bajazet as a prize to Roxane was to remind her of the uncertainty of her future should Amurath be defeated. Although Racine did not indicate this, however, the only solution to the predicament of Roxane should anything happen to the sultan on the battlefield was to be sent away to the Old Saray, which housed members of the harem of the dead or deposed sultans. Referred as the 'Palace of Tears' the Old Saray:

> is a very large place, immured with a very high wall, surpassing that of the King's *Seraglio*; the buildings are fair; it hath many inhabitants, all women and eunuchs, and is about three quarters of a mile compass, being seated in the noblest part of the city...the women which are therein, are those which are put out of the King's *Seraglio*, viz. such Sultanas as have belonged to the deceased *Grand Seignors*; those women, likewise, are fallen into disgrace with the King; and such as are infirm, or defective in what should belong to women for the company and bed of a King. (Bon, 117-118).

Contrary to the Western myths of the harem—based on information about a few notorious sultans—as a locus of Muslim promiscuity, family politics was the fundamental force in the harem (Peirce 3). Therefore, very few women of the imperial household could occupy the sultan's bed to achieve the title of sultana. Other than those captured in wars or taken from foreign nations, young women were sent to the sultan's court as gifts from the governors. While numerous harem women were Circassians and Georgians, most were encouraged to enter the harem by their families, as the life in the harem promised to be one of luxury and comfort (Croutier 30). It was possible for these women to rise through the ranks of the harem hierarchy and enjoy security through their power and position. (Croutier 33). Ultimately, the woman whose son became the sultan occupied the top of the hierarchy in the imperial harem, as Queen Mother. Since the harem was an institution to generate a ruling elite, loyal to the sultan and sharing a standard upbringing and customs, women in the harem were educated full time in the court culture before they were promoted to serve the dynastic family. Ultimately, dynastic continuity and procreation took precedence over sexuality in defining the roles in the harem. Therefore, the spacious domain of the royal family shrouded in a veil of secrecy and controlled by the Queen Mother who was followed by royal wives should not be regarded as a sign of promiscuity. Ultimately concubinage was a mechanism established in order to prevent the rise of a hereditary aristocracy that could challenge the legitimacy and continuity of the Ottoman dynasty. As Ottavio Bon, who provides a general description of the palace's architecture and institutional system in *Decrizione del Serraglio del Gransignore*, writes:

> ... Now in the women's lodgings, they live just as nuns so in nunneries ... The King doth not at all frequent, or see, these, unless it be at that instant when they are first presented unto him; or else in case that he desire one of them for his bed-fellow or to make him some pastime with musick and other sports ... And if it so falls out, that any one of them doth conceive him, and bring forth his first begotten child; then she is called by the name of *Sultana* Queen: and if it be a son, she is confirmed and established by great feasts and solemnitie; and forthwith hath a dwelling assigned unto her-a-part, of many stately rooms well furnished; and many servants to attend upon her. The King likewise alloweth her a large revenue, that she may give away, and spend at her pleasure, in whatsoever she may have occasion; and all they of the *Seraglio* must, and do acknowledge her for Queen, shewing all the duty and respect that she may be, both to herself and to them that belong to her.
>
> The other women (howsoever they bring forth issue) are not called queens; yet they are called *Sultanas*, because they had carnal commerce with the King: and she only is called Queen, which is the mother of her first begotten son, heir to the Empire ... Now if it happens that the first begotten son of the Queen, heir to the Empire, should die, and another of the *Sultana* should have a second son; then her son being to succeed the deceased heir, she is immediately made Queen, and the former shall remain a *Sultana* only, and be deprived of the aforesaid revenue and royalty. Thus the title of Queen runneth from one *Sultana* to another, by virtue of the son's succession ... married or not married, the mother of the heir is by everyone called and acknowledged for Queen (Bon 49-51).

In *Bajazet*, which is considered by some to be amongst the most noteworthy of Racine's plays because of its contemporary subject, its tragic scope and its portrayal of characters, the French dramatist manipulates centuries-old political hierarchies and royal protocol. Racine opens up time and place in a "free-play" (Romanowski 850) to examine how different forms of power can emerge in the continuum of absolute authority—hence begins a logic of transgression in the play. Ultimately, not only does Racine transgress and control the physical space but he simultaneously affirms his own authority through discursive and historical configurations. This transgression is intensified through his voyeurism and penetration through the boundaries of the palace courtyards and gates, which incidentally play a central role in the Ottoman system both architecturally and politically. One of the hallmarks of traditional Islamic society—segregation of males and females—as reflected in the sultan's palace is violated. To designate Roxane, as the ruler of the harem and the empire is to break the traditions, which have the force of law in the Ottoman society. Ultimately, though, Racine, like Roxane, who should have never set eyes on Bajazet is ready to take risks in the "Seraglio [which] is a ceremonial and mortal site":

> Rather like an arena in which Roxanne is the matador: she must kill, but under the eyes of an invisible judge who surrounds and watches her; as in the arena, where the bull is doomed and the man risks his life nonetheless, an improvised yet fatal game is played in the Seraglio. In either case the closing and opening of the circle are both norms and acts (Barthes 98).

3.2.4. Exotic Other

In constructing a play to arouse pity and fear to the extent that the "grande tuerie" (Knight 28) startled Mme de Sévigné as Atalide killed herself in front of the eyes of the audience, Racine had chosen a modern subject and relied sparingly on contemporary records. As R.C. Knight observes:

> Just as he avoided French subjects because they would inevitably suggest contemporary references, which would interfere with his selective and concentrated art, so in his treatment of ancient and alien societies he eliminated any details (Knight 28).

Bajazet, however, did not satisfy his critics' aesthetic and personal notions about the Ottoman society. Racine's tragedy, written with such epistemological rigour, had little place and validity for the viewers whose own image of the Other was the point of comparison and source of truth and value. As Said wrote in the opening page of his book: "The Orient was almost a European invention and has been since antiquity a place of romance, exotic beings, haunting memories and landscapes and remarkable experiences" (Said 1). In fact, what contributed to the invention of a vogue of *turquerie* in France was the reception of Suleyman Aga, the Ottoman Ambassador at the French court in 1669. Although the French had heard or read about the exotic beings from descriptions of travelers to the Orient such as the Chevalier d'Arvieux, the "theatricality" of their King's first encounter with an exotic other only "amplified the public's desire for Orientalist exoticism" (Behdad 38).

In the eighteenth century, although employed as an adjective, the term "exotic", according to the *Encylopédie*, referred particularly to foreign, alien flowers and plants (Pucci 146). Essentially, the sensation of exoticism was the notion of the different, the perception of Other. Since there was "a blending of subjectivity and objectivity" found in every form of the exotic, exoticism, the Western vision of the Other possessed a double status (Gilles de Van 79-92). In other words, exoticism which in essence stood as a metaphor of desire (an impetus for the other, an escape, a need to leave home) and a reality (one's own problems and conditions) while mirroring the Self through the perception of the Other, paralleled and complemented one's own internalized feelings. In Racine's case, his desire for the Orient was stimulated by the inaccessibility of the harem, which blocked his vision. Unlike Jean Tavernier, the French traveler to Istanbul in 1678, who began his account of the harem, "only to persuade the reader of the impossibility of really knowing them" (Yeazell 1) for Racine the veil rather than revoking his desire only aroused an urge to overcome the barrier. Because of its most apparent characteristics providing images of Istanbul, *Bajazet* represented the apex of the so-called Oriental tragedy (Wood 97) in French theatre. Yet the play also fulfilled the audience's desire for exoticism through its local colour, which was:

> Une certaine teinte, un aspect général de l'ouvrage qui invite le spectateur à replacer instinctivement les personnages et les événements dans leur milieu: elle permet de recréer ... le lieu géographique de l'action (Martino 200-1).

In Pierre Martino's view since "toutes les tragédies turques parues avant Bajazet étaient sans exotisme vrai... " (Martino 190) exoticism in *Bajazet* thus evoked a dual image of the Orient which was both "contradictory and consistent". This was because *Bajazet* was not only *the* play in the Racinian oeuvre referring to a contemporary historical subject based on an eye-witness report, but it was also his *only* work referred as an Oriental tragedy. Though set in the Holy Land, Racine's *Esther* (1689) and *Athalie* (1691) were regarded as biblical tragedies carrying medieval traditions of the classical forms. However, as Allen Wood points out:

> [T]he Holy Land is Western property, or so the Crusaders aimed to prove, and the Biblical stories had long been the patrimony of Western Christians. There was no need, nor desire, to distinguish characters as being different, Oriental, "other" (Wood 93).

As it was the case with his biblical tragedies, Racine's *Mithridate* (1673) was also a model for "Ancient Orientalism" (Wood 94) as it revolved around the King of Pontus (on the Turkish Black Sea Shore) and was set in the Classical antiquity. Thus it was considered to belong to part of the Western heritage. Beginning with Bounin's *La sultane* (1561) what constituted an Oriental tragedy in seventeenth-century France was the setting in the Ottoman Empire and the use of Oriental titles and character names—*Selim, Ibrahim, Mustapha, Amurath, Beyazid, Achmet and countless others*—and functional names with cultural codes—*sultans, sultanas, viziers, agas, bassas*—whose absolute authority presented "a rich texture of the onomastics of Otherness" (Wood 39). Furthermore, the references to the political and social institutions, which sustained poetic imagery and provided the play's Oriental context, also bore witness to the picturesque appropriations of Otherness. While the exotic fantasies revealed in the plays provided "mise en scene of a cultural appropriation of the spectacular aspects" (Greenberg 75) of Otherness, the exterior extravagance of the bejewelled and enturbaned exotic costumes, onomastics and bits of local colour were all external to the psychology of the characters and the conflicts of the action. Just like

Antoine Galland whose *Mille et une nuits* (1707-14) wove an endless series of tantalizing events, loves, deaths, voyages and magical transformations, Western writers, as voyeurs from a distance ultimately aspired to unveil the sultan's harem by emphasizing the excesses of power and love.

In Racine's case, it was virtually impossible for him to write the harem in its own terms and to portray Self and Other in simple conflicts of good and evil. Similarly, his critics' views, framed by a set of intertextual references primarily to the European representation alterity, mediated their relationship to "reality". What this revealed was a Western interrogation of its own image, discourse and ideology, which compared the oriental scene to an occidental one: if the French image was the model, the Ottoman image was considered its opposite. For example, the critics' declaration of Racine's play as "fausse turquerie" was a discursive strategy, which not only re-validated pre-existing myths about the Ottomans but also revealed prevailing occidental concepts about them. In the process of Orientalizing the Orient, "[t]ruth in short [became] a function of learned judgement, not the material itself, which in time seem[d] to owe even its existence to the Orientalist" (Said 67).

Racine wrote his tragedy about thirty years before Montesquieu's *Lettres persanes,* in which a more genuinely imagined harem figured as an exotic world of sexual and despotic licence. In Montesquieu's epistolary work when Rica arrived in Paris garbed in his native Persian dress with its marked and culturally specific difference, he attracted the attention of the Western onlookers who perceived him as an exotic, "rare object". Each time Rica appeared in his oriental clothes, he was almost flattered by "curiosité qui va jusqu'à l'extravagance" (Montesquieu 82). Yet once he was garbed in Parisian attire, he was stripped of his sudden appeal to the native onlookers in the city. While Rica complained about his loss of a privileged status and insisted that he was still Persian, he was faced with the question exemplifying the European appropriation of the Orient: "mais comment peut-on être persan?"[90] Despite the folly of this question, essentially exoticism as a sensation was based on the notion of the different and on the perception of the Other. It embodied a dual status which symbolized both desire and reality with the former functioning as an impetus for escapism and the latter as a reflection on one's own condition- a kind of introspection per se. Rica through a remarkable experience discovered that as an "exotic being" under scrutiny he had appeared as "a spectacle to the West" (Allen Wood 93)—always "watched": [S]ince its almost (but never quite) offensive behaviour issues out of a reservoir of infinite peculiarity; the European, whose sensibility tours the Orient, is a watcher, never involved, always detached" (Said 103). This reflected the condition of Louis XIV's court's desire for exoticism through the fantastic image of the Turk. Upon gazing at *Bajazet* at Hôtel de Bourgogne with a Western voyeuristic curiosity, if Mme Sévigné asked a similar question ["comment peut-on être ottomane?"] she seemed to have received her answer four years later. In 1676, in a letter that she wrote to her daughter in Aix-en-Provence, Mme de Sévigné was enthusiastic in drawing quite a flattering picture of a Grand Vezir under Sultan Mehmet IV. By making a minute comparison of the Other with the French self, she wrote:

> Je veux vous envoyer par un petit prêtre qui s'en va à Aix, un petit livre que tout le monde a lu et qui m'a diverti; c'est *l'Histoire des vizirs*. Vous y verrez les guerres de Hongrie et de Candie et vous y verrez, en la personne du grand vizir, que vous avez tant entendu louer et qui règne encore présentement, un homme si parfait que je ne vois aucun chrétien qui le surpasse (Chantal 309).

If Mme de Sévigné's frisky comparison of the Ottoman Turk with the French Self revealed the fluid nature of Orientalism as opposed to Said's monolithic[91] views about it, what Racine had

---

90 Two centuries after Montesquieu posed this intriguing question, another French writer Antoine de Saint Exupéry, addressed it in his encounter with another alien, the little prince. Rather than dwelling on an array of visual signifiers vested in a masquerade of differences of being the Other, Exupéry, he passed on a "secret" to his peculiar companion. "Il est tres simple: on ne voit bien qu'avec le coeur. L'essential est invisible pour les yeux" (Exupéry 87).

91 Said posits that the core of essential knowledge about the Orient is "effective

shown through the different and even peculiar "moeurs et coutumes" of its cultural Other was the "excesses of power, love and death" (Wood 98) inherent in the universal "coeur humain" (Adam 378).

As Antoine Adam writes in L'Histoire de la littérature française au XVIIe siècle, in Bajazet, Racine:

> voulait écrire une tragédie turque, mais nous devions plutôt dire qu'il avait décidé d'emprunter son sujet à l'histoire des sultans...parce que le 'coeur humain' fait plus franchement apparaître dans ces pays les excès dont il est capable (Adam 378).

If the characters, motivation and conflicts of the tragic action rested upon the "excesses" which seemed so "Oriental" in *Bajazet*, in fact they were central to "all tragedy of the seventeenth century" not just the so-called "Oriental" tragedy" (Wood 102). First of all, Racine's choice of an Ottoman subject to reveal the absolute power of the sultan was a timely demonstration for the age of Louis XIV, in terms of asserting the Sun King's supremacy. Despite the curiosity and novelty that the French-Ottoman treaty of 1670 aroused in its spectators, this "Oriental" play mirrored Louis XIV's own ambitions to assert his own privileges and to establish his personal rule and to strive to expand France's political and economic power.

In *Bajazet*, a story of power, although Amurath was absent, his rule was nonetheless effective as he held real military and political powers and within a state where he was recognized as absolute master. In a sense, Amurath, who reestablished his rule over the court and his empire, was a dramatic metaphor for Louis XIV, who was the presiding genius of the artistic and literary movement, which had shed much lustre on his reign. Considering his appetite for representations of oriental exoticism, the phantasm of the harem offered the Sun King an image of absolute and unlimited powers unto which he could project his own fantasies

... tested and unchanging" considering that "Orientals for all practical purposes were a Platonic essence, which any Orientalist (or ruler of Orientals) might examine, understand and expose" (Said 38).

and desire to dominate. After all, not only had *Bajazet* allowed Racine to add another loop in the chain of fantastical representations about the harem, but also his projection of Oriental despotism on stage had made the position of his own king as despot transparent.

3.2.5. The Sultaness (1717)

> *The theory of Ottoman government assumed that power resided in the hands of a strong sultan. In the absence of a watchful, powerful sultan, personal power was waiting to be seized, and there were many who wished to do that*
>
> (McCarthy 177).

The Sultaness, an English version of Racine's *Bajazet*, which was performed three times at the Drury Lane, was first presented on 25 February 1717. As Charles Johnson indicated in the Prologue (Spoke by Mr. Wilks) "Tis to the Great Racine he owes this Play ... /... 'tis hoped he'll meet a kinder Fate/Who strives some Standard author to translate/Than they who give you, without once repenting/Long-labour'd nonsense of their own inventing" (*The Sultaness*). Evidently, unlike Johnson's *The Victim* (1714), an adaptation of Racine's *Iphigénie*, in which the English dramatist gave free rein to his own imagination (Wheatley 139-153). *The Sultaness* was a translation of *Bajazet*. According to Dorothea Canfield who compared both plays, Johnson's play projected an accurate notion of its original:

> *The Sultaness*, far more than most Anglicizings of French tragedy in the eighteenth century ... is by no means a bad one ... With all its faults this is on the whole a very fair rendition, and deserves much praise for its fidelity to the construction of the first play (*Corneille and Racine*).

As F.Y. Ecclest argued however, "*The Sultaness* considered as a translation, [was] inadequate" (Ecclest 14). In a detailed comparison of the two plays, Katherine E. Wheatley concludes that although Johnson followed Racine closely, some of the changes that he made in the play demolished its dramatic effects (Wheatley 154-183). To be specific, in the English translation of *Bajazet*, Roxane disclosed to the prince "the Sultan's Orders" with "The

Mutes attend[ing]" (V.IV.60-61). As for Racine, he withheld information about Roxane's preparations for *Bajazet*'s execution. In other words, Racine achieved the climactic moment of the play with Roxane's famous line "sortez" which reflected her pride in her unprecedented power. *Bajazet*'s response to Roxane in the English version was not merely "heroic" as Wheatley suggests. Since Johnson made the prince utter the words "Obey the sultan" (V.IV.63), this was undoubtedly a more realistic approach to *Bajazet*'s imminent death as his fate had already been decided.

No one ever doubts that Racine's play was a fiction despite his claim to follow a rigidly historical point of view. It must be admitted that Racine's deviations from reality, however, were moderate in comparison to other plays within the same literary tradition. In fact, Racine's attempt to give the immediate determination of dynastic succession into the hands of Roxane mirrored Ottoman realities of the sixteenth and seventeenth centuries from the point of view of women's participation in the court intrigue by means of promoting the ascendancy of their own sons. In Johnson's case, although his avoidance of Roxane's terrible order "sortez" took away from the dramatic tension of Racine's scene, he might have been more faithful to *Bajazet*'s hypothetical response to his own situation. While the audience was deprived of Roxane's terrible outburst moments before the deaths of the protagonists, Johnson's mutilation of the tragic plot seems only to be an attempt to portray more faithfully the tragic realities of fratricide. Yet, Bajazet's fate was not solely left to the mercy of the sultan. Since he was under Roxane's commands, which reflected the power of the harem over the court, the prince's fate depended on his compliance to her. In a way, Racine could educate his audience about the arbitrary rule in his own society through an absent sultan and the execution of a young prince achieved through the violent emotions of the sultan's woman. Although Bajazet appealed to Roxane's love in order to save Atalide, it was ultimately Roxane who was in charge as she uttered the one word: "Sortez".

When Johnson wrote his play in 1717, the Grand Vizier Koprulu had effectively eliminated the influence of the harem women over court politics, forcing them to remain in the background. Therefore, in *The Sultaness* Johnson's emphasis on blind obedience to the power of the sovereign could be regarded as a warning to the audience against the possibility of arbitrary rule and the abuse of absolutism even at a time when autocracy was defeated and the parliamentary system had triumphed in England. It served as a safe way of demonstrating discontent with absolutism and arbitrary government, distinguished by the rule of a single person. As Bajazet's words revealed, this was a type of government which required the most pronounced and passive obedience.

It is interesting, however, to compare the historically verifiable events and characters with the universe of discourse in the play—a hypothetical world or rather an abstract system of thought based on certain assumptions. On the one hand, Bajazet's confinement in Amurath's palace governed by the arbitrary power of the sovereign and the blind obedience of the subjects enabled the audience to compare Europe and Asia from both moral and political aspects. On the other hand, Amurath's confrontation with a situation ripe for conspiracy and triggered by the Grand *Vezir* Acomat, who had won the loyalty of the Janissaries, reflected the issue of factionalism which had begun in England in the seventeenth century with the division between the Whigs and the Tories. Despite Queen Anne's preference for the Tories, the election of the Whigs to the House of Commons had allowed a rapid growth in the power and importance of the Cabinet during the reign of George I (1714-1727). And this had led to the emergence of the Whig politician Robert Walpole as "prime minister" to preside over the cabinet of both George I and George II from 1721 to 1742.

In Amurath's case, while he had power over the life and death of his subjects and over the workings of his government, he also had formidable challenges to his sovereignty. Unlike the mythical golden age of Suleyman the Magnificent, in the seventeenth century, the Ottoman Empire was undergoing a period of destabilization. Ottoman writers, in identifying the rapid changes in the Ottoman economic, political and social structures, focused on the withdrawal of the sultan from effective control over public affairs and the deterioration in the *kul* (slave)system.[92] Although Murad undertook a crusade to reinvigorate his empire, his brother Osman was assassinated mainly for his efforts in the state to put political reforms into effect. In theory although the sultans as the most absolute monarchs made the laws, in practice they had constraints. It was the Janissaries (slave soldiers) who had stormed the palace, seized Osman II and taken him to Seven Towers and strangled him after a horrifying assault. If Murad IV's reign was known as a reign of terror, this all stemmed from his urge to crush the tyranny of his military forces, who had developed into a subversive force within the empire and become a threat to the sultan's sovereignty. As Henry Blount wrote in 1636 about the limits of the sultan's absolutism:

> Wherefore he seems as absolute as a Tyrant, as happy as a King; and more establisht then either; yet he hath danger from both parts...This has shewed it selfe in the tumults of the *Janizzaries*, even as deepe as the bloud Royall (Blount 124).

If Osman had become subject to this own "slaves" it was, indeed, the Grand Vezir, holding the power and status of slave elite, who had ordered the assault. As Mansel indicates: "If sultans had grand viziers executed, viziers could also execute back ... In Western Europe, outside royalty's sacred circle, only Richelieu and Mazarin, who enjoyed both the power of a principal minister and the rank of a cardinal (equal to that of prince of the blood), had comparable status" (Mansel 134). Furthermore, owing to a run of feeble and young monarchs, the *valide* sultans exercised power like that of the Queen Mothers such as Catherine de Medici, Marie de Medici and Anne of Austria. Yet, at the apex of the

---

92 For *kul* (slave) system see: Cornell H. Fleischer, Ehud R. Toledana and Bernard Lewis.

official hierarchy stood the sultan's absolute deputy, the Grand *vezir*. Despite profound differences from other Western dynasties, the Ottoman shared with them similar problems such as religious extremism and weak monarchs. It is significant that by the time Racine wrote his tragedy and Johnson translated it for its English audience, the effective centre of the Empire was no longer the sultan's palace, but the palace of the Grand *vezir* at his gate Bab-i-Ali, which gave its name to the Sublime Porte. That is to say, the power of the dominating slave elite was clearly evident through the appearance of one of the ablest ministerial dynasties in the history of Europe—the Koprulu family of Albanian origin, who produced five chief Ottoman ministers that ruled the Empire in a statesmanlike spirit. As Naff indicates, however,

> [T]he dominant position of the grand vizier did not go unchallenged from various quarters, such the 'ayan' (provincial notables), the janissaries, the ulema, the harem or from among his own subordinates. The critical factor for a grand vizier's tenure was whether his power was based on the sultan or one of the aforementioned groups (Naff 94).

In *The Sultaness* as the political vacuum left by the sultan generates into violence and death, Acomat escapes the frenzied palace by sea leaving behind his unfulfilled desires to secure his position as the Grand Vezir. Obviously, the non-absolute form of power that Acomat takes hold of cannot compete with the absolute authority of Amurath. Thus, the moral of the play is that this mode of devious government is preferable to the tyranny of the sultan known to the English as "The Great Turk".

3.2.6. Turk's Head

The English audience was familiar with Murat IV's turbaned head which was displayed on a sign above the coffee-house entrances along with the words: "Morat ye Great Men did mee call". On the reverse side of the sign is a crescent next to the words "Where eare I came I conqver'd all" (Quoted from Matar 1998 115). Aside from theatre, the English encountered political and religious images of the Ottoman Turk—and particularly Murad IV—in the context of the coffee-house. Coffee-drinking was perceived as dangerous by the Puritans, who were alarmed that coffee might lead to apostasy and to Islam. The association of coffee with the publication of "Alcoran" touched on a fear that the secret ingredients of the drink might seduce Christians from their religion. As Matar writes:

> In 1665, an anomymous writer published The Character of a Coffee-House in which he denounced coffee as a product of the Interregnum religious toleration that had spawned the translation of Ross's "Alcoran" (Matar 112).

Ironically, though, if coffee, "Satan's drink" was made from a "sin-inducing" Mahometan berry and formulated with the "Turk's assistance to destroy Christendom" (113), during the reign of Murad IV all coffee-houses and taverns were closed down upon the sultan's orders. While advertisements appeared in London papers about new coffee-houses with Murad's head, the Ottoman sultan had already forbidden smoking and drinking coffee (*kahve*) and wine) on pain of death. Murad IV patrolled the streets by night and executed anyone found with a pipe or coffee. As for England's reaction to coffee in the seventeenth century, it obviously stemmed from a puritanical thought aimed at warning the Englishmen against drinking the "infidel berry" (Matar 113). The opposition to coffee was based on a conviction that this seductive drink conquered "both the Christian soul and Christian body" (ibid). Such fear was augmented by the crest of a grotesque Turk's head installed at the coffee-houses. Moreover, coffee in the English mind acquired a reputation as an aphrodisiac. This reportedly explained the licentious nature of the Turk. Paradoxically, though, when England denounced the Ottoman/Islamic drink within an ideological framework with Murad IV's head erected above the entrances of these places of leisure, the sultan was long gone. Although the Ottoman Sultan himself had already denounced coffee and ordered the closure of all coffee-houses throughout his own Empire long before the desire for the exotic surfaced in England, the anxiety for things Ottoman was, however, still alive. The link between coffee-drinking and apostasy/obscenity was as significant as the ramifications of Murad's Head installed at the coffee-houses as a symbol of a dangerous adversary. As Matar indicates, in the seventeenth century coffee generated a wide variety of literature. The negative effects of "the abominable liquor of the Infidels" (Matar 118) were blamed on Islam.

Johnson wrote his play in 1717, a time (especially for Habsburgs) of glorious campaigning against the Ottoman Empire. The Ottomans had already signed the Treaty of Karlowitz (1699). This marked the end of an era in the history of the Ottoman Empire. That is to say, the Ottoman Empire was no longer the expanding power Europe had known and feared for more than three centuries. The Treaty of Karlowitz was mediated by both Holland and England during the time when William Paget was the English Ambassador at the Porte. England also played the role of the mediator for the signing of the Treaty of Pasarowitz (1718) when the Ottomans finally yielded to the Habsburgs all that remained of Hungary, a great part of Serbia including Belgrade, Wallachia and an important part of Bosnia. This gave Charles VI the dominant position in Eastern Europe, which his predecessors had been unable to achieve.

As the power of the West with its rising nation-states began to outstrip the power of the Ottoman Empire, these chronological transformations revealed some changes in the English attitude towards the Ottoman Turks—as evidenced in Johnson's Epilogue, spoken by Mrs. Santlow:

> They'll say, we make our Turk too good a Christian:
> They are not so bad as you believe.
> You talk of virtue, but they virtuous live.
> Even the Seraglio, flocked with Royal Game
> Is not so vile in Practice, as in Fame.
> ...
> That place ... believe me Christians, 'tis most true,
> Is chaster than a Nunnery with you.

Johnson, in writing his "Epilogue" was aware that the European/Christian culture constituted itself on or against the defined

Other. That is to say, Johnson's audience would regard drama as a cultural and religious judgement of the Other and would measure the Turk against Western norms, Christian faith and virtue through a layering of value-judgements. Yet, Johnson's Epilogue hardly yielded itself to a binary model favoured by *Orientalism.* In fact, it deserved much praise as an effort undertaken by the dramatist to change the audience's perceptions regarding loose morality attributed to life in the harem. As much as this change in discourse was epistemologically based, historically this was a time when the Ottoman Empire was unlikely to contemplate further conquests in Europe.

3.2.7. Conclusion

In *Bajazet,* Racine, by distancing the death of an Ottoman prince from the spectator culturally and spatially—as he had done with his Roman and Greek subjects—constructed a superb tragedy which reconciled fratricide with "the decorum of French classicism" (Macgowan 16). In the Ottoman Empire, fratricide was an artifact of dynastic history, which ensured "peace" in the empire. Elimination of a threat to the throne was geared towards avoiding bloody civil wars that would have caused the deaths of many more than a few members of the ruling family. Obviously, from the sense of morality, this practice was to be condemned within and without the Ottoman Empire as revealed in Shakespeare's in *Henry IV, Part II* when Henry V greeted his younger brothers:

> Brothers, you mix your sadness with some fear:
> This is the English, not the Turkish court;
> Not Amurath an Amurath succeeds,
> But Harry Harry. (V.II.46-49)

The English audience was familiar with the archetypal tragedies of fratricide particularly at times when the future of England's throne was at stake. For example, in Sackville and Norton's *Gorboduc*, it was Porrex, the younger son of the king who killed his older brother Ferrex in a rivalry for the crown. Attempts to alter succession and overturn the rule of primogeniture did not merely reflect the anxieties of the Ottomans. The audience, who saw the play as foreign, non-western, Other, regarded it as a commentary on life in the West. Although very few members of the audience would go back to the 1640's, by the time Johnson had translated his work, many of Charles II's and James II's subjects had lived through the English Civil War, the beheading of Charles I, the military interregnum. While they contended with issues such as the succession of the crown, with George I on the throne in 1715, another difficult succession had been faced. By assuming that his audience was subliminally aware of some significant similarities between historical events in the Ottoman Empire and England, Johnson's changes in the translation even underlined some empirical connections between events at home and abroad. If Johnson indicated in the Epilogue that "The Turbant Sway/Is absolute ... they tremble and obey" (*Sultaness* 55) this was a reminder to the audience of its the autocratic system, though long gone by 1717's.

Although autocracy developed in England at about the same time it developed in France, by the eighteenth century the idea of absolutism had begun to lose its credibility and reliability among intellectuals. In the seventeenth century, Locke had established the view that since absolute power was not different than arbitrary power, to live under absolute monarchies was worse than living in a state of nature where humans had, at least, their freedom and were not supposed to submit to the unjust will of another (Locke, *Treatise* II:13:276). The restored Stuarts—Charles II (1660-1685) and his brother James II (1685-1688)—were at heart no less autocratic than their father and grandfather. In England although autocracy had been attacked by the Puritan Revolution and was destroyed by the "Glorious Revolution" in 1688 and 1689, during the reign of Louis XIV (1643-1715) it was in full action in France. In other words, when Racine wrote Bajazet in 1672, autocracy in France was not held in check. Louis XIV, the Grand Monarch, had taken the government of France into his own hands with a circle of literary men and artists basking in the sunshine of his presence. In this classic age of French literature and art, Racine too could only admire the Sun King's glory, take pride in his power and his court which depended upon the whim of one man.

Racine's great claim in *Bajazet*, was to a moral and sociological verisimilitude, it was precisely for this point that Corneille, Mme de Sévigné and Voltaire most criticized *Bajazet* and accused it of "fausse turquerie". Ironically, Racine's representation of the Ottoman Empire was internally consistent with the culture, ideology, epistemology and chronological time that produced it. This consistency was not only inherent in his tragedy, which allowed him to authenticate his ideological and textual strategies through the fictional discourses about the harem, but it also reflected the spectators. When Racine's viewers most severely criticized *Bajazet* by accusing it of "fausse turquerie", this criticism was rooted in their preconceptions about what it was to be an Ottoman. Evidently, the basis for the verisimilitude of Racine's play was not "reality" but an "eye-witness" report and the existing Orientalist discourse contained in a body of previous texts. Yet since any objection to Racine's representation of the Ottomans was based on false images and false knowledge, ironically they were twice removed from their origins and truth.

In sum: as it is the case with Racine's *Bajazet*, in plays representing the Ottomans, spatial and cultural configurations of the sultan's palace distance it in order to compensate for their intended historical/cultural proximity. As such, the relational and structural character of distancing not only places cultural and spatial difference *beyond* and *outside* the Western Self, but alienates it from the subordinate Other. Ultimately, cultural difference readily becomes a discursive system of judgement and coercion. That is "through talk, tales, stories, gossip, anecdotes, messages, pronouncements, news accounts...and the like definitions are presented and feelings are expressed...and a sense of group position is set" (Blumer 202-203). Such discourse on cultural differences within and between societies and civilizations manifests itself in recorded history. Yet, in order to justify for ideological domination and moral hierarchies, cultural differences are turned into "absolute natural oppositions" (Brown 660). Though writers might differ in their degree of setting the nature and boundaries of such oppositions, ultimately as much as difference becomes a "political deviance" (Brown 661) cultural representation becomes ideological authority.

3.3. Sultan Ibrahim (1640-1648)

I that of Ott'man blood remain alone,
Call'd from a Prison, to ascend a Throne.
My easy mind I bend to soft Delights.
Hate'ing th'unpleasant thoughts of Naval Fights.
Till Mad with Wanton Loves, I fall at first
Slave to my owne, then to my people's lust.

The Historie, 2:49

In 1679 Sir Thomas Browne wrote to his son Dr. Edward Browne that:

> Your sister Betty hath read unto me Mr. Ricauts historie of the last 3 Turkish emperours, Morat or Amurath the fourth, Ibrahim and Mahomet the fourth. It is a very good historie and a good addition unto Knolls his Turkish historie, wch will then make one of the best histories that we have in English (Keynes 166).[93]

Rycaut's *Continuation of the History* was not the only book that Elizabeth Littleton had recommended her father to read. As Berna Moran indicates, apart from other history books concerned with the Ottoman Empire, his daughter had also read Browne "all the Travells of Taverniere" and "all Sands his Travells" (Moran 1952, 380).

As Rycaut's books indicated, following the death of Osman II and Murat IV, the sole heir in male descent of the Ottoman dynasty was Ahmet I's son Ibrahim. Raised exclusively in the *saray*, in virtual imprisonment, Ibrahim (known to history as "Ibrahim

---

93 Browne writes about Rycaut's book in four other letters. See *The Works of Sir Thomas Browne* (Keynes 160, 169 and 170).

the Mad") with his trivial yet excessive desires had inherited none of his father's virtues. While Ahmet I's other sons Osman and Murat had no male children to survive them, it was not possible to persuade their uncle Mustafa (who was installed twice on the throne) to produce an heir. Therefore, the Ottoman House thrived when Ibrahim produced seven children, three of whom (Mehmet IV (1648-1687), Suleyman II (1687-1691 and Ahmet II (1691-1695) ruled the empire almost until the end of seventeenth century.

In *The History of the Turkes*, which elaborates at great length how the sultan was "swallowed in sensuality ... luxurious and wanton actions", (History 2:58) Ibrahim is referred to as the "Twelfth Emperor of the Turkes". The seventeenth-century English theatre-goers, however, knew him as the "Thirteenth Emperor of the Turks", thanks to Mary Pix, the author of a play about Ibrahim. Pix "beg[ged] pardon for the mistake in her "Preface" to the play in which the erotic life of Ibrahim became an intriguing spectacle. Going into a great detail about her source, Pix explained:

> I read some years ago, at a Relations House in the Country, Sir Paul Ricaut's Continuation of the Turkish History; I was pleas'd with the story and ventur'd to write upon it, but trusted too far to my Memory; for I never saw the Book afterwards till the Play was Printed, and then found Ibrahim was the Twelfth Empereour (The Preface).

Pix sought"pardon" from her "Criticks", emphasizing in the Epilogue that "The Author on her weakness, not on her strength relies". The facts, however, are that the twelfth and thirteenth "emperors" of the Ottomans, were Murad III (1574-1595) and Mehmet III (1595-1603) respectively. As for Ibrahim, he was the eighteenth "emperor" of the Ottoman State. Obviously, none of Pix's readers would "Arm on a Defenceless Foe" (Epilogue) considering that even major historians were prone to make historical gaffes. And in Pix's case, her error was indeed insignificant.

3.3.1. "Ott'man Blood"

From its foundation in 1299 as a small principality to its crumbling end in 1922, thirty-six sovereigns ruled the Ottoman sultanate. In the wide span of its rule, as the House of Osman emerged from the founding family of Osman, the Ottoman sultans projected numerous images of sovereignty. The reign of Ibrahim (whose frivolities such as his craze for scents, furs and women, did not endear him to his people, his government and his armed forces) corresponded to a period of decline of the Ottoman Empire. Inherent in the various elements of this decline lay the long wars in the seventeenth century and changes in the structure and institutions of the empire. Despite the signs and evidence of decadence within the sultanate, the decline of the empire was, however, neither rapid nor continuous. As the Ottoman State outlived many empires, monarchies, colonial and temporal powers of the Western world, the "seeds of decline", lay mainly in the "weakening of the Sultan's authority, through lack of serious concern with the affairs of the state" (Kinross 279).

If Ibrahim's brother Murad IV was recorded in history as a cruel "tyrant" who confounded to violence, despite his "iron rule" (Kinross, 310), he restored order in the empire and revived naval power. Before he died at the age of twenty-seven, he had made plans for fundamental military reforms. Unlike the period of regeneration during the reign of Murad, a strong-willed sovereign who had shown his military abilities as a commander, under the rule of his successor Ibrahim, the Ottoman Empire relapsed into disorder and destabilization.

While Ibrahim was labeled as "Ibrahim the Mad" because of his eccentric cravings, his son Mehmet IV (1648-1687) was known as "The Mighty Hunter". As Mehmet IV had no aspirations to govern the state, his reign of thirty-nine years was a significant turning point moving the effective centre of the government from the Sultan's palace to the palace of the grand *vezir*. Upon Mehmet's enthronement at the age of seven, the Ottoman throne was torn between the power struggles of his mother Turhan Sultan (of Russian origin) and his grandmother Kosem Sultan, both of whom competed for the position of the *valide sultan*. In turn, this created a partisan spirit and factions among the Janissaries and *sipahis* who played Turhan and Kosem against one another. By the time Mehmet's young mother matured politically and assumed the role of "guardianship and representative of the sultan" (Peirce 252), she willingly relinquished much of the authority from the *valide sultan* to the Grand Vezir Koprulu (of Albanian origin). While this move marked the end of the "sultanate of women", Mehmet himself was content to leave the government of the empire in the hands of the Koprulu family. This way, he could exert himself exclusively on sporting campaigns.

A century after Suleyman the Magnificent's reign, which had marked the zenith of the empire, the Ottomans began to fail disastrously in the very lands where for numerous generations their ancestors had been victorious. During their "reign", as the Koprulu's (father, son, brother) took drastic measures to halt corruption and injustice at any cost, their severe authoritarian government maintained a period of stability. As the Koprulus succeeded, once again, in turning the army into a disciplined force, the empire enjoyed a brief revival. Mehmet IV was to spend much of his life on horseback pursuing the "pleasures of the chase rather than the rigours of war" (Kinross 333). In the spring of 1683 when the Ottomans marched towards the West, Mehmet IV was induced to head the army. Yet, on reaching Belgrade, he decided to transfer its command, with the standard of the Prophet to Kara Mustafa Pasa. Kara Mustafa, then, revealed his intention and determination to march directly on Vienna itself—a decision, which brought the Ottoman Empire its greatest defeat and Christian Europe its long awaited victory.

3.3.2. The Conspiracy (1680)

Following Ibrahim's dethronement for debauchery and cruelty, he was executed in 1648. In Mehmet's case it was the Ottoman defeat at Mohac and the failures on the Austrian front that had led to his deposition in 1687. The failure of the army in the second siege of Vienna in 1683 had once and for all broken the prestige of the Ottomans as a conquering nation in the eyes of the world. In 1686 as Croatia and Buda passed into the hands of Austria and Hungary, this finally provoked a mutiny in the Ottoman army and led to dethronement of the sultan. Unlike his father who was executed with a sanction from the *mufti*, Mehmet IV's punishment in exile was to be banned from his favorite pastime of hunting.

In William Whitaker's *The Conspiracy or Change of Government*, when Mehmet IV is enthroned "in Imperial Robes" amidst the cries of "Love live Sultan Mehmet Han" (IV.I), Formiana, the sultaness who represents *valide* Turhan Sultan, laments:

> I wish they would forbear to crown my Son;
> I fear they raise him but to pluck him down.
> How happy Peasants, in their Children are!
> They're free from greatness, danger and from care:
> So happy, shu'd we be, to live below,
> If, with less pomp, we might more quiet know.
> But to the Gods, myself I must commit.
> I know what's pleasant; they know what is fit. (IV.I)

In *The Conspiracy*, which revolves around the regicide of Sultan Ibrahim (1640-1648) and ends with the simultaneous enthronement and dethronement of his son Mehmet IV (1648-87), the rebels "Crown young Solyman" (V.I). As the chief rebel Bektas puts it, Mehmet's Grand Vezir Kupreli "found the Sultan wanted wit/And always judg'd young Solyman more fit" (V.I). This parallels the sequence of historical events in Mehmet's life since it is the Grand Vezir Koprulu who instigates the deposition of the sultan in 1687.

Whitaker's play was written seven years prior to the dethronement of Mehmet IV. In that sense, it is intriguing to pose a hypothetical question as to kind of response an Ottoman audience would have given upon seeing on English stage representation, which constituted a kind of forewarning that Mehmet "shall be depos'd or slain/And that his Brother Solyman shall Reign"

(V.I). There is, however, historical evidence of Kosem's preemptive attempt to dethrone the child sultan. Following Ibrahim's death when Mehmet's mother became a challenge to Kosem's long-established power in the dynasty, the queen mother plotted to overthrow Mehmet and enthrone Suleyman, Ibrahim's son by another woman. Since Kosem found Suleyman's mother, Dilasub, a more complaisant rival, her idea of switching one child prince for the other was geared directly towards eliminating Turhan, who despite her tender age was quick in assuming her matriarchal role of authority. Yet, Kosem's plans for confiscation failed thanks to Meleki Hatun, a female servant who informed Turhan of the plot (Naima 5:107).

Joseph Trapp's *Abra Mule or Love and Empire* (1704) depicts the dethronement of Mehmet followed by the succession of his younger brother Soliman. In Trapp's play, Mahomet's dethronement through conspiracy is instigated solely for the purpose of fulfilling Soliman's desire for Abra Mule, a Muscovite, who is also loved by both the sultan and his Grand Vezir Phyrrhus. Trapp's source for the love-story woven into the plot of his tragedy is *Abra Mule or the True History of the Dethronement of Mahomet IV. Written in French by M.L. Noble. Made English by J.P. Printed for R. Clavel at the Peacock near St. Dunstan's Church in Fleet Street. 1697* (Moran 81).[94] In *Abra Mule* Trapp follows closely Le Noble's novel in which the purely invented love intrigue leads to Mahomet's deposition. The historical reasons for Mehmet's IV's dethronement, however, were primarily political.

The death or deposition of a sultan was always a time of disruption and crisis in the empire. In that regard, the primary role of the mother of the heir, who was simultaneously transformed into a sovereign, was to facilitate smooth transition. Following Ibrahim's death, while his seven-year-old successor Mehmet required a regent, he was blessed with two, as his grandmother

94 According to Berna Moran the English translator J.P. was John Phillips-1631-1706), who had also translated Mlle Scudery's *Almahide* (1677), Tavernier's *Six Voyages Through Turkey* (1677-8), Grelot's *Voyage to Constantinople* (1683) and *the Turkish Secretary* (1688) (Moran 1958, 81).

Kosem Sultan assumed the role of the "elder" *valide* sultan. Since the child sultan's mother, Turhan, was only about twenty-two years old, Kosem continued to exercise her sultanic authority. Furthermore, she received an honorific title *umm al-mu'minin* (Mother of the Muslim believers), an epithet bestowed upon the wives of the Prophet Muhammed (Naima, 4:318). This esteemed title extended her matriarchal role beyond the *Topkapi Saray* and the entire empire to the Muslim community at large. It was an abiding Ottoman custom that upon the accession of a new sultan, the mother of the old sultan would retire to the *Old Saray* and give up her office. In Kosem's case her reappointment to the duty of training and guardianship of Mehmet was natural.

In *The Conspiracy*, Whitaker faithfully depicts Mehmet as a "Child is yet a harmless thing". However, since "a good Prince may make a Tyrant King" (IV.I) Kiosem will "teach ... young Mahomet ... all the good [she] can" (IV.I). In fact, Bektas rejoices that:

> The Sultan being young, they will think fit
> The Government of all things to commit
> To Kiosem; whose skill in such affairs
> Renders her fit to serve out Turn and theirs;
> Then will the emperor be within our pow'r,
> When she commands and guides the Emperour. (IV.I)

Historically, what awaited Kosem, however, was a great challenge from Mehmet's young mother, Turhan, an emerging regent. In the play, Whitaker depicts the great tension between the two women prior to Mehmet's ascension to the throne. As Formiana blames Kiosem for the death of her husband Ibrahim, she cannot trust her, despite queen mother's invitation of friendship: "Come Daughter, come compose yourself to rest/And let more gentle thoughts possess your breast". When Formiana accuses Kiosem of shedding "Crocodile" tears over the death of Ibrahim, the Queen Mother's response is:

> Distrust, my Child, is the Soul's worst disease,
> A mortal symptom: when we once despair,
> We the true Prophets of our ruins are. (IV.I)

Formiana may be young and inexperienced, but since she is fully aware of the dangers of the position that she is swept into through forces beyond her control, she needs protection from Kiosem.

> Alas, what Amulet can us defend
> From the sad mischiefs, that her prayers attend?
> The Witch prays backward, if she prays at all. (IV.I)

Within the different factions formed around two women, Turhan's principal ally and protector was Suleyman Agha, the Chief Eunuch. As for Kosem, she befriended the ruling elite of the Janissary corps. In *The Conspiracy* Whitaker's factions represent the Ottoman political scene. As opposed to Solyman Aga, the Chief Eunuch, Kuperli, Ipsir and the Mufti, Whitaker clearly identifies the plotters conspiring to kill the sultan and his son:

> Janisar-Aga, and the Vizier
> In secret Counsels are and whisper soft:
> What they design to their own breasts they keep.
> For the Queen mothers, 'tis an old trick. (II.I)

At the beginning of the play, when Bektas, ensures Kiosem that "a Guard of sturdy Mutes" will give Ibrahim's "hated life a quick dispatch" the Queen Mother pleads that "it be gently done/[She] would by no means have 'em hurt [her] Son" (I.I). Later Bektas informs Kiosem:

> The deed is done, tho with difficulty, done:
> We're of our Sultan rid, you of your Son
> The safest way that I could think of since
> T'establish you, is to enthrone the Prince.
> To this Royalists consenting are:
> He shall the Title, you the Office bear. (IV.I)

There is historical evidence to suggest that the grand vezir and the *mufti* had formally appealed to Kosem Sultan to approve and facilitate the overthrow of her son. Although Kosem knew that Ibrahim's continued rule was harmful for the empire, the leading statesmen had to persuade her of the propriety and the legality of the deposition. Kosem, however, pleaded at great length against

Ibrahim's deposition before she gave her assent knowing that the conduct of her unbalanced son could no more be tolerated. Kosem's maternal compassion was obviously so strong that it overrode her own anger and sorrow at Ibrahim's mistreatment of her and her daughters, his disastrous administration and ruination of all the restorative work that his elder brother Murad IV had achieved. As Naima's lengthy and dramatic account of Kosem's dilemma and complex role in her son's deposition reveals, she would have never consented to the execution of her own son. Yet, Mehmet was put on the throne based on the *fetva*[95] that a child who was endowed with reason should rule. A madman should not reign whatever his age.

In *The Conspiracy* when "The City Rages in Rebellious Flame" and "The Commons are encouraged by the Peers" with "Vizier and Bektas head[ing] the Mutiniers" the Mufti declares that he is ready to die for Ibrahim: "I with joyful pride would shed my blood/To save a Prince, so pious and so good" (III.I). Ipsir and Kuperli, loyal friends to Ibrahim lament the "Sultan's Fate" saying that "Princes never, till their ruin, find/The inconvenience of being too kind" (III.I). In other words, Whitaker portrays Ibrahim as a virtuous and illustrious prince who is ill advised and surrounded by traitors. The fatal end that awaits him arises from Ibrahim's kindness: "Unhappy Prince! Thou'st too much innocence...Yet Princes never, till their ruin, find/The inconvenience of being too kind" (III.I). Ibrahim, however, is aware of some of the dangers to his crown through the apprehension of his loyal wife Formiana who tells Ibrahim: "[Y]ou my safety and Glory are/Not to be matched in kindness or in war/And yet I tremble" (I.I). Formiana's supernatural vision of Death in the form of a "grim Skeleton" is not the "Aery nothing" Ibrahim thinks. It beckons Ibrahim to "come" and "seems as if it call's [him] to a Tomb". (I) Ibrahim is indeed surrounded by "Traytor[s] and Hypocrite[s]" (II.I) such as

95 *Fetva* was a written answer to a legal question, issued by *seyhulislam* (head of the hierarchy of the doctors of Muslim canon law, tradition and theology) or by *mufti* (an officially appointed interpreter of the Islamic Law)] (Naima, *Tarih* 4: 303-318).

Oglar, who is enamoured with Formiana: "His Passion for the Queen will make" (I.I) him destroy Ibrahim as he will "venture ten lives for one Sultaness" (III.I) When the rebels reach the outward gate of the palace, Oglar suggests that he put on the Imperial Robe "that lie in a chair" (III.I) so that he can save Ibrahim from the raging crowd: "Taking the seeming Sultan for the true/Their swords shall murder" Oglar instead of Ibrahim. However, this is only a "hellish Plot" (II.I) as his ultimate goal is to enjoy "the sweets of his Sultana's bed" (III.I). Plots against the sultan are bountiful in Whitaker's play. As the crowds outside the Gate are shouting "Alla! Alla!" inside the palace Meleck Hamet, the Grand Vezir, who is a traitor, Bektas, a rebel, Kara and Kulchia, his adherents who have plotted against the sultan all along, now want "His head, his head his head" (III.I). As Flatra, the sultan's sister has already told Melek Ahmet, the Janissaries, Kiosem, the discontented *sipahees* "[a]ll plot the Sultan for different ends (I.I). Melek Ahmet, the grand vezir wants "[t]his day to kill, the next be Empereur" (II.I). Moreover, Melek who is looking for an opportunity to kill the sultan "for a Mistress and a Throne" (II.I) wants Ibrahim's sister as his royal bride. The transgressions in the palace reach such an extent that when all the rebels enter "the Queen's Bed Chamber" she desperately leads them to the sultan, who is in hiding. During the mutiny, while the people who quarrel are divided crying either "Poor Sultan, brave Prince, and the like words of kindness" or "Justice, Justice", Melek Ahmet stabs the sultan declaring that it is "time for [him] to die". Before the Mufti wraps up this scene of mutiny as "the sad effects of discord in a State" (III.I) Ibrahim dies asking Kuperli to avenge his death.

As Kinross writes in *The Ottoman Centuries* when the executioners "laid their hands on him" (317) Ibrahim died invoking the vengeance of heaven against his people for their infidelity. In *The Conspiracy*, although Ibrahim asks Kuperli avenge his death, in reality it was his other loyal friend Ipsir who amassed a huge number of troops in Anatolia and began to defy imperial orders on the grounds of avenging Ibrahim. In the play Kuperli warns

Ipsir ahead of time: "Ah, *Ipsir*! This, this is the Sultan's Fate/And we shall see his fall when 'tis too late" (II.I).

By the time he became *grand vezir* at the age of seventy, Koprulu, who had started his working life as a kitchen boy in the sultan's palace, had already ruled Damascus, Tripoli and Jerusalem. Before he took the *valide sultan*'s offer in 1656, Koprulu, whose family would guide the empire's destiny for half a century, had certain explicit conditions. He had these conditions confirmed with a *fetva* from the *mufti*: that his every act would be ratified without being examined either by young Sultan Mehmet or his mother Turhan. Thus before putting the House of Osman in order and regenerating the state, he had already become more of a regent than a *vezir*.

In *The Conspiracy*, when the Grand V*ezir* Melek Ahmet is alone on stage "with a bloody dagger" following his stabbing of Ibrahim, he is full of repentance:

> How could I hope the Sultan to succeed?
> His children claim that right
> ...
> Yet silly I, by senseless Passion led,
> Could hope to be the Turkish Empire's head.
> O Flatra! Thou hast fed this foolish flame.
> And thou must share the mischief and the blame. (III.I)

Whitaker portrays Flatra, the sister of Ibrahim, as one of the collaborators in the many plots organized against Ibrahim. When she prepares for a "Royal Nuptial" (III.I) with the Grand Vezir Melek Ahmet, her desire to be the wife of the highest military/administrative official of the empire is within the decorum of the Ottoman policy. As for her "Ambition" for the Grand Vezir to be "crown'd", Vezir Melek Ahmet, who repents his murder of the sultan will put an end to her "Ambition". He stabs Flatra saying that: "Cause you love Honor and a Crown so well/I do intend you shall go Reign in Hell" (III.I).

While sultans' daughters and sisters acquired and exercised power through kinship and marriage, as an assault on palace protocol, Ibrahim subjected his sisters Fatma, Ayse, Hanzade and her niece Kaya (daughter of Murad IV) to indignity. He made the princesses serve his concubines and made them attend like servants over meals, fetching the soap and pitcher to pour water for the women to wash their hands, etc. (Naima 4:317). Moreover, he took away the princesses' lands and jewels to distribute to his harem. Following his death, however, Princess Ayse was married to Ipsir, whom Mehmet's mother Turhan had appointed as grand *vezir*—thus making him an imperial *damad,* the royal son-in-law.

Since the reign of Mehmet the Conquerer, it was a norm in the House of Osman for the statesmen of *vezirial* rank to marry the sisters and daughters of the sultan. As Peirce writes about the pool of *damad* (husband of a princess and son and brother-in-law of the sultan) vezirs:

> Until the mid-fifteenth century or so, princesses had married rulers and princes of neighbouring Muslim states or members of the Ottoman ruling class. They ceased to make interdynastic alliances around the same time that their fathers and brothers did (Peirce 66).

While the significance of *damad*-princess alliances was always marked with lavish weddings and allocations of sumptuous palaces, assigning *damads* to the rank of provincial governors (*sanjakbeyi*) or offering them the status of governor-general (*beylerbeyi*) was common practice. Although this is not the case in *The Conspiracy,* Melek Ahmet had in fact, married Ibrahim's sister Fatma. She was in her late fifties and had previously been married several times. Melek Ahmet, who was in his seventies when he married her, had already acquired an enormous political importance (as governor of the province of Van) and wealth from his previous marriage to Kaya Sultan, daughter of Murat IV. After the death of the princess in child-birth, Melek's devastation and hysterical cries at the funeral created such a scandal that Koprulu soon arranged Melek's marriage to Fatma Sultan. Yet this was a miserable marriage which soon ended with the death of Ahmed Melek. Fatma, contrary to the fictional Flatra survived Melek. In *The Conspiracy* Flatra's words to her mother Kiosem reveal that Ibrahim's sister died yearning for power.

> O, I am dead: and by a subject slain!
> But shall I not have time one hour to reign?
> Yet make him emperor before I go:
> Or if you cannot make him, call him so.
> But fancy must your unkind sloth supply
> For in conceit, I will an Empress dy. (III.I)

Kosem Sultan, who was taken prisoner in the final act of *The Conspiracy*, in 1651, was murdered by Suleyman Aga, the Chief Eunuch, and his followers. Whether or not it was Turhan Sultan who had plotted her mother-in-law's murder, she had definitely sanctioned the undignified death of this widely feared yet equally loved and respected *valide* sultan, who had all along overshadowed her own power and authority. Following Kosem's death, Turhan's subordination to Kosem came to an end, and Mehmet IV's mother ultimately became the sole head of the Imperial Harem.

Upon her death, the enormous wealth of Kosem (like all the other *valide sultans* of the Ottomans) was returned to the empire through institutions and services that they established for the welfare of the public. While the *valide* sultans' roles as endowers of public institutions were inextricably linked to the sovereign power that they exercised, ultimately, as with Kosem, charities were financed from the extensive personal fortune provided to them by the House of Osman. In the late sixteenth, seventeenth and eighteenth centuries, with the exception of Sultan Ahmet I's magnificent mosque bearing his name, all the imperial mosques in Istanbul were built by or for the *valide sultans*. Unlike Turhan Sultan's "New Valide Mosque" (with a complex containing schools, public fountains and markets) which was the first mosque to be built by a woman to join the ranks of imperial mosques, Kosem's mosque complex in Uskudar was comparatively modest. According to Peirce this may be because:

> Murad IV, aggressively dominant in the second half of his reign and the greatest *ghazi* [warrior] sultan after Suleyman I, intended to construct an imperial mosque himself, as his father Ahmed had (Peirce 208).

Other than mosque complexes *valide* sultans founded other charitable structures such as public baths and *hans* (office spaces for merchants, craftsmen and tradesmen). Kosem's "Valide Han" built at the centre of Istanbul was the grandest *han* with its own mosque. Works displaying Kosem's piety and generosity were bountiful- ranging from provision of goods and stipends to orphaned young women who could not marry for lack of dowry, lodgings and furniture to the provision of water to pilgrims to Mecca and Medina.

> Every year in the month of Rejep, Kosem would leave the palace in disguise and personally arrange for the release of imprisoned debtors and other criminals (except murderers) through payment of their debts or recompense for their crimes (Peirce 209).

Thirty years after Kosem's death, when all the mosques and markets in Istanbul were closed for three days in mourning, Edward Ravenscroft wrote his Epilogue for Whitaker's play featuring the most renowned "political mother" in the Ottoman dynasty:

> Fancy you have two hours in Turky been;
> This was not Popish Plot, yet English too,
> For to say truth it was our Plot on you.

3.3.3. Conclusion

Whitaker's *The Conspiracy or Change of Government*, was performed at the Duke's Theatre the same time as Thomas Otway's comedy, *The Soldier's Fortune*. Like Otway's *Venice Preserv'd; or, A Plot Discovered*, which was performed in early 1682, in the wake of during the tumultous political events in England, Whitaker's *Conspiracy*, the title of which indicated its topicality, revolved around plots, conspiracies, violently opposed factions and divisions. *Conspiracy* was written and produced in the wake of the Popish Plot, a Roman Catholic conspiracy fabricated by Titus Oates. In this fictional conspiracy the alleged plan was to assassinate King Charles II in order to bring his brother James, Duke of York, to the throne. Not only did Oates' rumour increase hostility in England towards Roman Catholicism and the Jesuits, but it also led to the election of the Whig parliament at the height of national reaction to the Popish plot and the threat of arbitrary government. The Whig Parliament sought to pass an Act in 1678, excluding Roman Catholics from political life in England in England. By the time Otway wrote his political tragedy,[96] the Exclusion Bill, introduced by the Earl of Shaftsbury to prevent James II from succeeding Charles II, had died. The king dissolved the parliament in 1681, sent Shaftsbury to the Tower and recouped much of the Tory power representing the rights of the established Anglican Church. The prologue to *Venice Preserv'd* reveals the political turbulence of the times arising from the alleged Popish Plot which made the Whigs fear the reinstatement of Roman Catholicism by James as Mary had attempted in the sixteenth century:

> In these distracted times, when each man dreads
> The bloody stratagems of busy heads;
> When we have fear'd three years we know not what,
> Till witnesses begin to die o' th'rot,
> What made our poet meddle with a plot?

While Whitaker depicted in the play the regicide of Sultan Ibrahim (1640-1648), with the absence of a king in *Venice Preserv'd* the conspiracy was against the senators: "Curst be your Senate; curst your Constitution/The curse of growing factions and division/Still vex your councils, sake your public safety" (4.2.156-159). According to Phillip Harth the Venetian conspiracy, "spectacle of a disaffected minority planning to wreak revenge on their countrymen" paralleled "the Popish Plot"(Harth 352). As a Tory, though Otway did not approve of the alleged Popish Plot, at the same time he despised the Whigs and condemned their abuse of the conspiracy. In Whitaker's case, if the Ottoman's Divan represented the English court, his sympathies lay with the sovereign When every hour/A Prince is subject to the Subject's power (I.I). Whitaker had "no interest in representing the folly and madness

---

96 For a discussion of *Venice Preserv'd* as a political tragedy see *British Drama (1660-1779), A Critical History* (Kavenik 56-64).

of the eighteenth "emperor" of the Ottomans, who had put the Ottoman Empire in danger. In fact, as he put it in the Prologue:

> Tho Foreigners and Enemies be,
> Forget not what is due to Majesty.

It is interesting to note that despite the dramatists' comparisons of political events—such as factionalism, military interregnum, conspiracies, successions to the throne, regicides—between England and the Ottoman Empire, ultimately the Turk's Otherness sets the tone of drama's discursive structure. In other words, as the image of the Ottoman as "Foreigner/Enemy" carries its own specific meaning through discourse, representation as source of production of knowledge implicates broader issues of power. As Foucault writes, discourses produce truths and "we cannot exercise power except through the production of truth" (Foucault 1980, 93). For Foucault, the point is not where discourses come from nor what interest they represent, but what "effects of power and knowledge they ensure" and what makes their use necessary (Foucault 1984, 102). Based on Foucault' view, what produces discourses and truths in the seventeenth century stems from resistance to Ottoman's physical power. For Foucault, however, the concept of resistance takes the form of counter-discourses, which produce new knowledge and speak new truths as revealed from the benevolent and rational image of Ibrahim in Whitaker's play. The irony here is, however, the English dramatist picks for his subject, Ibrahim the Mad, an unworthy Ottoman sovereign, who, unlike many of his ancestors, does not merit this incontestable image. Yet again, for Foucault, as discourses located in *episteme* are inextricably linked with power, they represent one part of the multifaceted ideologies of Western theatre.

Chapter 4: Comic Representations of the Ottoman Turk

4.1. "New Beginnings"

> *Comedy is an imitation of an action*
> *that is luducrious and imperfect...*
> *through pleasure and laughter [it]*
> *effect[s] purgation of the ... emotions.*
>
> Aristotle

As Northrop Frye writes in his *Anatomy of Criticism*, "Comedy usually moves toward a happy ending, and the normal response of the audience to a happy ending, is 'this should be'"(Frye 167). While "the bitterest enemies" as Aristotle maintains "exit as friends at the conclusion" of the comedy and "nobody kills anyone else", it culminates in "joy, reconciliation and new beginnings"(Quoted from Nelson 2). One of the tenets of Frye's theory of comedy is that, as a dramatic form, comedy is about the reintegration of society in which the anti-comic character or "the blocking character" as Frye refers to it, can be dealt with by being purged of his ruling passion. This is what Ben Jonson calls a humour, and modern psychologists, a compulsion. In a comedy, the blocking character is ultimately included into the festive society unless he is too rigid to be converted. Otherwise, he is expelled from the final scene. While comic situations produce in the spectators a sense of superiority, there are different levels and techniques for achieving comic resolution.

In the Italian *commedia dell'arte* scenarios revolving around the Ottoman Turks, all the characters ultimately arrive at a happy and blissful ending either by reunion, rescue or liberation from enslavement or through conversion to Christianity. As Dante wrote in the *Divine Comedy*, comedy begins with harshness of some affair but its matter ends happily as it appears in Terence's comedies. Although *commedia* is not a morality play like Everyman or a divine comedy, in the scenarios not only is the Turk celebrated as a Christian, but his/her sudden conversion on stage stands as a metaphor for freedom or becomes a celebration of his/her integration into the society. For example, in *Flavio's Fortune*, when the Muslim Pasha's son is converted to Christianity in Rome and becomes Oratio, Francheschina, a servant to Pantolone, praises the "great generosity of his master Oratio": a "Turk who turned Christian": "all of Rome loves and honors him" (Scala 13).

George Meredith's view of comedy is that as a dramatic form it is "a version of the ordinary worldly understandings of social life" (Sypher 17) and thus cannot flourish apart from society, whose social gesture towards the comic is laughter. For Henri Bergson laughter as an interactive component is a testimony to comedy's social relevance. Yet, in accompanying a comic action, laughter for Bergson is essentially normative, a social correction to any forms of social abnormality. Ultimately, since laughter, as Bergson maintains, has a corrective function, it can also, in the same vein of the "thoughtful laughter" of George Meredith's "comic spirit" (Sypher 31-32) enable the society to question its ideologies.

Despite the spirit of freedom embodied in the Bakhtinian carnivalesque style, ultimately, the recurring motif in all the *commedia* scenarios revolving around the Ottomans' captivity and enslavement of the Christian figure establishes the widespread anxieties about the perilous Mediterranean world, of being captured, enslaved and converted. While the representation of the Turk/Muslim in *commedia* performances reveals a great deal about the collective psychology of fear produced by the Ottoman power in 'dangerous' zones, the characters' sudden conversions on stage become a means of mastering the threatening Other -a desire that goes back to the Crusades.

The relationship between fear and laughter is a complex compound. When elements that are fearful and comic are mixed, laughter turns into an Hobbesian celebration of superiority. In the *Leviathan*, Thomas Hobbes establishes his definition of laughter within a dichotomy of received social superiority and inferiority. Writing about the superiority theory of humour, he maintains that:

> Sudden glory is the passion which makes all those grimaces called laughter; and it is caused either by some sudden act of their own, that pleases them; or by the apprehension of some deformed thing in another by comparison whereof they applaud themselves (Hobbes I:6).

In this sense, while the ultimate freedom of enslaved characters becomes "a tale of trouble that turned to joy" (Coghill 4) Muslims' conversion to Christianity on stage exemplifies the superiority of laughter, first enunciated by Plato and Aristotle.

4.2. *Commedia dell'Arte* Scenarios (1611)

By the time Shakespeare's audience responded to his romantic comedies such as *A Midsummer Night's Dream, As You Like it* or *Twelfth Night* mostly through a laughter of delight, in English theatrical records there were specific references to performances by travelling *commedia dell'arte* troupes. Similarly, the many references to *commedia* characters by other Elizabethan and Jacobean playwrights were a testimony that the Italian players had performed in London during Shakespeare's era.[97] A *commedia dell arte* performance, which was based on improvised dialogue and routines, incorporated a set of stock characters, repartee and comic devices. Just like the plot devices, such as the use of twins, mistaken identities, disguises which were predominantly used by the Italian players of *commedia dell'arte*, the themes of captivity, enslavement and conversion also featured in the performances. Other than plot devices, some dozen stock characters, which constituted the backbone of the *commedia* repertoire, were later incorporated in the plays of Shakespeare, Ben Jonson, Molière, Ma-

---

97 In the sixteenth-century accounts of Italian players, performances in England began in Norwich in 1566. Visits also included performances in 1573 and 1577. Following Flaminio Cutesse's performance for Queen Elizabeth, the troupes visited England frequently for the next hundred years with Charles II witnessing a performance in 1678 (Scala xvii).

rivaux and other European dramatists.[98] The immortal *zannis* (buffoons) such as Scramuccia (Scaramouche) and Arlechiono (Harlequin); the elderly parent Pantolone (Pantaloon) and his pedantic friend Grattiano (Dottore); the alien Captain; the servants Columbine and Brighella and so on were evidently standard figures familiar to English audiences. Although the familiarity of these characters could not have been so widespread during the Elizabethan and Jacobean times, in a typical *commedia* scenario, which inspired European dramatists who modeled their comic characters on the *commedia* figures, the hero could perhaps be Flavio or Oratio and the heroine Isabella or Flaminia.

Evidence, such as Giacomo Franco's engraving dated 1610, which depicts and depicting the actors and charlatans performing in the Piazza San Marco, suggests that the Italian *commedia* players fascinated audiences from many different nationalities. In a single performance, which incorporated many regional dialects, the multilingual component of the shows also delighted the audiences through characters attempting to speak nonsense language or *grammelot*. In her doctoral study, Erith Jaffe-Berg defines *grammelot* as "the commingling of sounds and sound groups to evoke a language that is imaginary, but which, when performed, seems to make sense" (Jaffe-Berg 254). According to Jaffe-Berg, while *grammelot* did not comply with the linguistic form of any real national language, it allowed actors a great deal of flexibility in impersonating characters from different countries.

> In the renaissance, the mixture in *commedia* of confusion and comprehension provided the audience with a pleasurable duplication of their real life experience in a period of transition, of the instability resulting encounters with strangers which was both anxiety provoking and delightful, and the constancy of life which still provided continuities such as going to the theatre. The performances of *commedia* held up the mirror to this reality, but the mirror was on an ever fractured and refracting kind (Jaffe-Berg 255).

---

98 As a popular theatrical form, while *commedia* was contemporaneous with Shakespeare's, in *Italian Popular Comedy* Lea mentions passim to *commedia* roles by, Middleton, Nashe and Massinger (Lea 2: 339-455).

Jaffe-Berg, showing the mechanism of communication by the *commedia* troupes, refers to Domenico Biancoceli's description of a "Turkish Act" in *The Voyage of Scaramouche and Harlequin to the Indes* (1676) in which he plays the Harlequin:

> In the Turkish Act, Flautin tells me that he will give me a flute, and Scaramouche a bass fiddle, by which means we will obtain our freedom from the Sultan, and that he, Flautin will play the guitar (Quoted from Jaffe-Berg 1).

Jaffe-Berg suggests that the performers may also have incorporated in their show Turkish expressions considering that Francesco Andreini, well known for his role as Capitano, utilized Turkish along with other languages. As for his wife, Isabella Andreini, a *commedia* legend, particularly in her role in *The Madness of Isabella,* took on diverse identities as she launched into "a multilingual tirade" (Jaff-Berg 26). Like a movie actor of our era, Isabella Andreini had an international fame. In her role as a Turkish girl who was made a Christian in Majorca, her performance at the 1589 wedding of Grand Duke Ferdinando de Medici to Christine of Loraine (Clubb 263) gave "the most inexpressible pleasure to the bride, Her most Serene Highness" (Quoted from Clubb 263). Tommaso Garzoni wrote about Isabella Andreini's presence on the Italian stage and the poetic style of her improvisation:

> The gracious Isabella, dignity of the scene, ornament of the stage, a superb spectacle no less of [virtue] than of beauty, has so illuminated the style of her profession that while the world lasts, while the centuries endure, while times and seasons have life, every voice, every language, every cry, will echo the celebrated name of Isabella (Quoted from McGill 64).

It is most likely that Andreini had acted some other Turkish characters of the *commedia* scenarios that revolved around Ottoman themes. In fact, *The Madness of Isabella* was only one of the popular *commedia* scenarios (*canovacci*) published in the collection of Falminio Scala. In the fifty *canovacci* published by Scala under the title *Il Teatro delle favole rappresentative* (1611), other than *The Madness of Isabella,* the scenarios that revolved specifically around Ottoman themes were mainly, *The Old Twins, Flavio's Fortune, The Fake Blind Man* and *Isabella the Astrologer.*

In Scala's *A Theatrical Repertory of Fables or Comic, Pastoral, and Tragic Entertainment*, which is divided into fifty days, the scenario of *The First Day, The Old Twins*, revolves around two brothers, who on their way to Egypt are captured by pirates, made slaves and sold to a Turkish merchant. Like Shakespeare's *The Comedy of Errors, The Old Twins* has its source in Plautus' *Menaechmi* with the device of lost twins evoking many similarities. While the Plautine material of the Menaechmus brothers provided Shakespeare his plot, mistaken identity and the recovery of reunion of lost children had their source in ancient Greece towards the end of 4th century. As Anne Barton notes, the "obsessive preoccupation" with this theme, stemmed from:

> a Hellenistic world that was filled with displaced persons, where children were often "lost" by parents too poor or too distracted to cope with them at the time of birth, and where free citizens could become slaves overnight (Evans *Riverside Shakespeare*, 81).

As for the sixteenth century, with the rise of Barbary and Algerian corsairs in the Mediterranean, Europe was faced with the problem of Christian captives converting to Islam. In the seventeenth century, although the military and economic power of the Ottoman Empire was in decline, the European notion of identity was still threatened by cultural and religious differences of the Ottomans, who embodied the worst fears of the West. Unlike the Antipholus brothers (of Ephesus and of Syracuse) of *The Comedy of Errors*, Pantolone and his brother, who are the lost twins in Scala's scenario are the parents of Flavio and Oratio, who are captured and made slaves. In the scenario of *The Second Day*, entitled *Flavio's Fortune*, the title-character is also captured by pirates while at sea and "sold as a slave in Constantinople to a Pasha of great wisdom" (Scala 11). In *The Thirty-Fourth Day*'s scenario *The Fake Blind Man*, it is Pantolone's son Oratio, who is captured by the Turks, enslaved, taken to Algeria and given to the "viceroy, who was ruler and governor" (Scala 249). Later, when he is ransomed and the time for his departure to Rome comes, he will not leave Algeria without his friend Flavio. When the governor sees the strong bond of friendship between the two men, he frees them both; later, in Lyon, Oratio is reunited with his lover Isabella, who is also freed from slavery because of "a treaty between Turkey and France" and "all ended happily" (Scala 249-50). In *The Thirty-sixth Day*, while Isabella's lover Oratio is seized by pirates and brought to Algeria as a slave, her brother Flavio falls in love with Rabya Turca, a "young Turkish girl", who is the daughter of an "Arabian astrologer".

In *Flavio's Fortune*, the young Turk who is already determined to become a Christian before he sets sail in a small galley. As for his sister, who is disguised in man's clothes, she is also headed for the capital city in the same ship. After a series of unusual events and mistaken identities, the young Turkish girl (Turchetta), with whom the Captain falls in love, is reunited with her brother and her lover Flavio in Rome. In the end of play, the Turkish girl now named Alissa becomes "a Christian, and all live a joyful and happy life" (Scala 12). In *The Madness of Isabella*, the scenario of *The Thirty-Eighth Day*, when Oratio's ship is "ambushed by some Turkish vessels" he is sold to a captain who is married to a Turkish girl from the Seraglio. As Oratio falls in love with this "most graceful and beautiful creature" they plan to escape and marry in Genoa where she will become a Christian. While they are on board sailing in an armed boat on the high seas for Majorca, the Captain begins to follow the fugitives. When Oratio, with the help of other Turks on his boat, boldly opposes the Captain's galley they are able to continue their voyage. Then, as Scala narrates:

> They arrived at Majorca, where with great solemnity, the Turkish girl was made Christian. In short time they went from there to Genoa, where they lived happily for a while, but misery befell the Turkish girl, who became known as Isabella. After many misfortunes whereby she became mad, her beloved husband was restored to her, and they were made happy again (Scala 283).

In *Flavio's Fortune,* before the Pasha's son is converted to Christianity and becomes Oratio, not only has Flavio aroused a passion in the Turk for his beautiful sister in Rome, but he has also persuaded him to change his religion, a blocking element for the achievement of the comic end. In a typical *commedia* scenario revolving around conversions on stage, the audience's superiority arises from the ideology of the humour. In the eighteenth century the superiority theory was superseded by the incongruity theory, which posits that people find that which is incongruous funny. For Francis Hutcheson superiority is not a necessary condition for comic situations to arise for "generally the cause of laughter" is:

> The bringing together of images which have contrary additional ideas, as well as some resemblance in the principal idea: this contrast between the ideas of grandeur, dignity, sanctity, perfection, and ideas of meanness, baseness, profanity, seems to be the very spirit of burlesque; and the greatest part of our raillery and jest is founded upon it (Hutcheson 19).

We also find ourselves moved to Laughter by an overstraining of wit, by bringing resemblances from subjects of a quite different kind from the subject to which they are compared. Based on Hutcheson's view, comedy naturally arises in contexts where incongruous, contrasting or conflicting concepts, properties and categories are brought together. Yet, in literary representations governed by theological modes of thought, a sense of superiority towards the Muslim Other perceived as the embodiment of the most basic and general vices, ferocity and licentiousness, is not generically bound. Just like Shakespeare's tragedy of 1604 in which a typecast "lascivious Moor" (I.I.126) before "turning Turk" kills Brabantio's "fair" (122) daughter, in the eighteenth-century heroic play, *The Fair Captive*, when Isabella brings a dagger to Alphonso, the Spaniard hero tells her: "This glittering Steel/Points to a fatal Deed/This is a Heathen Liberty/Art thou not a Christian?" (IV.I.p.43)

In her article titled *Othello dell'Arte: The Presence of Commedia in Shakespeare's Tragedy*, Teresa J. Faherty suggests that even in a tragedy, *commedia*'s influence can be "broad and deep"(Faherty 182).

> From the opening scenes of the play, in which a Venetian *zanni* figure mocks a "Magnifico" and begins plotting to wreck the marriage of an old foreign captain and vivacious young woman, Othello looks very much like *commedia*, a resemblance [she does] not think a Renaissance audience could have failed to notice (Faherty 180).

Emphasizing how *Othello* is "after all, a tragedy" (180) and "this is not to argue, of course, that Shakespeare's play is *commedia*, (Faherty 193) Faherty states that:

> By *absorbing* commedia roles into his more free-styled characters, and by imposing a *commedia*-style shadow plot (via Iago), which his characters seem unable to entirely subvert, Shakespeare seems to entail by his superficial borrowings from *commedia* its notion of characterological determinism, the convergence of body, mind, reputation, and action, which constitutes a profound resistance to the possibilities of free will (Faherty 193).

In her article Faherty not only demonstrates how the setting of Shakespeare's tragedy conjures up local colour of a *commedia* scenario, but also how it evokes "an illusion of its microcosm and its rules" (Faherty 182). Based on Faherty's thought, it is indeed possible to visualize Othello as *commedia*'s alien Captain, a braggart soldier, who like the Miles Glorious of the Plautus comedy begins as an outsider and ends as an outcast. In the beginning, however, Othello, the Moor of Venice, rather than being an outsider or an alienated subject manifests a dual identity. Like the Capitano of the *commedia*, whose loud roar and threats of death are signals that he can be ferocious on a regular basis, Othello turns into a violent arbitrary tyrant at the end of the play. In *Othello* Venice's Christian civility is defined in relation to the Muslim/Turk, which is perceived as "alien, strange or hostile". Thus, this "threatening other—heretic, savage ... Anti-Christ—must be discovered or reinvented in order to be attacked and destroyed" (Greenblatt 1980 9). Stephen Greenblatt's views on self-fashioning echo in Said's words that "cultures have always been inclined to impose complete transformations on other cultures, receiving other cultures not as they are, but for the benefit of the receiver they ought to be" (Said *Orientalism* 67).

In *Arlequin sauvage*[99] set in Marseilles, Louis François Delisle de la Drevetière (1682-1756) challenges an ideological set of values when Lélio, in love with Flaminio brings Arlequin, a simple "savage" from America to Europe. In the play, Lelio is taken from the forests with all his ignorance so that his pure nature can be contrasted with the laws, arts and knowledge of civilized nations in Europe. On stage the elements of farce must have heightened the contrast between an inferior uncivilized savage, guided by brutish and unpolished nature and superior civilized nations which live according to law and order drawn from reason. Reason, as Lélio teaches Arlequin, enables one to differentiate between good and evil and laws teach one to make good use of one's life. The reply of the simple savage who is perceived as being unadorned with reason is: "Who the devil would have ever guessed that there were men in the world who needed laws to become good?" (I.IV). Similarly, if a *commedia* stock figure such as the foreign Captain, who like a Plautian Braggart Soldier with his ridiculous machine-like behaviour symbolizes "the cultural norm and the absence of that norm, either as nature or anti culture" (Bouissac 164) and evokes in the audience feelings of superiority, as Arlequin might say: "Who needs tragedies to look down on the Other as an inferior example of a person?"

In exploring the issues that have to do with Self and Other, Todorov in *The Conquest of America* opens up his discussion with the statement that his "subject" is "the discovery *self* makes in the *other*". In his study Todorov basically addresses the aspects of alterity through discovery and subjectivity. In discussing how we discover the Other in ourselves, Todorov's emphasis is on the "I" and the "Other" dynamic which points to the fact that we are not radically alien to that which we perceive is not us. Todorov identifies the problematics of alterity through value judgements (good or bad based on the values of the Self) and knowledge (ignorance of Other's identity). His emphasis on distancing in relation to the

---

99 Based on the French original, John Fenwick (1739-1823) has also written his own farce *The Indian*, which was performed at the Drury Lane.

Other emphasizes on a self-reflexive medium of self discovery. The role of such a medium as condition for perceptions of the Other involves imposing one's values and self-image on the Other; submission of Other to Self; embracing Other's values or adopting indifference. As the Self-Other dialectic central to representations of the Ottomans/Muslims reveal, discoveries of the Western Self are exclusively structured and essentially rooted in a fear of the loss of essence and identity. Consequently, the layering of value-systems on the East and West, Christian and Muslim configurations not only reinforces cultural and religious differences between Self and Other, but also imposes assimilation through conversion.

4.3. *Le bourgeois gentilhomme* (1670)

As Brian Corman writes in Genre and Generic Change in English Comedy (1660-1710):

> Stage comedy had emerged with most of its representative characteristics by the time Aristophanes and Menander offered their plays on the Athenian stage. Because of the loss of Aristotle's lectures on comedy, the theory of comedy remains less developed than the theory of tragedy (Corman 3).

In essence, for Aristotle while comedy is a forum for the representation of character types, imitation is that of ludicrous and imperfect action which enables the audience to purge emotions through pleasure and laughter. In the *Poetics*, however, Aristotle is quite particular as to proper subjects for comedy. While he defines tragedy as "an imitation (*mimesis)* not of men, but of action and life" and represents a noble hero as its object, comedy is "an imitation of characters of a lower type". In tragedies while authors imitated "noble actions" involving the pitiable and fearful dimensions of human existence, in farces and satires they imitate "actions of meaner persons" (Jovanovich 48-66). In comedy, the comic element arises from social relations. It is found in people, their movements, actions, trait of character, physical and mental expressions of their characteristics. The methods that can make people comic can serve a hostile and aggressive purpose in order to make them contemptible or to deprive them from their dignity and authority. Mimicry, disguise, unmasking, parody, etc. are devices that put the comic subject in a ridiculous situation inspiring laughter.

In Molière's (Jean Baptiste de Poquelin) *comédie-ballet, Le bourgeois gentilhomme* (1670), which has its roots in *commedia dell'arte,* when Cleonte in disguise enters the stage as the son of the Grand Turk to lead a burlesque ceremony, he confers the dignity of *mamamouchi* upon the unsuspecting Monsieur Jourdain. Monsieur Jourdain willingly accepts the so-called noble title since he is eager to become a person of "qualité". Instead he is deprived of his dignity and patriarchal authority and becomes an object of ridicule, a laughing stock in this farcical ceremony of *mamamouchi* (meaning "good for nothing in Arabic"). In *Le bourgeois gentilhomme* Molière's comic vision revealed through the interplay of culture and politics, incorporates several theatrical devices to make his audience laugh. M. Jourdain's comic character arising from his extravagance and vanity, his ridiculous outfit, the schemers' temporary fictive change of identity, the made-up rituals, invocations, chantings, the appropriation of *grammelots* to create an inaccessible language and finally the unmasking of his gullibility and folly on stage all lead to comic laughter.

The central motif in Bergson's theory of comedy in his *Essay on Laughter* is that "the mechanical encrusted upon the living (Quoted from Sypher 84) promotes laughter. Based on Bergson's analysis of comic vision, a human becomes an object of laughter because of his/her rigidity, lack of elasticity, inflexibility, puppet-like movements. Unlike a tragic figure, which touches our soul and attracts, absorbs, transforms and assimilates our diverse energies, we laugh at a comic character to humiliate and to correct him/her. Yet in order for that person to provoke laughter s/he must alienate our sympathy. Bergson's stress is on this creation of a critical distance in order for laughter to occur. According to Bergson, in order for the audiences to laugh at a "recognizable" member of their world, s/he must be singled out, separated and made different. While differentiation is achieved through the reduction of the comic figure's adaptability to a series of rigid and mechanical reflexes, separation is confirmed through the act of laughing which signifies the audience's collective judgement that the object of derision is not only different but also inferior.

In *Le bourgeois gentilhomme*, M. Jourdain is recognizable because he is French. Indeed, his French lessons dwell on the syntax of the French language and his pronunciation of the vowels and the consonants. His eccentric and extravagant behaviour is revealed through his obsessive desire to adapt to the social hierarchy in the French system in the seventeenth century. The play reflects the social realities of the times: the wars (starting in the 1620s) with the Huguenots, etc. Since victory of the French military depended on the availability of funds to pay the troops, "the investors who collected excise taxes for the king and who lent him money—investors known as *partisans*—made enormous profits" (Ranum 106). While the social rank of the investors remained obscure, the creation of this new wealth in the society had led to a passion of consuming goods such as fine clothing, new homes, jewelry etc. None of these *nouveaux riches* have the quality of birth necessary to be a *gentilhomme*, but the new wealth that they have acquired has often allowed them to outspend the nobility "on finery to wear at court, on receptions, and on the construction of prestigious residences (Ranum 106). *Le bourgeois gentilhomme* portrays changes in social class distinctions in seventeenth-century France in which the concepts of bourgeois and *gentilhomme* are mutually exclusive. Molière's comic vision reflects the dynamics between the rise of the bourgeoisie and the fall of the nobility and the disparity between men of different ranks and qualities based on an overt and explicit hierarchical society. In fact, the play is a satirical attack on the fraudulence and hypocrisy of seventeenth-century France in when the king reinforced the rise of the bourgeoisie for the sole purpose of exercising total authority and power over the nobles. As Larry W. Riggs writes:

> As the bourgeoisie developed, and especially as it tried to buttress its improving economic status with political gains, class distinctions became the explicit subject of ideological, literary, legal and social debates. Economic factors, and more or less deliberate government policies, contributed significantly to changes in both facts and perceptions about the social classes (Riggs 339).

In the play, M. Joudain's vice is his conviction that anything pertaining to social superiority can be bought through improved education and influence in the court. Coming from a cloth-merchant family, Jourdain enjoys the privileges of bourgeois rank, which makes him socially superior to common city people and the peasants. He is inferior, however, to the status of a noble and a *gentilhomme*. Therefore, in his aspiration to leap social hierarchies through his lifestyle, Jourdain will go in extremes such as having plans to have an affair with the marquise Dorimène, lending the count Dorante, a sum of money, an act which in turn will give give him "honor". Monsieur Jourdain belongs staunchly to the middle class and his concentrated efforts to enter the society of "les gens de qualité" appear eccentric. These superficial efforts to transform himself into nobility include imitating the dress code, taking language and fencing lessons, etiquette for greetings, the hosting of banquets etc. Thus his behaviour becomes exaggerated and distorted to the extent of making him different- thus laughable. Particularly, as the comic figure of a play performed for an audience of aristocrats at the court, he is cast out by means of laughter, which has "a social meaning and import (Quoted from Sypher 146). Thus, since Jourdain's flaw is his aspiration to move to the upper class, in the eyes of the aristocracy he is the bourgeois/Other and his non-aristocratic behaviour is contemptible by those who are antagonistic towards the members of his class.

Monsieur Jourdain's obsession with persons of *qualité* refers to the concept of the *ancien régime* that persons of noble birth are naturally superior to commoners. Based on the assumption that people with aristocratic blood inherit superior qualities of courage, virtue, and honesty and thus possess social and political superiority as a birthright, Monsieur Jourdain is not and can not be a person of quality. Despite the French monarchy's granting of nobility and the tax exemptions that go with it, the noblemen newly created by such favours are not accepted socially, as they are not the *gentilhommes*—those who are "born" noble. The commoner who acquires this title from the king is not considered a gentleman but his sons and daughters can be accepted as true *gentilhommes* and ladies.

In *Le bourgeois gentilhomme*, Molière, expands on the comic isolation of Jourdain's bourgeois Otherness by turning him into a Mamamouchi, which has further ideological, social and cultural implications. In the time of Louis XIV, as "political and other cultural activities had not yet separated into the distinct spheres which we recognize" (Riggs 2) today, as a cultural act, Molière's *comédie-ballet* with music by Lully participates in the influencing of awareness of the Ottoman/Muslim Other. Thus, on the one hand, Molière's comedy reflects the ideological crisis of class transformations in the seventeenth-century France with the eagerness of the bourgeoisie to claim social prestige based on wealth rather than nobility. On the other hand, the performance of a pseudo-Turkish wedding ceremony packed with the stereotypical portrayals of the Ottomans and full of caricaturized images of the dance of the Mevlevi Dervishes and *musique à la turque* makes the *turquerie* of the times the butt of the author's farcical fantasies.

Bergson defines laughter as a response to witnessing the machine inside the living so that we are amused with the spectacle of a cognizant being behaving in an automatic fashion that is rigorously contrary to its purported nature. He says that:

> [T]he laughable element ... consists of a certain *mechanical inelasticity* ... a certain inborn lack of elasticity of both senses and intelligence, which brings it to a pass that we continue to adapt ourselves to a past and therefore imaginary situation, when we ought to be shaping our conduct in accordance with the reality which is present (Sypher 66-67).

The staging of the *mamamouchi* Other arises from a clever plot schemed by Covielle, servant to Cléonte whom Jourdain denies the hand of his daughter Lucille as he is not a "gens de qualité". The stratagem is devised to fool the bourgeois Jourdain into believing that he is marrying his daughter to a noble- that is the son of the Grand Turk. In the hierarchical society of seventeenth-century France while it is only natural for a father to enjoy an unquestioned authority over his household, Jourdain is ultimately stripped of his traditional role. In that sense, as Jourdain's attempted domination represents the superiority that he seeks over the members of his family, the subversion of his authority also makes him ridiculous in the eyes of the onlookers. Before Jourdain ultimately agrees to make Cléonte his son-in-law,"Oui voila qui est fait, je consens au mariage/Yes, it is all right, I consent to the marriage" (V.VI), he is effectively isolated into the comic delusion of being the "noble" Other through a mumbo-jumbo ceremony. In this scene, as laughter thrives on difference, Molière's technique of working in terms of "realism" through Ottoman costumes and feigned characters, creates the ultimate effect of fantasy. Since the stratagem played on Jourdain is to "wheedle him into giving his daughter" (IV.V) to Cleonte, the *masquarade* creates on stage a carnivalesque energy released through self-exoticism. If Jourdain's initial blockage of the young lovers can be considered as an ambivalent sign of despotism, his eager acceptance of the *mamamouchi* title which "turns" him into a Turk both "visually and verbally", suggests the stereotyped oppressive policies of the Ottomans which will be portrayed on stage with carnivalesque exuberance.

The *masquarade* has a further ideological function in Molière's appropriation of his notion of Turkish language through stereotypical sounds, which are not altogether devoid of semantic form. By using *grammelot* as a tool in this comic performance, although Molière creates nonsensical words. His depiction of the Ottoman/Muslim alterity is not solely revealed through his reduction of the Other's culture and the language to the level of costumes, but also by the use of gibberish words. The Ottoman robe, which magically enables Monsieur Jourdain to become the Other with a status symbol, is seen by Madame Jourdain in her Occidental Self as a *momon*, a carnival mask. The Oriental outfit is thus an object of ridicule. The new title *paladin* ceremoniously invested upon Jourdain is his wife's appropriation of the expression is *baladin* meaning mountebank, a characteristic commonly attributed to the Islamic prophet Muhammed in the Christian West.

In the *mamamouchi* scene, the disguised "actors" who "perform" for Monsieur Jourdain are the Grand Turk, the Mufti, four dervishes, six dancing Turks and six musicians. The "religious ritual" presided over by the Mufti is easily recognized as a "bal masqué", that is "devoid of any cultural depth and specifity" (Behdad 44). Essentially, the characters' disguises are designed not only to aid the plot but also to get laughs from the audience by creating a ludicrous situation in which the Other, in terms of its customs, religion and language can be seen as different and inferior. The burlesque ceremony in Act IV Scene V begins with the Mufti's invocation of the prophet as "Mahametta per Giourdina" while M. Jourdain as a willing dope will be made a *mamamouchi (c'est-à-dire)* "un Paladina/de' Giourdina, de' Giourdina/Dar turbanta". When the Mufti asks his Turkish assistants the citizen's religion, they assure him that he is "Mahometan". Asked whether the citizen will be constant to his religion, the Turks respond him with "hi valla" (*eyvallah*), which is a common term of acknowledgement in Turkish. Then the Mufti proceeds to give the turban to the citizen saying "turbanta...turbanta" and puts it ceremoniously on Jourdain. He then presents the "Turca Giourdina" with the "Alcoran" and the sword. The Turks dance around him with sabres in hand, feigning to give him cuts and "bastonnade" him (pretend to beat him with sticks) chanting rhythmically "bastonorra bastonarra". Now, he is a Paladin, a dignity that has been ceremoniously endowed upon him. If Madame Jourdain's choice of the word "baladin" (mountebank) for "paladin" is not accidental so are the titles "Mahametta per Giourdina" and "Turca Giourdina" as the Turkish expression for infidel is "gavur", transcribed as "giaour" in Western languages.

The French desire to see a potent visual signifier of difference on stage is preceded by the royalty's first-hand experience of the presence of an Ottoman Ambassador in the court. In 1669, however, when Louis XIV ordered Molière and Lully to compose for the stage a superficial, light imitation of the Otttomans, he had already sent Jean de Caligny to join the European crusaders to defend Sicily against the invasion of the Ottoman Empire. When the king asked Molière to write his piece following the visit of Suleyman Aga to France, he had anxieties about the Ottomans' revoking France's exceptional commercial privileges in the Ottoman territories. By the mid-seventeenth century, however, the Ottomans' economic power had begun to decline due to the closing of old international routes in the Levant by the British and the Dutch. Yet, the West's fear of the military prowess of the Ottomans was confirmed when they regained their mastery of the Mediterranean in 1669 and continued to pose a threat to Europe. As Behdad suggests:

> The King's seemingly earnest demand for entertainment ... is inscribed within a whole series of epistemological, economic, political interests in the Orient; the staging of the lay was simultaneously embedded in and contributed to the circulation of these interests (Behdad 39).

Evidently, before the visit of Suleyman Aga, the Ottoman Ambassador, the King asked Chevalier d'Arvieux, known for his visits to Istanbul and his mastery of Eastern languages to brief the French court on the Ottoman culture.

> [T]he king made sure that d'Arvieux contributed his knowledge of the Orient to the production of *Le bourgeois gentilhomme*, and with the latter's diligent efforts the court thus took the task of re-presenting the Orient seriously. Not only did d'Arvieux spend eight days with Baraillon, the "maitre tailleur", to produce "authentic Oriental turbans and robes, but he also worked closely with Molière and Lully to give the play a "realistic" sense of Oriental culture (Behdad 32).

Louis XIV's demand that Molière prepare a theatrical event "où l'on put faire entrer quelques choses des habillements et des manières des Turcs" (Howard 221) followed Ambassador Suleyman Aga's visit to France. While the description of the theatricality of the Ottoman Ambassador's reception at the court was circulated in the Gazette, the diplomatic encounter with the Other, in turn contributed to the emerging fashion of *turquerie* in Paris. The desire for "turquerie" served cultural and political purposes as it was essentially aimed at fixing the identities of European self and Other. What is also significant here is that the comic representation of the Other through a *masquarade* created an Oriental identity that could be assumed temporarily in order to be rejected definitively. Considering that the cultural and religious difference of the Eastern Other posed a threat to the identity and unity of the Occident, it was not accidental that Molière end his comedy with a "ballet des nations" (presented by Dorante for the entertainment of "Son Altesse Turque") in which solely European nations were represented.

In the theatre, if to laugh is to laugh at someone from a position of superiority, Molière achieved his comic end. The play served its purpose in affirming the Self and in signifying Otherness through external differences such as Ottoman robes, turbans, nonsensical vagaries and gibberish language placed in the service of marginalizing and isolating the Turk as different and inferior. In 1670 when *Le bourgeois gentilhomme* was performed for Louis XIV and his court at Chambord, the great Renaissance château of the Loire Valley, the comedy must have enabled the audience to purge emotions through pleasure and laughter. More so, it must have given them a sense superiority arising from class, culture and religion.

Ultimately, though, as much as the comic *turquerie* in Molière's play provoked laughter, it also provided a "site for self-exoticism to lose oneself temporarily in the Other" (Behdad 42) by stimulating a desire for the Orient.

As Behdad suggests, Molière might have turned the king's demand for an Oriental "quelque chose" into "self-reflexivity" (Behdad 43) through Monsieur Jourdain's obsession with garments, his request from the music teacher for a *comédie-ballet* for his aristocratic friends, etc. In that case, the play's comic moments of self-presentation were indeed part and parcel of Louis XIV's commercial and colonial interests in the Ottoman Empire. This of course, foreshadowed Napoléon's imperial hopes for France: "I must go to the Orient: all the glory comes from there" (Quoted from Meyer 657).

4.4. *False Count* (1682)

Aphra Behn, the first Englishwoman to become a professional writer, had every right to boast that in seventeen years she had produced seventeen plays. She claimed that as a female author she had written "as many good comedies as any Man has writ in [her] Age". Yet, in these plays such as *The False Count: A New Way to Play an Old Game*, first performed at Dorset Garden in early 1682, it was apparent that she acted on a masculine set of values and authority passed on to her from her predecessors. In seeking to expose the discursive relationship between Western scholarship about the Orient and imperialism, while Said's discussions do not include women and gender, he never raises the question of the authority of the female author. Yet, for Said author is the source, origin and meaning of the text (Said *Beginnings* 83). This contradicts Roland Barthes' theory, which proclaims the death of the author. According to Barthes:

> To give a text to an Author is to impose a limit on that text, to furnish it with a final signified, to close the writing. Such a conception suits criticism very well, the latter then allotting itself the important task of discovering the Author (or its hypotheses: society, history, psyche, liberty) beneath that work: When the Author has been found, the text is 'explained' -victory to the critic (*The Death of Author*, 147).

When Barthes challenged author's role, he sought to explain the "text" as "a tissue of quotations drawn from the innumerable centres of culture", (Barthes 146) and he gave the reader the role of assigning meaning to the text. Irrespective of the author's gender or the reader's role, the emerging authorial voice discovered in *The False Count* was already inherent in the dominant culture of English society. It disclosed an ideology, which was homogeneous and all-encompassing in its portrayal of the image of the Ottomans. When Behn joined her male counterparts who had paved the way in exciting and interesting the audiences through the fantastical images of the Turk, she was fast in claiming an authority which allowed her to "speak" as a Turk, in place of the Turk, in the name of a Turk, for the Turk, or against the Turk:

> Francisco: Oh Lord, *Turk, Turks*!
> Guiliom: *Turks*, oh, is that all?
> Francisco: All -why they'll make Eunuchs of us, my Lord, Eunuchs of us poor men, and lie with our wives. (IV.I)
> ...
> Guiliom: Why where be these *Turks*? Set me to 'em, I'll make 'em smoke, Dogs...
> Isabella: Oh, the Insolence of these *Turks*!
> ...
> *Enter some* Turks *with the body of* Francisco *in chains and lay him down on a Bank.*
> I Turk: Christian, so ho ho, Slave, awake
> ...
> Fran: The Great Turk, -the Great Devil, why, where am I, Friend?
> I Turk: Within the Territories of the Grand Seignior, and this is a
> Palace of Pleasure, where he recreates himself with his Mistresses. (IV.II).

Whether or not Lady Mary Fielding, daughter of Earl of Denbigh and her husband Evelyn Pierrepoint, member of Parliament for East Retford in Nottinghamshire, had seen Behn's *The False Count*, it was only seven years after its first performance that their daughter Mary was born. It would be Mary, daughter of the Earl of Kingston (Pierrepoint inherited the title in 1690) and wife to Edward Wortley Montagu, who would in no time "set the terms of an alternative gender-specific discourse on the Middle East, one which [would evolve] alongside of the dominant discussion[s]" about the Orient (Melman 2). Contrary to Behn's female authorial voice which was influenced by patriarchal ideology and Western conventions that placed the Other outside the system of normality, Lady Mary's urgency was to reclaim this authority in order to normalize and humanize the Turk by making him/her familiar. In essence, Lady Mary with a visual and humanizing experience of the Other invoked an emergent feminist discourse on the Orient.

Two centuries later, Gayatri Spivak introduced in discussions of colonialism the question of women's representations.[100] Similarly, in the last decade, writers such as Leila Ahmed in *Women and Gender in Islam* and Fatima Mernissi in *Beyond the Veil* would begin to focus on historicising Middle Eastern women on exploring the relationship between colonialism and patriarchy in the East.

In Said's case, his "gender-blindness" reveals that his analysis of the Orient is based solely on "an analogy between orientalism and patriarchalism" (Melman xxii). In writing about the imaginative projections of the West and its "manipulative amassing of information" about the East, Said's discourse primarily displays the characteristics of "male gender dominance and patriarchy" (Melman 4). Even though in the segregated world of the harem, the power of the *valide sultans*, who were in charge of all affairs, could extend throughout the entire Ottoman Empire (the Orient), in Said's ungendered discourse, women had no place, no voice. As for Lady Mary, both as an author, who kept her "femaleness" in tact and an "authority" who actively participated in the eighteenth-century Ottoman social culture developed a consciousness untainted by any dominant ideology.

On 2 August 1716 when she left on board a yacht for a journey to Istanbul, Lady Mary was actually accompanying her husband Edward Wortley Montagu, who was appointed as the English Ambassador Extraordinary to the Ottoman Court. During the time that her husband was entrusted with this diplomatic task, Lady Mary's position as the Ambassador's wife, "enabled her to master normally masculine preserves of knowledge"(Lew 432) which she recorded in a series of letters. Written during the years 1717-1718 when she lived and traveled within the Ottoman territories, Lady *Mary's The Turkish Embassy Letters*, as they were called, were posthumously published in 1763. Although she was not able to publish anything that she wrote under her name in

100 Particularly, in the 1980s cultural critics and historians focused on the marginalisation of colonized women in India based on gender and race.

her lifetime, *Embassy Letters* soon possessed the status of a reference text about the Ottoman culture.

As she pronounced in her Epilogue, Behn was able to bring "forth with ease" a play about "fair slaves" and "ferocious Turks" as "one wish at the Devil" (III.I) in "five days"; her plot, the stage device, the rhetoric and perceptions about the Other and their harem system were all established by her predecessors. Contrary to Lady Mary's epistolary vision of the Ottoman Empire, drawn on an observable reality seen on the spot, naturally all these dramatic elements that helped shape the image of the Ottomans and their "Seraglio" were products of their authors' fantasy. In1668 Rycaut narrated in the *Present State of the Ottoman Empire* that although he had been able to come as far as the quarters of the "Eunuchs, which are the Black guard of the sequestered Ladies of the Seraglio" he was excluded from the "Captivated Ladies" (Rycaut 33-39). For Western writers the harem as a microcosm of despotism was projected antithetical to the benign ideals of absolute monarchies in Europe. In this context, Todorov's model of discovery and of identity involving distancing in relation to Other, underlies Western practice of knowledge, which does not necessarily imply an identification with the East. In fact, the textual strategies of Western discovery of the harem and the Muslim East, reveal the incongruity and difference that establish Otherness as such. Based on Lady Mary's discovery, however, the harem was neither foreign nor different. This naturally contradicted the ideas and information that appeared in the travelogues which gave writers a privileged position and power to reinforce and propagate myths surrounding this impenetrable place. The long series of travelers from Europe who preceded Lady Mary ranged from pilgrims and crusaders of the Middle Ages to traders, artists, renegades, soldiers, spies, etc. that followed in the later centuries. While their tales about the Ottoman Empire became instrumental in the formation and projection of images about the Turks, it was the harem that tied the notions of the Other together. As Bernard Lewis writes:

> It is now generally realized -it was not at the time- that the Christian informants of Western travelers in the Ottoman Empire conveyed a sectional and therefore somewhat distorted view ... The major disability of the travelers, of which their writings show the clearest evidence and the dimmest awareness is ignorance. It is of many kinds -diffident, and confident, simple and complex, ductile and rigid, elemental and compounded with prejudice, arrogance ... (Lewis *Some English Travellers*, 298-9).

It must be emphasized here, though, that if her gendered status allowed Lady Mary free interaction with upper-class Ottoman women, it gave her access only as far as the private apartments of a former favorite of the deposed Sultan Mustafa II. She could never get close to the harem of the sultan, which would always be left to the fantasy and imagination of writers. While no discovery about the harem was final, Lady Mary's first-hand knowledge, nevertheless, deconstructed previous apprehensions of the unknown Other that set the previous texts in motion. Lady Mary challenged all received representations of Ottoman society and set herself apart from other seventeenth-century travel writers. In redressing many of the misrepresentations, false conceptions and fantasies of Otherness attributed to the Ottomans, she wrote to her sister that "The manners of our mankind do not differ so widely as our voyage writers make us believe". In fact, since her "assimilation" in Ottoman culture inspired in Lady Mary a "most open and heart-felt admiration" (Desai xxvii) for the Other, she was adamant in refuting the erroneous representations of the Ottoman Empire given by these earlier travelers. Obviously, prior to her arrival in Istanbul Lady Mary brought with her images propagated through literary texts, polemical literature and travelers accounts -not to mention Gallands' *One Thousand and One Nights*, which conjured up female stereotypes and stereotypes of female sexuality. After she had the occasion to stay several years in Istanbul as Lady Mary wrote:

> You will perhaps be surprised at an account so different from what you have been entertained with by the common voyage-writers, who are very fond of speaking of what they don't know ... (Quoted from Desai 85)

> 'Tis a particular pleasure to me here to read the voyages to the Levant, which are generally so far remov'd from Truth and so full of Absurditys. I am very well diverted with 'em. They never fail giving you an account of the Women, which 'tis certain they never saw (104).

Real acquaintance with the Ottoman's culture, however, was different than reading accounts full of "melodramatic caricatures of exotic sexuality and barbarism in the seraglio for which orientalism is so famous"(Lowe 38). As one of Lady Mary's biographers notes, if her Letters had acquired the status of authority on things oriental, this was because "her sex and social rank allowed her a privilege not given to most travel writers -that of visiting Turkish court ladies in their harems" (Halsband 70). In Aphra Behn's case, as a writer, her desire to enter the world of the harem (even through a *masquarade*) that had been "terra ignognita" to the Westerners, was paradoxically a violation of many taboos in her time. Since the prevailing ideology in the seventeenth century was that writing was a male preserve, Behn's desire to write for the public was, of course, a momentous one. Yet, unlike Lady Mary's eye-witness experiences (irrespective of her borrowing ideas and literary devices from her predecessors and contemporaries), her comic vision in *The False Count* was based on imagination and fiction. Unlike Lady Mary whose husband's diplomatic presence in Istanbul had brought her prestige and comfort, Behn's challenge was to overcome the inhibitions which stood in the way of every woman who aspired to enter the literary world in her era. Women in the seventeenth century were kept from writing and publishing, not only by a conviction that wit belonged to a masculine domain (Goreau 19) but by fear of violating feminine modesty. As Angeline Goreau writes of Behn:

> Her example demonstrated that a woman -if lucky, if willing to surrender respectability, comfort, approval or even perhaps love; if prepared to risk ridicule, loss of reputation, vilification or attack -might declare autonomy and make a living by writing in an age when her only social and economic alternative was to marry or to find a wealthy 'protector' (Goreau 8).

While Lady Mary managed "to penetrate the Orient in ways no European male could" (Lew 434), Behn's achievement lay in her own ability to move out of the reinforced "feminine spheres" and circulate in the social milieu of courtiers, wits, poets, fops, etc. in London. Her literary aspirations were in defiance of the tradition of women's invisibility in the masculine domain of knowledge and literary circles. If women were restrained from writing and publishing in order not to violate feminine modesty, Charles II's abrupt return to the throne and his reversal of Puritan ethic allowed Behn to remove the "veil" of modesty and participate in the libertine ideology of her time. Thus, Behn eagerly embraced an ideal of sexual freedom and defied the rules of women's subjection to men. Ironically, *The False Count*, in which she eroticized the Ottomans through images of the harem, she ridiculed the shallowness of Isabella's ambitious desire to be the "She Great Turk". Yet as a woman writing in this era and exposing herself to the world, Behn had already taken a similar risk.

The False Count was a direct derivation from Molière's *Précieuses Ridicules* (1659) which was more than a satire about "ridiculous" women. It explored debates surrounding the "law" in an intensely patriarchal society. As a commentary on the gendered component of literary politics and social power struggles, Molière's comedy dealt with conflict in ideological and political order in the seventeenth century France. As Beasley writes, in Molière's comedy:

> The absolutist voice of the author, the father figure, brings back order to a chaotic state by pronouncing the condemnation of this monde à l'envers ("topsy-turvy world") in an aside addressed to the audience: [And you who are the cause of their folly, your back-brained absurdities, pernicious pasttimes of idle minds, novels, verses, songs, sonnets and moonets, may the devil take you all"] (Beasley 65).

Behn's "slight farce" as Elizabeth Barry announced in the Epilogue, had a satirical structure like Molière's play. *The False Count*, however, comically and critically targeted forced marriages. Yet, as her orientalist discourse revealed an ideological affirmation and superiority of Western values, the "morality" and customs of the Ottomans also made them an easy target for Behn. Since satire demanded that the audience be aware of two or more levels of discourse, *The False Count* through its sexually and racially aggressive language entertained the patriarchal structure of oppression and women's ambition for power through characters who "ventured life, liberty and wife to the mercy of the Heathen Turks...damned infidels" [IV.II]. On the one hand, Behn's obscene and racist language such as "Oh, damn'd circumcised *Turk*" or "Why, you're a *Mahometan* Bitch" [IV.II] threatened the moral aspect of a "satirical gesture" which had to be "essentially conservative" (Gill 156). On the other hand, the comic image of the Turk as "his Monstrousness", his "Barbarousness" fit into the parameters of a satire which operated by isolating and ridiculing some sort of abnormality and deviation. While abnormality implied a norm (which in this case was the Muslim/Ottoman culture, customs and religion), the comic effect in *The False Count* arose purely from the characters' disguise as Turks who terrorized the Christians on board. In the play, not only did Behn make the Turk the butt of her farcical fantasies, but she also ridiculed and severely satirized the Other's morality, religion and customs since they were perceived as deviations from the shared norms and standards of her audience.

In her comedy, drawn from a reservoir of ready types and plots, when Behn turned Antonio's fine villa into a pretense Seraglio (belonging to the Grand Seignior) where the "Tyrant" would regale himself with his "She-Slaves", Isabella also became the butt of the satirical joke. Although Guzman's project was to make the old wretch Fransisco a cuckold, it was his daughter Isabella, who was excited with the idea of being ravished by the Grand Turk and fascinated with the thought of being the "Queen of Turkey". Since Isabella's resolution was that "none should ravish [her] but the great Turk", she gave Guzman a jewel so that he would recommend her "to be first served up to the Grand Seignior" (IV.II). Considering that Behn predicted a whole new spectrum of possibilities for her sex, perhaps Isabella's enthusiasm to serve the sultan was packed not so much an allusion to her own violation of her modesty as it was a call for freedom of choice of mental partner. It was evident that Behn had transgressed the boundaries of the masculine and feminine spheres of her society through a kind of revolution. If the public exposure of her own work had revealed what ought to be hidden, ultimately the veiling and unveiling of Julia, Clara, Isabella and Jacinta through a masquarade in Act IV Scene II *[Enter ... Women veil'd ... Guzman unveils Jacinta ... Guzman presents Jacinta ... She is veil'd and set by: Then Clara is unveil'd ... Guzman unveils [Isabella] and leads her to Carlos, she making ridiculous actions of Civility]* had a direct link with the social hegemony of modesty, which controlled women. Behn, who like her literary colleagues Wycherley and Etherege wrote plays that dealt openly with sexual topics, had no qualms about openly violating the essential element of her gender - that is her modesty. Ultimately, if Isabella, with her misguided behaviour, was a foil for Behn, she also represented the "increasingly vulnerable and contingent position of women" (Goreau 11) in the seventeenth century.

While the image of the veiled Muslim woman epitomized the Other with respect to her Western counterparts, as Ayse Kadioglu indicates as Islam was viewed "innately oppressive to women. The veil and seclusion symbolized that oppression as well as the backwardness of Islam" (Kadioglu 651). Ironically, in terms of its historical roots, while women's veiling was not unique to Islam, in Lady Mary's opinion, its practice in the Ottoman society afforded women an anonymity that permitted them social and sexual license. She refuted the foreign travel writers' cultural constructions that women in the Ottoman Empire. Although Lady Mary saw an advantage in women's covering their face, a practice, which gave them liberty and freedom in society, veiling, however, was initially a foreign phenomenon for the Turkish people. In the Ottoman culture the adoption of veiling occurred through a process of assimilation of the customs of conquered peoples. In that sense, it is a complicated issue to analyze what is and is not unique, specific or intrinsic to the Ottoman/Muslim with respect to ideas about women and gender. It is a commonplace that throughout Ottoman history Islamic institutions and modes of thought constructed by early Muslim societies played a central role in defining women's place in society. Yet conceptions, assumptions, social customs and institutions relating to women and gender derived from the conquered lands of the Ottomans which included Byzantine and Islamic societies in which the subordination of women within the patriarchal power structure was "institutionalized within the rise of urban societies" (Ahmed 11). As the first urban centres of the Middle East arose in Mesopotamia between 3500 and 3000 B.C. in the valleys of Tigris and Euphrates rivers frequent warfare between city-states, the increasing military rivalry gave rise to male dominance. The Mesopotamian civilization, which spanned several millenia, included the rise and fall of a series of cultures such as the Sumerian, Akkadian, Babylonian, Assyrian and Sasarian. In these patriarchal societies, the family system, which entrenched women's subordination by vesting in men the control of society, became institutionalized and codified. As Leyla Ahmed writes:

> Women's sexuality was designated the property of men, first the woman's father, then her husband, and female sexual purity (virginity in particular) became negotiable, economically valuable property (Ahmed 11).

In the Mesopotamian region with the Code Hammurabi (1752 B.C.) and later Assyrian Law (1200 B.C.) authority resided exclusively in the male to whom the female owed absolute obedience. Although marriages were monogamous, it was the prerogative of the royalty to maintain large harems. While the Assyrian king had a harem consisting of about forty women, the Sasanian king, "shortly before the Muslim conquest ... consisted of some twelve thousand women" (Ahmed 14). Prior to Muslim conquest, this region was conquered by Alexander the Great, who after capturing the harem of King Darius with its three hundred and sixty-five concubines, even increased the number of women that the King of Persia had kept. In other words, prior to Muslim conquests of these regions—particularly during Sasasian times, concubines in the harems numbered in thousands. Under Islamic rule while the harem system became the norm among royalty, "veiling and confinement of women" (Ahmed 18) as a social practice was no longer restricted to the royalty and the elite. As Leila Ahmed writes:

> The veil was apparently in use in Sasanian society, and segregation of the sexes and the use of the veil were heavily in evidence in the Christian Middle East and Mediterranean regions at the time of the rise of Islam. During Muhammed's lifetime and only toward the end at that, his wives were the only Muslim women required to veil ... In those areas, as in Arabia, it was connected with social status, as was its use among Greeks, Romans, Jews and Assyrians, all of whom practiced veiling to some degree. It is nowhere explicitly prescribed in the Qur'an.[101] (Ahmed 5 and 55).

During the Christian era women's veiling and seclusion were practiced both on the northern shores of Mediterranean—as it was the case in the Byzantine society- and the south. Such practices and attitudes towards women, derived to some extent from cultural exchanges amongst the Mesopotamian, Persian, Hellenic, Christian and Islamic cultures. Ultimately, what was common to each culture was that the woman's humanity was submerged in the production of heirs to the throne. In these patriarchal societies as women's bodies defined the boundaries of their duties and aspirations, formulations of male dominance were quite explicit. During the Byzantine era, for example:

> Women were not supposed to be seen in public and were kept as "cloistered prisoners" ... and were always supposed to be veiled ... Daughters (and even sons) could be betrothed in infancy, and girls generally married at the age of twelve and thirteen...The system of using eunuchs to enforce separation of the sexes and to guard the enclosed world of women was fully in place (Ahmed 26).

In the West while the oppressive norms towards women were attributed to "oriental influences", in their "well-developed system of male-dominance" (Ahmed 28) the Byzantines were already oppressive towards women. The bias of the authors, who often distorted such information, often stemmed from a desire to distance oppression of women from Western societies. Yet, as Sarah Pome-

---

[101] The only verses that deal with women's clothing in the Quran are to be found in Sura, *Nur or Light*, 24:31-32. See Abdullah Yusuf Ali.

roy indicates, in the Classical period while males and females led separate lives, women "were usually secluded so that they could not be seen by men who were not close relatives" (Pomeroy 72). Most importantly, it was Aristotle who not only formulated the function of women as solely to provide heirs, but also attributed the subservient position of the female to her biologically, physically and mentally inferior capacities. Aristotle's influence regarding incapacities of women within the patriarchal power structure were widespread and enduring both in the Arab and European civilizations which systemized women's inferiority for centuries. Ultimately, irrespective of their sources, subordination of women and misogyny became the distinct characteristics of "Mediterranean and eventually Christian thought in the centuries immediately preceding the rise of Islam" (Ahmed 35). Later, regarding women as a source of danger, ultimately veiling and strict seclusion became a patriarchal mechanism to control the female gender in Islamic societies. As for the Christian world, church fathers such as Augustine even pondered why God had created the other sex, which was a source of temptation, corruption and evil.

When Islam arose in the seventh century and identified itself as a monotheistic religion in the Judeo-Christian tradition, misogyny was already a legitimized and justified concept. Despite ideological tendencies to attribute the seclusion and oppression of women to a non-Western source, it was Islam, as a new religion, which incorporated some of the already established norms into its system. As Ahmed observes, however:

> Nor is it only the Western world that developed historical constructs to serve vested political and ideological interests. Islamic civilization developed a construct of history that labeled the pre-Islamic period as the Age of Ignorance [Jahilia] and projected Islam as the sole source of all that was civilized- and used that construct so effectively in rewriting history that the Middle East lost all knowledge of the past civilizations of the region (Ahmed 37).

Ironically, in their efforts to recover of the knowledge of the ancient Middle Eastern civilizations, Western scholars do not acknowledge that Islamic civilization stems from a single source, and thus Islam is either totally "disinherited from that past" or not represented as "its direct heir" (Ahmed 37). It is a fact that the power of the Ottomans surpassed the ways of the conquered. This included the veil and the harem of the Arab and Byzantine societies.

Based on the first hand experience of Lady Mary, who had a particular position as a gendered observer, Ottoman women had at least as much liberty as their Western counterparts. Being a particularly learned woman, not only was Lady Mary engaged with the Ottoman culture in a specific intellectual context, but with her intimate knowledge of the domestic life in the *saray,* her urgency was to normalize and humanize life in the harem by making the Other familiar. Her letters that recorded her social visits with women who were free to create their own society, were a claim to subvert the stereotyped vision of an idle and oppressed women cloistered in an unfamiliar world. In *The Fair Captive,* for example, Eliza Haywood sought some compassion for Isabella, physically kept within the seraglio walls. In the Prologue to her play, she made a plea to her audience to think about the fair captive as her "Muse, and learn to pity then/A woman's suffering from a woman's pen". Before the curtain opened, Haywood had a frightened Englishwoman (played by no other than Aaron Hill who composed the epilogue) dressed in an "Ottoman" costume, running and pretending that she had escaped from the harem.

So I, broke loose, from a Seraglio life,
Will show, what 'tis to be a Turkish Wife!
Soft! -let me whisper! - shou'd some Husband gear,
'Twould cost our Petticoat Dominion dear!
No visits there -no plays-noCards-no Wooing;
Dull, downright Duty makes up all their doing.
...
All Women, there, obey, because they must.
Silent, they sit, in passive Rows, all day;
And musing, cross-legged, stitch strange thoughts away.
...
They feed, and fatten, for one Glutton's Dish.
...

> Blest in full Chastiti, and unbroke Slumber,
> They owe a spotless purity -to Number.
> Slow must five hundred Womens Virtue fall,
> Who have but one poor Man 'undoe 'em all! (*The Fair Captive*, Epilogue by Aaron Hill Esq.)

In 1721 if Aaron Hill had written this Epilogue in order to portray the seraglio as a nexus of slavery and abnormal sensuality with one male's erotic poweress could outdo the virtue of five hundred women, he also "claimed to have toured [!] the harem" (Beck 102) which, in the above epilogue gives a picture of a space populated by the seven deadly sins. A relation of the Ambassador, William Paget, Aaron Hill claimed that he saw the women's apartments in Adrionople during a temporary absence of the sultan and his ladies. As Yeazell writes:

> Assuming we believe Hill's repeated boasts of privileged access to the seraglio, we may still wonder just how a tour of the empty palace guaranteed this European visitor's superior knowledge of the sultan's private habits (Yeazell 16).

Hill's *The Full and Just Account of the Present State of the Ottoman Empire* (1710) ended with his "favourite" (Beck 102) account of: "A merry story of an English Cook who Caught some Turkish Ladies Naked in a Bagnio" (bath/*hamam*). Thus Hill's fabrications about the harem included fantasies about others' accounts of the secrets of the harem. Yet, Lady Mary was *the* only foreigner (later other Englishwomen claimed such visits) who had had the privilege of visiting the Ottoman ladies in their private apartments. She also visited other exclusively female spaces such as baths, which she perceived as a women's "coffee-house". Lady Mary wrote how these women were free to create their own society and how she admired the bonding between women adding that "there was not the least wanton smile or immodest Gesture amongst' em" (I, 313). Unlike Hill's vision which was based on imagination and fiction, as Lady Mary related her accounts of her visits to the Ottoman ladies, it was like being "in a drawing very different than that of England" where "no man enters" (I.266) and her opinion about these women was that they had "at least as much wit and civility; nay liberty, as ladies among us ... 'Tis not easy to represent to you the beauty of this sight (Desai 135). First of all, Montagu's eye-witness accounts and social interaction with the Ottomans revealed that despite the notions of tyranny and subjection of females arising from polygamy and concubinage, women had great liberty and freedom in the harem and that the Divan paid great respect to them. Furthermore, she was impressed with the financial privileges of the Ottoman women such as the custom of women's having control over their dowry and the financial obligation that the husband had upon divorce. Second of all, despite the stereotyped representations of the sultan's palace coloured with vivid images an unrestrained sensuality, it was not different than any aristocratic household in Britain at the time with the figure of libertine or a rake standing for a polygamous husband. As she wrote in The Embassy Letters:

> Now that I am a little acquainted with their ways, I cannot forbear admiring either the exemplary discretion or extreme Stupidity of all the writers that have given accounts of 'em. Tis very easy to see that they have more Liberty than we have, no Woman of what rank so ever being permitted to go in the streets without two muslims, one that covers her face and all but her Eyes and other that hides the whole dress of her head ... You may guess how effectually this disguises them, [so] that there is no distinguishing the great lady from the slave. 'Tis impossible for the jealous husband to know his wife when he meets her, and no man may dare touch or follow a woman in the street ... This perpetual masquerade gives them the entire Liberty following their Inclinations without danger of Discovery ... Neither have they much to apprehend from the resentment of their Husbands, those Ladys that are rich having all the money in their own hands, which they take with 'em upon a divorce with an addition which he is oblig'd to give 'em. Upon the Whole, I look upon the Turkish Women as the only free people in the Empire.
>
> ...
>
> 'Tis true their Law permits them 4 Wives, but there is no Instance of a Man of Quality that makes use of this Liberty, or of a Woman of Rank that would suffer it. When a Husband happens to be inconstant (as those things will happen) he keeps his mistress in a House apart and visits her privately as he can, just as 'tis with you (Quoted from Desai 71).

When Lady Mary refuted the construction of women in orientalist myths, challenged European norms and likened the English and Ottoman women in terms of their concerns and struggles within patriarchal societies, at the heart of her idealization of the "Turkish Ladies" lay the notion of "perpetual masquerade" which gave them liberty. [Lowe 44 & Lew 447). Terry Castle describes masquerade with its direct association to carnivalesque practices that subverted social practices, "for a brief moment, perhaps no longer than its duration, the masquerade effected an ecstatic liberation from the burdens of structure and hierarchy" (Castle 88). Lady Mary challenged the traditional and current interpretations of Orientalism by placing gender at the forefront of the hegemonic notions of the "exotic" and "different". She assimilated Ottoman culture to English modes of expression such as "masquerade", which in the eighteenth century social and moral context had connotations of sexual license as well as of defying traditional hierarchies. As Lowe writes:

> In the English concept of masquerade, disguises afforded an anonymity that permitted sexual and social promiscuity. Masked ladies could take lovers, courtiers could pretend to be peasants... Lowe 44).

In this sense, Lady Mary's metaphor "perpetual Masquerade" was another example of her intervention in the tradition of western writing about the Ottomans, which insisted on non-freedom, oppression and confinement of women in the Ottoman Empire. Essentially, Lady Mary was writing about the "liberty" of the Ottoman women, from the vantage of her own experience and awareness of the "unfreedom of the English women" (Lowe 44). In the case of Aphra Behn, whatever the "libertine ideology" of her time proclaimed, women could not renounce "at least the appearance of virtue" (Goreau 23). In this context,

> Wycherley's reference in a preface of his plays to that 'mask of modesty' all women 'promiscuity wear in public' is characteristic. This self-image was so deeply engrained that even woman of notorious reputation made an attempt at pretense (Goreau 23).

In *The False Count*, when Behn created her own masquerade, in which exoticism and spectacle added colour to her drama, she achieved her comic effect through the Bakhtinian carnavalesque energies of the ritual of the mask and disguise. For the audiences, Isabella who attempted to transgress the boundaries of feminine virtue in this masquerade remained an unsympathetic character. Ironically, the moral intent of Behn's comedy in terms of her bonding with female sufferers in a realm of patriarchal society, was hardly distinguishable from moral pretense.

Writing at a time when the prevailing ideology was that women were inferior to men in all aspects, she was participating in and responding to the needs of the historical moment. In that sense, she succeeded in asserting her power even through her potent language, which violated a customarily prescribed male privilege. If the patriarchal notion that the writers "fathered" their texts, had been all-pervasive in the Western literary civilization, Behn gave rise to an ideology of the female Other on stage. Evidently, Lady Mary's glimpses of the harem had changed *her* own perceptions of the Ottoman woman as being the absolute alien, ultimate Other. In fact, since Lady Mary's perspective was based on understanding the Other by making it familiar, she had even showed willingness to espouse the cultural practices of the Ottomans. She wrote to Lady Bristol that "you will imagine me half a Turk" (Desai 134). While it was her personal experience rather than external "authorities" that allowed Lady Mary to see beyond the stereotypes of Ottoman culture she was able to set a view that was neither monolithic nor a fixed world of any sort. In that sense, her views about the Orient were more complex and heterogeneous than Said's version of Orientalism.

Lady Mary, was in reality, a "reader" of culture and a writer. She brought to her "text" her unique experience. Indeed, she even portrayed herself as an actor in the scenes she described so vividly. She was simultaneously, character, author and interpreter or reader. She does not fit Said's binary model because of the dual complexity of her role and the sensitivity of her impressions, openness of her mind.

4.5. *A Peep into Seraglio* (1775)

> *At a famous ball held at Versailles in 1745, to celebrate the marriage of the Dauphin Maria Theresa of Span, Louis XV is said to have cast his handkerchief before Madame d'Etioles, the future Madame Pompadour, in a gesture understood to be that of the Sultan of Turkey in choosing his favorite. Whatever the truth of this episode, Charles des Glaces depicts numerous guests in Turkish dress, including many with gigantic Turkish headpieces consisting of face and turban and covering the heads and shoulders of the wearers ... There could be no more vivid experience of the fascination of turquerie* (Sweetman 44).

The myth of the imperial handkerchief, perceived as a custom for the sultan to choose his favourite, becomes a powerful symbol for patriarchal oppression in Isaac Bickerstaffe's *The Sultan; or A Peep into the Seraglio* (1787). Set in "An Apartment in the Seraglio", in *The Sultan* when Elmira, a Circassian woman, showed resistance to her captive position in the harem, the Chief Eunuch, intervened:

> Osmyn: Why then complain! You still possess his heart. Already you have been twice honour'd with the imperial handkerchief.
> Elmira: His heart! Does not this place contain a hundred beauties who equally share his love? (*The Sultan*, 6)

If the sultan's immense lust appealed to European fantasies of the harem with its stereotyped representations coloured with images of extravaganza, decadence and unrestrained sensuality, Bickerstaffe's rhetorical strategy through his peep into the *seraglio* was to transform its Oriental characteristics by affirming Occidental superiority. To begin with, the term *seraglio* was conveniently employed in the West not only for the women's lodging but also for the entire Topkapi Palace and all its buildings. As N.M. Penzer puts it:

> It would probably be impossible to think of any Eastern institution that is more familiar by name to the whole of the Western world but less understood in actual fact than the *harem*. From early childhood we have heard of the word harem and have been told that it is a place where hundreds of lovely women are kept locked up for the sole pleasure of one master ... There are perhaps two main reasons why such false ideas have lingered so long in the Western mind. In the first place, so great has been the secrecy which has always surrounded the Imperial *harem* that the first-hand and reliable information was seldom forthcoming. In the second place, the dividing line between fact and fiction, as far as the harem was concerned, was very thin and ill-defined (Penzer 13).

Following Antoine Galland's publication of the *Arabian Nights* in the eighteenth century, while the public was much intrigued by the novelty and fascination of the tales themselves, harem as an unfamiliar space for the Westerners eclipsed their curiosity. In the Western minds, the practice of the seclusion of women, slavery, polygamy and concubinage conjured up a cluster of powerful yet fantastical images "of a palace of women lazing about marble walls awaiting their master's pleasure" (Penzer 14). In *The Sultan*, while Solyman, much to the distress of his favourite Elmira, is enamoured by an "English slave" Roxelane, who demands liberty from him, "the Persian slave" Ismena, however, has no qualms about pleasing the sultan. In Act One of Bickerstaffe's farce: "Enter Ismena ... (kneeling) Your slave attends your pleasure". While Ismena begins to sing for the sultan "to express the effects of love", the sultan with his "hand" in Elmira's, is bewitched by the Persian girl's exquisite voice so much so that he will receive her "among the Sultana's attendants, and by that means [he] shall have an opportunity of hearing her often" (p. 8). As Elmira is "ready to burst with indignation and anger" arising from the sultan's infatuation with Ismena, enter the defiant Roxalana, led by Osymn, the Chief Eunuch, "that horrid ugly creature" (p. 9) as she calls him. The very presence of the English girl on stage, signals to the audience her radical attempt to change the status quo and make this Eastern setting inferior to the West:

> Sultan: Consider you are not now in your own country.
> Roxalana: No indeed; you make me feel the difference severely -There reigns ease, content and liberty; every citizen is himself a king, where the king is himself a citizen (p.9).

From the perspective of the audience, the belief that the harem is an inherently oppressive institution is a priori assumption. While the sultan advises Roxalana to alter her behaviour for "there are rigorous laws in the seraglio for such as are refractory" (p.9) the English girl's rhetoric is particularly targeted towards the policing regulations of the harem carried out by the Chief Eunuch:

> Roxelana: Oh, whispering -What is it that monster says? -that what-you-call-him, that good-for-nothing amphibious animal, who follows us like sheep here, and is ever watching us with his frightful glaring eyes, as if he would devour us —Is this the confidante of your pleasures —the guardian of our charity? — I must do him the justice to confess that if you give him money for making himself hated, he certainly does not steal his wages. We can't step one step but he is after us; by and by us, I suppose he will weigh out air and measure light to us; he wont's let us walk in the gardens, lest it should rain men upon us; and if it did, 'tis a blessing we've been long wishing for.
>
> ...
>
> If you follow my counsel I shall make you an accomplished prince—Let your window-bars be taken down—let the doors of the Seraglio be thrown open—let inclination alone keep your women within it; and instead of that ugly odious creature there, send a smart officer to us every morning (p. 10).

The sultan, though lulled by the English girl's violent condemnation of the harem can only admire her caprice as it is "the first time" that he has seen "in this place" such spirit of "independence. While the audience unquestioningly may have perceived polygamy, slavery and confinement as "Turkish" practices, originally, though, it was the Muslim tradition in the Ottoman Empire that concealed women—even those who held high positions that gave them financial security and power- from alien eyes. If Islam by nature was a patriarchal religion, Western writers used literary and dramatic strategies to make Eastern women inferior to women in the West through unexamined and stereotyped images. Yet, as far as Turkish people were concerned, as their religion prior to Islam was Shamanism, in their original home, which was Central Asia, matriarchal system prevailed. Changes in the climate had the forced the Turks to migrate to other parts of the world. Hence Turkish women in search of new lands left their home and traveled on horseback on the caravans with their husbands doing the same work as men. Women always shared the same rights and duties as men, and they were equally well equipped and trained as they jointly represented the state as *Hakan* and *Hatun* respectively (Inan 18). In the Orkhon inscriptions, in the eight century A.D. an order was not binding unless it began with "The King and the Queen Order". The two phrases "The Sovereign who continues the State " and "The Queen who knows the State" (Dogramaci 6) always went together. Both in the Orkhon inscriptions and the works of Uygurs, Turkish women were always mentioned with esteem. The birth of a baby girl did not bring dishonour to the family as it did in ancient Arabia and Greece. On the contrary, Turks even appealed to the mediatory prayers of the Oghuz Princesses for the gift of a baby girl. Tales of Dede Korkut (12 Oguzname), literary works of the times, indicated that it was customary for a girl to duel with the man who asked her to marry him. She would not marry the man unless defeated. With the spread of Islam, a Turkish monarch embraced its teachings and his people followed his lead. Although Turkish people remained faithful to their old and well-established matriarchal traditions even after they accepted Islam, eventually the social life of women began to be restricted. Since the practice of female slavery became a standard characteristic of Muslim dynasties, the preference of concubinage and the growing importance of slavery in the government system were reflections of the evolution of the Ottoman state along Islamic institutions and norms. Moreover, although the Turks were acquainted with the harem idea through the Persians and the Arabs, they were not interested in it until the fifteenth century when the Ottomans "found out that the Byzantines were enjoying" it (Cluegh 16). Following the conquest of Istanbul, as Mehmet II had divided the Ottoman Palace into two separate gendered sections, soon the *vezirs* and prominent members of the royal family introduced the harem life into their own homes and polygamy began to spread among a certain class of people. As Billie Melman writes:

> Although the Ottoman sultans modeled their harem-i-humayun or the Imperial Harem on the Byzantine 'gynecea', the pre-Islamic and non-Islamic origins of plural marriage and seclusion were not known to the West until the nineteenth century (Melman 59).

Despite the connotations of a slave institution as that of an uncivil society and arbitrary government, however, neither the female slaves of the imperial harem nor the corps of highly trained slaves that constituted the ruling elite of the dynasty should be thought of as "analogous to chattel slaves as we know of them from the history of Europe and America" (Peirce 40). As for polygamy, the social roots of which goes back to the beginnings of patriarchal society, it was established in the Islamic tradition to prevent immorality and abuse of the system. In Bickerstaffe's farce, however, for Roxalana, if domestic confinement is imprisonment, polygamy is a sexual slavery. Thus, now that she has gained "ascendancy over him" (p. 16) through her charms and her Western views, the sultan has even declared that: "but in every thing she is my superior" [p. 18]. Thus, you are my pupil", Roxalana tells Solyman, who is ready to be instructed in her ways.

> Ay, let me alone, now I have got the reins in my own hands, there shall soon be a reformation in this place, I warrant. Hey-day! What we got here? Cushions! What, do they think we are going to prayers? Let me die but I believe it is their dinner. What, do they mean to make me fit squat like a baboon, and tear my meat with my fingers?—Take away all this trumpery, and let us have tables and chairs, knives and forks, and dishes and plates, like Christians.—And, d'ye hear, lest the best part of the entertainment should be wanting, get us some wine ... I tell you, wine must be had.—-If there is none, go to the Mufty; he is a good fellow, and has some good wine, I warrant him. (p. 15).

In Bickerstaffe's comedy, the oppositional framework of acceptance and rejection forms much of the basis of his characters. Not only has Roxalana conquered and educated the sultan, but she has also brought "civilization" to his court. Thus Solyman even orders Osmyn "a true believer, a rigid Mussulman ... [to] obey ... and taste the horrible liquor" (p. 17) to the accompaniment of Ismena's song "Let men say whate'er they will/Woman, woman, rules them still" (p.18). Finally, as the sultan assumes and enforces his power, the handkerchief charade that he sets into motion only exemplifies the absurdity of his despotism in the *saray*:

> Sultan: I can rest no longer. (Gives the handkerchief to Roxalana).
> Roxolana: To me! Oh, no—Ismena, 'tis yours; the Sultan gives it as a reward for the pleasure you have given him with your charming song. [Gives the handkerchief to Roxalana).
> Elmira: (Faints) Oh!
> Sultan: (Snatching the handkerchief from Ismena, gives it to Elmira). Elmira! 'tis your's—look up Elmira.

In giving the handkerchief to Elmira, the sultan's plan is to "excite ... envy" in Roxalana and "leave her in everlasting jealousy" (p. 19) though the English girl will "never to consent to ascend his bed at night, at whose feet [she] must fall in the morning" and absolutely not in a polygamous relationship. In the eighteenth century, naturally, the image of "despotic sultans and desperate slave girls" was "a central part of an emerging liberal feminist discourse about the condition of women not in the East but in the West" (Zonana 594). Although, this is not to say that Bickerstaffe was a feminist, in the Enlightenment, assumptions about the East were aimed at both restructuring and transforming Western society itself. This allowed readers/audiences to contemplate their own problems by displacing the source of patriarchal oppression into the Muslim society. Yet, if one were to bring into focus the position of women in Islam, one is bound to dispel some myths particularly regarding the non-monogamous system allowed in the religion. According to a twentieth-century French surgeon Maurice Bucaille, a devout Christian, who learnt Arabic to study the Qur'an in depth:

> The totally erroneous statements made about Islam in the West are sometimes the result of ignorance, and sometimes a systematic denigration. The most serious of all the untruths told about it, are however, those dealing with the facts, for while the mistaken opinions are excusable, the presentation of facts running contrary to the reality is not. (Bucaille 110).

First of all, in an epoch in which women were considered a symbol of filth and evil, the prophet Muhammed's efforts to liberate them from their degrading position in the Arab culture in the seventh century were clearly seen in his Hadiths (sayings): "Woman is equal of man and the other half of the society" or "He who respects his wife is a good Muslim". With the revelation of Islam to Muhammed, the practice of murdering daughters which had been going on since the ancient Greeks, was prohibited: "... when the infant girl buried alive is asked for what crime she was slain ... then each soul shall know what it has done (*Qur'an*, Surah 81, Verses 8-11). Furthermore, for the first time, women could inherit properties under Islam, a great reform at that time. Islam introduced laws of marriage and divorce for the protection and the safeguard of women: "Either keep them honorably or part with them honorably" (*Qur'an*, Surah 65, Verse 2). As for polygamy, it was valid provided that absolute equality among the wives was maintained and the number of wives was limited to four. "... marry ... two, three or four of them. But if you cannot maintain equality among them marry only one. This will make it easier for you to avoid injustice" (*Qur'an*, Surah 4, Verse 3). This practice was acceptable as a response to the surplus of women in a warrior society and a way to build back the deteriorating family system in Arabia, where Islam had originated. As kindness to orphans and widows is much emphasized in the Qur'an, rich men mostly married widows for the protection of women and their children. Also the attitude of Islam to women's education was clearly defined in the prophet's words: "Search for knowledge is a strict duty of every Muslim man and woman. Seek for Science even if it is as far as China". In essence, while Islam brought great progress in Arabia during the time it was revealed to Muhammed thereafter, all its rules and teachings could not bring out the desired equality between sexes. As Mernissi argues, the medieval Muslim religious elite, which was uniformly composed of male members, aimed to preserve its authority over the society by exploiting Prophet Muhammed's saying that societies which entrust their "affairs to a woman will never know prosperity" (Abbott 175-76). She indicates that through the exploitation of the prophet's words the clerics distorted Islam's essential message of equality between the sexes.

In *The Sultan* when Roxalana turns the palace upside down and demands for "the gates of the Seraglio to be thrown open" (p. 21) Solyman hesitates:

> Sultan: But an emperor of Turks—
> Roxalana: May do as he pleases, and should be despotic sometimes on the side of reason and virtue.
> Sultan: Then there is our law—
> Roxalana: Which is monstrous and absurd.
> Sultan: The mufti, the vizirs, and the agas—
> Roxalana: Are your slaves—Set them a good example.

If Roxalana finds the Muslim law "monstrous and absurd", throughout the Ottoman history, the Islamic institutions and modes of thought played a central role in defining women's place in society. The issue of women was based on a set of laws and customs framed by the *ulema*, who were members of the corps of scholars and clerics. In that sense, Roxalana's displacement of the source of patriarchal oppression onto the Muslim society enables the audience to focus on the Other's problems by masking its own. This is, in fact, the essence of Orientalism, which is marked by distancing and differentiation.

In his article entitled *Lady Mary's Seraglio*, Joseph W. Lew points out that Lady Mary's masking of her cultural difference with the *yashmak* (veil) and *feradge* (long loose coat made in satin, taffeta or silk] "[s]tructurally parallels the paradox of apparent freedom for English women (which masks actual slavery) as opposed to apparent slavery of Turkish women (which disguises real freedom)" (Lew 447). If Lady Mary has reversed the Muslim woman's subjection of the veil and loose clothing as a symbol for personal liberty, in the late eighteenth century Lady Elizabeth Craven notes women's visibility on the streets in Istanbul. In fact, for Lady Craven, *yashmak*, not only "guarantees degrees of public freedom" for women, but also "makes them more mobile than their English sisters" (Melman 87). Moreover, Lady Craven brings into focus another detail on the condition of women in the harem with respect to women's desire for privacy and freedom-that is the custom of putting a pair of *cedik-pabuc* (yellow slippers for indoor wear) outside the door separating the men's quarters from the women's. As Julia Pardoe also observes, should a man, "on passing to his apartment, see slippers at the foot of the stairs, he cannot, under any pretense, intrude himself on the harem" (Quoted from Melman 110). Ultimately, unlike the myth of the handkerchief with its implications of women's subjugation and sexual exploitation, what the custom of yellow indoor slippers signifies is "the Ottoman woman's right for freedom "to refuse conjugal sex" (Melman 121). Based on the observations of Elizabeth Craven, Julie Pardoe and Fanny Janet Blunt, as Melman concludes:

> [M]arried middle and lower Englishwomen had no such privacy, and had little control on reproduction. The haremlik, seemed more protected from intrusion than middle class parlour (Melman 121).

In theatre, however, as the sexual proclivities of the sultan become a power symbol for his court, assumptions of the sexual, moral and political differences between the East and the West are portrayed on the basis of European perception of gender hierarchies and sexual behaviours of the Other. In 1775 when Isaac Bickerstaff's *The Sultan; or A Peep into the Seraglio* was produced at the Drury Lane with Frances Abington in the role of Roxalane, "responsible for its success" (Tasch 244). the story of a harem girl's reformation of the harem as depicted in this musical piece would later resound in Haydn's Symphony No. 63 called *La Roxelana. The Sultan*, a farce in two acts, was an adaptation of *Soliman II* or *Les trois sultanes* (1761), an *opera-comique* by Charles Simon Favart, who, in turn, had based his comedy on a prose-tale, titled *Contes moraux*_by Marmontel. Although, Favart referred to *Les trois sultanes* simply as a comedy since the play incorporated only a few song and dances, many composers later used it as a libretto for their operas.

Favart's staged comedy, which adhered closely to Marmontel's prose, revolved around three harem women- mainly the beautiful Circassian Delia, a stereotyped submissive Eastern slave and two Western women with minds of their own, the Spanish Elmire, and the Parisian Roxelane. The frontispiece to the book edition of *Les trois sultanes*, designed by Hubert Gravelot represented the musical divertissement with the women entertaining the sultan with music and dance. In this scene which probably was the highlight of the play, while Elmire danced, Roxelana played the harp as she sang a duet with Delia. Since the engraving rendered the long-necked flute and particularly the Turkish cymbals, which were at the time a novelty for Europeans, Favart explained "in a footnote their appearance and use" (Kurtz 1977, 314). Meanwhile Madame Favart's engraving after a drawing by Simonet was of particular interest because it depicted her in her famous authentic Ottoman costume, which was brought from Istanbul. Dressed in her exotic garb, what this "Parisian *gamine*" (Kurz 315) ultimately desired was to give liberty to all women in the harem.

On April 9, 1761, when Madame Favart in the habit of an Ottoman "sultana" featured in the Théâtre Italien production of *Les trois sultanes*, her husband's purpose in writing this *opera-comique*, was to portray the patriarchal oppression in the harem. In fact, as Yeazell argues, "where the harem is concerned ... Europeans were apt to see their own wishes and fears (sometimes both at once) as any unmediated reality" (Yeazell 7). Thus, in the eighteenth century, if the Favarts aspired to bring new political ideas of enlightenment to a despotic world, the historical Roxelana (Hurrem) had already made a great reform in the *saray* in the sixteenth century. In other words, more than two hundred years prior to the comic representation of Roxelana on the European stage, she had captivated Suleyman's affections and had convinced the sultan to free her. Once free, she had refused him any favours until he agreed to marry her. Following her marriage to the sultan, she had integrated the principally female side of the royal household into the imperial residence by moving the residence for royal women and children into the Topkapi Palace. Upon Roxelana's arrival at the Topkapi Palace, accompanied by an entourage of hundred of ladies-in waiting, a guard of eunuchs, servants, dress-makers, purveyors and various other household members, the harem, thus became all-powerful. In sum, Roxelana, for over a period of forty years within a legal marriage had received Suleyman's exclusive devotion. She was also allowed by the sultan to exercise an unprecedented power. This power shift in favour of the royal consort was significant in terms of reflecting the Ottomans' Central Asian Turkish heritage based on the principle that regardless of any gender boundary, authority emanated from both sexes. Evidently, before Suleyman had married her in contravention of Ottoman custom, Roxelana was presented to the sultan as a slave concubine, to which no stigma was attached. There are numerous historical records about the fact that Suleyman the Magnificent had remained constant to only one woman. As for the story circulated by the Europeans, including that of the English historian Rycaut who asserted that the sultans picked their "bed-fellow"s by throwing a handkerchief "where his eye and fancy directs" (Quoted from Yeazell 14) that was a source for false mythology. narrators. Ultimately, as J. Deny writes in *The Encyclopedia of Islam*:

> It is only in modern times that criticism has dealt with certain fables long believed, such as for example, the story of the handkerchief thrown by the sultan to his favorites (Deny 1113).

4.6. *Abduction from the Seraglio* (1782)

> *Osmin: This is Turkey, and here we do as the Turks do. I am the master; you're the slave! I command; you obey!*
> *Blonde: Your slave? I, your slave? Hah! As if any girl could be your slave. Don't make me laugh!*
> ...
> *Osmin: (Side) Poison and daggers for such a wench! By the beard of Mohammed, she makes me furious. And yet I love the little spitfire in spite of her crazy ideas. (Aloud) I command you to love me this very minute!*
> *Blonde: Hah...hah...hah...You just come a little closer. You'll feel my love all right!*
> *Osmin: You little vixen! Don't you know that you belong to me and that I can tame you if I want to?*
> *Blonde: Don't try to touch me if you value your eyes ... Your slave! I like that! It's women who pull the strings, and men do the jumping...*
> *Osmin: By my beard, in Turkey this is considered a treason.*
> *Blonde: Turkey, Turkey... I'm sick of your Turkey! A woman is a woman wherever she is!* (II.I)

Exactly a decade before the publication of Mary Wollstonecraft's *Vindication of the Rights of Woman* (1792) which turned the position of women in the harem into monitary images for women in the West, a feisty English girl took the centre stage to vindicate the rights of women in the seraglio. As Blondie told the lascivious and cruel Eunuch (referred to as overseer) Osmin:

> If you think, you old geezer, that I'm a Turkish slave who trembles at your feet, then you're sadly mistaken. European girls aren't like that. You see, we're accustomed to rather different manner. (II.I)

In his libretto for Wolfgang Amadeus Mozart, if the Prussian borne Gottlieb Stephanie (Younger), in reworking a libretto by the Austrian dramatist Christoph Friedrich Bretzner, identified the maidservant as English, this meant that even servants in England were freer than the "Turkish" wives confined to the harem. Unlike the tragedies, since Mozart's *Abduction from the Seraglio* (*Die Entfuhrung aus dem Serail)* approached the despotism of the passions in the harem in the spirit of comedy, even the tyrannical

Osmin, Blonde's would-be-master was made laughable by the very incarnation of his passions—lust, cruelty and vengeance.

During the second half of the eighteenth century, while plays with music, such as the *opéra-comique*, became an important feature in representing the Ottoman Turks on the French and English stages, the spirit of comedy soared in the imaginary seraglio. It is interesting to note that in La Scala's *commedia dell'arte* scenarios, the stock characters playing the lovers either flee the *seraglio* or convert to Christianity in the end. Similarly, in Favart's and Bickerstaff's comic operas, it was the French and the English girls, respectively, who converted the sultan to their ideas of freedom and introduced him to the concepts of virtue and freedom. Since a typical *seraglio* plot always revolved around the rescue of a captive girl kept in the harem against her will, "the loving couple, as the West imagine[d] them, [were] almost always engaged in trying to escape" (Yeazell 9). In fact, as Yeazell notes, strictly speaking, "both the possibility of being imprisoned in a seraglio and the chance of escape from one existed only in the European imagination" (Yeazell 1997, 86).

The number of comic operas produced between 1750 and 1800 was much higher than that of serious operas and some critics argue that *commedia dell'arte* groups were responsible for this popularity. Others refer to the two genres as "two branches growing from a common trunk" (Pirotta 305). In eighteenth-century operas such Mozart's *Abduction from the Seraglio*, while the arias provided the narrative and forwarded the plot, *opéra-comique*, as a sub-genre of musical theatre became a theatrical form, which was primarily sung. Charles Dibdin's comic opera, *The Seraglio* (1776), referred to as a musical entertainment, also incorporated airs and choruses to portray a noble and generous Ottoman Bassa (Abdalla) who initially came between two Christian lovers, Frederick and Lydia. In order to project their fascination with his power and splendour, the Chorus began with a hail to the "Grand Bashaw" at:

Whose steps one thousand slaves attend
Whose power with wonder we behold.
Whose mighty treasure's without end.
Whose palace shines with many gold (p.7).

Apart from rumours that Bickerstaff was writing for the composer Charles Dibdin (Tasch 244), the "best compliment that anyone [had] paid" (Tasch 247) *A Peep into the Seraglio* was that it had contributed to the plot of Mozart's *Abduction from the Seraglio.* Meanwhile Bickerstaff's *The Captive* (1769) was considered to be the source for Bretzner's libretto for *Belmont and Constanze* (1781), which, in turn, was the basis for *The Abduction from the Seraglio.* A two-act comic opera derived from Dryden's *Don Sebastian* in which Don Antonio, a noble Portuguese eloped with the daughter of the Mufti, in *The Captive,* the Cadi (Mufti) and his wife also escaped with the young lovers. Despite the political implications of Dryden's tragedy with a comic subplot, which satirized the meddling of the churchmen in state affairs, for *The Captive* Bickerstaff had eight different composers including Dibdin write "fourteen songs to sing away the lack of spoken wit" (Tasch 186).

As for Mozart's opera, which kept with the rational humanism of Enlightenment that so appealed to the composer, it vested the eighteenth- century *turquerie* fashion in music with deep resonances in the character of the magnanimous Selim Pasha. Just like the magnanimity of Selim in *The Abduction* which ended with a hymn of praise for the Pasha, the airs and choruses conveyed the generosity of the Abdalla in Dibdin's *The Seraglio.* Reason ultimately gave way to enlightened virtue with Lydia asking in Act II, "[I]s it peace or is it war? / Shall we quarrel or shake hands? / Which good Seignor are you for?" If the character of Selim fluctuated between that of an amorous cruel tyrant to that of a noble and generous pasha, such ambivalence also informed the very nature of Europe's political relationship with the Ottoman Empire in the eighteenth century.

In order to make his mark in Vienna, Mozart was anxious to work on Stephanie's libretto, which was chosen by the influential luminaries of the National Theatre particularly to please Emperor Joseph II who would be receiving the Grand Duke Paul of Russia. The text was solely chosen to appeal to the Austrian Habsburg Emperor Joseph and his propagandist campaign to seize lands from the Ottoman Empire, which had cut the gates to Vienna a century earlier. Moreover, both the libretto and the music appealed to the fashion of *turquerie*, reflecting a dual image, which, in the popular imagination, was at once as exotic and sensual, as it was cruel and despotic. This image helped to keep the memory of the Ottoman campaign for Vienna alive and continued to perpetuate the old myth of the vicious Turk" (Till 104) even though the Ottoman Empire had ceased to be a real threat to Europe. Yet, what needs to be kept in mind is that, although crippled by the 1683 defeat in Vienna, it would take at least another two hundred years for Ottoman Empire to cease to exist.

When Mozart was about to compose his opera, the Emperor was in the process of concluding a treaty with Russia for the Habsburgs to carve up some lands from the Ottoman Empire. The Treaty of Karlowitz in 1699 had demonstrated to the Ottomans that they were no longer militarily superior to Europe. In the eighteenth century, while the Ottoman army was still a formidable force, it was Russia, which had expanded at the expense of the Ottoman Empire. The first significant Ottoman losses to the Russians came during the reign of Catherine the Great (1762-96) whose forces had fought the Ottomans from 1768-72. Following the peace of Kucuk Kaynarca (1774), Ottoman territories on the Black Sea were given to the Russians, and Crimea, which had declared its independence, would soon be annexed by Russia in 1783.

Mozart and Stephanie had aimed at presenting *The Abduction* before Catherine The Great's emissary Grand Duke Paul, whose visit to Vienna entailed concluding a treaty with the Habsburgs against the Ottomans. Therefore, it would indeed be naïve to think that the music and the representation of the Ottomans in the opera were "well-intentioned". As Nicholas Till asserts:

> [T]here has never been a ruling power in history which was happy to encourage its people in favourable attitudes to a potential enemy, real or imagined. If Joseph II was willing to countenance Turkish music, it must have been because it was considered a just representation of the Turks themselves, its clashing and jangling aptly suggestive of the supposed barbarism of the oriental bogeyman. When Gluck in *Iphigenie en Tauride*, written three years before *Die Entfuhrung*, had come to portray the barbarian, human-sacrificing Scythians (whom Voltaire had suggested were the ancestors of the modern-day Turks) he gave them Turkish music for their bloodthirsty rituals. To our ears it may sound comically rustic; but Gluck intended his Scythians to be frightening representations of the primitive, savage unreason. And this is certainly how the Viennese audience would have heard the Turkish music in *Die Entfuhrung*: comic, yes but nonetheless crude and barbaric (Till 104-105).

If Mozart as a joke had given Osmin "one of the lowest bass roles in the operatic repertory" (Till 102) he had also given his longing for Blonde a touch of comic pathos. Like the harem-keeper, Selim Pasha with his lascivious and cruel nature embodied the stereotypical characteristics of "the barbarian" in Western thought, which stretched back to "Euripides' King Thoas" (Till 105). In the Western thought the sultan as an infidel conquering Christian lands, was a man to be feared as revealed in Dibdin's *The Seraglio*. Venture elaborates on his fear of the "horrid Turk" as he feels the "bowstring" at his throat and hears the "dreadful cries of murder" coming from the seraglio. In *The Abduction* when Constanze refuses his advances, the Pasha exhibits the characteristics of the cruel Turk, a tyrant who has the supreme decree over death and freedom. Although the worst features of the barbarian are loaded onto the ferocious and sinister harem-keeper, Selim Pasha's threats of torture to make Constanze submit herself to him are elaborated with Osmin's grotesque and manic outbursts to the accompaniment of a crashing and banging music complete with drums and cymbals. At the end of the play, in which the Pasha is given an opportunity to redeem himself, Belmonte, the Spaniard characterized as a knight-errant, who has arrived in Istanbul to rescue the captive Constanze, is recognized to be the son of Selim's archenemy. Yet, the opera comes to its expected happy ending as Selim with an act of magnanimity forgives and frees the captives and sends a message to his mortal enemy saying that "it is a far greater pleasure to repay injustices with kindness than evil with evil" (II.IX). Like the grateful lovers Lydia and Frederick of Dibdin's comic opera in which the Bassa by blessing them, is blessed, when Bellemonte and Constanze sing praises to his name to express their gratitude to Selim Pasha, the opera ends with a note that "nothing is hateful as revenge" (II.IX). This reflects the bourgeois Enlightenment's liberal vision, humane values and tolerance.

In both *The Abduction from the Seraglio* and *The Seraglio*, ultimately reason begot radiant virtue, the Enlightenment recognized passions, which through a careful observation, could be harnessed for the betterment of humanity. Contrary to the previous centuries' theological obsession with original sin, the Enlightenment's theoretical expansion of sexual freedom was made possible by a new sense of domestic morality, in which the family became an arena for the monogamous ideal. If the battle for sexual freedom was carried out in terms of the ideological reconstruction of the Enlightenment, passions still remained the source of all human creativity. If Rousseau claimed that "virtuous actions where I see no trace of ostentation or vain-glory always makes me tremble with joy, and even now they fill my eyes with tears of happiness" (Rousseau 101) James Boswell seemed to reject moral categories when it came to further mortal happiness. "Morals appear to me an uncertain thing" he said disclosing his secret fantasy for things Oriental, to Rousseau: "For instance, I should like to have thirty women. Could I not satisfy that desire?"

Rousseau: No!
Boswell: Why?
Rousseau: Ha! Ha! If Mademoiselle were not here, I would give you a most ample reason why.
Boswell: But consider: if I am rich, I can take a number of girls; I get them with child; propagation is thus increased. I give them dowries, and I marry them off to good peasants who are happy to have them. Thus they become wives at the same age as would have been the case if they had remained virgins, and I, on my side, have had the benefit of enjoying a variety of women.
Rousseau: Oh, you will be landed in jealousies, betrayals and treachery.
Boswell: But cannot I follow the Oriental usage?

> Rousseau: In the Orient the women are shut up, and that means keeping slaves. And mark you their women do nothing but harm, whereas ours do much good, for they do a great deal of work (*The Journals*, 112).

As the above brief section from Boswell's *Journals* revealed, not only did the pre-established images of the Orient gain the status of truth, but also discourse and ideology compared the oriental scene with the occidental one with fascination and repulsion. In this orientalist discourse, a non-monogamous system of sexuality, created a fantasy, which simultaneously disclosed Occidental identification with the Oriental male. Therefore, it was no surprise that Wollestonecraft, in vindicating the rights of women, recurrently referred to the conditions of the *seraglio* to identify the "present corrupt state of society" (Wollestonecraft 22).

Yet, in her identification of the East with despotism and tyranny, she took for granted that others shared her preconceived ideas about the *seraglio*, which she had never visited. If Favart's and Bickerstaff's Roxalanas stayed in the *seraglio* rather than fled it, this was because they had instructed the sultan to transform his lust for women to monogamous love. Moreover, they had converted him to ideas of the Enlightenment. Yet, based on Boswell's conversation with Rousseau, "a man is always a man wherever he is" as Blonde might say.

4.7. *The Russian Slaves: A Day In Turkey* (1792)

In 1792 when Hannah Cowley depicted the theme of enslavement and lack of freedom faced by the Russian slaves who were kept as captives by Ibrahim Bassa following the Russo-Ottoman war, she was inspired by the ideals of freedom emanating from the revolutionary zeal of France. Her comedy, *A Day in Turkey: or The Russian Slaves* acted (to the accompaniment of music, songs, dancing and spectacular stage effects) at the Theatre Royal in Covent Garden, however, was charged with such controversy that in the first edition of her play, she felt obliged to make a statement. As the "advertisement" read:

> Hints have been thrown out, and the idea industriously circulated, that the following comedy is tainted with POLITICS. I protest I know nothing about politics;—will Miss Wollstonecraft forgive me—whose book contains such a body of mind as I hardly ever met with—if I say that politics are *unfeminine*? I never in my life could attend to their discussion (*Advertisement*).

In the late eighteenth century, to be a Mary Wollstonecraft was to forsake conventional values and virtues by drawing a new focus to public and private spheres. If the prevailing ideology of her time was one that accepted women's inferiority as natural, as a pioneering feminist what Wollstonecraft advocated, was that women should have a political existence in the public sphere. Ironically, when Cowley attempted to alienate herself from the political realm, which she regarded as "unfeminine", she was already drawn into an ideological site. This was the ideological site of the Other, a centre per se, which automatically erased the gender-specific distinctions between a male and a female Western writer. Consistent with the ideological overtones of her comedy, which contrasted the manners and customs of the Ottomans with those of Europe, Cowley, like Wollstonecraft, focused on the importance of freedom and the humiliation of its loss. Ultimately, *The Russian Slaves; or A Day in Turkey*, which mingled the serious with the comic, conformed to a traditional orientalist structure that opposed the tyranny and licentiousness of the East to rational and civilized West. Furthermore, the cultural site that she created in her play, in a curious way, allowed her to ridicule and marginalize the Ottoman Turk in the farcical spirit of the entertainment. If she had anxieties about keeping her femininity in tact, Orientalism as a "style of thought based upon an ontological and epistemological distinction made between" the East and the West, had already given Cowley an "authority over" the Other (Said 2 and 3), which by itself was political in its inclinations. Thus, the overall impact of Cowley's play, relied on inconsistency: "tainted with politics" if it infringed upon the boundaries of the operative censorship determined by her state and her audience and apolitical when it implicated tyranny, nonfreedom and lack of love in another land -in this case "Turkey", which had to be endured only for "day". Consequently, Cowley's comedy permeated with such paradox reinforced a stereotyped vision of an alien culture by drawing attention to the morality, sexuality and cultural practices of the Other.

In the "Advertisement" while Cowley maintains that "[I]t is A LA GREQUE who speaks, not *I*; nor can I be accountable for *his* sentiments" she lets the servant of Orloff, a Russian Count, poke fun at "those vile turbans" of the Ottomans:

> A la Greque: ... Why you look as though you had all been scalp'd, and cover'd your crowns with your pillows.
> Turk: Christian, our turbans are too elevated a subject for your support.
> A la Greque: Dear Sir *[pointing to his turban, and then to the ground]* drop the subject, it will be a proof of national taste. (I.I).

As for Orloff, who is captured and enslaved by Ibrahim Bassa, he would rather be in "chains and dungeons" than be cheered with Turkish music, which he cannot "forbear" (I.I). While Orloff is yet unaware that his wife Alexina and her servant Paulina are also captured by Ibrahim, the countess, yearning for freedom and liberty, vows that she will kill herself if she cannot escape "these walls, the temple of loose desires, the abode of a tyrant and his slaves" (II.II). This mirrors the ecstatic readiness of Belmonte and Constanze's sacrifice of themselves in order to escape the imagined dangers of the *seraglio*. As for Paulina, who is the daughter of Alexina's father's vassal Petrowitz, she is fearless in her blunt protests against the Turks:

> Why, what wicked wretches you all are, then! Get out of my sight, do! You look so ugly I can't bear ye, and if I was a great man, I'd bring you altogether upon a rope that should reach from here to Saint Petersbourgh ... to be brought into such an odd, out-of-the way country as this—ha, ha, ha, ha. I have been here but an hour, and it seems an hundred—In one place a parcel of copper-colour creatures, without tongues, pop out, glaring with their sawcer eyes, and if you want to talk and be a little sociable, ba, ba, ba, is all you can get—I believe they learnt their alphabet of the sheep (III.I)

Later, as Ibrahim Bassa begins to woo her assuming that she is the Countess, Paulina objects: "Love! What, can you love? Such a hard-hearted—*Turkish*—creature as you love? ... I hate both you and your love (III.I). When Cowley seeks Wollstonecraft's forgiveness in the "Advertisement", she also defines "TRUE COMEDY" as being a "picture of life—a record of passing manners—a mirror to reflect to succeeding times the characters and follies of the present". Thus, as "a comic poet" she can mitigate tension in the theatre by drawing the audience's attention to the issue of enslavement in the Ottoman Empire. Yet, once she begins to evaluate the Western construction of freedom in the context of an ideology that allows slave trade in England, "hints" begin to circulate about the offensive nature of her play, which is now regarded to violate its performative agenda. If the comic scheme of the master servant configurations of Cowley's play diverts attention from similar subversive issues that are operative in the West, it also safely confronts and emphasizes the culture-specific perceptions of the Other. Once Cowley moves, however, from the distanced and differentiated Other to the ideological site of the familiar, the Self, she simultaneously undermines "what we have come to characterize as the Western humanist positions on the same issue" (Choudhury 495).

Following the Navigation Act (1680) resulting in the British monopoly of overseas trade and free trade policies which in turn led to the slave trade after the Revolution of 1688, England's interests permitted an ideology that justified the cultural subordination of colonial cultures. In Act I. Scene II Cowley touches on the issue of the freedom and liberty with reference to the ongoing slave trade in the West when Alexina begins to "melodiously [sing] her sorrows" as she puts it: "Blest freedom here ne'er lends her ray/Her bright steps here, we never trace". Then follows a witty conversation between Azim and Mustapha, which threatens and undermines the safe design of Cowley's comedy:

> Azim: *[snatching the paper from her hand]* Such a wailing about freedom and liberty! Why the Christians in one of the northern islands have established a slave-trade, and proved by act of parliament that freedom is no blessing at all.
> Mustapha: No, no, they have only proved that it does not suit dark complexions. Such a pretty creature as this, they'd think it is a blessing to give every freedom—and take every freedom.

> Later, in Act III. Scene I the dialogue between Paulina and Mustapha the theme of liberty in a similar fashion.
> Paulina: ... and if I could but see my father, and brother Peter.
> Mustapha: Well, if you begave discreetly—I'll buy your father, and brother Peter.
> Paulina: Buy! Buy! Why, you talk of buying us, as though we were baskets of eggs, or bales of cotton.
> Mustapha: Yes, it is the mode here—Every country has its fancies, and we are so fon of liberty, that we always buy it up as a rarity.

In this context, as Mita Choudhury, in her article, "Women Playwrights as Female Orientalists", comments:

> But how does his criticism of "Eastern" liberty square with the duplicity of the "Western" forms of liberty as signified in the logistics of the slave trade? The play resists delving into this quagmire. What emerges here is the Turkish slave's critique of the Eastern propensity to commodify freedom and liberty. It is the irony in Mustapha's observation that provides an oblique hint of the distorted principles upon which the West erected notions of free states and peoples. It is only an implication, and no attempt is made to unify Mustapha's sharply critical assessments within the context of his own enslavement which mirrors similar enslavements in the West (Choudhury 494).

The institution of slavery had been accepted and even legalized by the three monotheistic religions Judaism, Christianity, Islam. While it existed in all the ancient civilizations of Asia, Africa, Europe and pre-Columbian America, in the Middle East, it was practiced among the Sumerians, the Babylonians, the Egyptians, etc. In fact, one of the greatest powers in the Middle East, the Mamluk Empire (*mamluk* meaning 'owned') willingly remained as slaves. As Justin McCarthy indicates, however:

> It would be a mistake to think of the Mamluk slaves as comparable to slaves in the New World. Only in theoretical lack of individual freedom were they the same. Mamluks had power and wealth, both of which were denied to the slaves in America ... In the West, particularly in America, slavery is thought of as a lack of power as well as lack of freedom. Slaves in the southern United States were poor and had little control of anything, and were kept from gaining power that might threaten their masters. In the Middle East, military slaves often gained power and riches, but lack of freedom was still the defining quality of slavery. (McCarthy 84).

Before the American Civil War brought the issue of slavery sharply before Western opinion, the French Revolution had already given a new meaning to the ideas of liberty, equality and fraternity.

Thus, writers in the eighteenth century gave prominence to the ideal of freedom in the revolutionary fervour of France. In *A Day in Turkey,* Cowley, who is inspired by the French Revolution, turns the master and slave scheme into an ideological site of resistance to tyranny, oppression, lasciviousness, subjugation etc. In her comedy, the direct correlation between absence of law and freedom in the Orient has already been established by an epistemological framework, which operates through stereotypes and motifs brought together from different works. As a theatrical device while Cowley uses the motif of mistaken identity revolving around Orloff, Alexina, and Paulina, the Bassa assumes that the "lovely Russian who adorns" his harem is the Countess. And in a blissful and "transcendent moment" as the Bassa embraces the servant girl, in her lavish Ottoman garb, ultimately the object of his desire is the countess. By the end of the play as the comedy undermines the power of the Bassa, unambiguously, as Paulina confesses: "How hard it is when one sees a great gentleman, and so handsome withal, ready to die at one's feet" (V.I). Yet adds: "I can never be happy here—I hate the life people lead in harems—All is dismal, not even a window to the street! Nothing to look at but trees, fountains, and great whiskers and black slaves". As for Ibrahim, "[I]t is I who am your slave" he says. "You hold the chains of my destiny". In the final scene as Ibrahim Bassa will make Paulina his own by the holy rites of matrimony, Orloff whom the Bassa frees along with other captives, remarks: "Illustrious Turk! Love has taught thee to revere marriage, and marriage shall teach thee to honour love". Furthermore, as Alexina asks Ibrahim to forgive Azim, who has treated her cruelly during her captivity, the Bassa affirms that this "[c]harming magnanimity" must emanate from "the Christian doctrines" which must be "right". Thus he "will closely study them".

Originally, the encounter between the East and the West was one between Christianity and Islam not only as two religions but also as two cultures. The status of Islam within European culture was such that in terms of Western perceptions of gender hierarchies and sexual behaviours, it was the segregated Muslim woman, as a figure of alterity, who best represented the Christian West's ultimate Other. In the seventeenth century most of the accounts of the sultan's palace were written for Louis XIV who was fascinated with oriental despotism. The harem as a locus for Otherness continued to attract the curiosity of Western observers and led to a craze of *turquerie* in the eighteenth century. It was symbolized by the Ottoman palace, which stood as a microcosm of a despotic empire (despite the fact that the *ancien régime* in France is a universal model for despotism) and was contrasted to the supposedly benign ideals and Europe's absolute monarchies. As Mladen Dolar in an introduction to Grosrichard's *The Sultan's Court: European Fantasies of the East*, which deconstructs the Western accounts of "Oriental despotism" in the seventeenth and eighteenth centuries, writes:

> It is easy to expose the unreliability of sources, the use of highly dubious heresay, the blatant partiality and prejudice of the authors, their meticulous reports on which they, by their account, could not have witnessed (first and foremost, the seraglio) and so on (xiii).

Since it was the harem that stood for the opacity marking radical difference, the appropriation of the Oriental female confined in a space of nonfreedom, evil and lust, further led to constructions of European women as free, happy and loved. Particularly, the confinement of slave girls in the harem created in Europe a sense of Western women's unoppressed state. In the Ottoman system, however, since the dynastic lineage was perpetuated through the offspring of the slave concubines brought up in the palace—in order to curb the local autonomy of the aristocratic families-women achieved unprecedented levels of political power. Paradoxically, though, while this system diminished the power and position of the sultan himself, it also allowed slave women to rise from obscurity to notoriety by becoming mothers of princes eventually ruled the Ottoman Empire for a period that spanned over seven hundred years.

Cowley wrote *The Russian Slaves* in 1792 and portrayed "Turkey" as an oppressed land of non-freedom, which could only be endured for a day, during the reign of Selim III (1789-1807). Selim was installed as the twenty-seventh *padishah* of the Ottoman line, upon the death of his uncle Abdulhamid I, who like himself, was a passionate devotee of French liberalism. This is no surprising because Naksidil, Abdulhamid's royal consort, who was born and brought up in Martiniques was the first cousin of Josephine Bonaparte. With the sultan gone, the destiny that awaited his *haseki*, Naksidil Sultan (known in the West as Aimee Dubuc de Rivery) was to be transported to *the old saray*. Yet, while Selim made all the necessary arrangements for Naksidil to go back to France, she refused to go back. When Abdulhamid's son Mahmud acceded the throne, it was time for Naksidil, who was originally captured by the sultan and presented to the sultan as a gift, to reign peacefully and powerfully, in the Ottoman Empire as the *valide* sultan. Naksidil, like all the royal regents who preceded and followed her, had originally entered the *saray* as a slave girl. And like all these *valide* sultans, she was much honoured, loved and respected by the Ottoman populace. It is said that Mahmud granted Naksidil's last wish and let her die in compliance with the spiritual rites of the religion of her childhood - Christianity. Today, Naksidil, like all other Ottoman royal regents, lies in a most splendid imperial tomb. Her tomb is situated on the summit of the fourth of the seven hills of Istanbul, where the slender minarets and dome of the mosque of Fatih Sultan Mehmet the Conqueror glow.

4.8. Conclusion

Theatre is a potent vehicle for conveying dominant ideologies. In comedies although laughter seems to mask the ideological implications of representing the Ottoman Turks on the European stage, it does not eliminate them. Particularly, in the plays set in the harem, the Ottomans, whether in their fantastic or "realistic" guises, constitute the primary Other in the dramatic renderings of moral dilemmas. Consequently, the discursive relationships of tyranny and liberty, slavery and freedom, which help construct the imaginary locus of the harem, become fundamentally vital to the West's own self-definition and practices marked by differentiation and based on subjectivity.

In cultural representations of the East/Orient, difference creates ideological domination through discourse. Differences often lead to distinctions (racial, cultural, religious), hierarchies (superior/inferior, Christian/infidel), oppositions (good/evil, civilized/barbarian), stigmas (cruel, licentious) etc. As it is the case with tragedies, in comedies, too, the signifiers of difference establish visually the stereotypical images of the Other. Moreover, the comic spirit of the entertainment does not eradicate notions of the Orient as dangerous, evil and barbarous as opposed to the West. Thus, ideologically and discursively, cultural differences readily become systems of judgement for marking off and dominating the Other.

Todorov indicates that there are three responses possible in value judgements. On an "axiological level" one can accept the Other as good or bad based on the values of the Self. At a praxeological level one can embrace the values of the Other by identifying one's self with the Other or by distancing one may adopt indifference (neutrality). Finally, at an epistemic level, one can be ignorant of other's identity. All three of Todorov's options exist in Western responses to the exotic Other and to the harem, the private core of the Sultan's palace, the ultimate space of "Otherness". Conceptualized and defined in terms of its unfamiliarity and difference and perceived both as a locus of sensuality and incivility, harem as the primary indicator of alterity reinforces the West's "imaginative projections" or "structures of fantasy" (Yeazell 8). In this sense, the plays set in the *seraglio* are par excellence "narratives of space (récits d'espace)" [102] sustained by Orientalist assumptions of the Other's power, authority, morality and legiti-

102 See de Certeau, Chapter 9.

macy and operated through the voyeur's attraction and repulsion.[103]

Considering the ample interaction between the Ottoman Empire and the Italian States, the presence of the Turk/Muslim in Scala's *commedia dell arte* scenarios is not surprising. Although literary representations and imaginary constructs of Dante, Tasso and Ariosto have been instrumental in sustaining the idea of Muslim Otherness since the early modern age, in real life, amicability, trading and battles between the two states have gone hand in hand. Meanwhile as the *commedia* scenarios reveal, apart from commercial exchanges, privateering raids on the high seas have been so numerous on both sides that the themes of captivity, liberation and conversion display not only the comic genius of the players, but also reflect the real life dangers of travel.

In *Le bourgeois gentilhomme* the *mamamouchi* Otherness, which is seemingly a secondary theme, is in fact an essential element of the notion of Orientalism. In that sense, Moliére's *masquarade*, as an imaginary mode of representation becomes a cultural apparatus designed for purely strategic ends for "judgement, will to truth and knowledge" of the Other. In the play, not only does the ideology of humour display an imaginary encounter between two opposing paradigms of culture, but also difference at a variety of levels is ridiculed from the perspective of superior culture. Considering that Bergson's theory is based on the premise that the audiences laugh at a "recognizable" member of their world, the presence of the Turks even amidst the absurdity of the decorum, reminds the viewers of the Ottoman Empire's military, religious and political threat to Europe. In that sense, representation of the Ottomans in *Le bourgeois gentilhomme* partly functions as a means of mastering that fear.

In *The False Count* when Aphra Behn moves to the public world of writing and violates the rules of the gender-biased hierarchy of her society, her liberating attempt is already bound by

---

103 For the relations between voyeurism and Orientalism see Susan Robin Pucci (145-175).

all-pervasive ideological structures. Although the author discovered beneath her work may have attempted to reject patriarchal ideology, her Western values and perceptions of the Other reflect the psyche of her society. They are rooted in history. Yet, if Behn's main target in *The False Count* is forced and arranged marriage in a patriarchal society, the *seraglio masquarade* that she creates in her comedy is a dramatic device to deal with the complexities and contradictions of gender relations and sexual politics of Britain in the seventeenth century. Unlike Lady Mary, however, who has been able to subvert both patriarchy and the Orientalist discourse that conforms to a traditional perception of Eastern tyranny and licentiousness, Behn's comedy discloses an ideology is homogeneous and all-encompassing in its negative portrayal of the Ottomans.

In Bickerstaffe's two-act farce, in which Orientalist cultural assumptions are authenticated by ridiculing the sultan's power and authority, the Ottoman sovereign and an English slave girl define their positions vis-a-vis each other. When the sultan tells Roxalana that he will try to "render the Seraglio agreeable to you" (p.13), she is adamantly defiant of her status: "Yes, Sir, I do consider very well that you are the Grand Sultan; I am your slave; but I am also a free-born woman, prouder of that than all the pomp and splendour Eastern monarchs can bestow" (p. 13). Roxalana's identification of the Other as different is, essentially, to identify the Self as different.

In *The Conquest of America,* Todorov refers to Sepulvada as the defender of the intrinsic quality of Europe, an advocate of conquest in the name of European civilization. Roxalana's imposition of her civilized norms on the sultan and his "uncivilized" customs reflects Todorov's notion of imposing one's self-image and identity on the Other. The English girl's value judgements reveal that they are made exclusively in her own terms. In other words, when Roxalana sets up her propensities as the ideal (both in the ethical realm and in the realm of aesthetic judgements), her comparative method of judging the norms of the East and the West reveals her prejudice. On both social and ideological levels, Roxalana's self-image constitutes the basis of her conviction of the superiority of Western culture and of the Christian religion. The language of Self and Other employed by Roxalana in the cultural categories of "civilized" and "barbaric" forces the sultan think anew of his own Self.

As for Mozart's *Abduction from the Seraglio*, when Blonde, in defiance of Osmin, utters the words " I am an English woman born to freedom, and I defy anyone to enslave me" (II.I) the American Revolution notwithstanding, England is considered in the Habsburg Empire to be the advocate and guardian of freedom. Ultimately, however, in *The Russian Slaves: A Day in Turkey*, when Cowley through a complex interplay of power relations between Self and Other highlights the ideal of freedom in the revolutionary fervour of France, the ideology of her play can scarcely be regarded as solely protesting against slavery in the *seraglio*. Her authorial gaze is simultaneously drawn towards the ongoing slave-trade in the West. And that raises eyebrows in the theatre.

Conclusion

For Said Orientalism is a unified discourse that over the years has been coterminous with the Western consciousness of the East. This holds true for the Ottomans since from the time they invaded Europe, the danger they represented was abruptly revealed to the consciousness of the Christian West. In the sixteenth and seventeenth centuries as Europeans were well aware that the Ottoman Empire was not in a subservient position to the Western world, they challenged the Turk in fiction and exegesis, on stage and from the pulpit. As Matar observes the Western position with regard to the Ottomans "rested not on fact but on fabrication, not on achievement but on wishful thinking". It was only in "the imaginatively controlled environments of the theatre and the pulpit" (Matar 1998, 20), that the West was able to confront and engage the powerful Ottoman Empire. As long as the sphere of action was fabrication, then the Western writers of the sixteenth, seventeenth and even eighteenth centuries had an "authority of possessiveness" or "the security of domination" (Matar 1998, 11) over the Ottomans, which later developed to what Said refers as Orientalism.

If Orientalism is a "corporate institution for dealing with the Orient—dealing with it by making statements about it, authorizing views about it, describing it", then the current counter-hegemonic "regime(s) of truth" [Foucault '80, 131] that Said propagates, pose some historical and theoretical questions/challenges to this thesis. Although Said's main focus is on the post-Napoleonic period in which the European powers have begun the process of imperialism and colonization of the East, his work has been applied to the studies of Western encounters with Islam in different periods. In this respect, while Said's overgeneralization of the Orient is problematic and his general claims, made through a rough historical overview, are misleading, his binary opposition of the East and West through configurations such as weak/strong, inferior/superior, etc. are highly "complex and multifaceted" (Vaughan 27).

For Said, the image of the Other through which the West is able to identify itself is a European invention: " as both geographical and cultural entities—to say nothing of historical entities—such locales, regions, geographical sectors as 'Orient' and 'Occident' are man-made" (Said 4). Paradoxically, although Said's own designation of the "Orient" is "man-made", he asserts how European culture has partly defined itself in opposition to the East. He emphasizes that "Aeschylus and Victor Hugo, Dante and Karl Marx" (Said 3) stand together in Orientalism that has a continuity across the centuries based on a European distrust of Eastern cultures, that is said to be constitutive of Western identity.

The image of the Turk and Muslim, which has been for so long a myth and symbol of difference, has been historically shaped since the Crusades in representing values that are considered different from Christian and Western ones. In that sense, the Ottoman Turk is a conceptual given in the process of Christian Europe's self-understanding. In other words, as the texts studied reveal, the court of the Ottoman Turk with its intricate ceremonies and pageantries has offered a variety of themes to European drama, which have enhanced the visual splendour surrounding the Western theatrical performances. Yet, more essential to the texts than the exotic costumes, the spectacle, onomastics and bits of local colour that sustain images of the Ottoman Empire on stage, is the ubiquitous assumption that the despotic, irrational and licentious East is the West's Other. Yet, unless various misconceptions are exposed and the false polarity between the East and the West is dismantled, "real" differences cannot be revealed.

The traditional repertoire of Western cultural concepts about the Ottoman Turks is deeply rooted in history and ideology. Obviously, the Ottoman Empire as the paradigm and locale of the Other with its complex history and tradition of thought has a differentiating function through which European subjectivity has been defined since the Middle Ages. As the constructions of this subjectivity are built upon the dialectical interplay of Self and Other, subject and object, identity and difference, the Christian West constitutes itself on and against the defined Other. The Turk being both fearful and fascinating, tyrannical and evil, alien yet familiar allows Western identity to be defined. In that sense, in the London public theatres, when the public acquired its images of the alien Other through dramatized events, they also learnt about their own nation to a considerable extent. It helped them to affirm their identity through difference.

In Europe, not only were the travel accounts of Western visitors to Istanbul best sellers from the earliest days of the printed book, but illustrations in woodcuts, engravings and later in etchings and lithographs helped mold the European image of the Ottomans. Similarly, the constant menace to Europe of an Ottoman invasion coupled with a great interest in the character and customs of the Turk, perceived as treacherous and cruel, led to some of the bloodiest scenes displaying horrible court intrigues, rebellions and murders. Some of the stories taken from historical events inspired playwrights to write about complex Ottoman themes such as tyranny, captivity, war and conquests, fratricide, dynastic loyalties/disloyalties, rebellions, pride and humiliation and passions dictated by licentiousness. Following the watershed years of the late seventeenth century, when the Ottoman military threat began to wane, the fear of the Ottomans declined.

In the eighteenth century, the European image expanded to include diverse images of the Turk as noble, human, wise, generous, compassionate and magnanimous lovers. It is impressive that of the forty-seven plays representing different nationalities in Elizabethan drama, Turks are found in thirty-one of them. As Wann observes, this indicates that the European interest in this nation was stronger than in any other "oriental" race (Wann 427). In the carefully crafted plays which concentrated upon key characters who were predominantly Ottoman Sultans, the dramatists in exploring the motives and the consequence of the actions of these rulers, ultimately created heroes or villains who fulfilled the needs of drama as much as the discipline of the historian.

The relationship between the 'Turk', as a cultural and ideological composite Other constructed through diverse representational discourses (literary, linguistic, dramatic etc.), and the Ottoman Empire (real, material subject with its own history and tradition of thought) is one of the central questions that this thesis seeks to address. The connection between the Ottoman Empire as a historical subject and the re-presentation of the Turk produced by hegemonic discourse suggests that the Western writings have discursively "colonized" the material and historical world of the Ottoman Empire. Essentially, such discursive practices produced/re-presented a composite image of the Turk, which was not only arbitrarily constructed but also carried with it the authority of the West. With such a backdrop of the might and the power of the Ottoman imperialist system, it is no surprise that there was an outpouring of texts that vilified the Turks—not to mention a series of common prayers directed by ecclesiastical authorities for delivery of Christians from an Ottoman invasion. Since popular knowledge of Ottoman rule was limited to demonizing representations of the Turk, misrepresentations and misunderstandings about the empire's ethnically and religiously diverse society were inevitable.

In *Orientalism*, Said writes about what he calls—-after Foucault—the discourse of the nineteenth and twentieth-century Anglo-French Orientalism as it confronted the Islamic Near East. Said analyzes the assumptions, rooted in religious conviction, and conflict from which the nineteenth-century Islamic countries emerged. In dealing with the major features of Orientalism as a discourse which has been at work for centuries and in confronting the Orientalist apologias for colonial domination, he discusses structures and old oppositions, especially Islam counter-posed to Europe. In speaking of the essence of Orientalism through his schema of binary oppositions, he dwells on the ways in which putative knowledge about the "Orient" grew within a complex milieu of institutions, social and religious customs and the exercise of power. For Said Orientalism is a discourse of misrepresentation. In that sense, I share Said's conviction that the Western "ideas" about the "Orient" are largely gross representations ridden with bias and ideological concerns. Ideology, as Althusser puts it, is a "system (with its own logic and rigour) of representations (images, myths, ideas or concepts, depending on the case) endowed with a historical existence and role in a society" (Althusser 1969). In this sense, "systems of representations" about the Turks are ultimately indicative of the frameworks of sixteenth-century Western thought rooted in the fear of being conquered, captured and converted by the Ottoman Empire. As Hutcheon writes "be they fictive or historical" representations as constructs are "overtly politicized" and "inevitably ideological" (Hutcheon 6). Representations of the Ottomans on the European stage are not merely ideological; but as they occur within the systematic operation of what Foucault calls "discursive formations" constructed to ward off "powers and dangers" (Foucault 1981, 52), they constitute a "body of knowledge" or a "body of truth" (Hall 191).

The progression of events in the eighteenth century, however reveals this era as a time when not only were changes made within the Ottoman Empire with respect to its relations and patterns of affairs with Europe, but also as a period of Western reversals of trends in the representation of the Turks. The role of the feared villainous Turk is now downgraded in order to champion the noble and generous sultan and pasha with moral virtues. This is also an indication that theatre in the eighteenth century begins to provide a site for the geopolitical domination of the Ottoman Empire by turning the Orient into a feminine space through Seraglio themes. The interplay of culture and politics on stage points to the larger issue of European desire for hegemony over the Ottoman Empire. As the socio-political context of comedies and light musical plays provides the dynamic of the aesthetic representation of the Other, the dramatic subversion of the Ottoman Sultan under Western eyes, serves to invigorate the imperial ambitions of

Europe, which long had fascination with the Ottoman lands. The eighteenth century ushers in a time of defeat for the Ottoman Empire. With the emergence of the vogue of *turquerie,* the decline of the Ottoman Empire soon begins to inspire in the West a budding of "colonial"[104] fantasy in the Orient.

As far as the representation of the Ottomans on the European stage is concerned, the dramatic texts reveal the ambivalence, complexity and chronological transformations of Western attitudes towards the Ottoman Turks. In that sense "there is not a "master narrative or a singular orientalism, whether of influence or of comparison". Since the conception of orientalism is "heterogeneous and contradictory" (Lowe 5), the "essential relationship on political, cultural, and even religious grounds" between the Orient and Europe, cannot be simply defined as a fixed relationship "between a strong and weak partner" as Said claims it to be. Therefore, it is difficult to pin down the representation of the Turk in Said's monolithic discourse as a clear binarism. According to Lowe, on the one hand "orientalism consists of an uneven matrix of orientalist situations across different cultures and historic sites" and on the other hand "each of these orientalisms is internally complex and unstable" (Lowe 5). This holds true for the tradition of writing about the Turks as the plays reflect the ideological conformity of their writers to their social context and historic periods. Although the playwrights' perceptions about the Turks were devised rather than being faithfully reproduced, nonetheless, the tradition of writing about the Turks, bears a relationship to an underlying '"reality" about the Ottoman Empire. In short, Orientalism seems to have a complicated life of its own.

---

104 The terms "colonial" and "colonization" which have analytic values as categories of exploitative economic exchange between the West and the Ottoman Empire, denote a variety of phenomena in recent writings. In this thesis "colonization", as a problematic explanatory construct, is invoked predominantly as a "discursive" definition referring to a certain mode of appropriation and codification of "scholarship" and "knowledge" in the production of Western cultural discourse about the Other.

The critical intent of my study has been mainly to explore the historical basis for the distorted images of the Ottomans/Muslims on the European stage; and to assess the degree of the writers' faithfulness to "facts" considering that Ottomans/Muslims are constructed selectively with little regard for historical realities. However, when it comes to discussing the historical authenticity of the plays, one must first and foremost take the fictional quality of the dramatic texts for granted. In other words, the basic methodological problems that arise from too rigid an approach to exploring the representations of the Ottomans on the European stage are that a) drama being a product of imagination, need not correspond accurately to accepted historical knowledge and b) since we are dealing with fictional time, it is excusable for the dramatists to be ignorant about the Ottoman Empire and their affairs. Yet, as the patterns of deviations from "facts" indicate, in its construction of aesthetic knowledge and its dissemination of information, what film and TV have been to the twentieth century, drama was to the Renaissance and Restoration. Today, the plays about the Ottoman Turks in the English drama (1656-1792), may belong to a dead past just like the illusionistic world of the *Karagoz* shadow theatre. Yet, since these plays had a communal purpose in which national and religious identity was the prime focus of the sense of shared community, they played a great role in the constitution of the intellectual roots of modern Eurocentrism. Moreover, they participated in the creation and reinforcement of a highly biased picture of the Ottoman/Islam/East which still continues its political actuality to condition the West's perception of the Other.

In sum: at the close of the nineteenth-century while the Ottoman Empire attempted to survive in the victorious world of Western imperialism with its lands being carved up by the European allies, and their treasures "stolen, rather than sold" (McCarthy 195), the impoverished dynastic family of the empire was destined to belong to a dead past. Their fate was inextricably linked to that of the Western dramatists who aspired to give them life on the seventeenth and eighteenth-century stage:

> That curtain which they set up signifies the veil
> (that hides God from man's eyes)
> That candle is the light of the Creator's might.
> Behind the curtain of Divine Wisdom, incessantly
> The images of people appear, one by one.
> But when the candle goes out, the shadows vanish.
> Their person and their splendour are borrowed and transitory.
>
> (A Screen Ode to *Karagoz*).

WORKS CITED

A True Relation of the Murther of Osman the Great Turke, and fiue of his principal Bashawes, and the election and coronation of Mustapha his uncle in his stead... London, 1622.

Abbott, Nabia. *Aisha the Beloved of Mohammed.* Chicago: University of Chicago Press, 1942.

Abdul-Malek, Anwar. "Orientalism in Crisis". Diogenes 44 (1963): 102-140.

Adam, Antoine. *Histoire de la Littérature francaise au XVIIe siecle.* Paris: Domat, 1954.

Adams, Hazard, ed. *Critical Theory Since Plato.* San Diego: Harcourt, Brace, Jovanovich, 1971.

Agoston, Gabor. "Habsburg and the Ottomans: Defense, Military Change and Shift of Power". *The Turkish Studies Association Bulletin* 22 (1998): 126-141.

Ahmed, Leila. "Western Ethnocentrism and Perceptions of Harem". *Feminist Studies* 8 (1982): 521-534.

Ahmed, Leila. *Women and Gender in Islam: Historical Roots of Modern Debate.* London and New Haven: Yale University Press, 1991.

Aksoy, Nazan. *Ronesans Ingilteresinde Turkler. [Turks in Renaissance England]*, Istanbul: Cagdas, 1992.

Aksoy, Yildiz. "Onsekizinci Yuzyil Ingiliz Tiyatrosunda Turkler" [Turks in the Eighteenth Century English Theatre]. Unpub. Diss. University of Istanbul, 1973.

Ali, Abdullah Yusuf. *The Meaning of the Glorious Qur'an: Text, Translation and Commentary.* Cairo: Dar Al-Kitab, 1934.

Althusser, Louis. *For Marx.* Harmondsworth: Penguin, 1969.

And, Metin. *Culture, Performance and Communication in Turkey.* Tokyo: DAIWA, 1987.

And, Metin. *Karagoz Turkish Shadow Theatre.* Ankara: Dost Yayinlari, 1975.

And, Metin. *Turk Tiyatrosu 1839-1908.* [*Turkish Theatre*]. Ankara: Turkiye Is Bankasi Kultur Yayinlari, 1972.

Anderson, Sonia P. *An English Counsel in Turkey: Paul Rycaut at Smyrna 1667-1678.* Oxford: Clarendon Press, 1989.

Andrews, Kenneth R. *Trade, Plunder and Settlement: Maritime Enterprise and the Genius of the British Empire 1480-1630.* Cambridge: Cambridge University Press, 1984.

Aristotle. *Poetics I: With the Tractatus Coislinianus: A Hypothetical Reconstruction of Poetics II, The Fragments of the On Poets.* Trans. Richard Janko. Indianapolis: Hackett, 1987.

Artemel, Suheyla. "Turkish Imagery in the Elizabethan Drama". *Turkey: From Empire to Nation, Review of National Literature.* Ed. Talat Halman. New York: St John University Press, 1973. 82-96.

Atil, Esin. *The Age of Suleiman the Magnificent.* Washington: National Gallery of Art, 1987.

Baker, David Erskine, Isaac Reed and Stephen Jones. *Biographia Dramatica: A Companion to the Playhouse.* 3 vols. London, 1812.

Bartels, Emily C. *Spectacles of Strangeness: Imperialism, Alienation and Marlowe*, Philadelphia: University of Pennsylvania Press, 1993.

Bartels, Emily. "Othello and Africa: Postcolonialism Reconsidered". *William and Mary Quarterly* 54.1 (1997): 45-65.

Barthes, Roland. "The Death of the Author". *Image, Music, Text.* Ed. and trans. Stephen Heath. Glasgow: Fontana, 1977.

Barthes, Roland. *On Racine.* Ed. and trans. Richard Howard. New York: Hill and Bang, 1964.

Beck, Brandon. *From the Rising of the Sun: English Images of the Ottoman Empire to 1715.* New York: American University Studies, 1985.

Behdad, Ali. "The Orientalist Encounter: The Politics of turquerie in Molière". *L'Esprit Créateur,* 32.3 (1992): 37-49.

Behn, Aphra. *The Works of Aphra Behn.* 6 vols. Ed. Montague Summers. 1915. Reprint. New York: Phaeton Press, 1967.

Bell, John. *Bell's British Theatre, Selected Plays 1791-1802, 1797: Forty-Nine Plays Unrepresented in Editions of 1776-1781 and 1784.* 16 vols. 1797. Reprint. New York: AMS Press, 1977.

Bergson, Henri. *Laughter: An Essay on the Meaning of the Comic.* London: Macmillan, 1911.

Besterman, Theodore. *A World Bibliography of Bibliographies.* 4 vols. New York: Scarecrow Press, 1955.

Bevis, Richard W. *English Drama: Restoration and Eighteenth Century, 1660-1789.* London: Longman, 1989.

Bhabha, Homi. "The Other Question: The Stereotype and Colonial Discourse." *Screen* 24 (November-December 1983). 18-36.

Bhabha, Homi. "Dissemination: Time, Narrative and the Margins of the Modern Nation". *Nation and Narration.* London: Routledge, 1990. 291-322.

Bickerstaffe, Isaac. *The Sultan, or a Peep into the Seraglio.* London, 1787.

Bitterli, Urs. *Cultures in Conflict: Encounters Between European and Non-European Cultures, 1492-1800.* Trans. Ritchie Robertson. Cambridge: Polity Press, 1989.

Blount, Henry. *A Voyage into the Levant.* 1640. Reprint. Amsterdam: Theatrum Orbis Terrarum, 1977.

Boas, Fredericks. *An Introduction to Eighteenth-Century Drama 1700-1800.* Oxford: Clarendon Press, 1953.

Bodin, Jean *The Six Books of a Commonwealth.* Trans. Richard Knolles. London, 1606.

Boer, Inge E. "Despotism Under the Veil: Masculine and Feminine Readings of the Despot and the Harem". *Cultural Critique* 30-32 (1995-96): 43-73.

Bon, Ottaviano. *The Sultan's Seraglio: An Intimate Portrait of Life at the Ottoman Court.* Trans. R. Withers. 1650. Reprint. London: Saqi Books, 1996.

Boswell, James. *The Journals of James Boswell (1762-1795).* Ed. John Wain. New Haven: Yale University Press, 1991.

Botero, Giovanni. *Relations of the Most Famous Kingdomes and Commonwealthes of the World.* London, 1630.

Bouissac, Paul. *Circus and Culture: A Semiotic Approach.* Bloomington: Indiana University Press, 1976.

Boulanger, Nicolas Antoine. *The Origin and Progress of Despotism in Oriental and Other Empires of Africa, Europe and America.* Trans. John Wilkes. London, 1764.

Boyle, Roger. *The Dramatic Works of Roger Boyle, Earl of Orrery*. Ed. William Smith Clark. 2 vols. Cambridge: Harvard University Press, 1937.

Bradford, Ernle Dusgate Selby. *The Sultan's Admiral: The Life of Barbarossa*. New York: Harcourt, Brace and World, 1968.

Braudel, Fernard. *The Mediterranean and the Mediterranean World in the Age of Philip II*. Trans. Sian Reynolds. 2 vols. New York: Harper and Row, 1973.

Bridge, Anthony. *Suleiman the Magnificent*. London: Granada, 1983.

Bronson, Betrand Harris. *Johnson Agonistes and Other Essays*. Cambridge: Cambridge University Press, 1946.

Brown, John. *Barbarossa*. London, 1755.

Brown, Laura. *English Dramatic Form, 1660-1760: An Essay in Generic History*. New Haven: Yale University Press, 1981.

Brown, Richard Harvey. "Cultural Representation and Ideological Domination". *Social Forces* 71.3 (1993): 656-676.

Brummett, Palmira Johnson. *Ottoman Seapower and Levantine Diplomacy in the Age of Discovery*. Albany: State University of New York Press, 1994.

Buchan, John. *Prester John*. 1922. Reprint. London: Thomas Nelson, 1970.

Burian, Orhan. "Interest of the English in Turkey as Reflected in English Literature of the Renaissance". *Oriens* 5 (1952): 209-229.

Busbecq, Ogier Ghiselin. *Turkish Letters*. 2 volumes. Trans. E.S. Forster. 1881. Reprint. Oxford: Clarendon, 1927

Byzantium, Europe and the Early Ottoman Sultans (1373-1513), an Anonymous Greek Chronicle of the Seventeenth Century (Codex Barberinus Graecus 111). Trans. Marios Phillipides. New Rochelle: A.D.Caratzas, 1990.

Campbell, Killis. "The Sources of Davenant's 'The Siege of Rhodes'". *Modern Language Notes* 8 (1898): 354-363.

Canfield, Dorothea Frances. *Corneille and Racine in England*. New York: Columbia University Press, 1904.

Canfield, J. Douglas. *Nicholas Rowe and Christian Tragedy*. Gainesville: University Presses of Florida, 1977.

Caoursin, Guillamua. *The Siege of Rhodes*. Trans. John Kaye. 1482. New York: Delmar, 1975.

Castle, Terry. *Masquerade and Civilization*. Stanford: Stanford University Press, 1986.

Celebi, Evliya. *Seyahatname*. [Travelogue]. 10 volumes. Istanbul, 1896. Reprint. Istanbul, 1938.

Certeau, Michel de. *The Practice of Everyday Life*. Trans. Steven F. Rendall. Berkeley, Los Angeles and London: University of California Press, 1984.

Chambers, D.S. *The Imperial Age of Venice (1380-1580)*. London: Thames and Hudson, 1979.

Chew, Samuel. *The Crescent and the Rose: lslam and England During the Renaissance*. New York: Oxford University Press, 1937.

Child, C.G. "The Rise of the Heroic Play". *Modern Language Notes* 19 (1904): 167-173.

Choudhury, Mita. "Gazing at His Seraglio: Late Eighteenth-Century Women Playwrights as Orientalists". *Theatre Journal* 47 (1995): 481-503.

Clark, Donald B. "The Source and Characterization of Nicholas Rowe's 'Tamerlane'". *Modern Language Notes* 65 (1950): 145-152.

Clifford, James. *The Predicament of Culture: Twentieth-Century Ethnography, Literature and Art*. Cambridge: Harvard University Press, 1988.

Clot, Andre. *Suleiman the Magnificent, The Man, His Life, His Epoch*. London: Saqi Book, 1992.

Clubb, Louise George. *Italian Drama in Shakespeare's Time*. New Haven: Yale University Press, 1989.

Coghilll, Neville. "The Basis of Shakespearean Comedy". *Essays and Studies* 3 (1950): 1-28.

Coles, Paul. *The Ottoman Impact on Europe*. London: Harcourt, Brace and World, 1968.

Corman, Brian. *Genre and Generic Change in English Comedy 1660-1710*. Toronto: University of Toronto Press, 1993.

Covel, John. *Early Voyages and Travels in the Levant*. London, 1670.

Cowley, H. *A Day in Turkey: or, the Russian Slaves*. London, 1792.

Creasy, Sir Edward. *History of the Ottoman Turks.* London, 1878.

Croutier, Alev Lytle. *Harem: The World Behind the Veil.* New York: Abbeville Press, 1989.

Dallam, Thomas. *The Diary of Master Thomas Dallam, 1599-1600.* Ed. J.T. Bent. Hakluyt Series 87 (1893).

Dallmayr, Fred. *Beyond Orientalism.* Albany: State University of New York Press, 1996.

Daniel, Norman. *Islam and the West: The Making of an Image.* Edinburgh: Edinburgh University Press, 1960.

Davenant, Sir William. *Love and Honour and The Siege of Rhodes.* Ed. James W. Tupper, London: Heath, 1909.

Davenant, Sir William. *The Siege of Rhodes: A Critical Edition.* Ed. Ann-Mari Hedback. Uppsala: University of Uppsala, 1973.

Davey, Richard. *The Sultan and His Subject.* London: Chatto and Windus, 1907.

Denny, Walter B., ed. *Court and Conquest: Ottoman Origins and the Design for Handel's 'Tamerlano' at the Glimmerglass Opera.* Kent: The Kent State University Museum, 1999.

Dent, Edward J. *Foundations of English Opera: A Study of Musical Drama in England during the Seventeenth Century.* 1928. Reprint. New York: Da Capo, 1965.

Deny, J. "Walide Sultan". *The Enclyclopedia of Islam* 4 (1934): 1113-1118.

Desmond, William. *Desire, Dialectic and Otherness.* New Haven: Yale University Press, 1987.

Dibdin, Charles. *Airs, Choruses, etc. in The New Musical Entertainment of The Seraglio.* London, 1776.

Dobrée, Bonamy. *English Literature in the Early Eighteenth Century: 1700-1740.* Oxford: Clarendon Press, 1959.

Dobrée, Bonamy. *Restoration Tragedy.* Oxford: Clarendon Press, 1929.

Dodsley Robert. *A Collection of Poems.* 2 vols. London, 1768.

Donaldson, Hester Jenkins. *Ibrahim Pasha, Grand Vizir of Suleiman the Magnificent.* New York: Columbia University, 1911.

Dryden, John. *Of Dramatic Poesy and Other Critical Essays.* 2 volumes. Ed. George Watson. London: Dent, 1962.

Dumont, Jean. *A New Voyage to the Levant.* London, 1696.

Eagleton, Terry. *Criticism and Ideology.* London: New Left Books, 1976.

Eagleton, Terry. *Marxism and Literary Criticism,* Berkeley and Los Angeles: University of California Press, 1976.

Earle, Peter. *Corsairs of Malta and Barbary.* London: Sidgwick and Jackson, 1970.

Eccles, F.Y. *Racine in England.* Oxford: Clarendon Press, 1922.

Ekstein, Nina C. "Narrative Reliability and Spatial Limitations in 'Bajazet'". *Neophilologus,* 68.4 (1984): 498-503.

Ercan, Yavuz. *Image: Culture in the Ottoman State* Part 1. Istanbul: 1991.

Evans, G. Blakemore, ed. *The Riverside Shakespeare.* Boston: Houghton Mifflin, 1972.

Eysturlid, L.W. "Where Everything is weighed in the Scales of Material Interest: Anglo-Turkish Trade, Piracy, and Diplomacy in the Mediterranean during the Jacobean Period". *Journal of European Economic History,* 22.3 (1993): 613-625.

Faherty, Teresa J. "Othello dell'Arte: The Presence of 'Commedia' in Shakespeare's Tragedy", *Theatre Journal* 43 (1991): 179-194.

Feigl, Erich. *A Myth of Error: Europe, Turkey and Public Opinion.* Vienna: Amalthea, 1999.

Ferguson, Robert. *Representing Race, Ideology and the Media.* New York: Oxford University Press, 1998.

Fleischer, Cornell, H. *Bureaucrat and Intellectual in the Ottoman Empire,* Princeton: Princeton University Press, 1987.

Foster, W., ed. *The Travels of John Sanderson in the Levant, 1584-1602.* London: Hakluyt Society, 1931.

Foucault Michel. *Power/Knowledge: Selected Interviews and Other Writings 1972-1977.* Ed. and Trans. Colin Gordon. New York: Pantheon Books, 1980.

Foucault, Michel. *The Archaeology of Knowledge.* Trans. A.M. Sheridan Smith. New York: Pantheon, 1972.

Foucault, Michel. *The History of Sexuality.* Volume I. Trans. Robert Hurley. New York: Vintage Books, 1980.

Foucault, Michel. *The Order of Things.* New York: Vintage, 1973.

Frye, Northrop. *Anatomy of Criticism: Four Essays.* Princeton: Princeton University Press, 1957.

Fussner, F. S. *The Historical Revolution: English Historical Writing and Thought,* 1580-1640. London: Routledge, 1962.

Genest, John. *Some Account of the English Stage, from the Restoration in 1660 to 1830.* 10 vols. Bath, 1832.

Gentleman, Francis. *The Sultan: or, Love and Fame.* London, 1770.

Gibb, H.A.R. and H. Bowen. "Islamic Society and the West". *Islamic Society in The Eighteenth Century.* 2 vols. London: Oxford University Press, 1950-1957.

Gibbon, Edward. *The History of the Decline and Fall of the Roman Empire.* 3 vols. 1776-81. Reprint. New York: Modern Library, 1983.

Gibbons, Herbert Adams. *The Foundation of the Ottoman Empire,* Oxford: Clarendon Press, 1916.

Gill, Pat. *Interpreting Ladies: Women, Wit, and Morality in the Restoration Comedy of Manners.* Athens: University of Georgia Press. 1994.

Gillilands, Thomas. *The Dramatic Mirror.* London, 1808.

Gocek, Fatma Muge. *East Encounters West: France and the Ottoman Empire in the Eighteenth Century.* New York and Oxford: Oxford University Press, 1987.

Goffman, Daniel. *Britons in the Ottoman Empire (1642-1660).* London and Seattle: University of Washington Press, 1998.

Goreau, Angeline. "Aphra Behn: A Scandal to Modesty". *Feminist Theorists: Three Centuries of Key Women Thinkers.* Ed. Dale Spenser. New York: Pantheon Books, 1983. 8-27.

Greenblatt, Stephen. *Marvelous Possessions: The Wonders of the New World.* Chicago: University of Chicago Press, 1991.

Greenblatt, Stephen. *Renaissance Self-Fashioning from Marlowe to Shakespeare.* Chicago: University of Chicago Press, 1980.

Greg, W.W., ed. *Henslowe's Diary.* London: A.H. Bullen,1904.

Greenberg, Mitchell. "Racine's Berenice: Orientalism and the Allegory of Absolutism". *L'esprit Createur* 32.3 (1992): 75-86.

Grosrichard, Alain. *The Sultan's Court: European Fantasies of the East.* Trans. by Liz Heron with an introduction by Mladen Dolar. London and New York: Verso, 1998.

Grout, Donald Jay. *A Short History of Opera.* Volume I. New York: Columbia University Press, 1965.

Guleryuz, Naim. *The History of the Turkish Jews.* Istanbul: Rekor Ofset, 1992.

Gunny, Ahmad. *Images of Islam in Eighteenth Century Writings.* London: Grey Seal, 1996.

Hakluyt, Richard. *The Interpretation of the Letters in Hakluyt's The Principal Navigations, Voyages, Traffiques and Discoveries of the English Nation.* 8 vols. Glasgow: James MacLehose, 1904.

Hale, J. Rigby, ed. *Renaissance Venice.* London: Faber and Faber, 1974.

Hall, Stuart, ed. *Representation: Cultural Representations and Signifying Practices.* London: Sage Publications/Open University, 1997.

Halman, Talat Sait. "Comic Spirit in the Turkish Theatre". Theatre Annual, 31 (1975): 16-42.

Hammer, Joseph, Freiherr von Hammer-Purgstall. *Histoire de l'Empire ottoman depuis son origine jusqu'a nos jours.* 18 vols. Trans. J.J. Hellert. Paris: Bethuen, 1835-43.

Hanley, William. '"Vicissitudes of the Literary lnquisition: The Case of Voltaire's 'Mahomet'". *The Stage in the Eighteenth Century.* Ed. J.D. Browning. New York: Garland Publishing, 1981. 87-107.

Harth, Phillip. "Political Interpretations of Venice Preserv'd" *Modern Philology,* 85 (1988): 345-362.

Hasluck, F.W. *Christianity and Islam under the Sultans.* Oxford: Clarendon Press, 1929.

Haywood, Eliza Fowler. *The Fair Captive.* London, 1721.

Highfill, Philip H. Jr., Kalman A. Burnim, and Edward A. Langhans. Eds. *A Biographical Dictionary of Actors, Actresses, Musicians, Dancers, Managers, and Other Stage Personnel in London, 1660-1800,* 16 vols. Carbondale: Southern Illinois University Press, 1973-93.

Hill, Aaron and William Popple. *The Prompter. A Theatrical Paper (1734-36).* Ed. William Appleton and Kalman A. Burnim. New York: B. Blom, 1966.

History of the Life and Death of Sultan, Solyman the Magnificent, Emperor of the Turks, and of his son Mustafa. London, 1739.

Hobbes, Thomas. *Leviathan.* 1651. Reprint. New York: Liberal Arts Press, 1958.

Hoffman, Kathryn A. "The Space of Difference in Racine's 'Bajazet'". *Romantic Review* 77 (1986): 104-115.

Houlton, Robert. *A Review of the Musical Drama of the Theatre Royal, Drury Lane for the years 1797-1800.* London, 1801.

Hourani, Albert. *Islam in European Thoughts.* Cambridge: Cambridge University Press, 1991.

Howarth, W.D. *Molière, A Playwright and his Audience.* Cambridge: Cambridge University Press, 1982.

Hughes, Leo. *A Century of English Farce.* Princeton: Princeton University Press, 1956.

Hughes, Leo. *The Drama's Patrons: A Study of the Eighteenth-Century London Audience.* Austin: University of Texas Press, 1971.

Hume, Robert D. *The Development of English Drama in the Late Seventeenth Century.* Oxford: Clarendon Press, 1976.

Hume, Robert D., ed. *The London Theatre World, 1660-1800.* Carbondale: Southern Illinois University Press, 1980.

Hutcheon, Linda. *A Poetics of Postmodernism: History, Theory, Fiction.* New York: Routledge, 1988.

Hutcheson, Francis. *Reflections upon Laughter and Remarks upon the Fable of Bees.* 1750. Reprint. Glasgow: Garland Publishing, 1971.

Inalcik, H., P.L. Picon and K. Kevenk. *Turkish-Jewish Relations in the Ottoman Empire.* Chicago: United Turkish American Associations, 1982.

Inalcik, Halil, ed. *An Economic and Social History of the Ottoman Empire (1300-1914).* Cambridge: Cambridge University Press, 1994.

Inalcik, Halil. "Istanbul: An Islamic City". *Journal of Islamic Studies* 1 (1990): 1-23.

Inalcik, Halil. *The Ottoman Empire Classical Age: 1300-1600.* Trans. Norman Itzkowitz and Colin Imber. London: Weidenfeld and Nicholson, 1973.

Itzkowitz, N. "Eighteenth Century Ottoman Realities". *Studia Islamica* 16 (1982): 73-94.

Jaffe-Berg, Erith. "Towards a Paradigm of the Polylingual Performance: Linguistic and Metalinguistic Functioning in the Commedia dell'Arte", Unpublished Ph.D. Thesis, Graduate Centre of Drama, University of Toronto, 1998.

Jenkins, Hester Donaldson. *Ibrahim Pasha, Grand Vizir of Suleiman the Magnificent.* New York: Columbia University, 1911.

Johnson, Charles. *The Sultaness.* London, 1717.

Johnson, Samuel. *Irene.* London, 1749.

Johnson, Samuel. *Lives of the English Poets.* 1779-81. Reprint. Ed. John Wain. London: Everyman, 1975.

Kabbani, Rana. *Europe's Myths of the Orient.* London: Macmillan, 1986.

Kadioglu, Ayse. "Turkey: Is Islam really the villain?" in *Middle East Journal,* 48.4 (1994): 645-660.

Kafadar, Cemal. *Between Two Worlds: The Construction of the Ottoman State.* Berkeley and Los Angeles: University of California Press, 1995.

Kamps, Ivo. *Historiography and Ideology in Stuart Drama.* Cambridge: Cambridge University Press, 1996.

Kavenik, Frances M. *British Drama-1660-1779: A Critical History,* New York: Twayne, 1995.

Keynes, G., ed. *The Works of Sir Thomas Browne.* 6 volumes. London: Faber and Faber, 1931.

Kinross, Patrick Balfour, Baron. *The Ottoman Centuries: The Rise and Fall of the Ottoman Empire.* New York: Morrow Quill Paperbacks, 1977.

Knolles, Richard. *The General History of the Turks [1603].* Sixth Edition. London, 1687.

Kritovoulos, Michael. *History of Mehmet the Conqueror.* Trans. C.T. Riggs. Princeton: Princeton University Press, 1954.

Kunt, Metin I. *The Sultan's Servants: The Transformation of Ottoman Provincial Government. 1550-1650.* New York: Columbia University Press, 1983.

Kurtz, Otto. "A Gold Helmet Made in Venice for Suleyman the Magnificent". *Gazette des Beaux-Arts* (1969): 249-258.

Kurtz, Otto. *The Decorative Arts of Europe and Islamic East.* London: The Dorian Press, 1977.

Kyd, Thomas. *The Tragedye of Solyman and Perseda.* London, 1599.

Lea, K.M. *Italian Popular Comedy.* 1934. Reprint. New York: Russell and Russell, 1962.

Van Lennep, William, Emmett L. Avery, Arthur H. Scouten, George Winchester Stone and C. Beecher Hogan. *The London Stage: 1600-1800.* 11 volumes. Carbondale: Southern Illinois University Press, 1960-1969.

Lew, Joseph. Lady Mary's Portable Seraglio, *Eighteenth Century-Studies,* 24 (1991):423-451.

Lewis, Bernard. "Some English Travelers in the East", *Middle Eastern Studies,* 4, (1967-68): 269-315.

Lewis, Bernard. "Eurocentricism Revisited" *Commentary,* 98 (1994): 47-51.

Lewis, Bernard. "Some Reflections on the Decline of the Ottoman Empire". *Studia Islamica,* 9 (1958): 111-127.

Lewis, Bernard. *Islam in History.* London: Tauris, 1991.

Lewis, Bernard. *Istanbul and the Civilization of the Ottoman Empire.* Norman: University of Oklahoma Press, 1963.

Lewis, Bernard. *The Muslim Discovery of Europe.* New York: Norton, 1982.

Lewis Bernard. *Race and Slavery in the Middle East.* Oxford: Oxford University Press, 1990.

Lillo, George. *The Christian Hero.* London 1735.

Lipson, Ephraim. *Economic History of England. The Age of Mercantilism.* 2 vols. London: Black, 1931.

Lithgow, William. *The Total Discourse of the Rare Adventures and painefull Peregrinations of long Nineteene Travayles.* London, 1632.

Locke, John. *Two Treatises of Government [1690].* Ed. Peter Laslett. Cambridge: Cambridge University Press, 1991.

Loftis, John. ed. *Restoration Drama: Modern Essays in Criticism.* New York: Oxford University Press, 1966.

Lowe, Lisa. *Critical Terrains, French and British Orientalists.* London and Ithaca: Cornell University Press, 1991.

Lowe, Robert Manly. *A Bibliographical Account of the English Theatrical Literature from the Earliest Times to the Present Day.* New York: Nimmo, 1888.

Lybyer, A.H. *The Government of the Ottoman Empire in the Time of Suleiman the Magnificent.* Cambridge: Harvard University Press, 1913.

Lybyer, A.H. "The Ottoman Turks and the Routes of Oriental Trade". *English Historical Review,* 30 (1915): 577-588.

Mackenzie, John. M. *Orientalism, History, Theory and the Arts.* Manchester: Manchester University Press, 1995.

MacMillan, Dougald, ed. *Drury Lane Calendar (1747-1776).* Oxford: Clarendon, Press, 1938.

Mallett, D. *Mustapha.* London, 1739.

Mansel, Philip. "Art and Diplomacy in Ottoman Constantinople". *History Today,* 46.8 (1996): 43-49.

Mansel, Philip. *Constantinople: City of the World's Desire (1453-1924).* London: Penguin Books, 1995.

Marcus, Julie. *A World of Difference: Islam and Gender Hierarchy in Turkey.* London: Atlantic Highlands, 1992.

Marlowe, Christopher. *Tamburlaine The Great.* Ed. Una M. Ellis-Fermor. 1930. Reprint. New York: Gordian Press, 1966.

Marmontel, Jean Francis. *Soliman the Second. Marmontel's Moral Tales.* Ed. and Trans. George Saintsbury. London, 1895.

Martino, Pierre. *L'Orient dans la littérature française au XVIIe et XVIIIe siècles.* Paris: Hachette, 1906.

Martinovitch, Nicholas N. *The Turkish Theatre.* 1933. Reprint. New York: Benjamin Blom, 1968.

Matar, Nabil. "Turning Turk: Conversion to Islam in English Renaissance Thought". *Durham University Journal,* 86 (1994): 33-41.

Matar, Nabil. *Islam in Britain (1558-1685).* Cambridge: Cambridge University Press, 1998.

Matar, Nabil. "The Traveller as Captive: Renaissance England and the Allure of Islam". *LIT* 7 (1996): 187-196.

Matar, Nabil. *Turks Moors and Englishmen: In the Age of Discovery.* New York: Columbia University Press, 1999.

McCarthy, Justin. *The Ottoman Turks, An Introductory History to 1923.* London and New York: Longman, 1997.

McGill, Kathleen. "Women and Performance: The Development of Improvisation by the Sixteenth-Century Commedia dell'Arte'", *Theatre Journal* 43 (1991): 59-69.

Melman, Billie. *Women's Orients: English Women and the Middle East, 1718-1918.* Ann Arbor: University of Michigan Press, 1995.

Mernissi, Fatima. *The Veil and the Male Elite: A Feminist Interpretation of Women's Rights in Islam.* Trans. Mary Jo Lakeland. Reading: Addison-Wesley, 1991.

Merriman, Roger Bigelow. *Suleiman the Magnificent.* Cambridge: Harvard University Press, 1944.

Meyer, Eric. "'I Know Thee not, I loathe Thy Race': Romantic Orientalism in the Eye of the Other". *ELH* 58.3 (1991): 657-699.

Miller, Barnette. *Beyond the Sublime Porte.* New York: AMS Press, 1970.

Miller, James. *Mahomet.* London, 1745.

Minchinton, W.E. *The Growth of Overseas Trade in the Seventeenth and Eighteenth Centuries.* London: Methuen, 1969.

Molière, Jean-Baptise Poquelin. *Œuvres*, "Grands Écrivains de la France". Volume 8. 1873-1900.

Molière, Jean-Baptiste Poquelin. *Plays.* 8 volumes. Ed. and Trans. A.R. Waller. Edinburgh: J. Grant, 1926.

Montagu, Lady Mary Wortley. *The Complete Works of Lady Mary Wortley Montagu.* Ed. Robert Halsband. Vol. I, Oxford: Clarendon 1967.

Montagu, Lady Mary Wortley. *Turkish Embassy Letters.* Ed. Malcolm Jack. London: William Pickering, 1993.

Montesquieu, Charles de Secondat Baron de. *Persian Letters.* Trans John Ozell. 1743. Reprint. 2 vols. New York: Garland Publishing, 1972.

Moran, Berna. "The Irene Story and Dr. Johnson's Sources". *Modern Language Notes* 71 (1956): 87-91.

Moran, Berna. "Sir Thomas Browne's Reading of the Turks", *Notes and Queries* 197 (1952): 380-383, 403-406.

Moran, Berna. *Turklerle Ilgili Ingilizce Yayinlar Bibliyografyasi: Onbesinci Yuzyildan Onsekizinci Yuzyila Kadar* [The Bibliography of the English Publications About the Turks from the 15th Century to the 18th Century]. Istanbul: Istanbul University Press, 1964.

Moseley, R.D., ed. *The Travels of Sir John Mandeville.* London: Penguin, 1983.

Naff, Thomas and Roger Owen, eds. *Studies in the Eighteenth-Century Islamic History.* Carbondale: Southern Illinois University Press, 1977.

Naima, M. *Annals of the Turkish Empire from 1591-1659.* 9 vols. Trans. C. Fraser. London, 1832.

Naima, Mustafa. *Tarih.* [History]. 6 vols. Istanbul, 1280/1863-1869.

Necipoglu, Gulru. "Suleyman the Magnificent and the Representation of Power in the Context of Ottoman-Hapsburg-Papal Rivalry". *Art Bulletin,* 71.3 (1989): 401-427.

Nelson, T.G.A. *Comedy: An Introduction to Comedy in Literature, Drama and Cinema.* Oxford: Oxford University Press, 1990.

Nicholas, Nicolay de. *The Navigations, Peregrinations and Voyages.* London, 1585.

Nicoll, Allardyce. *A History of English Drama, 1660-1900.* 6 vols. 1952-59. Reprint. Cambridge: Cambridge University Press, 1965.

Osborne, Francis. *Political Reflections Upon the Government of the Turks.* London, 1656.

Painter, William. *The Palace of Pleasure: Elizabethan Versions of Italian and French Novels from Boccacio, Bandello, Cinthio, Straparola, Quen Margaret of Navarre and Others.* 3 vols. Trans. Joseph Jacobs. London, 1890.

Pavis, Patrice. *Théâtre: Modes d'Approche.* Brussel: Meridiens Klincksieck, 1987.

Payne, H.N. *The Siege of Constantinople.* London, 1675.

Penzer, N.M. *The Harem.* Revised ed. London: Spring Books, 1967.

Pepys, Samuel. *The Diary of Samuel Pepys, ed. John Dump.* New York: Washington Square Press, 1964.

Pepys, Samuel. *The Diary of Samuel Pepys.* 9 vols. Ed. Robert Latham and William Matthews. Berkeley: University of California Press, 1970.

Pierce, Leslie. *The Imperial Harem: Women and Sovereignty in the Ottoman Empire.* New York: Oxford University Press, 1993.

Pirrotta, Nino. "Commedia dell'Arte and Opera". *Musical Quarterly.* 16 (1955): 305-324.

Pix, Mary. *Ibrahim the Thirteenth Emperour of the Turks.* London, 1696.

Pomeroy, Sarah. *Goddesses, Whores, Wives, and Slaves: Women in the Classical Antiquity.* New York: Schocken, 1975.

Porter, Dennis. *Haunted Journeys: Desire and Transgression in European Travel Writing.* Princeton: Princeton University Press, 1991.

Pucci, Suzanne Rodin. "The Discrete charms of the exotic: Fictions of the Harem in Eighteenth Century France". *Exoticism in the Enlightenment,* ed. G.S. Rousseau and Roy Porter. Manchester: Manchester University Press, 1990.

Purchas, Samuel. *Hakluytus Posthumus or Purchas His Pilgrimes.* 20 vols. New York: AMS Press, 1965.

Racine, Jean. *Bajazet.* Ed. Margaret M. McGowan, London: University of London Press, 1968.

Ranum, Orest. "Visions of Nobility and Gallantry: Understanding the Jourdains Historically". *Approaches to Teaching Moliere's Tartuffe and Other Plays*". Ed. James F. Gaines and Michael S. Koppisch. New York: MLA, 1995. 104-109.

Ribeiro, Aileen. "Turkey and the West". *Court and Conquest.* Kent: Kent State University Museum, 1999. 19-28.

Richards, Kenneth. *The Commedia dell'Arte: A Documentary History.* Oxford: Blackwell, 1990.

Riggs, Larry W. *Molière and Plurality: Decomposition of the Classicist Self.* New York: Peter Lang, 1989.

Riggs, Larry W. "The Issues of Nobility and Identity in 'Don Juam' and 'Le bourgeois Gentilhomme'". *The French Review* 59.3 (1986): 399-409.

Robinson, Francis, ed. *Islamic World.* Cambridge: Cambridge University Press, 1996.

Rogers, J.M. and R.M. Ward. *Suleyman the Magnificent.* London, British Museum Publications, 1988.

Rolls, Albert. *The Theory of the King's Two Bodies in the Age of Shakespeare.* New York: Mellen, 2000.

Romanowski, Sylvie. "The Circuits of Power and Discourse in Racine's 'Bajazet'". *Papers on French Seventeenth Century Literature,* 18 (1983). 849-867.

Rossiter, Johnson, ed. *The Great Events by Famous Historians.* 22 vols. New York: The National Alumni, 1926.

Rothstein, Eric and Frances M. Kavenik. *The Designs of Carolean Comedy.* Carbondale: Southern Illinois University Press, 1988.

Rothstein, Eric. *Restoration Tragedy: Form and the Process of Change.* 1967. Reprint. Westport: Greenwood, 1978.

Rouillard, Clarence D. *The Turk in French History, Thought and Literature (1520-1660).* Paris: Boivin, 1938.

Rowe, Nicholas. *Tamerlane, A Tragedy.* Ed. Landon C. Burns, Jr. Philadelphia: University of Pennsylvania Press, 1966.

Rycaut, Sir Paul. *The History of the Turkish Empire From The Year 1629 to the Year 1677.* London, 1687.

Rycaut, Sir Paul. *The Present State of The Empire.* London, 1668.

Said, Edward. *Beginnings,* New York: Basic Books, 1975.

Said, Edward. *Culture and Imperialism.* London: Chatto and Windus, 1993.

Said, Edward. *Orientalism.* 1978. Reprint. London: Penguin, 1985.

Said, Edward. *Covering Islam: How the Media and Experts Determine How We See the Rest of the World.* New York: Pantheon Books, 1981.

Said, Edward. "Representing the Colonized: Anthropology's Interlocutors", *Critical Inquiry* 15 (1989): 205-225.

Said, Edward. *The World, The Text and The Critic.* Cambridge: Harvard University Press, 1983.

Sandys, G. *Travels (1610).* London, 1652.

Saint Exupéry, Antoine de. *Le Petit Prince.* New York: Harcourt, Brace and World, 1971.

Savage, John. *The Turkish History.* Abridged from Knolles and Rycaut. 2 vols. London, 1701.

Scala, Flaminio. *Scenarios of the Commedia dell'Arte:Flaminio Scala's Il teatro delle favole rappresentative.* Trans. and Ed. Henry F. Salerno. New York: New York University Press, 1967.

Schwoebel, Robert. *The Shadow of the Crescent: The Renaissance Image of the Turk (1453-1517).* New York: St. Martin's Press, 1967.

Seaton, Ethel. "Fresh Sources for Marlowe" in *Review of English Studies* 5 (1929): 385-401.

Setton, Kenneth, Meyer. *The Papacy and the Levant.* 4 volumes. Philadelphia: American Philosophical Society, 1976-78.

Shaw, Stanford J. and Ezel Kural Shaw. *History of the Ottoman Empire and Modern Turkey.* Cambridge: Cambridge University Press, 1977.

Shirley, Sir Anthony. *Travels into Persia in Hakluytus Posthumous or Purchas His Pilgrimes.* New York: AMS, 1965.

Shirley, Thomas. "Discours of the Turkes by Sr. Thomas Sherley'. Ed. Denison Ross. *Camden Miscellany* 16 (1936).

Silverberg, Robert. *The Realm of Prester John,* Garden City: Doubleday, 1972.

Siyavusgil, Sabri Esat. *Karagoz.* Istanbul: Turkish Broadcasting and Tourist Department, 1961.

Skilliter, Susan A. "Three Letters from the Sultana Safiye to Queen Elizabeth I. Documents from Islamic Chanceries". *Oriental Studies* 3 (1965). 120-157.

Skilliter, Susan A. *William Harborne and the trade with Turkey (1578-1582): A Documentary Study of the first Anglo-Ottoman Relations.* Oxford: Oxford University Press, 1977.

Smith, J.C. and E. de Selincourt, eds. *Spenser: Poetical Works.* 1912. Reprint. Oxford: Oxford University Press, 1985.

Solbrig, Ingeborg. "The Theatre, Theory and Politics: Voltaire's 'Le Fanatisme ou Mahomet le Prophete' and Goethe's 'Mahomet, Adaptation'". *Michigan Germanic Studies* 16.1 (1990): 21-43.

Solomon, Samuel, trans. *The Complete Plays of Racine.* New York: Random House, 1967.

Southern, R.W. *Western Views of Islam in the Middle Age.* Cambridge: Harvard University Press, 1977.

Sox, David. *The Gospel of Barnabas.* London: George Allen and Unwin, 1984.

Spence, Leslie. "Tamburlaine and Marlowe". *Modern Philology* 23 (1930): 604-622.

Spencer, Terence. *Fair Greece Sad Relic: Literary Philhellenism from Shakespeare to Byron*, London: Weidenfeld and Nicolson, 1954.

Starr, Herbert W. "Sources of David Mallet's 'Mustapha, A Tragedy'", *Notes and Queries* 181 (1941): 285-287.

Stavrianos, L.S. *The Balkans Since 1453.* New York: Rineheart, 1958.

Stephanie, Jr. G. *The Abduction from the Seraglio.* [Original German Text by C.F. Bretzner, English adaptation by Moron Siegel and Waldo Lyman]. New York: International Music Company, 1989.

Swedenberg, H. T., Jr. *The Theory of the Epic in England, 1650-1800.* Berkeley: University of California Press, 1944.

Sweetman, John. *Oriental Obsession: Islamic Inspiration in British and American Art and Architecture (1500-1920).* Cambridge: Cambridge University Press, 1988.

Sypher, Wylie, ed. *Comedy.* 1956. Reprint. Baltimore: Johns Hopkins University Press, 1980.

Tasch, Peter, A. *The Dramatic Cobbler: The Life and Works of Isaac Bickerstaffe.* Lewisburg: Bucknell University Press, 1971.

Thaler, Alwin. "Thomas Heywood, D'Avenant, and The Siege of Rhodes". *PMLA* 39 (1924): 624-641.

Thorp, Willard. "A Key to Rowe's 'Tamerlane'" *JEGP* 39 (1940) 124-127.

Tiddy, R.J.E. *The Mummers Play.* Oxford: Clarendon, 1923.

Till, Nicholas. *Mozart and the Enlightenment: Truth, Virtue and Beauty in Mozart's Operas.* London and Boston: Faber and Faber, 1992.

Todorov, Tzvetan. *The Conquest of America: the Question of the Other.* Trans. Richard Howard. New York: Harper and Row, 1984.

Toledana, Ehud. R. *The Ottoman Slave Trade and Its Suppression*: 1840-1890. Princeton:Princeton University Press, 1982.

Trapp, Joseph. Abra-Mule: or, Love and Empire. London, 1704.

Tyerman, Christopher. *England and the Crusades 1095-1588.* Chicago: University of Chicago Press, 1988.

Ulucay, M. Cagatay. *Harem.* Ankara: Turk Tarih Kurumu Basimevi, 1992.

Ulucay, M. Cagatay. *Padishalarin Kadinlari ve Kizlari* [*Wives and daughters of the Sultans*]. Ankara: Turk Tarih Kurumu Başimevi, 1992.

Uzuncarsili, Ismail Hakki. *Osmanli Tarihi* [*Ottoman History*]. 4 volumes. Ankara: Turk Tarih Kurumu Basimevi, 1947-1959.

Valensi, Lucette. *The Birth of the Despot: Venice and the Sublime Porte.* Trans. Arthur Denner. Ithaca: Cornell University Press, 1993.

Valensi, Lucette. '*The Making of Political Paradigm: The Transmission of Culture in Eastern Modern Europe.* Eds. Anthony Grafton and Ann Blair. Philadelphia: University of Pennsylvania Press, 1990. 173-203.

Van, Gilles de. "Fin de Siècle Exoticism and the Meaning of Far Away". *Opera Quarterly 11* (1994-1995): 78-94.

Vaughan, Dorothy M. *Europe and the Turk: A Pattern of Alliances (1350-1700).* Liverpool: Liverpool University Press, 1954.

Vaughan, T Alden and Virginia Mason Vaughan. "Before Othello: Elizabethan Representations of Sub-Saharan Africans. *William and Mary Quarterly* 54.1 (1997): 1944.

Vaughan, Virginia Mason. *Othello: A Contextual History.* Cambridge: Cambridge University Press, 1994.

Visser, Margaret. "Worship your Enemy: Aspects of the Cult of Heroes in Ancient Greece", *Harvard Theological Review* 75.4 (1982): 403-428.

Vitkus, Daniel. "Turning Turk in Othello: The Conversion and Damnation of the Moor". *Shakespeare Quarterly* 48.2 (1997): 145-174.

Voltaire, François-Marie Arouet, *Oeuvres complètes*, Paris: Garnier, 1878.

Walker, Hallam. *Molière*. Boston: Twayne Publishers, 1990.

Wann, Louis. "The Oriental in the Elizabethan Drama". *Modern Philology* 12 (1915): 423-447.

Ward, A.W. *History of English Dramatic Literature to the Death of Queen Anne.* 2 vols. London, 1899.

Weinstein, Donald. *Ambassador from Venice: Pietro Pasqualigo in Lisbon, 1501.* Minneapolis: University of Minnesota Press, 1960.

Wheatcroft, Andrew. *The Ottomans.* London: Viking, 1993.

Wheatley, Katherine E. *Racine and English Classicism.* 1956. Reprint. Westport: Greenwood, 1973.

Whitaker, William. *The Conspiracy, or Change of Government: A Tragedy.* London, 1680.

White, Hayden. *Tropics of Discourse.* Baltimore: Johns Hopkins University Press, 1987.

Wilcox, John. *The Relation of Molière to Restoration Comedy.* New York: Columbia University Press, 1938.

Wilson, M. Daniel. "Turks on the Eighteenth-Century Operatic Stage and in European Political, Military and Cultural History". *Eighteenth Century Life* 2 (1985): 79-92.

Withers, Robert. *A Description of the Grand Signor's Seraglio or Turkish Emperors's Court.* London, 1650.

Wollstonecraft, Mary. *A Vindication of the Rights of Women.* Ed. Carol H. Poston. New York: Norton, 1988.

Wood, A.C. "The English Embassy at Constantinople: 1660-1762". *English Historical Review* 15 (1925): 533-61.

Wood, Alfred C. *A History of the Levant Company.* 1935. Reprint. London: F. Cass, 1964.

Wood, Allen. "Murder in the Seraglio: Orientalism in Seventeenth-Century Tragedy". *Papers on French Seventeenth Century Literature* 12 (1979-80): 91-107.

Woodhead, Christine. "The Present Terror of the World' Contemporary Views of the Ottoman Empire c1600". *History* 2 (1987): 20-37.

Yapp, M.E. "Europe in the Turkish Mirror". *Past and Present* 137 (1992): 134-155.

Yeazell, Ruth Bernard. "Harems for Mozart and Rossini". *Raritan* 16 (1997): 86-105.

Yeazell, Ruth Bernard. *Harems of the Mind.* London and New Haven: Yale University Press, 2000.

Yucel, Yasar. *Sultan Suleyman The Grand Turk.* Ankara: Turk Tarih Kurumu Basimevi, 1991.

Zilfi, Madeline C., ed. *Women in the Ottoman Empire, Middle Eastern Women in the Early Ottoman Era.* Leiden: Brill, 1997.

Zonana, Joyce. "The Sultan and the Slave: Feminist Orientalism and the Structure of Jane Eyre", *Signs* 18.3 (1993): 592-614.